MINISTRY AND THEOLOGY
IN
GLOBAL PERSPECTIVE

MINISTRY and THEOLOGY
in
GLOBAL PERSPECTIVE

Contemporary Challenges
for the Church

Edited by

DON A. PITTMAN
RUBEN L. F. HABITO
and
TERRY C. MUCK

WILLIAM B. EERDMANS PUBLISHING COMPANY
GRAND RAPIDS, MICHIGAN / CAMBRIDGE, U.K.

© 1996 Wm. B. Eerdmans Publishing Co.

255 Jefferson Ave. S.E., Grand Rapids, Michigan 49503 /

P.O. Box 163, Cambridge CB3 9PU U.K.

Printed in the United States of America

01 00 99 98 97 96   7 6 5 4 3 2 1

Library of Congress Cataloging-in-Publication Data

Ministry and theology in global perspective: contemporary challenges for the church /
edited by Don A. Pittman, Ruben L. F. Habito, and Terry C. Muck.

p.   cm.

Includes bibliographical references and index.

ISBN 0-8028-0844-1 (pbk.: alk. paper)

1. Christianity and other religions.   2. Missions — Theory.
3. Religions — Relations.   4. Religion and culture.
I. Pittman, Don Alvin, 1948-   . II. Habito, Ruben L. F., 1947-
III. Muck, Terry C., 1947-

BR127.M56   1996

261 — dc20   95-50493

CIP

Contents

Foreword, *by Robert J. Schreiter, C.PP.S.*   xi

Preface   xiv

INTRODUCTION
THE GLOBAL CONTEXT FOR MINISTRY

Christian Ministry and the Globalization of Community   3

I. TOWARD A CHRISTIAN
THEOLOGY OF RELIGIONS

Christian Theology and People of Other Faiths   33

READINGS

Pre–Twentieth-Century Christian Views

    Justin Martyr   67

    Tertullian   70

    Augustine   73

CONTENTS

Nicholas of Cusa   77

Friedrich Schleiermacher   81

Contemporary Roman Catholic and Eastern Orthodox Views

Karl Rahner   87

Georges Khodr   94

Raimundo Panikkar   100

Hans Küng   107

Paul F. Knitter   115

Gavin D'Costa   123

Contemporary Protestant Views

Ernst Troeltsch   133

Karl Barth   141

Hendrik Kraemer   149

Paul Tillich   155

John Hick   162

John B. Cobb Jr.   170

Choan-Seng Song   177

Marjorie Hewitt Suchocki   182

Diana L. Eck   189

Lesslie Newbigin   196

James A. Borland   204

Don A. Pittman   210

Contents

II. MISSION AND MINISTRY

Global Mission Today: Seven Key Questions   219

READINGS

Four Views of Mission

Redemptoris Missio   237
  Pope John Paul II

Contemporary Evangelical Theology of Mission   247
  Donald A. McGavran

Mission and Evangelism — An Ecumenical Affirmation   254
  WCC Central Committee

Theology and Strategy of Pentecostal Missions   265
  L. Grant McClung

Mission in Non-Christian Religions

Mission-Minded Hindus Going Global   273
  Swami Palimi

A Comparative Religious Study of Missionary
Transplantation in Buddhism, Christianity, and Islam   277
  Frank Whaling

On the Nature of Islamic Da'wah   283
  Isma'il al-Faruqi

Issues in Mission

The Absolute Claim of Christianity:
The Justification of Evangelization or an Obstacle to It?   291
  Alexandre Ganoczy

Dialogue and Mission: Conflict or Convergence?   297
  Michael Amaladoss

We Are the World   304
  James Engel

CONTENTS

Mission and Mammon: Six Theses   309
  Jonathan J. Bonk

Contextualization from a World Perspective   315
  Robert J. Schreiter

Fundamentalisms Observed   328
  Martin E. Marty and R. Scott Appleby

The Mission Fields

The Enduring Validity of Cross-Cultural Mission   335
  Lesslie Newbigin

Christian Mission in the Pluralist Milieu:
An African Experience   339
  Lamin Sanneh

Christian Mission and the Peoples of Asia   348
  D. Preman Niles

Contextual Evangelization in Latin America:
Between Accommodation and Confrontation   355
  Mortimer Arias

A Great New Fact of Our Day:
America as Mission Field   361
  Craig Van Gelder

The Mission Challenge

Vision for Mission   371
  David J. Bosch

Justice, Peace and the Integrity of Creation   380
  World Council of Churches

Contents

III. DIALOGUE AND MINISTRY

Interreligious Dialogue as a Christian Task   385

READINGS

The Why and How of Dialogue

Cosmic Dialogue   399
    David Lochhead

Dialogue, Encounter, Even Confrontation   408
    John R. Stott

Speaking the Truth in Love   415
    Pinchas Lapide and Karl Rahner

Dialogue and the Prophetic-Mystical Option   418
    David Tracy

Evangelicals and Interreligious Dialogue   425
    David J. Hesselgrave

Fruits of Dialogue: Toward Inner Transformation

Meeting Other Religious Traditions and
Rethinking My Own   431
    Minoru Kasai

A Journey with the Unknown   435
    Bettina Bäumer

Christians and the Practice of Zen   441
    Yamada Koun Roshi

Taking Heart: Spiritual Exercises for Social Activists   445
    Joanna Macy

Toward the Meeting of Mystical Paths   455
    Ewert Cousins

CONTENTS

Tasks for Interreligious Cooperation

Shalom: Complementarity   465
Jacob Neusner

Social Activism and Spiritual Alternatives —
An Islamic Perspective   472
Chandra Muzaffar

Hinduism and Social Action
from Women's Perspective   480
G. Shanta

Buddhism and Social Values   485
Sulak Sivaraksa

A Tradition of Thanksgiving   493
Audrey Shenandoah

Ten Global Issues for Christian Reflection   499
Jocele Meyer

Pastoral Recommendations on Dialogue:
A Joint Statement by Protestant and
Catholic Churches in Asia   503

Acknowledgments   507
Index of Subjects and Names   513
Index of Scriptural References   523

Foreword

The phenomenon called globalization can be said to have begun when European explorers began their planet-encircling voyages at the end of the fifteenth century. Since that time it has been possible — in theory at least — to think of the world as a single, interconnected place. For that is the essential meaning of globalization: that the world is an interconnected — and increasingly, interdependent — single place.

But it has really been in the last third of the twentieth century that globalization has become more than a notional possibility. As one theorist of globalization has put it, we are now experiencing a compression of time and space. Nearly instantaneous communication is possible to almost all parts of the globe. Satellite-linked television makes it possible for the entire world to be witnesses in historical events. Fax and computer networks now interlink people around the globe in ways that make hierarchies of communication superfluous. Long-distance air travel has redefined the nature of our perception of space, allowing peoples to move and mingle on an unprecedented scale. Consequently, boundaries of time and space are being radically redrawn, and with them, the boundaries of our cultural, social and personal identities.

While all of this may seem exhilarating, it does have its ominous side as well. The compressions of time and space bring with them the development of worldwide or global systems. Such systems are now in evidence in economics, science, medicine, education, and to some extent in the media. These systems bring with them a growing uniformity in language, behavior, and custom. In popular culture, there is a similar kind of system, driven by U. S. entertainment, leading to a standardization in clothing (T-shirts, denim jeans, athletic shoes), food (Coca-Cola, McDonald's), and music. All of these global systems threaten to overwhelm local cultures, especially those which are already quite fragile. The pressure of these systems has the paradoxical effect of heightening senses of local particularity, as cultures resist the power of standardization and reassert local values. This reassertion takes on a variety of forms, ranging from what are sometimes mistakenly called fundamentalisms through nativism to revitalization movements.

But even more ominous than the struggle for cultural particularity and identity is the growing ecological threat. Where the threats to the ecosystem touch the atmosphere, all are at risk, no matter how sound their ecological practices may be locally. Sustainability becomes a new watchword, tempering the headlong rush to what has been called "progress."

Christians find themselves very much caught up in the tides of globalization. Protestant Christianity was born at the time of the beginnings of globalization in the sixteenth century. In retrospect, one can see that that form of Christianity would not have been possible without technological advances like the printing press, which made unmediated access to the Scriptures possible for the first time for all Christian people. The worldwide mission movement of the nineteenth and twentieth centuries created a globe-embracing network of Christian communities, and spawned an ecumenical movement. That same compression of time and space experienced in other sectors of human life is now making itself felt in religion as well. The pressures of uniformity are creating new particularity in religion, as religion becomes the badge for ethnic and cultural particularisms. The new networks of communication are eroding mediating structures in the churches: judicatories and denominational structures become harder to sustain and support as congregations seek direct contact with their areas of interest.

The three theologians who have prepared this volume on how ministry and theology are taking shape in this globalized world have done us all a great service. Globalization processes are changing the fabric of our social and cognitive structures in ways as profound as those in the sixteenth century when the combination of technological progress, the rise of capitalism, and the beginnings of the European empire altered the shape of societies around the planet. Where exactly globalization at the end of the twentieth century will take us is still unclear. But the compilers of this book have chosen three areas that are already clearly being influenced by these powerful forces.

Religions are being brought into contact with one another in unprecedented ways. Consequently, issues of religious pluralism press in upon Christians as never before. The interaction of religious communities and

the displacement of many religious communities to new locations introduce forces within religious traditions that will inevitably change them in
ways we cannot foresee. The outcome of all of this for Christianity has yet
to be discerned. The essays and the readings chosen here will first help set
a framework for thinking about these questions as we search together for
resolutions of how to live in a genuinely plural world.

Second, if religious pluralism is changing how Christians think about
themselves, it is also changing how the churches see their mission. The
Christian mission of the nineteenth and first half of the twentieth centuries
saw itself territorially, expanding the frontier of Christian presence
throughout the world. Under those same forces of compression of time
and space experienced in other sectors, Christians must now rethink what
Christian mission will mean, both in light of the religious geography of the
world and from the perspective of the majority of Christians, who now live
outside the North Atlantic cultural sphere. Mission is more than growth
strategy; it has to do with the very heart of Christian identity. Who are
Christians and how are we called to live in the world? In a world so rapidly
changing, these questions of identity take on special urgency.

And thirdly, what shall be the nature of Christian communication
with the other religious communities of the world? Christianity still represents the largest single religious tradition in the world, but it could well be
overtaken by Islam early in the twenty-first century. With religions no
longer confined to large cultural areas, but now elbow-to-elbow in urban
centers around the world, the ability to communicate effectively and non-
violently becomes imperative. This is especially so when religion becomes
the banner under which ethnic hatred and bigotry march.

Religious interest in globalization as such began in the late 1970s,
about a decade or so after it had already begun to receive attention in
business and educational circles. The latter half of the 1980s and the first
half of the 1990s have been a period of intense preoccupation and interest
in how this larger phenomenon is both shaping religion and the wider
world to which religion is trying to respond. We all owe Don Pittman,
Ruben Habito, and Terry Muck a debt of gratitude for bringing together
their own thoughtful reflections and those of other authors, past and present, to help those concerned about how the churches will respond faithfully
and prophetically to the challenges that globalization poses for Christianity
today. This book serves as a benchmark for measuring how well we will be
able to make that response.

ROBERT J. SCHREITER

Preface

In making their 1988 report to the thirty-sixth biennial meeting of the Association of Theological Schools in the United States and Canada (ATS), the association's Committee on Global Theological Education listed a number of its basic assumptions regarding the contemporary global context that suggested the need for a new vision for the mission of Christian theological schools in the twenty-first century. The contemporary global reality, the committee observed, is commonly viewed by Christians as either an ominous threat or an exhilarating opportunity. In addition to the citation of fundamental economic, military, technological, sociological, cultural, and theological assumptions concerning the new global reality that confronts the church today, the committee began its statement with two of its general assumptions concerning human life on this planet. "There is," the committee remarked, "a profound connectedness of human life worldwide, which opens up the possibility of mutual enrichment through dialogue and reciprocal learning; [and] there is also a deeply disturbing threat to the planet itself from human conflict, inequities and exploitation, and from the misuse of technology."

This textbook and reader, grounded in extended collegial conversations of a team of theological educators concerning both this *profound connectedness* and this *disturbing threat to the planet,* represents one effort to provide important resources for reflection on contemporary Christian ministry and theology in global perspective. In 1991, at the request of the Executive Committee of the Council of Southwestern Theological Schools (COSTS), a teaching and research team was formed with the charge of contributing to the globalization of theological education in the member schools of the region through the design of an innovative interseminary course. Invited to participate on the team were Don A. Pittman, an ecumenical or "mainline" Protestant scholar affiliated with the Christian Church (Disciples of Christ), who at the time taught history of religions, mission, and interreligious dialogue at Brite Divinity School, Texas Christian University, before joining the faculty of the Tainan Theological College and Seminary, Tainan, Taiwan, in 1994; Ruben L. F. Habito, a Roman Catholic scholar from the Philippines who was educated as a Jesuit missionary in Japan and now teaches world religions and spirituality at Perkins School of Theology, Southern Methodist University; and Terry C. Muck, an evangelical scholar with a Baptist heritage who has lived in Sri Lanka and who served for a number of years as senior editor of *Christianity Today* prior to joining the faculty of Austin Presbyterian Theological Seminary to teach in the area of comparative religion and mission.

It should be noted that all three of us who participated on the team were trained as historians of religion. Therefore, both our interseminary course and, by extension, this textbook and reader deal with topics, methods, and literature beyond the usual boundaries of our discipline. This is especially true in the area of missiology. Yet mission and evangelism are such crucial parts of globalization, both affected by and affecting theology of religions and interreligious dialogue, that we decided we must cover it in this context and from these perspectives. Thus, in this blatant act of "academic poaching," we learned a great deal, and hope we did it responsibly enough to have made a contribution to the interdisciplinary nature of the global challenge facing the church.

After a year of consultation regarding important issues that should be addressed in a proposed interseminary course, as well as discussion of the diverse practical theological perspectives presented at the 1990 ATS Summer Institute on the Globalization of Theological Education a syllabus was designed to highlight (a) *the global context for contemporary Christian ministry,* with special attention to the profound interdependence of the human community within a deeply wounded world; (b) *options for a Christian theology of religions,* with an exploration of the range of theological positions expressed in the church's history and its present life; (c) *the nature of Christian mission,* with an examination of the church's historical and contemporary debates on mission priorities and procedures; and (d) *interreligious dialogue as a Christian task,* with discussion of the promise and problems of dialogical engagement, variously conceived, with peoples of living faiths and ideologies. The graduate course was offered in the fall of

PREFACE

1992, with student participation from six seminaries and a wide variety of Christian traditions. In addition to assigning one required book in each of these four areas, the instructors also prepared an initial draft of the collection of readings now included in this volume to further enhance what turned out to be for all who participated in the course an exciting series of exchanges on important practical theological issues in Christian ministry today.

In 1993, the Association of Theological Schools in the United States and Canada, with primary funding from The Pew Charitable Trusts, generously awarded the teaching and research team a globalization grant to help facilitate the final preparation and publication of these edited materials with introductions, so that the collection could be shared with a broader community of theological educators who are seeking models and resources that may inform new globalization efforts within both the classical and practical theological disciplines. The original collection has been revised and augmented in view of constructive criticisms offered by colleagues interested in the project. Although inclusive language has been utilized in the introductory essays, no attempt has been made to alter the language of previously published work in this regard. For the limitations of the textbook, the authors assume all responsibility.

We would like to express our appreciation to the Council of Southwestern Theological Schools and the students who shared in its 1992 interseminary course; to the Association of Theological Schools, its associate director Gail Buchwalter King, and The Pew Charitable Trusts; and to the consultants who reviewed drafts of the manuscript and offered helpful suggestions, including David J. Gouwens, Brite Divinity School; Pete Hendrick, Austin Presbyterian Theological Seminary; George Hunsberger, Western Theological Seminary; Paul O. Ingram, Pacific Lutheran University; Michael K. Kinnamon, Lexington Theological Seminary; Henry N. Smith, Center for the Study of World Religions, Harvard University; Robert J. Schreiter, Catholic Theological Union; and Max L. Stackhouse, Princeton Theological Seminary. We also wish to express appreciation to Nancy Claire Pittman and other technical assistants, including Shirley D. Bubar, Robin Gray, Pamela G. Holt, Barbara Hunt, Susan Smith, and Christopher Wilson; to the Reverend Thomas M. Potter and the members of Central Christian Church, Waco, Texas, who graciously provided hospitality and meeting space for the authors on several occasions; to editor-in-chief Jon Pott and the editorial staff of Wm. B. Eerdmans Publishing Company; and to all of the members of our families who supported this work with their encouragement and patience. We sincerely hope that this book proves to be a useful resource for students and faculty from different denominational and disciplinary backgrounds who are concerned with the critically needed globalization of theological education.

Don A. Pittman
Ruben L. F. Habito
Terry C. Muck

THE GLOBAL CONTEXT
FOR MINISTRY

Christian Ministry and the Globalization of Community

Christian ministry has always entailed seeking to understand ever more comprehensively both the nature of the world's brokenness and the good news of God's healing presence in the life, death, and resurrection of Jesus Christ. It has always required a discernment of the ongoing salvific mission of God's Spirit in the world for a corresponding definition of the reconciling mission of the Christian church. In our own time, accordingly, an increasing number of persons called to Christian discipleship have recognized that our prayer life, our primary dialogue with God, has to be paralleled by a sincere commitment to a dialogue with one another within the church, and with persons of all faiths and ideologies, regarding our common human joys and sorrows and the redemptive will of God for the whole creation. Indeed, as our personal and corporate Christian prayers constitute a profound opening of our lives to God and a listening for God's healing word, so authentic dialogues with our neighbors represent a sincere opening of our lives to one another and a listening for the ways that healing words have been and need to be expressed in a deeply wounded world. The discernment of our Christian mission requires a continual relating of these two fundamental dialogues.

A Simple Paradox and the "Kin-dom"

Jesus not only instructed us to love our neighbors as ourselves, but in response to a direct inquiry and through parable, he provocatively defined

3

"neighbor" in a universal manner (Luke 10:25-37). Compliance along the disciples' way has never been easy, of course. Yet given our contemporary matrix of complexly interwoven sociopolitical and economic global networks and the critical condition of our global ecosystem, the universal love of neighbor now presents unprecedented and formidable challenges to our will and intellect. Indeed, only within the last few decades have we started to realize how truly interdependent is our world community and how much what some of us on this planet do, or do not do, may affect the rest of us on our one endangered galactic home. Only within recent years have most of us become more alarmingly enlightened concerning how much is at stake for the whole human family in the spirited debates currently taking place on a wide range of critical eco-justice issues in the global public forum.[1]

Moreover, as we have engaged others in critical reflection on the requirements of a "just, participatory, and sustainable" global society,[2] we have learned in many unique and life-changing ways that we cannot love others unless we sincerely try to know them, and to know them in their own terms and as they understand themselves. Paradoxically, we have also become much more aware of the correlative truth that we cannot truly understand others unless we first love them, unless we first respect and value them as precious children of God equal to all others. All of our local Christian ministries, inspired and informed by the global vision of our Lord, surely have to be grounded in this simple paradox about relationships between children of the one majestic God: we cannot really love others whom we make no serious attempt to understand, and at the same time we cannot truly understand others whom we do not really love.[3]

Through a dialogical process of discernment, therefore, which must be engaged on the broadest possible scale and with the greatest particularity possible, many in the church today are seeking to understand more clearly, and to embody more faithfully, the will of God for the whole creation. Not infrequently, in our indecision and faithlessness, we Christians close our hearts to what we see and hear and rationalize away what the Spirit com-

---

1. The commonly employed term "eco-justice" points to the intrinsic interrelatedness of the well-being of all sentient life to the well-being of the natural ecosystem.

2. The reference to a "just, participatory, and sustainable" global society acknowledges the contribution of the 1975 World Council of Churches' General Assembly held in Nairobi.

3. Portions of this chapter are adapted with permission from Don A. Pittman, "Dialogical Discernment and the 'Kin-dom' of God: On Globalizing Ministries in North America," *Lexington Theological Quarterly* 28, no. 4 (winter 1993): 319-31.

municates in moments of true discernment. Nevertheless, through the grace at work within us — the grace that will not let us go — we all dream of realizing what the Cuban theologian Ada María Isasi-Díaz has referred to as the "kin-dom" of God, the solidarity that rightly characterizes the whole family of God.[4] As members of the church of Jesus Christ, we universally confess to have been claimed by that holy dream and to be convicted, through Scripture and tradition, of the transforming truth that we humans are in fact, and more perfectly will be through God's saving activity, kin to one another.

Historically, the practice of loving others, as Isasi-Díaz points out, has most commonly been conceived of by Christians in terms of "charity," a basically one-sided affair in which we give out of our abundance to those we judge to be in need. Rather, she argues, we ought more appropriately to define love of neighbor in terms not of charity but of *solidarity.* Solidarity is a dialogical rather than a one-sided ideal. It requires mutual discernment within community. It involves trying to realize within the circumstances of our own local situation, globally conceived, the crucial yet paradoxical link between loving and understanding others. It calls us beyond expressions of disinterested altruism to engagement in relationships. Comments Isasi-Díaz, "Solidarity is *not* a matter of agreeing with, of being supportive of, of liking, or of being inspired by, the cause of a group of people. Though all these might be part of solidarity, solidarity goes beyond all of them. Solidarity has to do with understanding the interconnections among issues and the cohesiveness that needs to exist among the communities of struggle."[5]

In seeking prayerfully to discern and manifest the kin-dom of God, in seeking earnestly and holistically to become authentically a human *family* in relation to divine reality, we will surely have to commit ourselves in the future ever more resolutely to *mutuality,* to attempts to deparochialize our perspectives in order to see the world through the eyes of "others" and to

---

4. Ada María Isasi-Díaz, "Solidarity: Love of Neighbors in the 1980s," in *Lift Every Voice: Constructing Christian Theologies from the Underside,* ed. Susan Brooks Thistlethwaite and Mary Potter Engel (San Francisco: Harper & Row, 1990), 31-48. She remarks in a footnote, "There are two reasons for not using the regular word employed in English Bibles, *kingdom.* First, it is obviously a sexist word that presumes that God is male. Second, the concept of the kingdom in our world today is both hierarchical and elitist — which is why I do not use the word reign. The word kin-dom makes it clear that when the fullness of God becomes a day-to-day reality in the world at large, we will all be sisters and brothers — kin to each other" (304).

5. Ibid., 32-33.

place ourselves at their sides in their situations. This educative and trans-formative process, which Paulo Freire calls "conscientization," is not merely a mental exercise in imaginative identification, or a "center-complex voy-eurism" in Kosuke Koyama's terms.[6] It involves praxis, that is, the actual formation of community. It means being present to one another and being willing to examine critically our own lives in relation to the lives of all those whom God has created as our kin.[7]

Yet for most of us in the church that conscientization process in dialogue with God and with our global neighbors both near and far will be a very disquieting, even terrorizing one. For in that process we may see and hear things that we do not want to see and hear. For example, we may become aware as never before of how much our privileged affluence has been achieved through the exploitation of others and how much our wealth has effectively insulated us from the desperately poor of the world. We may begin to recognize how poorly we have understood the implications of Jesus' teaching of universal neighborliness, how inappreciably we have been moved by the marginalization and suffering of others, and how little we have been willing to do to participate more fully in the kin-dom that God is bringing into reality in God's own way and time. We may begin to understand more comprehen-sively especially how those of us who live in industrialized societies have dangerously abused the ecosystem and recklessly ignored the relation of economic development to environmental viability. We may begin to realize how significantly many of our most well-intended individual and corporate actions have been compromised by self-interest, as well as how frequently, if unwittingly, our efforts to serve others have been tainted by our need to control and dominate. We may begin to see how narrow and ill-informed has been our prayer life and how often we have tried to shield our souls from the Spirit's searching and guiding presence. Discipleship in solidarity and mutu-ality with our neighbors, globally embraced, will undoubtedly mean new visionary and ethical paradigms for Christians who sincerely seek the gra-cious kin-dom of God which, through divine self-emptying, drew near to us in Jesus Christ (Phil. 2:5-7).

6. See Kosuke Koyama, "Theological Education: Its Unities and Diversities," *Theo-logical Education,* Supplement 1 (autumn 1993): 95.

7. Paulo Freire writes, "The term *conscientização* refers to learning to perceive social, political, and economic contradictions, and to take action against the oppressive elements of reality." See *Pedagogy of the Oppressed,* trans. Myra Bergman Ramos (New York: Herder and Herder, 1970), 19.

Decentering and the Global Crisis

The practical envisioning of new human paradigms for the future requires in all cases *decentering*. That is, for any of us to be able to imagine and live in a different reality than the one in which we currently exist, we must first come to entertain the possibility that our own personal experiences, judgments, and actions may not be universally shared, comprehensively valid, or fully appropriate to our situation. We must first come to doubt seriously that our own individual experiences, judgments, and actions are, and unquestionably should be, without further prayer, reflection, and testing in dialogue with others, the fully adequate and normative center point for all. Accordingly, within the Christian community in recent years, many thoughtful persons from different backgrounds and perspectives have aimed to raise fundamental questions about what faithful discipleship requires of us in our time. Some, such as liberation theologians of all varieties, have called for a radical identification with the poor and the marginalized and the practice of a "hermeneutics of suspicion" with regard to ideologies that may mask oppression. Others, unable to accept the basic categories and approaches of liberation theologies, have called rather for a reclamation of the profound truths of humility and service as taught by Jesus in the Beatitudes. Indeed, all of those Christians who have promoted conscientization in one form or another have recognized that we do live in a deeply wounded and divided world. They have realized that if questions concerning faithfulness in Christian discipleship can be effectively posed they may engender prayerful and conscientious drives within a global context to reconsider the nature of the church's catholicity, to investigate the unique character and texture of our neighbors' life experiences, to seek understanding of the joys and sorrows that contribute to or diminish our neighbors' well-being, and to work toward solidarity within the bonds of a more expansively defined global community.

Authentic efforts to listen empathetically to others and to see the universe from others' perspectives, however difficult such endeavors might be, always produce change. A creative, comparative hermeneutics, if earnestly pursued, not only entails a measure of *disorientation*, but provides a wider experiential context in which an appropriate *reorientation* to the realities of a more broadly conceived community becomes possible.[8] Min-

---

8. See Mark Kline Taylor and Gary J. Bekker, "Engaging the Other in a Global Village," *Theological Education* 26, Supplement 1 (1990): 52-85. They comment, "It is

imally, as a result of such an interpretive enterprise, one's own experiences, judgments, and actions cannot again be naively interpreted a priori as those of all human beings of whom one need take account. Therefore, for the Christian community, "globalization," insofar as it is directed toward mutuality and toward an ever greater measure of participation in God's kin-dom, refers not to the universalization of a single human perspective, but to the enrichment of all perspectives through attentiveness to God and an expansive encounter with human otherness. It refers to being transformed by the global vision of Christ and by our embrace of all others in a common quest for adequate expressions of the good and the true.

An openness to God and to the life experiences of our neighbors on the widest possible scale today will, of course, guide us inevitably toward a direct confrontation with the piercing realities of a profoundly hurting world in which justice, equal participation, and sustainability are unrealized dreams. It will lead us to see "spaceship Earth" as imperiled by tragically myopic concerns that have effectively blinded members of the human family to their interdependency and to the long-term well-being of the whole. It will surely motivate us to ask more searchingly where God is at work in the cosmos, how the Spirit's multidimensional healing activities may be identified, and how we might become more significantly a part of the story of which God is the ultimate author. It will unquestionably encourage us to reexamine our biblical and theological understandings of the gospel of Jesus Christ in relation to our stewardship for the earth, to the meaning of other faiths, to the nature and scope of the church's global mission, and to opportunities for interreligious dialogue. Through divine grace, it may even inspire us in humble confession to seek reconciliation with God and neighbor to the end that our own lives might be more nearly aligned in solidarity with all of our kin within God's holy reign, which from a biblical perspective is both already and not yet.

One fact that such an openness to our global neighbors will searingly impress on our minds is the staggering and increasing inequity between the living standards of the rich and the poor, an inequity that poses a fundamental moral challenge to the sustainability of our present global

---

our experience that students (and professors) from North American contexts, after experiences of intercultural engagement abroad, do in fact return home often dazed, disillusioned — but for all that productively reoriented for growth in faith and intellect" (82).

society. How is it possible, we may ask, for many human beings to live in absolute luxury while so many others — in fact more than one quarter of humankind — live in "absolute poverty," defined by the lack of income sufficient even to afford the minimal dietary requirements for health and other non-food essentials? How is it possible for more than 85 percent of the world's income to benefit only 23 percent of the world's population, for the ratio of the wealth of the top 20 percent to that of the bottom 20 percent to be 150 to 1, and for more than one billion people to survive on less than one U. S. dollar per day?[9] How is it possible for many individuals to suffer from an obvious over-consumption of food while so many others are seriously malnourished, with more than 177 million children — one-third of those under the age of five in developing nations — so poorly nourished that their physical and mental development has been permanently impaired?[10] How is it possible in a world of plenty that more than 40,000 young children die from hunger-related causes each day, more than 25 each minute?[11] How can it be, in view of such desperate and dehumanizing poverty, suffering, and death that the world's nations can spend more than $1.8 million on military armament every minute, with a total annual expenditure of approximately $1 trillion?[12] How can it be that the church of Jesus Christ is not galvanized worldwide in vocal protest and active response to these facts which assail our souls? Addressing Western Christians, the evangelical Mennonite missiologist Jonathan Bonk has observed prophetically:

9. See Sandra Postel, "Denial in the Decisive Decade," in *State of the World 1992: A Worldwatch Institute Report on Progress Toward a Sustainable Society,* ed. Lester R. Brown (New York: Norton, 1992), 4; see also Wesley Granberg-Michaelson, *Redeeming the Creation: The Rio Earth Summit: Challenges for the Churches* (Geneva: World Council of Churches, 1992), 68; and *Earthkeeping in the Nineties: Stewardship of Creation,* ed. Loren Wilkinson (Grand Rapids: Eerdmans, 1991).

10. Cited in "Most Frequently Asked Questions About Hunger," Background Paper No. 124 (Washington, D.C.: Bread for the World, spring 1992).

11. Arthur Simon, "Fact Sheet on Hunger," Background Paper No. 99 (Washington, D.C.: Bread for the World, August 1987), citing a UNICEF report.

12. Wesley Granberg-Michaelson, *Redeeming the Creation,* 41. See also Postel, "Denial in the Decisive Decade," 6. Consult further the preparatory document for the Seoul convocation in March 1990 on *Justice, Peace and the Integrity of Creation,* cited in Hans Küng, *Global Responsibility: In Search of a New World Ethic* (New York: Crossroad, 1991), 2; as well as *The Ecumenical Review* 41, no. 4 (October 1989), devoted to the issues addressed at the convocation.

Global poverty is an acute material problem, no doubt; but Western affluence is a profoundly spiritual one. Is it not at least as difficult for us members of the Western church to overcome our affluence as it is for our poverty-stricken brothers and sisters in the rest of the world to survive their poverty? Unless we come to see our Western world through the eyes of Jesus, we shall continue to excuse the personal and collective covetousness and greed that have made us "great," and above the locked door to the heart of the richest church the world has ever seen will be written — in splendid gilt lettering — the word ICHABOD [meaning "the glory of God has departed," (1 Sam. 4:21)]. And the Savior will remain on the outside (Rev. 3:17-20).[13]

Herman Daly and John Cobb have pointed out that our prevailing understanding of basic economic progress in the West was first developed in the eighteenth and nineteenth centuries and was related to a utilitarian philosophy that recognized "no other regulatory principle than that of individual egoism."[14] Since that time, they argue, a great many persons have been persuaded that any significant community control of self-interested economic activity would tend to be counterproductive to the well-being of the whole group, while acknowledging the unfortunate possibility of some limited human costs at the bottom of the socioeconomic ladder in unrestrained competitive development. They comment:

Modern economic theory has taught that these inhibitions of the quest for wealth are not needed for the sake of the general good and that, indeed, they impede its realization. Where each individual seeks to maximize economic gain, the total product of society increases and hence all people benefit. If government was once expected to influence economic activity for the sake of justice to all, now its interventions are seen as preventing that increase of total product which alone can bring widespread prosperity. *Homo economicus* has little incentive to moderate the

---

13. Jonathan J. Bonk, "Missions and Mammon: Six Theses," *International Bulletin of Missionary Research* 13, no. 4 (October 1989): 178. See also Ronald J. Sider, *Rich Christians in an Age of Hunger* (Dallas: Word, 1990).

14. Herman E. Daly and John B. Cobb, Jr., *For the Common Good: Redirecting the Economy toward Community, the Environment, and a Sustainable Future* (Boston: Beacon Press, 1989), 4, quoting Joseph Schumpeter, "The Future of Private Enterprise in the Face of Modern Socialistic Tendencies," *History of Political Economy* 7, no. 3 (1975): 294-98.

quest for wealth by other concerns. . . . *Homo economicus* abstracts from human feelings about what happens to others and about one's relative standing in the community. It abstracts from the sense of fairness and from judgments of relative value.[15]

To an increasing number of persons, however, it now seems that the material inequities have become so great, the human suffering so severe, the growth of the world's population so accelerated, the irresponsible depletion of the earth's natural resources so frightening, the despoliation of the planet so advanced, the debt of the two-thirds world to the first world so unbearable, and the long-term sustainability of our international economic practices so much in doubt, that a new socioeconomic paradigm must be envisioned. The basic socioeconomic question concerning our immediate future is surely not whether we shall have an international market economy or not, but rather what community values shall define the success of that market. Few naively question whether or not we shall continue aggressively to utilize our technological capabilities for further development, given the remarkably advantageous scientific advances of this century and the promises for new breakthroughs. Yet many are now appropriately questioning what kinds of technological processes the human family ought to invest in and to what ends for all concerned. The summary eco-justice question is what we shall sincerely and confidently be able to affirm, in view of our critical global circumstances, concerning a just and *replicable lifestyle* for the future of all those on the small lifeboat that is planet Earth. In the midst of a divided and yet interdependent world, this question is of profound importance for the entire human family and requires that all voices be heard, including voices from the advantaged as well as the marginalized socioeconomic underside. It is a question that we Christians will surely recognize as intrinsically related to our own spiritual quest for what we are able to say concretely in our time about the healing mission of God's Spirit and about the correlative reconciliatory mission of the church.

In the current global debates concerning what achieving sustainability might require of us, unquestionably a number of the most difficult practical issues are directly linked to the growth rate of the world's population. It took more than sixteen centuries, from the first century of the common era to 1650, for the population to double from 250 million to 500 million. Yet, it took only 150 years for the population to double again to 1 billion

15. Ibid., 89, 95.

in 1800. It took only 130 years for it to double once more to 2 billion in 1930, and it took only another 45 years for it to double again to 4 billion in 1975. The population reached 5 billion in 1987 and will reach 6 billion before the year 2000. Population projections through the next century vary widely, given the uncertainties surrounding family planning programs and other regional factors. The United Nations Fund for Population Activities forecasts a population of at least 10 billion by the year 2050, with 95 percent of the population increase in the underdeveloped countries of the Southern Hemisphere.[16] The "carrying capacity" of the planet and the precise relation of the world's population to the problem of hunger remain controversial subjects, as does, of course, the divisive issue of population control.[17]

Most scholars in the field have concluded that currently there are sufficient food resources, and should be in the foreseeable future, to eliminate hunger-related suffering and death completely, were the human community to make that a priority. Nevertheless, relatively few of these scholars would venture to project that over the long term the current lifestyle expectations of most individuals in the wealthy industrialized countries of the world — predominantly in the Northern (and predominantly Christian) Hemisphere — are sustainable. Despite anticipated technological advances, few would claim that living "lighter on the earth" will not be necessary. Why? Because it has become increasingly clear that popular expectations for an ever more affluent standard of living in the industrial nations of the first world — as commercialized globally by large multinational corporations — are indirectly and directly linked to the rapid depletion of the earth's nonrenewable mineral resources and fossil fuels; to soil erosion, desertification, and deforestation; to the acidification of the atmosphere, global warming, and ozone depletion; to the pollution of land and water with hazardous waste; to the endangerment and extinction of many life-forms; and to the impoverishment of many communities, especially in developing nations of the Southern Hemisphere. Technological innovations and socioeconomic paradigms for the future will be recognized as valuable to the extent that they presuppose and address this tragic fact.

16. Cited in *Christian Faith and the World Economy Today: A Study Document of the World Council of Churches* (Geneva: WCC Publications, 1992), 23. See also *Wealth and Poverty,* ed. Robert Clause (Downers Grove: InterVarsity Press, 1984).

17. Consult for statistics, projection models, and a summary of perspectives: "Population," in The Hunger Project's *Ending Hunger: An Idea Whose Time Has Come* (New York: Praeger, 1985), 22-93.

Although debates continue with regard to specific statistical evidence presented to document the seriousness of our situation, some researchers have concluded, for example, with regard to nonrenewable mineral resources, that "for the rest of the world to use as much energy (not to mention consumer goods) per capita as the United States does, it would have to burn 300 percent more coal, 500 percent more petroleum, and 1,100 percent more natural gas," posing an immediate ecological nightmare.[18] Merely given current rates of depletion — that could markedly discriminate against the aspirations of the developing nations — energy supplies of oil and natural gas that are economically feasible to recover in the U. S. will last only until about the year 2020, while the world's supplies will last only thirty years longer to 2050.[19] With regard to arable land, severe over-grazing and over-cultivation have resulted in alarming rates of soil erosion and irreversible losses of topsoil worldwide, rapidly diminishing agricultural production and the promotion of desertification in many regions. Over 1 billion tons of valuable topsoil are lost each year in Europe and more than 25 billion tons in Asia.[20] Currently, the cutting of trees and the clearing of forests for wood pulp and land development significantly exceed natural regrowth and tree planting; lost each year are over 17 million hectares of valuable tropical forests alone, an area about half the size of Finland.[21] Moreover, throughout the world, air pollution and acid rain are threatening the viability of a great number of biological organisms and damaging plant life. In some parts of the world, the environmental crisis has already progressed to the point that fish can no longer survive in numerous freshwater lakes, while many established forests have been irreparably damaged by sulfur deposition. The widespread use of chlorofluorocarbons has contributed to the frightening rate of stratospheric ozone loss, not only over the Antarctic but at all latitudes. In the heavily populated

18. Christopher Manes, *Green Rage: Radical Environmentalism and the Unmaking of Civilization* (Boston: Little, Brown and Company, 1990), 32.

19. Consult *Keeping and Healing the Creation: A Resource Paper Prepared by the Presbyterian Eco-Justice Task Force* (Louisville: Committee on Social Witness Policy, Presbyterian Church U.S.A., 1989), 15, citing a study conducted by the Complex Systems Research Center of the University of New Hampshire.

20. Cited in Rex Ambler, *Global Theology: The Meaning of Faith in the Present World Crisis* (London: SCM Press, 1990), 43.

21. Lester Brown, "A New Era Unfolds," in *State of the World 1993: A Worldwatch Institute Report on Progress Toward a Sustainable Society* (New York: Norton, 1993), 5.

latitudes of the Northern Hemisphere, for example, the protective ozone shield is thinning twice as fast as many scientists projected just a few years ago, which some estimate could lead in the next five decades to an additional 200,000 skin cancer fatalities in the U. S. alone and millions worldwide.[22] The atmospheric concentration of carbon dioxide has increased more than 25 percent since the industrial revolution and the emission of all greenhouse gases has increased more than 9 percent in the last twenty years, threatening to warm the global atmosphere 3 to 8 degrees centigrade by the end of the next century, with potentially catastrophic consequences.[23] While the demand for water has tripled since 1950, surface reservoirs and underground aquifers are increasingly being contaminated by refuse and the more than a million tons of hazardous wastes that are generated each day throughout the world.[24] In fact, more than 1.2 billion people now lack safe drinking water.[25] Biodiversity has also been endangered; according to some scientists, as many as 40,000 species of plants and animals per year are becoming extinct, meaning that within the next century or so the world will lose "at least one quarter, possibly one third, and conceivably one half" of all species.[26]

All of these threatening and perplexing environmental issues have contributed to the summary judgment of many that the maintenance of the affluent lifestyle currently idealized in the industrialized West would likely require within the very near future a ravaging of the earth's ecosystem beyond repair. Some have suggested, moreover, that it would mean facilitating the further devolution that is already in progress of "spaceship Earth" to "slaveship Earth." This is so because the elites within the most powerful

---

22. Ibid., 10, citing a 1991 report by epidemiologists at the U. S. Environmental Protection Agency. See also Postel, "Denial in the Decisive Decade," 3.

23. *The State of the Environment* (Paris: The Organization for Economic Cooperation and Development, 1991), 20-30. See also Brown, "A New Era Unfolds," 4.

24. Sandra Postel, "Facing Water Scarcity," in *State of the World 1993: A Worldwatch Institute Report on Progress Toward a Sustainable Society* (New York: Norton, 1993), 22.

25. Postel, "Denial in the Decisive Decade," 4.

26. See Norman Myers, "The Environmental Crisis: How Big, How Important?" *Report and Background Papers of the Meeting of the Working Group, GDR, July 1986* (Geneva: WCC Publications, 1986), 101-14, cited in Jay B. McDaniel, *Of God and Pelicans: A Theology of Reverence for Life* (Louisville: Westminster/John Knox, 1989), 51. See also Norman Myers, *The Sinking Ark: A New Look at the Problem of Disappearing Species* (New York: Pergamon, 1979).

modernized states recognize that their comfortable lifestyles are rooted in fundamental inequities. They will continue to endure through the exploitation and suppression of those in marginalized societies who provide the necessary labor and resources but fail to attain just benefits, with the exception of the co-opted managerial elites within those societies.[27] How shall the church characterize and respond to these difficult issues in accordance with the redemptive purposes of the triune God?

Toward a Kin-dom Form of Spirituality

In view of these profound eco-justice dilemmas and the decimating wars and virulent explosions of racial, ethnic, and religious strife in the world — all of which testify to human sinfulness and highlight aspects of our failed stewardship of the earth and the shallowness of our concern for one another — followers of Jesus Christ are universally called to reexamine critically the nature of their witness. Given different perspectives on biblical authority, divergent methods of interpreting scripture, diverse forms of Christian piety, and distinct disciplinary traditions and spiritual communities within the church, there will be, of course, no single understanding of what faithfulness means within our historical context. As H. Richard Niebuhr recognized so ably, there have always been multiple answers to the relation between Christ and culture and we may remain certain that God employs all our various works in accomplishing God's own.[28] Nevertheless, this certainty about God does not at all diminish the need for those of us who would be disciples of Jesus Christ to maintain a responsible openness to challenges concerning our own particular interpretations of Christian faith and order, as well as to criticisms concerning our practical witness to those interpretations, i.e., to the potential need for both reformulated doctrines and redirected deeds. Our confidence in God's sovereignty ought not to obscure the fact of our own *pilgrimage toward faithfulness*, lest we fall into the trap of transforming our own perspectives and practices into divisive political programs and rigid legalisms. On this very point, Max Stackhouse remarks insightfully:

27. See James Garbarino, *Toward a Sustainable Society: An Economic, Social and Environmental Agenda for Our Children's Future* (Chicago: Noble Press, 1992), 40-41.

28. See H. Richard Niebuhr, *Christ and Culture* (New York: Harper & Row, 1951), 2.

Christianity offers more a coherent foundation to guide *praxis* than it does a prescribed orthopraxy. Faith, hope, and love, for example, are taken to be formative virtues that incline people to justice, and all social dynamics can be evaluated accordingly as they are faithful to the laws of God, anticipatory of the purposes of God. However, such a way of understanding Christian ethics implies that the debate is always, in some measure, an open one regarding which actions, precisely, are the most complete embodiments of these virtues or principles in any specific context. To judge some one or some group to be beyond the pale of God's justice because they do not immediately endorse a particular orthopraxis is to prematurely preclude the exercise of Christian conscience and open ethical debate about public decisions.[29]

Recognizing the frightening complexity of the eco-justice wilderness in which we find ourselves, as well as the bewildering diversity of voices within our global public forum — voices of Christians who represent different theological positions and forms of piety than our own, of missionaries representing other religious traditions who may be highly critical of the church, or of nonreligious individuals and organizations who may advocate forms of religio-ethical relativism or secular forms of absolutism — many devout Christians have experienced in recent years a new and unsettling degree of uncertainty about aspects of their witness. Many churches have become polarized about how to define the gospel, how to relate it to various social issues, and how to delineate norms for catholicity. As disciples of Christ have tried to consider what a general movement toward a more just, participatory, and sustainable global society might require, within increasingly pluralistic and professionally highly specialized societies, many have felt poorly prepared for the responsible exercise of Christian conscience, for public apologia, and for intercultural and interreligious encounter. Yet, as Koyama reminds us, it was in a similarly frightening and barren wilderness that God's people Israel first came face to face with both the overwhelming dangers and the immeasurable opportunities of a covenantal relationship with the divine. It was there that the people were prepared, albeit with God's slow, divine patience over a long period of years, to listen to God's instructions and to respond. It was there, Koyama asserts, that the people were called to go beyond a "pro-

---

29. Max L. Stackhouse, *Apologia: Contextualization, Globalization, and Mission in Theological Education* (Grand Rapids: Eerdmans, 1988), 186.

16

tection-from-danger religion" and a "happy-ending religion" to a "trust-God religion."[30]

Is it possible, therefore, it may be asked, that our own modern eco-justice wilderness may become for us a cathartic wandering in a threatening Sinai in which, despite all intimidating signs to the contrary, we shall be granted through God's patient grace a more perfect understanding of our call to share in God's kin-dom, a foretaste of which the Spirit provides as manna for our frightened and hungry souls? Is it possible that through divine forgiveness and instruction we might even begin to live in God's new heaven and new earth more meaningfully in the here and now with a renewed confidence in ourselves and in God, even if all aspects of the dramatic changes to which God is surely leading *all of us* are not entirely clear to *any of us?* Despite all of our human frailties, our resistance to God and our insensitivity to others, is it possible in the midst of our perilous eco-justice wilderness — the full dimensions of which the exodus flock of Moses could simply not have imagined — that we will also be mysteriously guided, as were they, to a more faithful *trust-God way of life?*

Through Spirit-led efforts to discover how we should relate to each of our neighbors and to the whole creation by discerning more comprehensively how in fact God relates to them, we shall surely see and hear things that we do not want to see and hear. It has always been that way for disciples of Jesus Christ who respond selflessly to the invitation to pick up a cross and follow, as the New Testament depictions of *metanoia,* of "turning around" in the face of that which is ultimately real, would suggest (cf. Mark 10:17-22). So how do those of us who too often suffer from contextual myopia (a self-centered near-sightedness) and from individualistic forms of spirituality turn around to expand our sphere of vision more globally and to embrace a deprovincial-ized, *kin-dom form of spirituality?* In scriptural terms, how do we open ourselves to a divinely inspired contrition in view of the world's wounded-ness, to a "godly grief" that "produces a repentance [*metanoia*] that leads to salvation" (2 Cor. 7:10)? How within our sin-ful context and from our self-limited perspective do we find traces of the global *missio Dei,* the creative mission of redemption in which God is engaged throughout God's world, and begin anew to share in the "abundant life" that it promises? More accurately, in accord with the apostolic Christian witness, how do we respond to the amazing fact that God has already lovingly found us?

30. Kosuke Koyama, *Three Mile an Hour God: Biblical Reflections* (Maryknoll: Orbis Books, 1979), 4.

17

Q 10

(1)

    A partial answer surely includes at least the following five elements of spiritual discipline, each of which involves and requires the others in an integrated, transformative process of personal and communal dimensions. First, we must begin by committing ourselves once again to *prayer*, a spiritual practice often atrophied in our daily lives, despite Jesus' instruction to "pray always" (Luke 18:1). Dialogical discernment of where God is leading us today involves most fundamentally *conversations with God*, the ground of our being. Accordingly, formal liturgical prayers of the church and all forms of spontaneous prayer should facilitate both our communication with the One who seeks always to communicate reconciliation to us, as well as our communion with our neighbors for whom we offer prayers of intercession. Christian prayer, in fact, constitutes a direct challenge to the principalities and powers of destruction. As David J. Bosch observes, even to utter sincerely the Lord's Prayer is a "subversive activity." To speak from the heart "Your kingdom come," he claims, is "a word of defiance."[31] Prayer subverts our blissful ignorance of our own failings and our potential for greater wholeness as one created in the image of God, as well as our selective ignorance of the failings and potentialities of all others within God's family. Prayer subverts our preference for thinking that, although the kin-dom has not fully come, surely the life-world that will characterize its dawning will not be radically different from our own. Prayer subverts the unspoken hope of each of us that while being Christian we will not have to be a subversive.

(2)

    Second, we have to attend with greater seriousness to the *study of Christian Scripture and tradition*. Too many of us know too little about the Word Incarnate because we do not read the words of our Bibles, choosing, because of more pressing and practical priorities, to be satisfied with a "general sense" of the apostolic witness contained therein. In addition, too many of us know too little about the diversity of Christian experience and expression that has enlivened the church down through the centuries, choosing, because of the comfortable certainty that it provides, to imagine that our own denominational heritage represents not only the best basis for Christian unity but is worthy of exact replication around the world. Study of Scripture may remind us, as Lesslie Newbigin has commented, that the worldview of the Bible is essentially a "relational" one, a worldview that emphasizes our cosmic network of kinship with all others. We may

---

31. David J. Bosch, *Transforming Mission: Paradigm Shifts in Theology of Mission* (Maryknoll: Orbis Books, 1991), 34.

discover, correspondingly, he claims, that in the Bible salvation is understood in three tenses — we have been saved; we are being saved; and we look for salvation, the completion of God's whole work — and that the salvation, the healing, of any one individual within the family of God — which in this life is never certain — is ultimately related to God's desire that everyone be saved (1 Tim. 2:4).[32] The complementary study of Christian tradition may remind us of the faithful heroism of the many saints who have gone before us and of the glorification of the Holy that has been visibly expressed when the church has taken up the cross of Christ in servant ministry. It may also sober us when we recall the church's sins of sectarian divisiveness; its hateful denunciations of Jews, Muslims, and others outside the church as though they were despised by God; and its lamentable identifications of the kin-dom with the institutional church. It may force us to acknowledge instances of the church's compromise with the powerful and privileged at the expense of those less fortunate and of apostasy when the cost of an incarnational ministry in the footsteps of Jesus has been deemed too high. Our congregations need a renewed discipline in the study of both Scripture and tradition.

Third, we need to *celebrate more actively with one another in word and deed the gift of the Holy Spirit,* through whom is manifest our call to be witnesses to what God has accomplished in Jesus Christ. Acknowledging that "in Christ God was reconciling the world to himself" (2 Cor. 5:19), we ought rightly to celebrate our gratitude for God's healing acts by proclaiming in Jesus' name repentance and the forgiveness of sins to all the peoples of the world (Luke 24:47). We are aware that there are many of our global neighbors who have yet had little contact with Christian ministries and possess no significant knowledge of Jesus Christ, and many others who, while they perhaps know of Christianity, have encountered no explicit or compelling witness to the gospel. Therefore, we need to embrace energetically and humbly the life of a church truly evangelical, a church concerned about the more than one billion of our neighbors who remain unevangelized and the billions who do not recognize in Jesus Christ the revelation of life's central meaning.[33]

Moreover, if we are to give adequate account of the hope that is within

32. Lesslie Newbigin, *The Gospel in a Pluralist Society* (Grand Rapids: Eerdmans; Geneva: WCC, 1989), 171-72, 178.

33. See David B. Barrett, "Annual Statistical Table on Global Mission: 1993," *International Bulletin of Missionary Research* 17, no. 1 (January 1993): 22-23. Annual reports, with notes, are published each year in the journal's January issue.

us (1 Pet. 3:15), and if that hope anticipates the inviting and all-encompassing kin-dom of God for whose sake Christ lived, died, and was resurrected, then our discipleship has to maintain an integrity between our verbal witness and our deeds. It must embrace actively the Word Incarnate whom we encounter in the hungry, the thirsty, the stranger, the naked, the sick, and the imprisoned, even as Jesus said (Matt. 25:40). In fact, our Christian mission both near and far involves far more decisively than most of us have been willing to acknowledge that we must be "doers of the word, and not merely hearers who deceive themselves" (James 1:22). We have found "hearing," or more precisely *selective* hearing, confined to occasional Sunday morning gatherings, to be much more compatible with what we have come to define as a "normal" Christian lifestyle than is the sacrificial way of the cross. We must confess that we are very much afraid of losing ourselves for the sake of the gospel.

Keith Miller once observed in a meditation on Christ's commission to his disciples to be witnesses "to the ends of the earth" (Acts 1:8), that most of us tend to think of the "ends of the earth" as some geographically far off place. This is because we generally think of the *center* of the world as wherever *we* are, as a result of our unfortunate contextual myopia. "But where then is the end of the earth from God's perspective?" he inquires. "If the heart which beat in Jesus Christ was in any sense the heart which throbs at the center of the universe," Miller continues, "then the 'end of the earth' from God's perspective may be wherever the influence from that heartbeat stops."[34] Globalizing our Christian ministries involves developing our gifts for a distinctly spiritual perspective that views the whole as an interconnected reality, the healthiness of which depends on the healthiness of all its various parts. It entails a vision in which local and global witness become theologically and practically interdependent.

Fourth, we ought to recognize that we desperately need one another in discerning God's will. In addition to prayer, we need both *intrafaith and interfaith dialogue* on a global scale if we are to see more clearly dimensions of the *missio Dei* in our time. Because our own individual perspectives are necessarily limited and far too often distorted by self-interest, our faithfulness frequently depends on challenges posed by others who see and hear something critically important that we do not. The Christian ecumenical movement of this century has surely shown this to be true. Within the bonds of the universal church, with all of its diversity, we need to continue in a spirit of humility our intratraditional dialogue on the nature of our

34. Keith Miller, *The Taste of New Wine* (Waco: Word Books, 1965), 116.

20

ministry in the name of Jesus Christ and on the limits of acceptable diversity. We must continue to struggle earnestly with the meaning of Christ's prayer that we may all be one (John 17:11).

Moreover, because we believe that God "has not left himself without a witness in doing good" in any time or place (Acts 14:17), and because we affirm the sovereignty of the Holy One whose very nature is *agape* (self-giving love), we ought not to think of God's healing activity as being confined only to the institutional church. Rather, we should humbly enter into dialogue with people of all living faiths and ideologies to give as well as to receive. As the World Council of Churches has confessed, in such encounters "we come not as manipulators but as genuine fellow-pilgrims, to speak with them of what we believe God to have done in Jesus Christ who has gone before us, but whom we seek to meet anew in dialogue."[35] As Newbigin has aptly suggested, such dialogue need not focus primarily on the question of *who* is going to be saved — a question that remains according to the Bible the prerogative of God to answer — but rather on the question, "What is the meaning and goal of this common human story in which we are all, Christians and others together, participants?"[36]

Fifth, we have to manifest a renewed *trust in God and in one another.* In both the Jewish and Christian traditions, "faith" is characterized not so much by "belief that" as "belief in." Being faithful means going beyond accepting the truth of certain propositions about God to *trusting in,* with all of one's life, the compassionate, saving presence of God. Christianity is defined less by beliefs about Jesus as the Christ than by belief *in* him, though of course the two are closely related. Intellectual affirmations about Jesus are important, but a holistic relationship with him is fundamental; trusting in Jesus Christ is foundational for all else.

Similarly, then, as Choan-Seng Song has argued, dialogical relationships between Christians, and between persons of all religious and ideological commitments, need to be firmly established on the basis of a mutual trust.[37] With honesty and humility, one must be able to say to one's brother and sister, "I believe in you; I respect you as a person, as I ask for similar

35. World Council of Churches, *Guidelines on Dialogue with People of Living Faiths and Ideologies* (Geneva: WCC, 1979), 11.

36. Lesslie Newbigin, *The Gospel in a Pluralist Society,* 182.

37. Choan-Seng Song, *Tell Us Many Names: Story Theology from an Asian Perspective* (Maryknoll: Orbis Books, 1984), 138. See also William Dyrness, *Learning about Theology from the Third World* (Grand Rapids: Zondervan, 1990).

respect; I trust in your sincerity and conviction, even if we do not agree."
A principle Christian concern must be the creation of an authentic global
community, i.e., a place of *global communion,* a locus of mutuality in which
the struggles for peace with justice may be addressed and in which all voices
may be freely heard. That kind of vulnerability and trust in other human
beings, who so often disappoint us as we disappoint ourselves, must be
rooted, if it is to last, in our utter trust in the triune God. In that very
vulnerability lies our strength. The God whom we worship we certainly
cannot claim to comprehend fully, for God's judgments are unsearchable
and God's ways inscrutable (Rom. 11:33). We cannot know precisely where
discipleship shall lead us. Yet, guided by the Spirit we can say with the
apostle Paul, "If God is for us, who is against us?" (Rom. 8:31), and with
the psalmist, "The Lord is the stronghold of my life; of whom shall I be
afraid?" (Ps. 27:1).

From biblical times to the present, of course, the *real* church has often
been afraid. Yet, the *ideal* church, which is always on the horizon before us,
always in our future and not in our past, beckons us ever forward in our
servant ministries in the name of Christ. The church that knows "the first
fruits of the Spirit" (Rom. 8:23) is to be a sign of the kin-dom that is to
come. Bosch writes, "Living in the creative tension of, at the same time,
being called out of the world and sent into the world, it is challenged to be
God's *experimental garden on earth,* a fragment of the reign of God."[38] As
a sign, as a sacrament, the ideal church always mediates graces as it points
beyond itself to the Gracious One who gives it life.

The eco-justice issues that confront us in our global village are so
increasingly complex and far-reaching that they are beyond the capacities
of any one group of us without the others to understand sensitively and to
address adequately. Egocentric and ethnocentric fragmentation, isolation,
alienation, and domination may be the response of many. Yet, the serious
global crises of our time — social, political, economic, ecological — may
also provide new opportunities for spiritual renewal and change both personal and communal. They may offer to those of us who would be disciples
of Jesus Christ, even in our own story of constantly drawing near to and
of falling away from the kin-dom, new possibilities of witnessing and participating in healing ways in the stories of others within our expanded
family and in God's great story of creation and redemption. They may

---

38. David J. Bosch, *Transforming Mission: Paradigm Shifts in Theology of Mission,*
11. Emphasis mine.

furnish us an impetus to pursue a new and more comprehensive sense of the truth that shall set us free (John 8:32), as we listen for the whisper of God's Spirit and learn from brothers and sisters whom we have never known before. They may present to us a captivating call to a *metanoia*, a turning around, to a more globally envisioned ministry in the name of Christ even right where we live, "at the ends of the earth."

Globalization and Theological Education

Recognizing that "the very nature and content of our Christian confession draws Christians to pay the closest attention to the realities of the world as it has developed under God's creative, disciplinary, and redemptive rule," and reflecting concerns variously expressed within Roman Catholic, Orthodox, Evangelical Protestant, and Ecumenical Protestant churches, the World Council of Churches urged its membership in 1979 to promote new educational programs "to enhance the understanding of the cultural, religious and ideological traditions of humankind." Furthermore, it called for theological seminaries and colleges "to prepare Christian ministers with the training and sensitivity necessary for interreligious dialogue."[39] At the same time, the Association of Theological Schools in the United States and Canada, while seeking closer relations with other theological associations around the world, established a Committee on Global Theological Education which, through three biennial periods, 1980-1986, effectively brought the issues of globalization and contextualization to the forefront of discussions among theological educators. In the fall of 1987, the mandate of the committee was expanded and its membership enlarged in a reconfigured Task Force on Globalization, charged with "providing the needed research and organizational structures to make the 1990s a decade to implement global theological education in North American schools."[40] At the heart of all of these efforts to reenvision forms of education for ministry that are appropriate to our profoundly interconnected and threatened world, and to the church's efforts to relate the unchanging gospel that is for *everyone* to the realities of a changing world that has failed to affect the lives of *no*

39. World Council of Churches, *Guidelines on Dialogue with People of Living Faiths and Ideologies*, 3, 18.
40. The Association of Theological Schools in the United States and Canada, *36th Biennial Meeting Program and Reports* (San Francisco, June 19-21, 1988): 70-71.

one, is the simple but elusive quest for Christian faithfulness, individual and corporate. In that sense, what is involved for the church is both ancient as well as new. As Stackhouse has commented:

> Globalization involves the possibility of a gracious recovery and re-casting of the catholicity of the faith. The very term suggests that the church, amid a diverse and pluralistic yet singular and increasingly unified world, can move beyond the fissiparous tendencies of sectarianism and dogmatism and beyond the mere pragmatism of adjusting to the demands of the moment. It thus requires a new quest for excellence; a renewed dedication to mission, ecumenicity, dialogue and justice; and fresh approaches to learning and teaching. Above all, it calls for courage and wisdom to speak of God in ways that signal the divine universality, reform the church, and guide the reconstruction of civilization.[41]

Those Christian leaders engaged today in one way or another in the globalization of theological education and in the globalization of the church's ministries at every level — local, regional, national, and international — inevitably encounter, among the many issues that need to be addressed, three critical questions that represent the particular foci for this textbook and reader: First, *what can we affirm about the meaning of other faiths?* Second, *how in our time shall we define the church's mission priorities in relation to God's mission?* Third, *why and in what sense need we understand interreligious dialogue to be a Christian task?* These three interrelated questions press each of us to reexamine the very foundations of our faith. They lead us to ask, in the company of those whose Christian experience may be different from our own, or others who may not at all share our religious heritage or commitments, what it is that we believe and why. They represent critical concerns about which there is clearly no consensus within the church today and with which Christians must continue to be in dialogue as together we seek our role in Christ's ministry of reconciliation into the twenty-first century.

The Meaning of Other Religious Traditions

The first major section of the book examines elements of the controversy within the Christian church about the *meaning* of other faiths. Since we

41. Max L. Stackhouse, "The Global Future and the Future of Globalization," *The Christian Century* 111, no. 4 (February 2-9, 1994): 118.

live in increasingly pluralistic societies, shaped by many religious and cultural traditions, it has now become more important than ever to be able to state our own faith *in relation to the faith of others*. Wilfred Cantwell Smith has framed the essential question quite provocatively: "We explain the fact that the Milky Way is there by the doctrine of creation, but how do we explain the fact that the Bhagavad Gita is there?"[42] For example, is the Gita, one of the most important texts of modern Hinduism, the product of human delusion or demonic possession, an element of a tradition that serves only to lead people "away from God and hold them captive from God?"[43] Or could the Gita in any way be related to a genuine experience of the one God that we Christians claim to have encountered in Jesus? Could the Gita represent or contain a divinely inspired message especially relevant to Hindu culture? Or could it be relevant even more universally to all human beings, including those of us in the church? Does it contain truths that we need to hear? How would we even begin to formulate an answer to such questions, especially if we have never read the Bhagavad Gita or heard it interpreted by a knowledgeable Hindu? Would such a reading on our part or a Hindu interpretation be unnecessary if we have already read the Bible?

The introductory essay for section 1 begins with a general discussion of the nature of religion, providing a comparative perspective on spiritual commitments and communities as a prolegomenon for our theological reflections. The essay also includes a brief historical survey of various ways in which Christian leaders prior to the twentieth century expressed their convictions concerning salvation in Jesus Christ in view of the reality of those who existed outside of the institutional church. Finally, the essay presents a concise description of a commonly employed typology which delineates three major theological options with regard to our relation to people of other living faiths and ideologies: *exclusivism, inclusivism, and pluralism*. The edited readings for the section include a few short selections from Christian works prior to the twentieth century. Most of the readings, however, highlight the diversity found in writings of twentieth century Christian leaders — Roman Catholic, Eastern Orthodox, and Protestant — that in some way illuminate dimensions of the problem and exemplify types of responses.

---

42. Wilfred Cantwell Smith, *The Faith of Other Men* (New York: The New American Library, 1963), 133.

43. Edmund Perry, *The Gospel in Dispute: The Relation of Christian Faith to Other Missionary Religions* (New York: Doubleday, 1958), 83.

The Global Challenge to Missions

Section 2 of the textbook and reader focuses on priorities for Christian mission globally conceived. Its introductory essay acknowledges the new sense of global cooperation and mutuality among churches around the world, as well as the unparalleled opportunities and dangers presented to the church in our more technologically, economically, and politically integrated global context. It proceeds, then, to pose seven key questions for the church with regard to contemporary Christian mission. The first question, *what is mission?* leads to a consideration of the diverse and sometimes ambiguous ways that Christians employ basic biblical and theological terms, such as mission, evangelism, salvation, and uniqueness. Second, the question, *why engage in mission?* points to the different goals that Christians may emphasize. Some Christians, for example, would say that the purpose of mission is to save souls from eternal separation from God through conversion, while others would define it primarily in relation to faithful efforts to help those in need, to work for peace and justice, to provide spiritual encouragement, or to plant churches. Specific criteria for determining success in mission are defined in each case in relation to the principal goals envisioned. Third, the question, *who are the missionaries?* facilitates a review of the trends from foreign to indigenous missionaries, from professional to lay missionaries, from career to short-term missionaries, and from Western to Eastern and Southern missionaries.

A fourth key question, *who are the missionized?* prompts a discussion of parallels between Christian perspectives on mission and those expressed within other missionary-minded world religions, as well as of divergent views within the church concerning the primary targets for evangelization. A fifth question, *where do we do mission?* leads to a discussion on the relation between local and global ministries, as well as on the practice of some churches to initiate foreign mission work only in direct response to specific requests for assistance from indigenous churches overseas. *How do we engage in mission?* a sixth question, presses us to consider various mission methodologies in relation to the issues of power, money, and technology. A final seventh question, *what is the nature of the competition?* encourages reflection on various expressions of opposition to Christian mission in the world. The edited readings that follow the essay are intended to represent a diversity of viewpoints within the church on a variety of important issues relevant to contemporary missiology. The section's selection of readings, while not exhaustive of all judgments or issues worthy of attention, should provoke considerable reflection and discussion by representing different options for interpreting our call to be disciples to the ends of the earth.

Interreligious Dialogue

Section 3 of the textbook and reader focuses on *interreligious dialogue as a Christian task*. Its introductory essay begins with a discussion of what Mark Kline Taylor has described as a critical postmodern trilemma, our call "to acknowledge some sense of tradition, to celebrate plurality, and to resist domination."[44] Posed here for Christians is the question of how we shall give witness to the good news that we have encountered in Jesus Christ, while at the same time sharing life and struggling with common issues more significantly and more sensitively than ever before with persons of other faiths and ideologies, and also while recognizing and resisting all those forces in the world that tend toward dehumanization and domination.

The essay reviews divergent responses to our contemporary trilemma by noting, first, the contributions of several Christian scholars from different theological perspectives who have considered *the why and how of interreligious dialogue*. Some argue that dialogue is both a practical as well as a theological necessity. As a needed corrective to the church's traditional and predominantly monological approach, for these Christians it is an activity directed toward mutual transformation. Others, while affirming that dialogue may be fully consistent with belief in the finality of Jesus Christ, remain suspicious of mutual transformations, and so are especially concerned to delimit the kinds of dialogues in which Christians may be appropriately engaged. All are intent on confirming that disagreements concerning ultimacy need not be accompanied by disrespectful or distrustful relationships.

Second, the essay considers perspectives on the kinds of *inner transformations* that interreligious dialogues may foster. It raises the question of how we shall evaluate the testimonies of individual Christians who claim that it is, indeed, possible to receive nourishment from two or more spiritual traditions in ways that do not compromise essential aspects of those traditions. It thus poses the issue, for example, of how Christians should respond to invitations from Buddhist masters, Muslim imams, or Hindu saints to

44. Mark Kline Taylor, *Remembering Esperanza: A Cultural-Political Theology for North American Praxis* (Maryknoll: Orbis Books, 1990), 23.

explore spiritual enrichment through profound experiential encounters with Buddhists, Muslims, and Hindus, i.e., with the range of beliefs and practices of sincere persons committed to other religious traditions. Some Christians wish to emphasize the creative possibilities of a "global spirituality"; some want to warn of the dangers of syncretism and the potential for a diminished sense of commitment to any particular religious way.

Third, the essay illuminates the responses of several contemporary religious leaders within different traditions — Jewish, Muslim, Hindu, Buddhist, and Christian — concerning *the tasks for interreligious cooperation.* It raises the question not only of how persons of different faiths might cooperate in ventures that are made necessary by circumstances, but it also asks, in view of our divergent understandings of ultimacy, whether it is possible to move beyond mere tolerance of the other toward "a universal spiritual vision of human dignity and social justice." It recognizes that all of us must return to the resources of our own faiths to find bases for understanding and cooperating with our neighbor, for addressing the paradox of embracing the other *as other* but not as *mere other.* The edited readings which follow the section's introductory essay are intended to elicit critical discussion of all of these issues on the cutting edge of the practical theological work of the church.

Aware of the profound connectedness and deep woundedness that characterizes the human condition, given to dream our Lord's dream of a just and peaceable kin-dom, and lured by the Spirit to live into that gracious reality of the future in the confusing here and now, we are called to engage in our time in a new measure of prayerful reflection and debate on the meaning of Christian faithfulness. Our responsibility as ambassadors of Christ is a daunting one, a fact about which there is no disagreement amidst the diversity of concerns and viewpoints expressed by Christians in the three sections of the book that follow. In conversation with God and one another on the directions for ministry and theology in our global context, we struggle to find ways of responding to the fundamental questions of how we shall glorify God and how we shall love others as God in Christ first loved us. Yet we know how far we are from formulating compelling answers to those transformative questions and living them out gracefully in the contemporary world. So we continue to wrestle with God and with one another for more perfect answers to embody. That is our enduring vocation in the world: trying through grace to integrate our small stories with God's great story. Along the paths of Christian discipleship, we may encounter evidence of how far-reaching our own modest witness in word and deed can be for a church in which local and global ministries are interdependent. Yet whether or not we ever learn of the myriad ways in which our own witness may have changed the lives of others, as pilgrims we will undoubtedly encounter the infinite mercy of the mysterious One who forgives us our sins and whose holy will shall surely come to be.

Together these three sections should help you the reader address the question, What does globalization mean to me and my calling? In a very real, almost ironic sense, globalization only becomes real when we realize that it is at the local level — our local level — that mission is done.

Discussion Questions

1. Is the love of God and neighbor more difficult in our time than in earlier periods of Christian history? Why would you agree or disagree with those who say that it is?

2. What do the authors mean by Christians' need for a "dialogical process of discernment" in relation to human hopes for a more just, participatory, and sustainable global society?

3. What will realizing a greater degree of mutuality and communion with our global neighbors require of us? What has been and should be the role of the church in this quest?

4. Many Christians are calling for a conscientization process. What might this mean in terms of greater openness to God and neighbor? In what ways do you feel that you are prepared for the changes that it may entail? How do you think such a conscientization process might be a disturbing or frightening experience for the church universal, for your local congregation, for members of your own family, and for you?

5. Have you ever experienced "decentering" in your life? What were the circumstances? How did it feel at the time? How did it change you?

6. How would you explain "globalization" in ministry in relation to the authors' definition? Is this an important element in your own Christian witness?

7. In view of the statistical evidence of dimensions of the world's current ecological crisis and related concerns for the carrying capacity of the earth, how do you articulate in ministry a Christian sense of stewardship for creation?

8. In view of voices from the suffering socioeconomic underside that testify to another dimension of the world's woundedness, how shall we

envision and work toward a replicable lifestyle for all members of the human family?

9. What are the implications of the fact that there will undoubtedly be many different Christian responses to these difficult eco-justice issues? How shall the church express its unity in the midst of its plurality? How will you share your own witness in relation to Christians who embody different forms of piety?

10. How do you understand the five elements of a kin-dom form of spirituality which the authors describe? What other valuable elements in integrating our own human stories with God's great story of redemption could be helpfully discussed?

For Further Reading

Cobb, John B. Jr. *Sustainability: Economics, Ecology, and Justice.* Maryknoll: Orbis Books, 1992.

Evans, Robert A., Alice F. Evans, and David A. Roozen, eds. *The Globalization of Theological Education.* Maryknoll: Orbis Books, 1993.

Granberg-Michaelson, Wesley. *Redeeming the Creation: The Rio Earth Summit: Challenges for the Churches.* Geneva: WCC Publications, 1992.

Küng, Hans. *Global Responsibility: In Search of a New World Ethic.* New York: Crossroad, 1991.

McDaniel, Jay B. *Of God and Pelicans: A Theology of Reverence for Life.* Louisville: Westminster/John Knox, 1989.

Schreiter, Robert J. *Constructing Local Theologies.* Maryknoll: Orbis Books, 1985.

Sider, Ronald J. *Rich Christians in an Age of Hunger.* Dallas: Word, 1990.

Stackhouse, Max L. *Apologia: Contextualization, Globalization, and Mission in Theological Education.* Grand Rapids: Eerdmans, 1988.

Thistlethwaite, Susan Brooks, and Mary Potter Engel, eds. *Lift Every Voice: Constructing Christian Theologies from the Underside.* San Francisco: Harper & Row, 1990.

Wilkinson, Loren, ed. *Earthkeeping in the Nineties: Stewardship of Creation.* Grand Rapids: Eerdmans, 1991.

World Council of Churches, Christian Faith and the World Economy Today. Geneva: WCC Publications, 1992.

TOWARD A CHRISTIAN THEOLOGY OF RELIGIONS

Christian Theology and People of Other Faiths

Christian theology is a contextual activity. It involves discerning and articulating within particular and ever changing historical circumstances authentic, credible, and relevant ways for disciples of Jesus Christ to express ultimate truth in word and deed. This prayerful and critically reflective activity presupposes experience within Christian community and a willingness to test constantly the authenticity, credibility, and relevance of any Christian expression both within that faith community and within the larger human community. Christian theological reflection, therefore, is a dynamic, dialogical endeavor conducted on the broadest possible scale under the guidance of the Holy Spirit. *Authenticity* as a criterion for truth requires that all Christian expressions be responsibly evaluated in light of the biblical witness to God's disclosure in and through Jesus and in light of the traditions and experiences of discernment of the worldwide Christian church. Critical reflection on the *credibility* of any Christian expression must refer to the conditions for inspiring belief as judged by common human experience and reason. In our religiously plural world, as Schubert Ogden has argued, there must be offered in the public forum "reasons purporting to establish its credibility in terms of what all of us somehow experience and understand, if only implicitly."[1] *Relevance* requires that Christian words and deeds meaningfully express the transformative truth concerning the reign of God drawn near to us in Jesus in ways shaped by and appropriate to the particularity of each context for witness. "Shaped

1. Schubert M. Ogden, *On Theology* (San Francisco: Harper & Row, 1986), 140.

33

by" refers to the need for *indigenization,* i.e., for an inculturated expression of the gospel selectively adapted to visionary and ethical dimensions of each receptor's world of meaning; "appropriate to" refers to the need for *contextualization,* for a localized expression of the gospel transformatively addressing the human condition as concretely manifested within each particular community.

Christians in our time are becoming ever more cognizant of, if not always more sensitive to, the complexities within every human context that make spiritual discernment and faithful action difficult. We are becoming acutely aware of the multiplicity of competing perspectives and judgments within the church on virtually every issue of substance. Indeed, in view of the controversies that threaten to alienate and divide us, our polarized churches are often striving simply to find ways to continue a real dialogue within a covenantal relationship. Among the defining practical theological issues of our time that are surrounded by debate, perhaps none poses a more difficult set of interrelated foundational questions than the relation of Christians to people of other living faiths and ideologies. It is this perplexing and unavoidable issue, therefore, and its evaluation in terms of the potential authenticity, credibility, and relevance of contemporary Christian witness in a religiously plural world, that is the focus of this section.

Understanding Religion

In recent years, historians of religions and other scholars in the field of religious studies have developed general theories concerning the nature of religion that may provide an advantageous frame of reference for our consideration of religious pluralism as a theological issue. Therefore, as a prolegomenon to an exploration of the history of the contemporary debate within the church concerning approaches for developing an adequate Christian theology of religions, it may be helpful — while recognizing concerns about the distinctiveness of Christianity — to begin with a brief consideration of two concepts in a general theory of religion that could inform aspects of our discussion: *religion as a form of human labor* and *religion as a processual reality.*

As Jonathan Z. Smith has observed, "what we study when we study religion is one mode of constructing worlds of meaning, worlds within which men [and women] find themselves and in which they choose to dwell."[2] Employing sacred symbols, linguistic and behavioral, religious persons establish these worlds of meaning by giving expression to revelatory experiences of ultimacy that are believed both to correspond to reality as well as to shape it.[3] Grounded in deep mystery, these symbols both salvifically delineate the absolute context for human existence and define the normative modes of action appropriate to it. Accordingly, as Frederick Streng has asserted, religion may be understood fundamentally as "a means to ultimate transformation."[4] That is, religion concerns knowledge and power for holistic change. In response to the universal experiences of suffering and lack of fulfillment that characterize the finite human condition, religious persons pursue a pathway of illumination and transformation toward the threshold of an alternative, spiritual universe in which suffering may become meaningful and ultimate fulfillment possible.

Most of us initially experience a religious world of meaning at a young age as an objective fact in a socialization process. It is experienced as a sacred portrait given to us in our familial or cultural context of the way the world is in relation to the way it should be. It is accepted as a symbolic map of reality offering us a sense of who we are in relation to all things. It provides us with an important basis, however dimly perceived, for beginning to understand our value, purpose, and location in the cosmos. It offers us a "home" in the most profound and comprehensive sense. It makes us aware of the boundaries between safety zones and realms of danger in the universe and directs us to the narrow but well-worn paths which may keep us from getting lost along our way.

Recognizing the compelling power of these "inherited" religio-cultural worlds, with their visionary and ethical dimensions, we can freely acknowledge that had we been born to different parents in a different community in a different time or place — in Beijing or Banaras, Katmandu or Cairo, Lhasa or La Paz — we would probably be very different persons religiously than who we are. We are able to recognize that spiritual orientation, to a significant extent, is a function of an individual's socio-temporal context and that our religious identity is Christian — and not Buddhist,

2. Jonathan Z. Smith, *Map Is Not Territory: Studies in the History of Religions* (Leiden: E. J. Brill, 1978), 290.

3. See Clifford Geertz, "Religion as a Cultural System," in *The Interpretation of Cultures* (New York: Basic Books, 1973), 87-125.

4. See Frederick J. Streng, *Understanding Religious Life*, 3rd ed. (Belmont, Calif.: Wadsworth, 1985), 2.

Hindu, Muslim, or Shinto — largely because of the givenness of our particular historical circumstances. Correspondingly, we are fully aware that the vast majority of persons whom God has created to live on the earth since the beginning of humankind have not been Christian because of the givenness of their particular circumstances.

Moreover, we can now acknowledge that despite twenty centuries of active missionary efforts on the part of the church, Christians remain a minority people. While Christianity currently ranks as the largest institutional religion, Christians of all varieties still only constitute approximately thirty-three percent of the world's population. Two-thirds of humanity today, about four billion people, live outside the church. Although Islam is growing more rapidly than Christianity, the size of the Christian community relative to the world's population will most likely remain approximately the same for the foreseeable future.[5] Historically, "the vast majority of converts [to Christianity]," as Paul Knitter has noted, "have come from polytheistic or animistic religions or from religions that had already lost their personal hold on the hearts of their peoples."[6] Relatively few persons have ever converted to Christianity from another vital major religious tradition such as Buddhism, Hinduism, or Islam. Religious pluralism, therefore, appears to be an enduring characteristic of the human situation as we know it, a fact directly related to the multiplicity of religio-cultural circumstances in which we human beings are socialized.

Yet while commonly introduced to each of us as objective realities, as trustworthy "corrective lenses" inherited from our ancestors (biological and/or spiritual), religious worlds of meaning at some point must also be explicitly chosen. They must be internalized as *our own orientation* to the universe. Born simply human, in some sense we have to *become* Christian or Buddhist or Sikh or Taoist. Not that the worldview that we accept will explain completely and provide satisfactorily for all of the incongruities and mysteries of life and death that we encounter in this world, but it has for us a certain integrity and inner coherence, a certain wholeness and healing power, that no other worldview with reference to transcendence has. Many religious traditions require that as a sign of spiritual maturity members make some ritual affirmation of the validity of the shared visions

5. See David B. Barrett, "Annual Statistical Table on Global Mission," *International Bulletin of Missionary Research* 17, no. 1 (January 1993): 22-23.

6. Paul F. Knitter, *No Other Name? A Critical Survey of Christian Attitudes Toward the World Religions* (Maryknoll: Orbis Books, 1985), 4.

and norms which effectively bind their community of discernment and transformation together. Yet every individual within the community remains personally engaged in world construction as he or she constantly strives to apply those shared understandings creatively and appropriately within the unique rhythm and texture of his or her own life.

Religion, then, as Smith suggests, can be understood as one form of "human labor."[7] For just as spiders work so diligently to spin their gossamer webs, their "homes," so human beings also persistently and carefully labor to spin around themselves webs or structures of signification. As Clifford Geertz has asserted, unlike all other forms of life, humans obviously require more than intrinsic, biochemical or genetic information in order to structure their existence.[8] All other forms of life, apparently, never have to contemplate their particular vocation in the order of creation; that information is included in their highly specific genetic coding. However, the intrinsic information provided in the inherited genetic coding for humans is much more generalized and not too specific when it comes to troubling issues like human identity and destiny. Therefore, convincing answers to such crucial questions have to be constantly formulated and reformulated out of human experience and transmitted through extrinsic, symbolic sources of information: through mythic narratives and doctrinal expositions, religious rites and moral codes, structures of holy community and guidelines for relating to those outside of our community in the larger world.

Human beings, then, uniquely as far as we know, construct the reality in which they live. They must always be about the task of applying their most fundamental and comprehensive insights and deeply held convictions about meaning and value to the particular, often ambiguous, and messy details of daily living. This "exegetical" task, based on the sacred canon of one's religious community, is most crucial when it is most difficult: at times of frustration, fear, and failure.[9] Such experiences remind us of our intellectual, moral, and biological limits, the human finitude that we cannot

---

7. Jonathan Z. Smith, *Imaging Religion: From Babylon to Jonestown* (Chicago: University of Chicago Press, 1982), 43.

8. See Clifford Geertz, *The Interpretation of Cultures*, 91-94.

9. See Jonathan Z. Smith's argument that religion is primarily *exegesis*, that "if there is anything that is distinctive about religion as a human activity, it is a matter of degree rather than kind, what might be described as the extremity of its enterprise for exegetical totalization," in *Imaging Religion: From Babylon to Jonestown*, 44.

escape. Moreover, they threaten us because in many instances they may portend and contribute to an even greater threat to our existence, the experience of utter meaninglessness. One of the greatest threats to human survival appears to be the feeling that our lives contribute finally to nothing, that in the end we don't really matter. Indeed, human religiosity seems to be founded on the conviction that life in this world must in some significant sense matter, that what we think, feel, and do in this world must be related to some more ultimate reality or dimension of experience. Religion involves remembering from moment to moment the sacred character of our fleeting existence here from cradle to grave. It involves acknowledging that our lives must, beyond our penultimate aims, contribute to some individual or communal destiny beyond the limits of our particular time and space. Religion may be understood as our human labor in stubborn defiance of that feeling of despair to bring what we experience as sacred and ultimately meaningful to the very center of our existence and the center of our culture.

This general understanding of religion is obviously one which recognizes the relation of the products of this persistent exegetical work to the ever changing circumstances of life and the unique personalities of individual persons. Indeed, beyond interpreting religion as a form of human labor, it may also be helpful for Christians reflecting on the nature of religious commitments and communities to understand the religious life, as Wilfred Cantwell Smith has aptly suggested, as *participation in a process.*[10] This perspective on the religious life involves at least several important aspects.

It involves, first, the realization that religious communities are complex realities that commonly permit, if not actively encourage, multiple forms of piety. "Pieties" here refer to dispositions of thought and action that are both the means and ends of transformational disciplines. We need to acknowledge, accordingly, that all Christians are not the same, all Baha'is are not the same, all Jews are not the same, and so forth. Within each community, for example, some persons may be advocates of what might be termed a "visionary piety." That is, there are those who tend to emphasize the attainment of mental dispositions, the "seeing" of the true nature of things. Some persons, on the other hand, may practice a form of "ethical piety." That is, there may be those who tend to emphasize ultimate trans-

10. Consult Wilfred Cantwell Smith, "Religious Life as Participation in Process," in *Towards a World Theology: Faith and the Comparative History of Religion* (Philadelphia: Westminster Press, 1981), 21-44.

formation through normative activities, the "doing" of truth. Internal disagreements may frequently arise, of course, within similarly structured forms of piety, as individuals and groups debate which specific aspects of the visionary or ethical norms should be understood as most significant and how to balance experiential intensity and expressional clarity. In fact, it would appear that virtually all religious traditions that have survived for any extended period of time have valorized multiple forms of piety and, at least to that extent, the intrafaith conflict they have usually engendered.

Furthermore, this perspective on religious life entails the recognition that the terms "Christianity," "Hinduism," "Jainism," "Judaism," and so on, which we commonly employ to refer to certain historical religious traditions, are essentially theoretical constructs. That is, we never encounter another religious tradition per se; we encounter only the creative witness and presence of uniquely individual human beings who, given the compelling options which they find in their setting, are inspired to identify themselves with a particular world of meaning as they interpret and give concrete expression to central visions of ultimacy and paradigms for public and private behavior. We tend to reify cumulative faith traditions by failing to recognize their fundamental dynamism. Indeed, as Wilfred Cantwell Smith has claimed, Christianity itself, as with any tradition, is always "under construction." This means that the historic and contemporary witness of millions of Christians around the world — in many cases remarkably similar, yet in some cases significantly different — and their joint participation in the on-going Christian process, as the church constantly struggles to determine its essential message and the limits of acceptable diversity, continually defines and redefines what anyone might mean by the abstract concept of "Christianity." Smith writes likewise with regard to Buddhism:

> From Sri Lanka to Japan, and at one time from Samarqand to Sumatra . . . each Buddhist has added to, subtracted from, or in some way modified some part of the Buddhist tradition that he has inherited from his forebears and that he passes on to his children; or she, from and to hers. Our task is to study not simply the teachings of the Buddha, but rather what men, women and children — many millions of them — have done with these teachings, or through them, or because of them, in interaction with them; have done or felt, or realized, or become. Every Buddhist who has ever lived has added his or her own particular brick to the structure of the continuingly growing Buddhist movement.

Not every one has been brilliantly creative, or even significantly so:

in many cases the bricks have been small, and remarkably like previous bricks in the structure. On the other hand, from time to time persons, or groups, have come along who have introduced new types of brick, or new types of architectural pattern altogether, or new windows or doors or balconies or towers. As the movement in its geographic spread reached new areas, persons added to the growing structure of bricks in a new style: often the traditional style of their locality, perhaps quite different from those in other Buddhist countries. Yet in each case these men and women would not have been able to add their particular innovations, however novel, had they not had the previous structure to build on, and had the previous structure not inspired them to feel that taking part in this project was worthwhile.[11]

Finally, expanding on the religious contrast between the world as it is in relation to the way it should be, this perspective leads us to recognize that to be a religious person means to be committed to certain spiritual ideals that humans rarely, if ever, seem able to live up to. Our spiritual ideals always transcend our spiritual realities. There are back-sliding Baptists and back-sliding Buddhists. Employing the unique languages of our various religious communities, we all commonly name what we hope to become and dream of doing in the future far more than we celebrate who we actually are and what we have concretely accomplished in the past. Indeed, through interreligious dialogue, we Christians have come to discover that those committed to other spiritual paths are people much like us: people who want to believe what they often doubt; people who sincerely aspire to become what they nevertheless fail to achieve; people who recognize that their ultimate hope lies less in what they achieve through their own unaided insights and abilities than in some form of grace that may come their way. Thus, reflecting on the dynamic struggles through time of his own Christian community, Smith comments:

> "To be a Christian," I am happy enough both to propose for others and to accept for myself, means — has always meant — to participate in the Christian Church: to take on its past, perhaps not without criticism yet, for all its aberrations, without ultimate embarrassment, and indeed with decisive appreciation; to take on its present, again certainly not without criticism, even not without tears, but in the end also not without

11. Ibid., 25.

hope; to contribute what one can to its future, in full seriousness and responsibility and with a devastating sense of one's own inadequacy and yet leaving the outcome to God. . . . We choose to participate in the historical Christian process because through it we find God; more strictly, of course, because through it God finds us.[12]

These two basic ideas from comparative studies in religions — religion as a form of human labor and religion as a processual reality — are instructive, therefore, in several ways as we proceed to consider the current debate within the church on different approaches for developing a Christian theology of religions. They may be more significant for this theological engagement than one might initially imagine. Why? First, they may serve to remind us of the dialectic between the givenness and the chosenness of any religious vision and way of life. As will be noted below, a fuller understanding of this dialectic emerged within the Christian church when knowledge of other religious cultures outside the Mediterranean world increased. As a result, leading Roman Catholic theologians in Europe felt it necessary to consider reformulations of certain early medieval teachings that appeared to be too restrictive concerning possibilities of salvation outside the institutional church.

Second, in the face of ultimate mystery, these comparative interpretations may cause us to reflect more deeply on the nature of our own religious efforts and those of others to discern the ultimate truth and to relate it to all aspects of life. We may be led to reflect broadly on what religious commitment is and what it involves, how the worldview of a holy community may be taught and how its ethos may be "caught."

Third, acknowledging the reality of religious change and the diverse forms of piety within all cumulative faith traditions, these religio-historical concepts may tend to encourage our active participation in intrafaith and interfaith dialogue with our neighbors near and far. They may serve to stimulate our engagement in reasoned apologetics, as we share what it is that we deeply believe and why, and as we invite others to do likewise. Correspondingly, they may discourage our embrace of either the stance of religio-philosophical relativists, who assert that all truth claims are elements of noncomparable "language games," or the position of spiritual inquisitors, who wish to proceed in dialogue with a prosecutorial manner.

Fourth, these perspectives on religion may provoke us to examine

12. Ibid., 34.

more carefully the historical development of our own religious tradition, as well as the traditions of others. We may be motivated in that study to consider the various ways that Christians have encountered persons of other religious communities in the past and how they could or should potentially interact with them in the future.

Fifth, focusing on the personal dimension of spirituality, these ways of thinking about religious commitments may encourage us to recognize the seriousness of our own representative roles in the ongoing development of the Christian heritage, as we humbly add our own bricks to that religious edifice, or "sacred canopy," that helps to shelter us from anomie.[13] Paradoxically, they may also lead us simultaneously to a more generous and imaginatively playful entertainment of theological ideas and forms of piety, as we explore within covenantal community, and in relation to the larger human community, the authenticity, credibility, and relevance of any expression that would claim to be Christian. The maintenance of this complementarity of attitude — of critical seriousness and at the same time of generosity in theological exploration — will be essential for full participation in the critical intrareligious and interreligious dialogues that are now taking place in the global forum on a whole range of difficult eco-justice issues, issues that are constantly leading members of the Christian church to consider anew their relationships to people of other living faiths and ideologies. Thus, it is to a brief historical summary of Christian judgment concerning those outside the church and to present options for developing a Christian theology of religions that we now turn.

The Church and Unbelievers: Developments in Christian Perspective

In 1958, Canon Max Warren, then general secretary in London of the Church Missionary Society, insightfully predicted that the extensive theological reflection that had been required of the church in the confrontation between Christianity and agnostic science would eventually appear to be mere child's play when compared to the challenging reconsiderations made necessary by the modern encounter of Christianity and other religions. Summarizing the contemporary crisis in Christian mission theory and

---

13. See Peter L. Berger, *The Sacred Canopy: Elements of a Sociological Theory of Religion* (Garden City, N.Y.: Doubleday, 1967).

practice, and pointing to the central question of the *meaning* of other faiths, Warren remarked expressively, "We have marched around alien Jerichos the requisite number of times. We have sounded the trumpets. And the walls have not collapsed."[14]

This sense of crisis in Christian mission is related not merely to the fact that two-thirds of the world's population still remains outside the church. It is also related to the widely experienced dissonance between the Christian calling to be involved in and supportive of evangelization aimed at church growth and the Christian calling to remain sensitive to, appreciative of, and in relationship with persons sincerely and resolutely committed to other religious ways. Thus the crisis concerns not merely the fact that Christians are discovering, as John Cobb has observed, "that what seemed most self-evidently important is something that in another community they do without marvelously," but the deep uncertainties within our own Christian community about what to make of that challenging fact.[15] Twentieth-century interpretations of and responses to this acutely experienced dissonance and uncertainty vary considerably, as we shall see. Yet, it would be inaccurate, of course, to suppose that religious pluralism constitutes a wholly new issue for the church and that those who would wrestle with it in our time have nothing to learn from the past. Indeed, Christians have always lived in situations characterized by a multiplicity of spiritual options. In professing what they have understood to be God's "good news," members of the church have always had to respond to troubling questions concerning the particularity and universality of God's revelation in Jesus Christ and to envision a faithful and a compassionate form of discipleship in mission.

The Christian church has traditionally grounded its efforts in world-wide evangelism in authoritative New Testament Scriptures which proclaim eternal salvation through Jesus Christ and describe the disciples' commission to carry the gospel to the ends of the earth. In John's Gospel, for example, Jesus declares to his followers, "I am the way, and the truth, and the life; no one comes to the Father, except by me". (John 14:6). In the longer version of Mark's Gospel, the resurrected Jesus appears to the eleven

14. An address delivered at Scarborough, Ontario, Canada, October 18, 1958; cited in Wilfred Cantwell Smith, *The Faith of Other Men* (New York: New American Library, 1963), 121.

15. Remark made by John B. Cobb Jr. at the 1987 International Conference on Buddhist-Christian Dialogue, Berkeley, California. Consult the videotape documentary, "Buddhism & Christianity: Toward the Human Future."

disciples and exhorts them, "Go into all the world and proclaim the good news to the whole creation. The one who believes and is baptized will be saved; but the one who does not believe will be condemned" (Mark 16:15-16). The apostle Paul writes to the Corinthian church concerning the Christian's call to be "separate from" those who are "unclean," saying, "What partnership is there between righteousness and lawlessness? Or what fellowship is there between light and darkness? What agreement does Christ have with Beliar? Or what does a believer share with an unbeliever? What agreement has the temple of God with idols?" (2 Cor. 6:14-15). In *The Acts of the Apostles,* Peter proclaims, paradigmatically, "There is salvation in no one else, for there is no other name under heaven given among mortals by which we must be saved" (Acts 4:12). As Willard Oxtoby has remarked, in view of such texts, "two millennia of Christian evangelists have shared the confidence of their first-century predecessors that on Jesus' authority they had the truth, the whole truth, and nobody but them had the truth."[16] *Extra Ecclesiam nulla salus* (outside the church no salvation), a doctrine that many Christians would still unreservedly affirm on the basis of Scripture, was thus classically stated in the medieval period by the Council of Florence, which declared in 1442:

> [The sacrosanct Roman Church] firmly believes, professes, and proclaims that those not living within the Catholic Church, not only pagans, but also Jews and heretics and schismatics cannot become participants in eternal life, but will depart "into everlasting fire which was prepared for the devil and his angels" (Matt. 25:41) unless before the end of life the same have been added to the flock; and that the unity of the ecclesiastical body is so strong that only to those remaining in it are the sacraments of the Church of benefit for salvation. . . . No one, whatever almsgiving he has practiced, even if he has shed blood for the name of Christ, can be saved, unless he has remained in the bosom and unity of the Catholic Church.[17]

Church leaders, however, from a very early date were forced to confront the scandal of the particularity of God's self-disclosure in Jesus. In fact, directly posed to early Christian evangelists by both Jews and Gentiles

16. Willard G. Oxtoby, *The Meaning of Other Faiths* (Philadelphia: Westminster Press, 1983), 31.
17. *The Sources of Catholic Dogma,* trans. Roy J. Deferrari from the 30th ed. of H. Denzinger's *Enchiridion Symbolorum* (St. Louis: B. Herder, 1957), 230.

were penetrating queries, such as, If Jesus is the only true guide and redeemer of all people, how is it that a God who is supposedly good has
waited until now to reveal him? Why did he who is called the one universal
Savior hide himself for so many ages? What became of the souls of all those
millions of people who were deprived of the grace of Christ until the time
when he finally appeared? What will become of those even now in our time
who die without confessing Jesus as Lord?

One of the first of the early church fathers to offer a carefully crafted
and biblically based response to what essentially constituted a challenge to
God's justice was Justin Martyr, who was executed in Rome between 163
and 165. For Justin, the eternal Word of God, the *Logos,* through whom all
things were made and in which all things partake, was fully incarnate in
Christ. This eternal Word, incarnate in one time and place, was revealed
nevertheless to be the same true light which enlightens every human being.
Moreover, in line with Paul's argument in the first chapter of *Romans,* Justin
argued that God's nature and purposes were sufficiently, if not fully, revealed in creation, so that all persons in all times and places were without
excuse if they had failed to live as God intended. He roundly condemned
those devoted to pagan religions, for they were worshipping "gods" that
were really demons. Yet he boldly claimed that those individuals who had
lived in accordance with the mind of God, in harmony with the eternal
Logos, should be confident and unafraid. He asserted, in fact, "those [of
every age] who lived reasonably are Christians, even though they have been
thought atheists; as among the Greeks, Socrates and Heraclitus, and men
like them."[18]

Despite the stern warnings of Tertullian (c. 160–c. 225) and others
about the dangers of compromising the radical distinctiveness of Christian
belief and the purity of Christian practice, most early church leaders like
Irenaeus (c. 130–c. 200), Clement of Alexandria (died c. 215), and Origen
(c. 185–c. 254) found it appropriate to affirm the continuity of God's saving
activity through every generation to the advent of Christ. For example,
Origen wrote:

> [Celsus, a pagan] raises a new objection saying: "Is it only now after
> such a long age that God has remembered to judge the life of men? Did

18. *The Ante-Nicene Fathers: Translations of the Writings of the Fathers Down to*
A.D. *325,* 9 vols., ed. A. Roberts and J. Donaldson (Grand Rapids: Eerdmans, 1973),
1:178.

he not care before?" We will reply to this that God has at no time not desired to judge the life of men, but He has always cared for the reformation of the rational being and given opportunities of virtue. For in each generation the wisdom of God, entering into souls which she finds to be holy, makes them friends of God and prophets. In fact, in the sacred books you could find holy men in each generation who were receptive of the divine Spirit, and who devoted all their powers to converting their contemporaries.[19]

If many of the leaders within the early church maintained this broader perspective concerning God's provisions for salvation in all generations, how did the church arrive at the more particularistic view exemplified by the Council of Florence? As Francis Sullivan has ably shown, the answer to this question is related, first, to the church's increasing concerns about heretics and schismatics and, second, to the altered situation of Christianity in the post-Constantine era.[20] To begin with, it is important to understand that the earliest assertions to the effect that there was no salvation possible outside the church emerged in relation to heightened concerns not about unconverted Jews and Gentiles, but about Christians who, having once been a part of the household of faith, left that wonderful ark of salvation in order to join a heretical or schismatic sect. Many of the early church leaders who could affirm with certainty God's saving activities among all peoples from the beginning of time, when confronted by threats to the unity of the church could just as unequivocally warn those separated from the body of Christ, either by their own actions or those taken by church authorities, that they had absolutely no hope of salvation. Cyprian, for example, who was martyred in 258, was among the most definitive of the early church fathers in addressing those who would not submit to the guidance of the church. "Let them not think," he wrote, "that the way of life or salvation exists for them, if they have refused to obey the bishops and priests. . . . For they cannot live without, since the House of God is one and there can be no salvation for anyone except in the Church."[21] Although Cyprian's statements were

---

19. Origen, *Contra Celsum*, trans. with an introduction and notes by Henry Chadwick (Cambridge: Cambridge University Press, 1953), 188-89.

20. Francis A. Sullivan, *Salvation Outside the Church? Tracing the History of the Catholic Response* (Mahwah, N.J.: Paulist Press, 1992), 14-27.

21. Cyprian, Letter 4.4, in *The Fathers of the Church: Saint Cyprian, Letters (1-81)*, trans. Rose Bernard Donna (Washington, D.C.: Catholic University of America, 1964), 51:13.

often later cited by Christians who wished to apply them more generally to all unbelievers, his own specific concern was divisions within the church.

During the first three centuries, then, the majority of leaders within the church were willing to believe that God had provided for the possibility of salvation for all those who lived prior to Jesus Christ, while they were unwilling to imagine that those separated by heresy or schism from the church, the body of Christ on earth, had any hope of life eternal. It was only after the reign of Constantine and his three sons in the fourth century, when Christianity made a rapid transition from a persecuted religion to a tolerated religion to the officially supported religion of the Roman empire, and when a majority of the empire's citizens were joined to the institutional church, that the teaching "no salvation outside the church" came to be applied more broadly to all Jews and Gentiles. By the late fourth century, prestigious bishops of the church, such as Ambrose (340-397), were even able to influence official state policy and to enlist the state's support for the church's own efforts to suppress heretical teaching. By the fifth century, Christian leaders were able to assume that virtually everyone in the known world had heard the gospel of Jesus Christ and had opportunity to join the church. Therefore, if any individuals remained outside the church and did not believe in its orthodox faith, it could summarily be concluded that such persons, through their own stubborn obstinacy, had rejected God's graces and were justly subject to damnation.

This position is clearly represented in the extensive writings of Augustine of Hippo (354-430). One of the dominant figures in church history, Augustine may be considered, according to Hans Küng, the inaugurator of the medieval Roman Catholic paradigm for Christianity.[22] In fact, his basic interpretation of Christian belief and practice has remained an authoritative one within the church, although it is quite distinct from that of Thomas Aquinas (1225-1274), the next major theologian whose work eventually influenced the church in a similarly sweeping way. As with earlier authorities, Augustine affirmed that those who lived a godly life before the time of Christ could be saved. Of course, in every such case — and he judged that there were surely many — salvation involved election by the one true God. The church could recognize neither the possibility of multiple

---

22. See Hans Küng, *Theologie im Aufbruch: Eine ökumenische Grundlegung* (Munich: Piper Verlag, 1987), 258. For a chart of paradigm shifts in the history of the church, see Küng's *Theology for the Third Millennium: An Ecumenical View,* trans. Peter Heinegg (New York: Doubleday, 1988), 128.

agents of salvation nor the manipulation of God's sovereign will. Augustine taught, therefore, that from the beginning of humankind, as it seemed timely to God, God granted salvation to worthy men and women. Yet Augustine also firmly held that if anyone now remained an unbeliever outside the church they would be justly condemned.

David Bosch has aptly suggested that Augustine's ultimate theological position — which evolved over several decades as he confronted the crises spawned by the sack of Rome by the Goths in the year 410, the Pelagian debates, and the Donatist controversy — constituted an "individualization" as well as an "ecclesiasticization" of salvation.[23] In the first place, the individual human soul, taught Augustine, was not merely confused and in need of perfection, but was depraved, powerless, lost, and in need of a radical transformation. Christ's death on the cross, he averred, served objectively to ransom human souls from Satan's hold, thus providing an opportunity for human beings subjectively to appropriate that great salvific act, something which only God's elect could do. This subjective appropriation of an objective gift, for Augustine, entailed an inward experience of true conversion, as the individual soul accepted its redemption through grace and was reoriented toward its heavenly reward.

This interpretation of redemption, according to Bosch, tended to be both other-worldly and individualistic. Nevertheless, he observes, paradoxically this "spiritualization and introversion which began with Augustine also paved the way for large-scale externalization."[24] For example, in response to the Donatists' rigid assertion that sacramental actions of the church were dependent on the moral purity of the officiants who represented Christ's body, Augustine argued that sacramental authority adhered to the church as a holy institution, despite the sinfulness of all those who participated in its corporate life and ministry. The ark of salvation was an institution more perfect than those who represented it. Salvation, in fact, he argued, could no longer be found apart from that one apostolic institution and its sacraments. Heretics and schismatics, as well as unbelieving Jews and Gentiles, therefore could never belong to God's elect.

Augustine admitted in one of his many letters that he realized there were some barbarian tribes located in the distant southern reaches of Africa that remained unaware of Jesus Christ and geographically beyond the cur-

23. David J. Bosch, *Transforming Mission: Paradigm Shifts in Theology of Mission* (Maryknoll: Orbis Books, 1991), 214-61.
24. Ibid., 217.

rent ministries of the church. Yet, in order to maintain both his ecclesial perspective on salvation and the justice of God, he asserted that the gospel had not been made known to these people precisely because it was foreknown by God that they would not believe. Thus, they were *predestined* to be among the damned and not the saved. Given the troubling case of infants who died before being baptized, Augustine concluded that since they were outside of the ark of salvation, they too were justly damned. They were damned, however, not because of their unbelief, but because of either a contracted original sin inherited from Adam, or sins that they committed by their own selfish infant deeds. In both cases, in the condemnation of either unknowing adults or infants, Augustine wrote, "we see what is due all, so that those He delivers may thence learn what due penalty was relaxed in their regard and what undue grace was given."[25] Since Augustine could not imagine that what the sovereign God willed would not actually come to pass, he found it necessary to interpret the "all" in 1 Timothy 2:4, where it is said that God "desires all persons to be saved and to come to the knowledge of the truth," to mean only "the many whom He wishes to come to the grace."[26]

Although theological perspectives associated with this individualization and ecclesiasticization of salvation continued to shape the church's views of unbelievers, with unfortunate consequences in particular with regard to Jewish-Christian and Muslim-Christian relations, the formative writings of Aquinas in the thirteenth century began to provide the building blocks for a less narrow perspective. Interestingly, this happened indirectly as the nature of the church and its holy sacraments were more fully explored. As Sullivan points out, Aquinas fully concurred with the traditional view that faith in Christ was absolutely necessary for salvation. Moreover, he claimed that if any Gentiles were saved prior to the coming of Christ it was because of the fact that their sincere faith in the existence and sovereignty of God constituted an *implicit,* if not explicit, faith in Christ. In the present age, Aquinas believed, the one catholic and apostolic church existed as the only true mediator of divine grace in the world. Because the church was the body of Christ on earth, saving grace was available only through the appropriation of its sacraments, most efficaciously through baptism and the eucharist. However, citing an example of a person who

---

25. Augustine, *Contra Julianum* 4.8, in *The Fathers of the Church: Against Julian,* trans. Matthew A. Schumacher (New York: Fathers of the Church, 1957), 35:207.
26. Ibid., 206.

intended to be baptized but who died suddenly before receiving the sacrament, Aquinas introduced the idea that incorporation into the body of Christ might, through the mysterious grace of God, take place *mentally* though not actually, that is, by *desire* though not in fact.

In the mid-fifteenth century, shortly after the stern pronouncements of the Council of Florence concerning those outside the church, and concurrent with the anti-Islamic hostilities associated with the fall of Constantinople in 1453 to Turkish Muslims, the German bishop Nicholas of Cusa (1401-1464) responded with a remarkably more inclusive perspective on the meaning of other faiths. In keeping with the long-held view that God had always provided help to those who earnestly sought it, and in harmony with Aquinas's provision for incorporation into the church by desire, Nicholas imagined that the world's great religious teachers and prophets were inspired to desire truth passionately and to order their faith and life so as to honor the divine. Christ, the incarnate Word, he asserted, was mercifully sent to illuminate and clarify by reason the truth of God that all desired and through which all would become one. In many ways, Nicholas's position prefigured the rationalism of Immanuel Kant (1724-1804) and other writers of the Enlightenment three hundred years later.

In the sixteenth and seventeenth centuries, after the startling discovery of the New World and its innumerable peoples, and after further exploration of the tremendous expanse of Asia with its vast population, the distinction between an implicit and explicit faith and the teaching of an incorporation into the body of Christ by desire became the keys for many subsequent attempts to reflect theologically on the status of these millions of souls who had never heard of Jesus Christ nor been introduced to the institutional church. A growing number of Christians, especially Roman Catholics, judged it no longer appropriate to try to maintain the rhetoric of the traditional doctrine of no salvation outside the church in view of the overwhelming numbers of innocent persons, past and present, involved. The expanded experience of the world in the early modern period led some to argue that the old doctrine, when applied to those who had never heard of Christ, was attitudinally arrogant and morally problematic. Some went on to suggest that even after the church's initial efforts at evangelization the old doctrine ought not to be immediately or rigidly applied to all these people. Initial efforts at conversion might be unconvincing and a considerable period of time might be required to present a compelling case for Christianity, particularly amidst impressive and highly organized non-Christian religio-cultural systems.

Other theologians eventually ventured on to argue that not only individuals who lived prior to the coming of Jesus Christ could be saved through an implicit (unconscious) rather than explicit (conscious) faith in Christ, but that persons presently living could be so saved. Any persons, they asserted, who were doing what was possible within the givenness of their context, within the horizons of their own limited experiences, to draw near to God and to the mystical body of Christ surely would not be left without the means for their eternal salvation. The famous Jesuit missionary to China, Matteo Ricci (1552-1610), when asked if Confucius (551-479 B.C.E.) was in hell, responded, "All those who know God and love Him above all things, and who pass out of this life with such knowledge and love, are saved. If Confucius knew God and loved Him above all things, and passed out of this life with such knowledge and love, without doubt he is saved."[27] The extension of this attitude regarding the possible salvation of those who lived before Jesus Christ to all persons who have lived outside the church since the time of Christ began to gain even wider acceptance in the eighteenth and nineteenth centuries.

Especially among Roman Catholic scholars, therefore, the critical distinction came to be stated as existing between those who were *culpable* and those who were *inculpable*. If a person were truly open to the mysterious inward workings of divine grace within the interiority of his or her own soul, such a person might be *oriented toward* the church even if he or she had never heard of it and thus, from God's perspective, inculpable. While adamantly opposed to pronouncing any human opinion concerning a divine judgment of inculpability with regard to specific individuals or groups, some theologians, however, eventually suggested that even some contemporary Jews or Muslims might be inculpable if, because of their complete socialization within their own religious communities, they did not fully understand the necessity of adherence to the teachings of the Christian church, and if they remained sincerely open to God's guidance. Although some remained hesitant about this theological trend, the Roman Catholic Church by the end of the nineteenth century had clearly found a way to affirm the ancient doctrine "no salvation outside the church," in accord with more exclusivistic Scriptures, while creatively defining what the doctrine actually meant in relation to other more inclusive scriptural injunctions and images concerning a loving and just God who wishes the salvation of all. Roman Catholics intended to envision a vigorously active

27. Ralph R. Covell, *Confucius, the Buddha, and Christ: A History of the Gospel in Chinese* (Maryknoll: Orbis Books, 1986), 60.

missionary church, but one that had to define carefully and sensitively the content and presentation of its good news. As Pope Pius IX (reigned 1846-1878) wrote to his bishops in 1854:

> With all the skill and learning at your command, you should prove to the people committed to your care that the dogmas of the Catholic faith are in no way opposed to the divine mercy and justice. Certainly we must hold it as of faith that no one can be saved outside the apostolic Roman Church, that this is the only ark of salvation, that the one who does not enter this is going to perish in the deluge. But nevertheless, we must likewise hold it as certain that those who labor in ignorance of the true religion, if that ignorance be invincible, will never be charged with any guilt on this account before the eyes of the Lord. Now who is there who would arrogate to himself the power to point out the extent of such ignorance according to the nature and variety of peoples, regions, talents, and so many other things.[28]

Most Protestant theologians were unwilling to go this far. With a strong christocentrism, the leaders of the Protestant Reformation, such as Martin Luther (1483-1546), Ulrich Zwingli (1484-1531), and John Calvin (1509-1564), tended to emphasize human sinfulness, justification through faith in Jesus Christ, and the finality of the Christian religion. They set a spiritual pattern for Protestants in which holy Scripture was valued over reason and tradition, in which the individual's direct relationship with God through Christ was emphasized over gifts and graces supposedly mediated through a hierarchically structured and liturgically centered religious institution, and in which God's sovereignty was frequently understood in terms of predestination. Any religious belief and practice, therefore, which in any way contradicted or diminished the centrality of the Bible, the sinner's atonement through the life, death, and resurrection of Jesus Christ, or the absolute sovereignty of God was subjected to harsh critique, whether the target was a self-serving papacy or Jewish legalism. Luther, for example, raged not only against the pope as Antichrist, but also against the Jews as a miserable and demonic people doomed to hell, whose books should be seized, synagogues burned, and residence in Christian territories no longer tolerated.[29]

28. *Singulari quadam, Acta Pii* IX, I/1, 626. Quoted in Sullivan, *Salvation Outside the Church?* 113.

29. Consult Martin Luther, "On the Jews and Their Lies," trans. M. H. Bertram, in *Luther's Works*, 55 vols. (Philadelphia: Fortress Press, 1971), 47:121-306.

Although a number of the early Protestant leaders held that the great commission represented an apostolic obligation that no longer applied to the church, and that God called the elect without the need of human assistance, others encouraged missionary outreach as a natural response to the grace experienced in Jesus Christ. Nicholas von Zinzendorf (1700-1760) and other leaders of the Pietist movement, in particular, zealously challenged Christians to engage in personal evangelism and service. By the nineteenth century, Protestants characteristically stressed the radical discontinuity between Christianity and other religions and the importance of an active conversionary mission. Numerous new Protestant mission organizations were founded in Europe and the United States and the evangelization of the entire world became an exciting dream, a dream not unrelated in many minds — both Christian and non-Christian — to the Western domination of the world. The "Great Century" of Christian mission (1800-1914), according to Kenneth Scott Latourette, was preeminently a Protestant century and one, most unfortunately, intertwined with a new colonialism.[30]

An increasing number of Protestants, however, shaped by the spirit of the Enlightenment and of German Romanticism, came to acknowledge more openly the continuity between Christianity and other faiths, while nevertheless attempting to demonstrate in comparative terms the finality of the Christian religion. These latter Protestants were primarily influenced by the works of Immanuel Kant (1724-1804) and G. W. F. Hegel (1770-1831), who emphasized human rationality and historical progress, as well as by the writings of Friedrich Schleiermacher (1768-1834), who described the religious a priori, the universal element in human experience — that of absolute dependence — which defined religion in all its forms, including Christianity. From these religio-philosophical perspectives, which were to provide the foundations for modern Protestant liberalism, the distinctiveness of Christianity was clearly more of degree than kind, and any claim to Christian finality, accordingly, required an apologetic defense. It was this tradition, then, which those like Ernst Troeltsch (1865-1923) inherited, as they struggled in the early years of the twentieth century with the perplexing problem posed by the commonly experienced need for absolute religious certainty in a world in which modern historical consciousness had awakened to the relative nature of all knowledge.

---

30. See Kenneth Scott Latourette, *A History of the Expansion of Christianity,* vol. 6, *The Great Century in Northern Africa and Asia,* A.D. 1800–A.D. 1914 (New York: Harper & Brothers, 1944), 440-56.

Contemporary Options for the Church

Several insightful typologies of theological options have been offered in the emerging field of the Christian theology of religions in the last twenty-five years. In 1969 Owen C. Thomas, for example, characterized six principal Christian attitudes toward other religions (truth-falsehood, relativity, essence, development-fulfillment, salvation history, and revelation-sin). More recently, John B. Cobb has identified five major patterns for responses in the history of Christian theology (Logos Christology, universal history, religious a priori, dogmatic confession, and pluralistic confession). Paul F. Knitter has surveyed four primary models for addressing the question of the meaning of other faiths (the conservative evangelical model, the mainline Protestant model, the Catholic model, and the theocentric model).[31] In each case, these authors have sought to develop their own positions in relation to these historic paradigms.

Perhaps the most widely employed typological distinction in the current debate among those concerned with developing an adequate Christian theology of religions is that which distinguishes between theological exclusivism, inclusivism, and pluralism.[32] Any typological classification has both advantages and disadvantages, of course, precisely because it identifies disparate phenomena as belonging to a single category. Therefore, typologies must be carefully defined and employed so that they illuminate more than distort. Since exclusivism, inclusivism, and pluralism are terms often used ambiguously in contemporary discussions, it will be necessary to define

31. See Owen C. Thomas, ed., *Attitudes Toward Other Religions: Some Christian Interpretations* (New York: Harper & Row, 1969); John B. Cobb, Jr., *Beyond Dialogue: Toward a Mutual Transformation of Christianity and Buddhism* (Philadelphia: Fortress Press, 1982); and Paul F. Knitter, *No Other Name? A Critical Survey of Christian Attitudes Toward the World Religions.* Consult also John Sanders, *No Other Name: An Investigation into the Destiny of the Unevangelized* (Grand Rapids: Eerdmans, 1992).

32. See, for example, the exploration of this threefold typology in Alan Race, *Christians and Religious Pluralism: Patterns in the Christian Theology of Religions* (Maryknoll: Orbis Books, 1983). This typology is also relevant to several important monographs and collections of essays, including John Hick and Paul F. Knitter, eds., *The Myth of Christian Uniqueness* (Maryknoll: Orbis Books, 1987); Gavin D'Costa, *Theology and Religious Pluralism: The Challenge of Other Religions* (Oxford: Basil Blackwell, 1986) and *Christian Uniqueness Reconsidered* (Maryknoll: Orbis Books, 1990); and William Crockett and James Sigountos, eds., *Through No Fault of Their Own? The Fate of Those Who Have Never Heard* (Grand Rapids: Baker Books, 1991).

briefly, along a spectrum of Christian judgment, the range of theological options that are represented in these three commonly cited types.

Theological Exclusivism

Those Christians whose positions may be identified with theological exclusivism firmly maintain that no salvation exists apart from the atoning action of the triune God known in the life, death, and resurrection of Jesus Christ and that no spiritual community other than the Christian church is a God-inspired mediator of saving grace. On the basis of holy Scripture, some exclusivists affirm the ancient axiom "no salvation outside the church" in the strictest of terms. For them, the church constitutes the only ark of salvation and all those outside of it remain destined to eternal separation from God. Other exclusivists affirm that there is no salvation apart from the triune God and the Christian church, and yet at the same time, as we have seen, find ways theoretically to include other individuals within this ark of salvation because of God's gracious acts of election which may have mysteriously oriented certain souls toward Jesus Christ and the church. While exclusivists claim that they do not wish doctrinally to limit the sovereign will of God to save whom God chooses, they find no compelling scriptural evidence to support the claim that salvation may be available apart from what God has accomplished in Jesus Christ. Therefore, if any individual is saved by God outside the institutional church it is assuredly *despite of,* rather than in any sense *because of,* their non-Christian beliefs and practices. While some exclusivists even wish to affirm universal salvation as a Christian hope, if not a Christian doctrine, no other spiritual community may be considered a God-intended vehicle of salvation.

Although it cannot be attributed uniformly to all theological exclusivists, many maintain that there is a fundamental discontinuity between human reason and divine revelation paralleled by a discontinuity between religiosity and Christianity. The revelation or self-disclosure of God in Jesus Christ, it is asserted, is *sui generis,* one of a kind. In one time and place did God reach out in a definitive way, in the Word Incarnate, to save human beings who are utterly unable to save themselves. Forms of spiritual practice founded on any other basis merely represent the feeble attempts of human beings to reach for God, the unsuccessful efforts of finite creatures to grasp for the infinite. This evaluation is intended, such exclusivists would assert, neither to denigrate human achievement nor to deny that the Spirit of God has been active in human history. Yet human achievements, however honorable, are always flawed by sin. Moreover, the gracious activities of God outside the one saving revelation in Jesus Christ must be understood only as luring, orienting, and preparatory acts of a distinctly lesser order than an incarnational revelation. In Jesus Christ, once and for all, humans receive something totally new through the unwarranted grace of God.

Some exclusivists argue that it is possible to state this discontinuity too forcefully. Therefore, they maintain that while in Jesus Christ we receive something *radically* new, it is not *totally* new. These exclusivists concur in an emphasis on the discontinuity between Christianity and other religions, but they also want to acknowledge that Christians have reason to regard the other great living religions of the world as embodiments of an ongoing interactive drama between God and humankind. Christians should recognize, they argue, the sincere, God-inspired piety of many individuals who live outside of the church and within other spiritual communities. Yet, such an acknowledgment certainly does not reflect the view that in Jesus Christ we receive *fully* what previously the world has received *partially* or that other religious communities, as communities, are legitimized as vehicles of salvation. Indeed, for such exclusivists, God's overtures at self-disclosure throughout history prior to the coming of Jesus Christ were consistently ignored and rejected. Therefore, while in some sense it may be appropriate to speak of a "general revelation" prior to the "specific revelation" of God in Jesus Christ, this should in no way suggest an atoning revelation outside the Christ event described in the New Testament.

Theological exclusivists of all varieties emphasize that the Christian church is the sole religious community in the world with a legitimate missionary mandate. Personal evangelism tends to take precedence over other forms of mission because of the importance placed on profession of faith and obedience in baptism. The mission of the church is to proclaim Jesus Christ as Lord and, through word and deed, to convert the world to worship. The primary question is the one that Jesus asked of Peter: "But who do *you* say that I am?" The Christian religion constitutes the true religion only to the extent that it announces and embodies the right answer to that question, to the extent that Christians attend to and are claimed by the reconciling self-disclosure of God in Jesus Christ. That unique revelation judges Christians and the Christian religion, of course, as it judges all else. Therefore, there is no place in Christian mission for an attitude of arrogance or for a dismissal of others, since all fall short of the glory of God, whose grace is always undeserved. In fact, cooperation and dialogue with persons of other living faiths is even encouraged by some exclusivists as long as the foundation of the Christian faith is not compromised. All would resolutely maintain that the reign of God, which is both already and not yet, has uniquely and with finality drawn near to us in the Word Incarnate, Jesus Christ, apart from whom there is abundant life neither in this world nor in the world to come.

Theological Inclusivism

The Second Vatican Council, which met in Rome 1962-65, approved several documents of considerable importance for a theology of religions. *Nostra Aetate (Declaration on the Relation of the Church to Non-Christian Religions)*, for example, stated boldly that the Catholic Church maintains a sincere respect for those ways of acting and living which, though they may differ in some respects from what the church professes, nevertheless reflect the true light which enlightens all humankind. The bishops affirmed that God's plan of salvation extends to all persons who, through no fault of their own, do not know Jesus Christ and are not joined to the church, but who, moved by grace, seek sincerely to do God's will. Special appreciation was expressed for the Jews, who remain dear to God, as well as the Muslims, who venerate Jesus and his mother Mary, anticipate a day of judgment, and pursue a moral life.

It was especially in *Lumen gentium (Dogmatic Constitution on the Church)* and *Unitatis redintegratio (Decree on Ecumenism)*, however, that the council took a provocative new step. With these pronouncements the Roman Catholic Church officially recognized the ecclesial nature of non-Catholic Christian communities. That is, for the first time, such communities were formally declared to be actual recipients of God's gifts and graces and to know in fact, if only imperfectly, what the Roman Catholic Church knew. The "Mother Church," while recognizing her offspring as true churches, and celebrating the continuity that existed between their ministries and hers, also called for these ecclesial communities to sublimate and renew their faith and order in pursuit of the unity with the Mother which was their true destiny.

A number of Roman Catholic theologians have been willing to extend this line of argumentation even further to claim that non-Christian religions *in their institutionality* may also be considered mediators of true grace, albeit imperfect mediators in need of correction. Some Eastern Orthodox and Protestant theologians, in a parallel manner, have asserted that non-Christian religious traditions, *qua traditions,* can lead one nearer to God. These are declarations that theological exclusivists are uniformly unwilling to make. Characteristically emphasizing the *continuity* rather than the discontinuity between Christianity and other religions, theological inclusivists within the church have sought an appropriate way to affirm simultaneously the redeeming gifts and graces of God that may be operative in non-Christian religions as well as the finality of the revelation of God in Jesus Christ, which provides the criterion of every healing and saving process.

While acknowledging that God has never in any time or place been without witness (Acts 14:16), inclusivists insist that in the life, death, and resurrection of Jesus of Nazareth God has been encountered definitively, incarnationally. Christianity, therefore, can be said to have no equal and ought to be rightly considered in the present age the absolute religion intended for all. Yet the gracious God that we have come to know most fully in Jesus Christ, the Lord of the universe who desires that all persons be saved (1 Tim. 2:4), has always been healingly active in the world. Non-Christian religious traditions, therefore, may reflect in many of their elements an authentic divine-human interaction and may be regarded as legitimate vehicles of salvation, included in God's great plan of redemption, to the extent that they serve positively to bring persons into a right relationship with God and neighbor. The claim is not that every religion *is,* in fact, a vehicle of salvation, but that any religion *may* be so.

Since religion must exist in a social form, we should expect, most inclusivists would suggest, that God saves people through, and not wholly apart from, the religious forms available to them in their own situation. Non-Christian religio-social forms, then, while imperfect, may in many respects anticipate and point toward Christ and the church. Accordingly, individuals committed to these religious traditions must be understood and approached as "pre-Christians," or even "anonymous Christians," despite, in some cases, their obvious hostilities toward institutional Christianity. The point of personal culpability and obligation to profess faith explicitly in Jesus Christ and to be baptized in his name arises within the unique circumstances of an individual's life only when the gospel is compellingly proclaimed and Christian discipleship becomes a viable spiritual option. However, the exact point of any specific person's culpability is known only to God.

The Christian church, as it attends to the biblical witness, testifies to and institutionalizes the ultimate criterion of truth. In mission, it is called to manifest the abundant life shaped by that truth and humbly to call others to believe and to share in its reconciling work. In so doing, inclusivists insist, the church should remain confident about the transforming power of God's gracious activity within the lives of all persons and communities faithful to Jesus Christ, responsible in mission, and open to new possibilities for interreligious cooperation and dialogue. If the Christian community can be so confident, faithful, responsible, and open, then, it is argued, others outside the institutional church may surely, through the mysterious work of the Holy Spirit in their midst, finally come to find fulfillment in naming the name above all others, Jesus Christ.

Theological Pluralism

While appreciative of the intent of inclusivists to develop a position that challenges the church's traditional exclusivism, pluralists have sought to articulate an even less ecclesiocentric and more theocentric Christian perspective. In accomplishing this, they have focused attention on the relativity of all human knowledge, on the mutual sharing of religious experiences, and on the dialogical exploration in a multi-religious context of criteria for the discernment of truth. While remaining committed to Christ and the church, theological pluralists have asserted that such a commitment ought not imply either a pre-judged negation or diminution of other ways of ultimate transformation.

To begin with, Christian pluralists characteristically emphasize that all human knowledge is conditioned knowledge, always limited by the particular circumstances of finite creatures. Thus, all things are necessarily known according to the unique mode of the knowers. This is an especially important confession to make in the case of religious knowledge, it is argued, because such knowledge can only be expressed in a highly symbolic manner. Therefore, religious symbols, i.e., finite metaphors for the infinite, must always remain open to criticism in light of further religious experience. Accordingly, to employ Christian terms, none of us knows fully the mind of God and all our images of God are partial.

Recognizing both similarities and differences in Christian and non-Christian symbolic language concerning ultimacy, Christian pluralists maintain that it is important to pursue such criticism through inner-personal, intra-traditional, and inter-traditional dialogue on the broadest possible scale. As we make sincere efforts to understand what others have come to "know," and to present coherently to others what we, and others within our own tradition, have experienced to be true, all of us are likely to benefit. This process most fully engaged involves a form of crossing empathetically over into other religious worlds of meaning and returning to our own, crossing over and coming back. Such spiritual journeys may enhance or even alter one's perspectives on ultimacy, leading finally perhaps to a rather limited or more significant reconceptualization of faith. Yet, most Christian pluralists would argue that to such spiritual adventures, which offer us options beyond that of a rigid absolutism or a debilitating relativism, the church is now being led by the Holy Spirit.

That God *may* have provided multiple paths to salvation (to right relations with God and neighbor both in this world and beyond it), is affirmed by all Christian pluralists. Given the reality of the many diverse cultures that have developed in relative isolation from one another in human history, most pluralists tend to proceed with the working hypothesis that a single saving revelation is improbable and that God has, in fact, so graciously provided. Unlike exclusivists, they will not affirm a priori that there is no salvation outside the church; to base such doctrinal claims on the *confessional* language of certain New Testament passages, they argue, is inappropriate. Moreover, they charge, such a position ignores important scriptural texts which suggest that inheriting eternal life has more to do with service to others and faithfulness to God than a profession of faith in Jesus Christ as the only Son of God and Savior of the world (e.g., the separation of the sheep and goats in Matt. 25:31-46, or the parable of the good Samaritan in Luke 10:25-37); that God is never without a witness in any nation or generation (cf. Acts 14:7); and that, in the case of the Jews in particular, they remain "beloved" by a God whose gifts and calls are "irrevocable" (cf. Rom. 11:28-29). Unlike inclusivists, they will not claim a priori that in Christianity all other religious ways find their true completion and fulfillment, and so should ultimately be displaced by it; such a position, they assert, represents only a slightly modified form of absolutism that provides no real opportunity for dialogical learning.

Christian pluralists tend to claim not only that spiritual isolationism is no longer possible, but that it is not actually desirable. Some envision a future convergence of the great religious traditions into a single religious heritage, albeit one that recognizes special devotional traditions (Buddhist, Christian, Islamic, etc.) that continue to contribute to it. The valuing of "unity with diversity" within the modern Christian ecumenical movement has provided for some a model of how this might be conceived. Most

Christian pluralists do not project such a convergence, and are concerned with the relativization of Jesus Christ that it potentially represents, yet they do expect that mutual interactions and influences in the future will shape all of our continually developing religious traditions in ways that we are presently unable to predict. All pluralists acknowledge that Christianity has developed through syntheses with other religio-philosophical perspectives and practices in the past and anticipate that syntheses will likely continue, if not accelerate. The Christian mission, realistically speaking, some suggest, may lie more in influencing those in other traditions to incorporate something of Christ's spirit into their own practice than in leading them explicitly to renounce their heritage in order to become Christians. While recognizing that inter-tradition dialogue, joint religious practice, and a reinterpretation of the Christian mission will occasion difficult and emotional intra-tradition dialogue within the Christian community on the authenticity, credibility, and relevance of various new practical theological proposals from Christians so engaged, pluralists characteristically welcome such dialogues as activities central to responsible contemporary discipleship. This is because, from their perspective, the human community has clearly moved beyond what Knitter calls the *micro phase* of religious history, in which the major spiritual traditions developed largely in isolation from one another, to the *macro phase* of religious history, in which "each religion will be able to grow and understand itself only through interrelating with other religions."[33]

An Invitation to Theological Reflection and Discussion

The readings that follow in this section of the book constitute an invitation for you to engage with other Christians in reflection and dialogue on one of the most important and potentially divisive theological issues of our time. They invite you to think about the nature of religious commitments and communities and to consider theological options for speaking of the meaning of other faiths. They encourage you to find your own voice in relation to the typology described or to find ways to go beyond it in new directions.

Although the edited selections are relatively short, they are intended to provide you with concise, coherent statements of the authors' basic positions.

33. Paul F. Knitter, *No Other Name?* 225.

The readings are arranged under three headings: pre-twentieth-century Christian views, contemporary Roman Catholic and Eastern Orthodox views, and contemporary Protestant views. Within each category, they have been arranged according to publication date of the source from which they were excerpted. In order to provoke inquiry and discussion, no effort has been made to group them according to the typology of exclusivism, inclusivism, and pluralism. Indeed, you are encouraged to judge for yourself how the selections relate to the typology described, or another typology, and to compare the differently nuanced positions that may belong to the same general type. A range of theological opinions are represented in these resources, although, of course, the collection cannot be exhaustive. The selections were made on the basis of their original contribution to the discussion or their pedagogical usefulness in highlighting controversial issues. For more complete argumentation by the authors, please consult the original source for each selection, as well as the section bibliography for other study resources.

Discussion Questions

1. What assumptions seem to be held by the authors of the excerpted selections concerning the nature of religion and the process of forming communal perspectives on ultimacy? How do you define religion?

2. What do these authors claim about the nature of the Christian gospel? In what terms do you share the Christian gospel with someone who is outside the church?

3. What do these authors deem to be the primary sources of religious authority? How do you describe the primary sources of religious authority within the church?

4. How important for the authors are comparative studies in religion for formulating a Christian theology of religions? How important are comparative historical studies for your own theological position?

5. How do the authors perceive the scope of Christian mission? How do you define the mission of the church?

6. To what extent is interreligious dialogue encouraged and why? In your own judgment, do Christians have anything to learn in interreligious dialogue?

7. How do you relate your own tradition-specific criteria for truth as a Christian to the problem of conflicting truth claims in a religiously plural world?

8. Where should the author be located along the spectrum of Christian judgment concerning a Christian theology of religions? Where do you locate yourself at the present time? Has your position changed in recent years?

9. How are the authors' positions to be evaluated in your own judgment in relation to the criteria of authenticity, credibility, and relevance?

For Further Reading

D'Costa, Gavin, ed. *Christian Uniqueness Reconsidered: The Myth of a Pluralistic Theology of Religions.* Maryknoll: Orbis Books, 1990.

Dupuis, Jacques. *Jesus Christ at the Encounter of World Religions.* Maryknoll: Orbis Books, 1991.

Hick, John, and Paul F. Knitter, eds., *The Myth of Christian Uniqueness: Toward a Pluralistic Theology of Religions.* Maryknoll: Orbis Books, 1987.

Knitter, Paul F. *No Other Name? A Critical Survey of Christian Attitudes Toward the World Religions.* Maryknoll: Orbis Books, 1985.

Newbigin, Lesslie. *The Gospel in a Pluralist Society.* Grand Rapids: Eerdmans, 1989.

Ogden, Schubert M. *Is There Only One True Religion or Are There Many?* Dallas: Southern Methodist University Press, 1992.

Pinnock, Clark H. *A Wideness in God's Mercy: The Finality of Jesus Christ in a World of Religions.* Grand Rapids: Zondervan, 1992.

Race, Alan. *Christians and Religious Pluralism: Patterns in the Christian Theology of Religions.* Maryknoll: Orbis Books, 1983.

Sanders, John. *No Other Name: An Investigation into the Destiny of the Unevangelized.* Grand Rapids: Eerdmans, 1992.

Sullivan, Francis A. *Salvation Outside the Church? Tracing the History of the Catholic Response.* Mahwah, New Jersey: Paulist Press, 1992.

Swidler, Leonard, ed. *Toward a Universal Theology of Religion.* Maryknoll: Orbis Books, 1987.

PRE–TWENTIETH-CENTURY CHRISTIAN VIEWS

Justin Martyr

Teacher and author, Justin was among the most important apologists for Christianity in the second century. Born in Samaria around 100, he was martyred in Rome between 163 and 165. Justin was especially concerned to demonstrate Christ's fulfillment of prophecies found in the Hebrew Scriptures and to emphasize the continuity between Christian revelation and Greek philosophy. In the following selections, he defends Christians against the charge of atheism and employs the Stoic idea of the "seminal logos," also important in the prologue to John's Gospel, to describe the Word in the world before Christ. Source: *The Ante-Nicene Fathers: Translations of the Writings of the Fathers down to A.D. 325,* ed. Alexander Roberts and James Donaldson, vol. 1 (Grand Rapids: Eerdmans, 1973).

The First Apology of Justin

Reason directs those who are truly pious and philosophical to honour and love only what is true, declining to follow traditional opinions, if these be worthless. . . . We have come not to flatter you by this writing, nor please you by our address, but to beg that you pass judgment [on Christianity], after an accurate and searching investigation. . . . As for us, we reckon that no evil can be done us, unless we be convicted as evil-doers, or be proved to be wicked men; and you, you can kill, but not hurt us. . . .

Since of old . . . evil demons, effecting apparitions of themselves, both defiled women and corrupted boys, and showed such fearful sights to men, that those who did not use their reason in judging of the actions that were done, were struck with terror; and being carried away by fear, and not knowing that these were demons, they called them gods, and gave to each the name which each of the demons chose for himself. . . . Not only among the Greeks did reason (Logos) Himself prevail to condemn these things through Socrates, but also among the Barbarians were they condemned by Reason (or the Word, the Logos) Himself, who took shape, and became man, and was called Jesus Christ; and in obedience to Him, we not only deny that they who did such things as these are gods, but assert that they are wicked and impious demons, whose actions will not bear comparison with those even of men desirous of virtue.

Hence we are called atheists. And we confess that we are atheists, so far as gods of this sort are concerned, but not with respect to the most true God, the Father of righteousness and temperance and the other virtues, who is free from all impurity. But both Him, and the Son (who came forth from Him and taught us these things, and the host of the other good angels who follow and are made like to Him), and the prophetic Spirit, we worship and adore, knowing them in reason and truth, and declaring without grudging to every one who wishes to learn, as we have been taught. . . .

We forewarn you to be on your guard, lest those demons whom we have been accusing should deceive you, and quite divert you from reading and understanding what we say. For they strive to hold you their slaves and servants; and sometimes by appearances in dreams, and sometimes by magical impositions, they subdue all who make no strong opposing effort for their own salvation. And thus do we also, since our persuasion by the Word, stand aloof from them (i.e., the demons), and follow the only un-begotten God through His Son. . . .

But lest some should, without reason, and for the perversion of what we teach, maintain that we say that Christ was born one hundred and fifty years ago under Cyrenius, and subsequently, in the time of Pontius Pilate, taught what we say He taught; and should cry out against us as though all men who were born before Him were irresponsible — let us anticipate and solve the difficulty. We have been taught that Christ is the first-born of God, and we have declared above that He is the Word of whom every race of men were partakers; and those who lived reasonably are Christians, even though they have been thought atheists; as, among the Greeks, Socrates and Heraclitus, and men like them; and among the barbarians, Abraham, and

Ananias, and Azarias, and Misael, and Elias, and many others whose actions and names we now decline to recount, because we know it would be tedious. So that even they who lived before Christ, and lived without reason, were wicked and hostile to Christ, and slew those who lived reasonably. But who, through the power of the Word, according to the will of God the Father and Lord of all, He was born of a virgin as a man, and was named Jesus, and was crucified, and died, and rose again, and ascended into heaven, an intelligent man will be able to comprehend from what has been already so largely said. . . .

The Second Apology of Justin

For I myself, when I discovered the wicked disguise which the evil spirits had thrown around the divine doctrines of the Christians, to turn aside others from joining them, laughed both at those who framed these false-hoods, and at the disguise itself, and at popular opinion; and I confess that I both boast and with all my strength strive to be found a Christian; not because the teachings of Plato are different from those of Christ, but be-cause they are not in all respects similar, as neither are those of the others, Stoics, and poets, and historians. For each man spoke well in proportion to the share he had of the spermatic word, seeing what was related to it. But they who contradict themselves on the more important points appear not to have possessed the heavenly wisdom, and the knowledge which cannot be spoken against. Whatever things were rightly said among all men, are the property of us Christians. For next to God, we worship and love the Word who is from the unbegotten and ineffable God, since also He became man for our sakes, that, becoming a partaker of our sufferings, He might also bring us healing. For all the writers were able to see realities darkly through the sowing of the implanted word that was in them. For the seed and imitation imparted according to capacity is one thing, and quite another is the thing itself, of which there is the participation and imitation according to the grace which is from Him.

Tertullian

Often referred to as "the father of Latin theology," Tertullian (ca. 160 – ca. 225) was a highly educated and outspoken North African Christian apologist from Carthage. An influential rigorist who appreciated Christian asceticism and emphasized the sinful condition of humanity and the need for God's grace, Tertullian died as the leader of a heterodox Montanist sect. In the following selection, from "The Prescription Against Heretics," Tertullian contrasts human foolishness with divine wisdom and seeks to restrict Christian inquiry regarding truth. Source: *The Ante-Nicene Fathers: Translations of the Writings of the Fathers down to A.D. 325,* ed. Alexander Roberts and James Donaldson, vol. 3 (Grand Rapids: Eerdmans, 1951).

The Prescription against Heretics

The character of the times in which we live is such as to call forth from us even this admonition, that we ought not to be astonished at the heresies [which abound] neither ought their existence to surprise us, for it was foretold that they should come to pass, nor the fact that they subvert the faith of some, for their final cause is, by affording a trial to faith, to give it also the opportunity of being "approved." . . .

The Lord teaches us that many "ravening wolves shall come in sheep's clothing." Now, what are these sheep's clothings, but the external surface

70

of the Christian profession? Who are the ravening wolves but those deceitful senses and spirits which are lurking within to waste the flock of Christ? Who are the false prophets but deceptive predictors of the future? Who are the false apostles but the preachers of a spurious gospel? . . .

These [heresies] are "the doctrines" of men and "of demons" produced for itching ears of the spirit of this world's wisdom; this the Lord called "foolishness" and "chose the foolish things of the world" to confound even philosophy itself. For [philosophy] it is which is the material of the world's wisdom, the rash interpreter of the nature and the dispensation of God. . . . Whence spring those "fables and endless genealogies" and "unprofitable questions," and "words which spread like a cancer?" From all these, when the apostle would restrain us, he expressly names *philosophy* as that which he would have us be on our guard against. Writing to the Colossians, he says, "See that no one beguile you through philosophy and vain deceit, after the tradition of men, and contrary to the wisdom of the Holy Ghost." He had been at Athens, and had in his interviews [with its philosophers] become acquainted with that human wisdom which pretends to know the truth, whilst it only corrupts it, and is itself divided into its own manifold heresies, by the variety of its mutually repugnant sects. What indeed has Athens to do with Jerusalem? What concord is there between the Academy and the Church? What between heretics and Christians? Our instruction comes from "the porch of Solomon," who had himself taught that "the Lord should be sought in simplicity of heart." Away with all attempts to produce a mottled Christianity of Stoic, Platonic, and dialectic composition! We want no curious disputation after possessing Christ Jesus, no inquisition after enjoying the gospel! With our faith, we desire no further belief. For this is our palmary faith, that there is nothing which we ought to believe besides. . . .

At the outset I lay down [this position] that there is some one, and therefore definite, thing taught by Christ, which the Gentiles are by all means bound to believe, and for that purpose to "seek," in order that they may be able, when they have "found" it, to believe. However, there can be no indefinite seeking for that which has been taught as one only definite thing. You must "seek" until you "find," and believe when you have found; nor have you anything further to do but to keep what you have believed, provided you believe this besides, that nothing else is to be believed, and therefore nothing else is to be sought, after you have found and believed what has been taught by Him who charges you to seek no other thing than that which He has taught. . . .

As for us, although we must still seek, and *that* always, yet where ought our search to be made? Amongst the heretics, where all things are foreign and opposed to our own verity, and to whom we are forbidden to draw near? What slave looks for food from a stranger, not to say an enemy of his master? . . . No man gets instruction from that which tends to destruction. No man receives illumination from a quarter where all is darkness. Let our "seeking," therefore, be in that which is our own, and from those who are our own, and concerning that which is our own — that, and only that, which can become an object of inquiry without impairing the rule of faith.

Augustine

Aurelius Augustine (354-430), one of the most important early leaders of Western Christianity, was born and educated in North Africa. As a teacher of rhetoric in Milan, he came under the influence of the great Christian preacher Ambrose, who baptized him in 387. Returning to Africa, Augustine subsequently served the church at Hippo for more than thirty years. He was a prolific writer, recognized for his theological acumen in controversies especially with the Manichaeans, Donatists, and Pelagians. The following selection is excerpted from his letter (no. 102, ca. 409) to Deogratias, a priest at Carthage, who sought Augustine's counsel in answering questions from a non-Christian whom he hoped to convert. Source: *The Fathers of the Church: Saint Augustine, Letters,* vol. 2, trans. W. Parsons (New York: Fathers of the Church, Inc., 1953).

Of the Time When the Christian Religion Appeared

They say: "If Christ says He is the way, the grace, and the truth, and He places in Himself alone the approach of believing souls to Him, what did the men of so many centuries before Christ do? . . . What, he says, became of the innumerable souls, who were entirely guiltless, if He in whom they could believe had not yet lent His presence to men? The world, also, as well as Rome, was devoted to the religious rites of its temples. Why, he says, did He who is called the Savior, hide Himself for so many ages? . . ."

The answer to this objection is that they themselves should first say whether the worship of their own gods, which was established at definite times, was beneficial to men. . . . If they defend their religion, and claim that it was wisely and usefully ordained, then I ask what became of those who died before it was established; surely they were cheated of its salvation and benefit. And if these were able to be cleansed of sin in some other way, why was this way not handed down to their descendants? What was the use of setting up new religious rites which had not existed of old?

If they say at this point that the gods themselves always existed, and had always been equally able to save their worshippers everywhere, but that on account of changes of temporal and earthly circumstances, which they knew accorded with certain time and places, they willed to be served under one name or another, in one way in one place, in another in another, why do they introduce this question into the Christian religion? It is a matter in which they either cannot answer us about their gods, or, if they can, by that very fact they would answer themselves about our religion, and they would agree that it makes no difference with what various rites a worship is carried on, according to diversities of time and places, so long as what is worshiped is holy, just as it makes no difference with what various sounds speech is uttered, according to diversities of language and hearers, so long as what is said is true. But it does make a difference that by a common agreement men are able to select the sounds of the language by which they communicate their meaning to each other, and that those who are truly wise follow the will of God in selecting the acts of worship which befit the Divinity. What is needed for salvation has never been wanting to the goodness and devotion of men, and, if the forms of worship are carried out in different ways by peoples in one or another place, though joined by one and the same religion, in so far as this happens it is very important that human weakness be supported and tolerated, and that the divine authority be not opposed.

Therefore, when we say that Christ is the Word of God, through whom all things were made, we say also that He is the Son because He is the Word; not a word spoken or uttered, but Himself unchanged remaining unchangeably with the unchangeable Father, by whose authority every creature, spiritual and corporeal, is governed in a manner suitable to its time and place. In guiding and governing creatures, He knows and understands what should happen and when and where. . . .

Therefore, from the beginning of the human race, all those who believed in Him and knew Him and lived a good and devout life according to His commands, whenever and wherever they lived, undoubtedly were saved by Him. Just as we believe in Him, both as remaining with the Father and as having come in the flesh, so the ancients believed in Him, both remaining with the Father and about to come in the flesh. We should not think that there are different kinds of faith, or more than one kind of salvation, because what is now spoken of in the course of time as something accomplished was then foretold as something to come; and, because one and the same thing is foretold or preached by diverse rites or ceremonies, we are not to think that they are different things or that there are different kinds of salvation. Let us leave to God the choice of when anything is to happen, which tends to the salvation of souls of the faithful and the good, and for ourselves let us hold to obedience. . . .

What will they answer, if for the sake of brevity in explaining this question we say only this, that Christ willed to appear among men, and to preach His doctrine to them at the time when and the place where He knew there would be souls to believe in Him? . . . As long as the mind of man is small and weak, it will not yield to divine truth. Is it any wonder, then, that Christ, knowing that the world was so full of unbelievers in the early ages, was justly unwilling to appear or to preach to them who He foreknew would believe neither in His words nor in His miracles? . . .

Yet, from the beginning of the human race, sometimes obscurely, sometimes openly, as it seemed to His providence to suit the times, He did not cease to prophesy, and before He appeared in the flesh there were not lacking men to believe in Him, from Adam to Moses, among the people of Israel, which by divine ordinance was the prophetic race, and among other peoples. In the sacred books of the Hebrews there is mention of many from the time of Abraham, who were not of his stock, nor of the people of Israel, nor were they joined by any chance alliance to the people of Israel, yet were partakers in His worship; so why should we not believe that sometimes there were other men, here and there among other races, who were worshipers of Him, although we do not find mention of them in the same sacred Books? The saving grace of this religion, the only true one, through which alone true salvation is truly promised, has never been refused to anyone who was worthy of it, and whoever lacked it was unworthy of it. From the beginning of human history to the end, this is made known for the reward of some and the punishment of others. And that is why it is not made known at all to some, because it was foreknown

75

that they would not believe, yet it is also made known to some who will not believe, as a warning of the former. As to those to whom it is made known and who do believe, they are being made ready for the kingdom of heaven and for the companionship of the holy angels.

Nicholas of Cusa

A German philosopher, bishop of Brixen, and cardinal, Nicholas of Cusa (1401-1464) has been remembered for his Neoplatonic mysticism and for his influence on the later rationalism of the Enlightenment. In view of the Christian hostilities expressed toward Islam provoked by the fall of Constantinople to Muslim forces in 1453, Nicholas's more reasoned, dialogical (if not utopian) response to such interreligious strife in *De pace fidei (On the Peace of Faith)* is remarkable. The text, from which the following selection is excerpted, is written as the witness of a Christian who is granted an extraordinary vision of a celestial discussion of religious unity and diversity in the court of God. Source: *Nicholas of Cusa on Interreligious Harmony: Text, Concordance and Translation of* De Pace Fidei, ed. James E. Biechler and H. Lawrence Bond (Lewiston, N.Y.: Edwin Mellen Press, 1991).

On the Peace of Faith

You know, O Lord, that a great multitude cannot exist without considerable diversity and that almost everyone is forced to lead a life burdened with sorrows and full of miseries and to live in servile submission under the subjection of the rulers who reign over them. Therefore, only a few have enough leisure that they can proceed to a knowledge of themselves using their own free choice. For they are distracted by many bodily cares and duties; and so they are not able to seek you who are a hidden God. Therefore, you appointed for your people different kings and seers, who are called prophets; in carrying out the responsibility of your mission many of them have instituted worship and laws in your name and taught the unlettered people. They accepted these laws as if you, the King of kings, had spoken to them face to face, and they believed they heard not them but you in them. You sent the different nations different prophets and teachers, some at one time and others at another. However, it is a characteristic of the earthly human condition that a longstanding custom which is taken as having become nature is defended as truth. Thus not insignificant dissensions occur when each community prefers its faith to another.

Therefore, come to our aid you who alone are able. For this rivalry exists for sake of you, whom alone they revere in everything that all seem to worship. For each one desires in all that he seems to desire only the good which you are; no one is seeking with all his intellectual searching for anything else than the truth which you are. For what does the living seek except to live? What does the existing seek except to exist? Therefore, it is you, the giver of life and being, who seem to be sought in the different rites by different ways and are named with different names, because as you are you remain unknown and ineffable to all. For you who are infinite power are none of those things which you have created, nor can a creature grasp the concept of your infinity since there is no proportion between the finite and the infinite. But you, almighty God, who are invisible to every mind, are able to show yourself as visible to whom you will and in the way in which you can be grasped. Therefore, do not hide yourself any longer, O Lord; be merciful and show your face, and all peoples will be saved who are no longer able to forsake the source of life and its sweetness when they have had even a little foretaste of them. For no one withdraws from you unless he does not know you. If thus you would deign to do this, the sword and the bilious spite of hatred and all evil sufferings will cease; and all will know that there is only one religion in the variety of rites. . . .

In response to the archangel's supplication, when all the heavenly citizens together bowed to the highest King, he who was seated on the throne said that he had left man to his own choice and had created him capable in his choice for fellowship with God. But the animal and earthly man is held in ignorance under the Prince of Darkness and walks in accordance with the conditions of the sensible life which is from nowhere else but the world of the Prince of Darkness and not in accordance with

78

the intellectual inner man whose life is from the realm of his origin. Hence, he said that with much care and diligence he had recalled man from his wrong way through various prophets who, by comparison with others, were seers. And finally when all the prophets themselves could not sufficiently overcome the Prince of Darkness, he sent his Word, through which he had also created the world. This Word he clothed with humanity so that at least in this way he might illuminate the docile man having a most free choice and so that he might see that he should walk not according to the outward man but according to the inner man, if he hoped to return one day to the sweetness of eternal life. And since his Word put on the mortal man and with its blood bore witness to this truth: man is capable of eternal life for the attainment of which the animal and sensible life is to be regarded as nothing, and eternal life itself is nothing except the ultimate desire of the inner man, namely, the truth which alone is desired and which, as it is eternal, nourishes the intellect eternally. . . .

The incarnate Word, holding chief position among all the heavenlies, replied on behalf of all: "Father of Mercies, even though your works are most perfect and nothing has to be added for their completion, nevertheless, since from the beginning you decreed that man stay a being of free choice and since in the sensible world nothing remains stable and because of time opinions and conjectures as well as languages and interpretations vary as things transitory, human nature needs frequent visitation so that the erroneous notions of which there are a great many concerning your Word might be rooted out and truth might continuously shine forth. Since truth is one and since it is not possible that it not be understood by every free intellect, all diversity of religions will be led to one orthodox faith.

The King agreed. And after the angels who are set over the nations and languages were called forth, he instructed each angel to lead one who is quite knowledgeable to the incarnate Word. And at once there appeared before the Word the more eminent men of this world, as if caught up into ecstasy. The Word of God addressed them thus: "The Lord, King of heaven and earth, has heard the groans of the slain and the bound and of those reduced to servitude who suffer because of the diversity of religions. And since all those who either cause this persecution or suffer it are led only by the belief that in this way it is expedient to be saved and pleasing to their Creator, therefore, the Lord has had mercy on his people and has decided that by the common consent of all men all diversity of religions be brought peacefully to one religion to remain inviolable from now on. He commits this responsibility of ministry to you as the elected men and from his court gives you as assistants the ministering angelic spirits who are supposed to guard and direct you, and he deems Jerusalem as the place best suited for this. . . . You will find that not another faith but the one and the same faith is presupposed everywhere. . . . There can be only one wisdom. For if it were possible for there to be plural wisdoms, they would have to derive from one wisdom, for before all plurality is unity."

Friedrich Schleiermacher

Influential German philosopher and theologian, Friedrich Daniel Ernst Schleiermacher (1768-1834) was educated in the Moravian tradition. During the last twenty-five years of his life he was a professor of theology and dean of the faculty at the University of Berlin. Reacting against the German rationalist heritage of Kant, Schleiermacher defined religion in terms of a *feeling* of absolute dependence, a human self-consciousness in relation to the divine that is expressed most adequately in monotheism. In the following selection, he discusses the superiority of Christian piety in view of religious diversity. Source: *The Christian Faith,* ed. H. R. Mackintosh and J. S. Stewart (Edinburgh: T. & T. Clark, 1928).

The Conception of the Church: Propositions Borrowed from Ethics

The common element in all howsoever diverse expressions of piety, by which these are conjointly distinguished from all other feelings, or, in other words, the self-identical essence of piety, is this: the consciousness of being absolutely dependent, or, which is the same thing, of being in relation with God. . . . It can indeed be said that God is given to us in feeling in an original way; and if we speak of an original revelation of God to man or in man, the meaning will always be just this, that, along with the absolute dependence which characterizes not only man but all temporal existence, there is given to man also the immediate self-consciousness of it, which becomes a consciousness of God. In whatever measure this actually takes place during the course of a personality through time, in just that measure do we ascribe piety to the individual. . . .

The religious self-consciousness, like every essential element in human nature, leads necessarily in its development to fellowship or communion; a communion which, on the one hand, is variable and fluid, and, on the other hand, has definite limits, i.e. *is a Church.* . . . If the feeling of absolute dependence, expressing itself as consciousness of God, is the highest grade of immediate self-consciousness, it is also an essential element of human nature. . . . The truth [is] that every essential element of human nature becomes the basis of a fellowship or communion. . . . Fellowship, then, is demanded by the *consciousness of kind* which dwells in every man, and which finds its satisfaction only when he steps forth beyond the limits of his own personality and takes up the facts of other personalities into his own. . . .

The various religious communions which have appeared in history with clearly defined limits are related to each other in two ways: as different stages of development, and as different kinds. . . . Our proposition does not assert, but it does tacitly presuppose the possibility, that there are other forms of piety which are related to Christianity as different forms on the same level of development, and thus so far similar. But this does not contradict the conviction, which we assume every Christian to possess, of the exclusive superiority of Christianity. . . .

Our proposition excludes only the idea, which indeed is often met with, that the Christian religion (piety) should adopt towards at least most other forms of piety the attitude of the true towards the false. For if the religions belonging to the same stage as Christianity were entirely false, how could they have so much similarity to Christianity as to make that classification requisite? And if the religions which belong to the lower stages contained nothing but error, how would it be possible for a man to pass from them to Christianity? Only the true, and not the false, can be a basis of receptivity for the higher truth of Christianity. . . .

Those forms of piety in which all religious affections express the dependence of everything finite upon one Supreme and Infinite Being, i.e. *the monotheistic forms, occupy the highest level; and all others are related to them as subordinate forms, from which men are destined to pass to those higher ones.* . . . As such subordinate stages we set down, generally speaking, Idol-worship proper (also called Fetishism) and Polytheism; of which, again, the first stands far lower than the second. . . .

Idol-worship proper is based upon a confused state of the self-consciousness which marks the lowest condition of man, since in it the higher and the lower are so little reflected as arising from a particular object to be apprehended by the senses. So, too, with Polytheism: in its combination of the religious susceptibility with diverse affections of the sensible self-consciousness, it exhibits this diversity in such a very preponderant degree that the feeling of absolute dependence cannot appear in its complete unity and indifference to all that the sensible self-consciousness may contain; but, instead, a plurality is posited as its source. But when the higher self-consciousness, in distinction from the sensible, has been fully developed, then, in so far as we are open in general to sensible stimulation, i.e., in so far as we are constituent parts of the world, and therefore in so far as we take up the world into our self-consciousness and expand the latter into a general consciousness of finitude, we are conscious of ourselves as absolutely dependent. Now this self-consciousness can only be described in terms of Monotheism, and indeed only as we have expressed it in our proposition. . . .

It can therefore justly be said that as soon as piety has anywhere developed to the point of belief in one God over all, it may be predicted that man will not in any region of the earth remain stationary on one of the lower planes. For this belief is always and everywhere very particularly engaged, if not always in the best way, in the endeavour to propagate itself and disclose itself to the receptive faculties of mankind; and this succeeds eventually, as we can see, even among the rudest human races, and by a direct transition from Fetishism without any intermediate passage through a stage of Polytheism. On the other hand, there is nowhere any trace, so far as history reaches, of a relapse from Monotheism, in the strict sense. . . .

On this highest plane, of Monotheism, history exhibits only three great communions — the Jewish, the Christian, and the Mohammedan; the first being almost in process of extinction, the other two still contending for the mastery of the human race. Judaism, by its limitation of the love of Jehovah to the race of Abraham, betrays a lingering affinity with Fetishism; and the numerous vacillations towards idol-worship prove that during the political heyday of the nation the monotheistic faith had not yet taken fast root, and was not fully and purely developed until after the Babylonian Exile. Islam, on the other hand, with its passionate character, and the strongly sensuous content of its ideas, betrays, in spite of its strict Monotheism, a large measure of that influence of the sensible upon the character of the religious emotions which elsewhere keeps men on the level of Polytheism. Thus Christianity, because it remains free from both these weaknesses, stands higher than either of those other two forms, and takes its place as the purest form of Monotheism which has appeared in history. Hence there is strictly no such thing as a wholesale relapse from Christianity to either Judaism or Mohammedanism, any more than there is from any monotheistic religion to Polytheism or idol-worship. Individual exceptions will always be connected with pathological states of mind; or, instead of religion, it will prove to be simply one form of irreligion that is exchanged for another, which indeed is what always happens in the case of renegades. And so this comparison of Christianity with other similar religions is in itself a sufficient warrant for saying that Christianity is, in fact, the most perfect of the most highly developed forms of religion. . . .

The widest diversity between forms of piety is that which exists, with respect to the religious affections, between those forms which subordinate the natural in human conditions to the moral and those which, on the contrary, subordinate the moral to the natural. . . . These two fundamental forms [active *teleological* religion and passive *aesthetic* religion, respectively] are definitely opposed to each other, in virtue of the opposite subordination of the elements which are common to both. . . . In the realm of Christianity the consciousness of God is always related to the totality of active states in the idea of a Kingdom of God. . . . That figure of a Kingdom of God, which is so important and indeed all-inclusive for Christianity, is simply the general expression of the fact that in Christianity all pain and joy are religious only in so far as they are related to activity in the Kingdom of God, and that every religious emotion which proceeds from a passive state ends in the consciousness of a transition to activity. . . . Thus the monotheistic stage appears divided, the teleological type being most expressed in Christianity, and less perfectly in Judaism, while Mohammedanism, which is quite as monotheistic, unmistakably expresses the aesthetic type [because of its predeterminism]. All this points us for our present task to a definitely limited field, and what we are going to establish as the peculiar essence of Christianity must no more deviate from the teleological line than it may descend from the monotheistic level.

CONTEMPORARY ROMAN CATHOLIC AND EASTERN ORTHODOX VIEWS

Karl Rahner

One of the leading Roman Catholic theologians of the twentieth century, Rahner (1904-1984) was an important consultant at the Second Vatican Council. In the following selection, the Jesuit theologian gives further definition to the new inclusivist position with regard to non-Christian religions which emerged in the documents approved at Vatican II. Source: *Theological Investigations,* vol. 5, *Later Writings* (1962), trans. K. Kruger (London: Darton, Longman & Todd, Ltd., 1966).

Christianity and the Non-Christian Religions

1st Thesis: We must begin with the thesis which follows, because it certainly represents the basis in the Christian faith of the theological understanding of other religions. This thesis states that Christianity understands itself as the absolute religion, intended for all men, which cannot recognize any other religion beside itself as of equal right. This proposition is self-evident and basic for Christianity's understanding of itself. . . . Since the time of Christ's coming — ever since he came in the flesh as the Word of God in absoluteness and reconciled, i.e. united the world with God by his death and resurrection, not merely theoretically but really — Christ and his continuing historical presence in the world (which we call 'Church') is *the* religion which binds man to God. . . . It has not always and everywhere been *the* way of salvation for men — at least not in its historically tangible

87

ecclesio-sociological constitution and in the reflex fruition of God's saving activity in, and in view of, Christ. As a historical quantity Christianity has, therefore, a temporal and spatial starting point in Jesus of Nazareth and in the saving event of the unique Cross and the empty tomb in Jerusalem. It follows from this, however, that this absolute religion — even when it begins to be this for practically all men — must come in a historical way to men, facing them as the only legitimate and demanding religion for them. It is therefore a question of whether this moment, when the existentially real demand is made by the absolute religion in its historically tangible form, takes place really at the same chronological moment for all men, or whether the occurrence of this moment has itself a history and thus is not chronologically simultaneous for all men, cultures and spaces of history. . . .

We maintain positively only that, as regards destination, Christianity is the absolute and hence the only religion for all men. We leave it, however, an open question (at least in principle) at what exact point in time the absolute obligation of the Christian religion has in fact come into effect for every man and culture, even in the sense of the *objective* obligation of such a demand. Nevertheless — and this leaves the thesis formulated still sufficiently exciting — wherever in practice Christianity reaches man in the real urgency and rigour of his actual existence, Christianity — once understood — presents itself as the only still valid religion for this man, a necessary means for his salvation and not merely an obligation with the necessity of a precept. It should be noted that this is a question of the necessity of a *social* form for salvation. Even though this is Christianity and not some other religion, it may surely still be said without hesitation that this thesis contains implicitly another thesis which states that in concrete human existence as such, the nature of religion itself must include a social constitution — which means that religion can exist only in a social form. This means, therefore, that man, who is commanded to have a religion, is also commanded to seek and accept a social form of religion. . . .

2nd Thesis: Until the moment when the gospel really enters into the historical situation of an individual, a non-Christian religion (even outside the Mosaic religion) does not merely contain elements of a natural knowledge of God, elements, moreover, mixed up with human depravity which is the result of original sin and later aberrations. It contains also supernatural elements arising out of the grace which is given to men as a gratuitous gift on account of Christ. For this reason a non-Christian religion can be recognized as a *lawful* religion (although only in different degrees) without thereby denying the error and depravity contained in it. . . .

We must first of all note the point up to which this evaluation of the non-Christian religions is valid. This is the point in time when the Christian religion becomes a historically real factor for those who are of this religion. Whether this point is the same, theologically speaking, as the first Pentecost, or whether it is different in chronological time for individual peoples and religions, is something which even at this point will have to be left to a certain extent an open question. We have, however, chosen our formulation in such a way that it points more in the direction of the opinion which seems to us the more correct one in the matter although the *criteria* for a more exact determination of this moment in time must again be left an open question. . . .

If we wish to be Christians, we must profess belief in the universal and serious salvific purpose of God towards all men which is true even within the post-paradisean phase of salvation dominated by original sin. We know, to be sure, that this proposition of faith does not say anything certain about the *individual* salvation of man understood as something which has in fact been reached. But God desires the salvation of everyone. And this salvation willed by God is the salvation won by Christ, the salvation of supernatural grace which divinizes man, the salvation of the beatific vision. It is a salvation really intended for all those millions upon millions of men who lived perhaps a million years before Christ — and also for those who have lived after Christ — in nations, cultures and epochs of a very wide range which were still completely shut off from the viewpoint of those living in the light of the New Testament. If, on the one hand, we conceive salvation as something specifically *Christian*, if there is no salvation apart from Christ, if according to Catholic teaching the supernatural divinization of man can never be replaced merely by good will on the part of man but is necessary as something itself given in this earthly life; and if, on the other hand, God has really, truly and seriously intended this salvation for all men — then these two aspects cannot be reconciled in any other way than by stating that every human being is really and truly exposed to the influence of divine, supernatural grace which offers an interior union with God and by means of which God communicates himself whether the individual takes up an attitude of acceptance or of refusal towards this grace. It is senseless to suppose cruelly — and without any hope of acceptance by the man of today, in view of the enormous extent of the extra-Christian history of salvation and damnation — that nearly all men living outside the official and public Christianity are so evil and stubborn that the offer of supernatural grace ought not even to be made in fact in most cases, since these individuals have already rendered themselves unworthy of such an offer by previous, subjectively grave offences against the natural moral law.

If one gives more exact theological thought to this matter, then one cannot regard nature and grace as two phases in the life of the individual which follow each other in time. It is furthermore impossible to think that this offer of supernatural, divinizing grace made to all men on account of the universal salvific purpose of God, should in general (prescinding from the relatively few exceptions) remain ineffective in most cases on account of the personal guilt of the individual. For, as far as the gospel is concerned, we have no really conclusive reason for thinking so pessimistically of men. On the other hand, and contrary to every merely human experience, we do have every reason for thinking optimistically of God and his salvific will which is more powerful than the extremely limited stupidity and evil-mindedness of men. However little we can say with certitude about the final lot of an individual inside or outside the officially constituted Christian religion, we have every reason to think optimistically, i.e., truly hopefully and confidently in a Christian sense — of God who has certainly the last word and who has revealed to us that he has spoken his powerful word of reconciliation and forgiveness into the world. . . .

Our second thesis goes even further than this, however, and states in its second part that, from what has been said, the actual religions of 'pre-Christian' humanity too must not be regarded as simply illegitimate from the very start, but must be seen as quite capable of having a positive significance. This statement must naturally be taken in a very different sense which we cannot examine here for the various particular religions. This means that the different religions will be able to lay claim to being lawful religions only in very different senses and to very different degrees. But precisely this variability is not at all excluded by the notion of a 'lawful religion,' as we will have to show in a moment. A lawful religion means here an institutional religion whose 'use' by man at a certain period can be regarded on the whole as a positive means of gaining the right relationship to God and thus for the attaining of salvation, a means which is therefore positively included in God's plan of salvation. . . . We must therefore rid ourselves of the prejudice that we can face a non-Christian religion with the dilemma that it must either come from God in everything it contains and thus correspond to God's will and positive providence, or be simply a purely human construction. If man is under God's grace even in these religions — and to deny this is certainly absolutely wrong — then the possession of this supernatural grace cannot but show itself, and cannot but become a formative factor of life in the concrete, even where (though not only where) this life turns the relationship to the absolute into an explicit theme, viz. in religion. It would perhaps be possible to say in theory that where a certain religion is not only accompanied in its concrete appearance by something false and humanly corrupted but also makes this an explicitly and consciously adopted element — an explicitly declared condition of its *nature* — this religion is wrong in its deepest and most specific being and hence can no longer be regarded as a lawful religion — not even in the widest sense of the word. . . .

It must be borne in mind that the individual ought to and must have the possibility in his life of partaking in a genuine saving relationship to God, and this at all times and in all situations of the history of the human race. Otherwise there could be no question of a serious and also actually effective salvific design of God for all men, in all ages and places. In view of the social nature of man and the previously even more radical social solidarity of men, however, it is quite unthinkable that man, being what he is, could actually achieve this relationship to God — which he must have and which if he is to be saved, is and must be made possible for him by God — in an absolutely private interior reality and this outside of the actual religious bodies which offer themselves to him in the environment in which he lives. . . . That which God has intended as salvation for him reached him, in accordance with God's will and by his permission (no longer adequately separable in practice), in the *concrete* religion of his actual realm of existence and historical condition, but this fact did not deprive him of the right and the limited possibility to criticize and to heed impulses of religious reform which by God's providence kept on recurring within such a religion. . . . If we say that there were lawful religions in pre-Christian ages even outside the realm of the Old Testament, this does not mean that these religions were lawful in *all* their elements — to maintain this would be absurd. Nor does it mean that *every* religion was lawful. . . .

3rd Thesis: If the second thesis is correct, then Christianity does not simply confront the member of an extra-Christian religion as a mere non-Christian but as someone who can and must already be regarded in this or that respect as an anonymous Christian. It would be wrong to regard the pagan as someone who has not yet been touched in any way by God's grace and truth. . . . If it is true that a person who becomes the object of the Church's missionary efforts is or may be already someone on the way towards his salvation, and someone who in certain circumstances finds it, without being reached by the proclamation of the Church's message — and if it is at the same time true that this salvation which reaches him in this way is Christ's salvation, since there is no other salvation — then it must be possible to be not only an anonymous theist but also an anonymous Christian. And then it is quite true that in the last analysis, the proclamation of the gospel does not simply turn someone absolutely abandoned by God and Christ into a Christian, but turns an anonymous Christian into someone who now also knows about his Christian belief in the depths of his grace-endowed being by objective reflection and in the profession of faith which is given a social form in the Church. It is not thereby denied, but on the contrary implied, that this explicit self-realization of his previously anonymous Christianity is itself part of the development of this Christianity itself — a higher stage of development of this Christianity demanded by his being — and that it is therefore intended by God in the same way as everything else about salvation.

Hence, it will not be possible in any way to draw the conclusion from this conception that, since man is already an anonymous Christian even without it, this explicit preaching of Christianity is superfluous. Such a conclusion would be just as false (and for the same reasons) as to conclude that the sacraments of baptism and penance could be dispensed with because a person can be justified by his subjective acts of faith and contrition even before the reception of these sacraments. The reflex self-realization of a previously anonymous Christianity is demanded (1) by the incarnational and social structure of grace and of Christianity, and (2) because the individual who grasps Christianity in a clearer, purer and more reflective way has, other things being equal, a still greater chance of salvation than someone who is merely an anonymous Christian. If, however, the message of the Church is directed to someone who is a 'non-Christian' only in the sense of living by an anonymous Christianity not as yet fully conscious of itself, then her missionary work must take this fact into account and must draw the necessary conclusions when deciding on its missionary strategy and tactics. We may say at a guess that this is still not the case in sufficient measure. . . .

4th Thesis: It is possibly too much to hope, on the one hand, that the religious pluralism which exists in the concrete situation of Christians will disappear in the foreseeable future. On the other hand, it is nevertheless absolutely permissible for the Christian himself to interpret this non-Christianity as Christianity of an anonymous kind which he does always still go out to meet as a missionary, seeing it as a world which is to be brought to the explicit consciousness of what already belongs to it as a divine offer or already pertains to it also over and above this as a divine gift of grace accepted unreflectedly and implicitly. If both these statements are true, then the Church will not so much regard herself today as the exclusive community of those who have a claim to salvation but rather as the historically tangible vanguard and the historically and socially constituted explicit expression of what the Christian hopes is present as a hidden reality even outside the visible Church. To begin with, however much we must always work, suffer and pray anew and indefatigably for the unification of the whole human race, in the one Church of Christ, we must nevertheless expect, for theological reasons and not merely by reason of a profane historical analysis, that the religious pluralism existing in the world and in our own historical sphere of existence will not disappear in the foreseeable future. We know from the gospel that the opposition to Christ and to the Church will not disappear until the end of time. If anything, we must even be prepared for a heightening of this antagonism to Christian existence. . . .

If this Christianity, thus always faced with opposition and unable to expect seriously that this will ever cease, nevertheless believes in God's universal salvific will — in other words, believes that God can be victorious by his secret grace even where the Church does not win the victory but is contradicted — then this Church cannot feel herself to be just *one* dialectic moment in the whole of history but has already overcome this opposition by her faith, hope and charity. In other words, the others who oppose her are merely those who have not yet recognized what they nevertheless really already are (or can be) even when, on the surface of existence, they are in opposition; they are already anonymous Christians, and the Church is not the communion of those who possess God's grace as opposed to those who lack it, but it is the communion of those who can explicitly confess what they *and* the others hope to be.

Georges Khodr

When the Central Committee of the World Council of Churches met in Addis Ababa in January 1971 to consider issuing a policy statement on the relationship of Christians to people of other living faiths and ideologies, Mgr. Georges Khodr, who served as Metropolitan of Mount Lebanon, a diocese of the Greek Orthodox Patriarchate of Antioch, was invited to address the committee because of his considerable experience in interreligious dialogue in the Middle East. In the following excerpt from that address, Mgr. Khodr considers as complementary the salvific economies of Word and Spirit and argues that "any exploration of the religions is an exploration into Christ." Source: *Living Faiths and the Ecumenical Movement,* ed. Stanley J. Samartha (Geneva: World Council of Churches, 1971).

Christianity in a Pluralist World: The Economy of the Holy Spirit

Contemporary theology must transcend the notion of "salvation history" in order to recover the meaning of the *oikonomia.* The economy of Christ cannot be reduced to its unfolding in history; the heart of it is the fact that it makes us participants in the very life of God. It must involve reference to eternity and to the work of the Holy Spirit. For inherent in the term "economy" is the idea of mystery. To say mystery is to point to the power and inspiration of the event; but also to the freedom of God, whose providential and redemptive work is not tied to any mere event. The Church is the medium of the mystery of the nations' salvation. She is the sign of God's love for all men. She is not set over against the world of which, from one point of view, she is a part. Rather she is the very heart of mankind, the image of mankind to come, thanks to the light she has received. She is the life of men even if these are unaware, the "cosmos of the cosmos" as Origen puts it. If the Son, as Origen also says, is the "cosmos of the Church," then the Church's function must be so to read, in the light of the mystery she signifies, all the other signs that God has set in the passing years, even in the religions, that she can make known to the world of the religions the God who is hidden in it and so bring on the final and actual unfolding of that mystery.

This economy is of old. It begins with the creation, a manifestation of God's *kenosis.* Like Jacob after his fight with the angel, the cosmos bears the mark of God. In the time before the law, God enters into a covenant with Noah. Here the primal dialogue of creation is pursued in a dialogue with mankind. It is a cosmic covenant which abides alongside the particular covenant with Abraham, and in which those peoples live who have not received the word addressed to the father of believers. The scriptures tell us that such nations have angels watching over them. Origen, referring to these angels, tells us that it was they who told the shepherds of the Savior's birth and who thus fulfilled their mission. We may well agree, if this is taken to mean that the Savior who himself became the true covenant between God and the cosmos thereby completed the covenant with Noah by filling it out with his salvation. The messianic Archetype is implied in that Old Testament figure who is his "shadow cast before."

The election of Abraham is yet more clearly an election for the sake of all nations upon the earth. They are — in him — the purpose of God's choice. In leaving his country, Abraham enacts a first Exodus. The second is then that of the people journeying to Canaan through the desert until the day when Jesus will be nailed to the cross like a stranger. Here Israel figuratively lives out the mystery of the divine economy. Israel rescued from the waters on its way to the Promised Land stands for rescued mankind; she is a figure of the Church rescued by Christ. The election is of one man, while the economy of the mystery has to do with all men. Israel is saved as the type and representative of mankind as a whole. The Old Testament, moreover, makes it clear that the saving events to which it witnesses are antitypes of the salvation in the Exodus. The Hebrews saw them not so much as a linear succession of saving events but as proto-typical facts which other facts then imitate — the continuity lying only in God's faithfulness to himself. As the place where the Lord is made known, and as the people constituted by their obedience to the Lord — and only by that — Israel stands in solidarity with all other nations who have been visited by God "in fragmentary and varied fashion," to whose fathers and prophets God has spoken, those whom the Fathers of the Church consider the saints and just men among the Gentiles. What matters is that the stories of Abraham, of Moses, and of David were spiritually rich with the divine presence. Their historical progression is of little weight. Like Matthew in his genealogy, the writers of the Old Testament were only interested in the spiritually significant, in that which had to do with the Messiah they were hoping for or had known manifested.

This relationship in meaning with Christ is also true beyond Israel, in so far as the nations have had their types of Christic reality, whether in persons or in teachings. It is of little account whether their religion was historical or a-historical, or whether or not any given religion considers itself incompatible with the Gospel. For Christ is everywhere hidden in the mystery of his self-effacement. Any exploration of the religions is an exploration into Christ. When grace visits a Brahmin, a Buddhist, or a Muslim reading his scriptures it is Christ alone who is received as light. Whoever dies a martyr for truth or is persecuted for what he believes to be right is in communion with Christ. It was the single *agape* of St. John that was lived out by the Islamic mystics, those great witnesses to the crucifying love. If the tree is to be known by its fruit, then there can be no doubt whatever that the poor and the humble in all nations who are consumed by their yearning for God are already receiving that peace which the Lord grants to those on whom his favor rests.

This salvation at work outside Israel according to the flesh and outside the historical Church is the outcome of the Resurrection, which fills all things with the fullness of Christ. The coming of the Christ in whom all things "are held together" (Col. 1:17) has brought all mankind into true existence. Moreover it gives rise to notable spiritual movements, particular economies that can take charge of men's souls until he comes. The Church loses none of its mediating function. But God's freedom is such that he can raise up prophets outside the sociological confines of the New Israel no less easily than he could outside the Old Israel. Yet these callings to prophecy or wisdom outside the sanctuary are secretly linked with the power of the Risen Lord; they do not in the least conflict with the singularity of the economy of Christ.

The fullness of Christ can be obscured in history by human sin. The Church can fail to be seen as the bearer of the power and glory of her Lord. The visible is often far from pointing to the Kingdom of God. Yet to those to whom it has not been given to see the exalting splendor of Christ in his face that has been bloodied by our shortcomings and in his robe torn by our divisions, God can send witnesses and manifest a power far greater than we would suspect from the teachings outside the Bible. True fullness will be lived in the second coming, and it is thus in function of that end and ultimate meaning of all that the economy of salvation is even now being realized. The economy of Christ cannot be understood apart from the economy of the Spirit.

"God says, 'This will happen in the last days: I will pour out upon everyone a portion of my Spirit'" (Acts 2:17). This must be understood as referring to a universal Pentecost arising out of the first coming. Indeed, we read in the Book of Acts that "the gift of the Holy Spirit (was) poured out even on Gentiles" (10:45). The Spirit is everywhere present, filling all things, and this in an economy distinct from that of the Son. Irenaeus calls the Word and the Spirit the "two hands of the Father." The point of this is not only to affirm their hypostatic independence but to show that the coming of the Holy Spirit into the world is not subordinate to the Son, is not a mere function of the Word. "Pentecost," says Lossky, "is not a 'continuation' of the Incarnation. It is its sequel, its result. The creature has become fit to receive the Holy Spirit" [Vladimir Lossky, *The Mystical Theology of the Eastern Church*, 159]. Between the two economies there is a reciprocity and a mutual service. The Spirit is another comforter.

It is he who fashions Christ within us. Since Pentecost it is he who makes Christ present. It is he who here and there makes Christ inwardly available; Irenaeus puts this well, "Where the Spirit is, there the Church is also." The Spirit works by his own energies and in his own economy. In this perspective the non-Christian religions may be considered as places where his inspiration is at work.

All those visited by the Spirit are the people of God. The Church constitutes the first-fruits of all mankind as called to salvation. "In Christ all will be brought to life" (1 Cor. 15:22) because of the Communion which is the Church. In the present, the Church is the sacrament of that future unity formed by those she has baptized together with those, in Nicholas Cabasilas's wonderful phrase, who have been baptized by the Bridegroom of the Church. When we now partake of the Body of Christ we are united with all those whom the Lord enfolds in his life-giving love. They are all there in the eucharistic cup, waiting to form at the Parousia the one glorious body of the Savior, when all signs and symbols will disappear in front of "the throne of God and of the Lamb" (Rev. 22:3).

Open Both to Receive and to Give

If the bases of this theology are accepted, how then are we to define the Christian mission? What should be the attitude of a Christian community towards a non-Christian community?

1. The man of faith, who knows that within God's plan the great religions are as it were disciplines of his mercy, will be marked by an attitude of profound peace, of utterly gentle patience. This is to obey the purpose being realized by the Spirit, to wait for the coming of the Lord, to yearn to eat the eternal Passover and secretly to be in communion with all men in the economy of the Mystery within which we are moving slowly towards the final consummation, when all things will be gathered up in Christ.

2. An awareness of the universal religious community will enrich our experience as Christians. What matters here is not so much the objective historical or literal meaning of the non-Christian scriptures but that they be read in the light of Christ. For just as without the Holy Spirit the Hebrew words can conceal revelation, Christ being the only key to the Old Testament, so we can choose either a cold and critical scholarship to describe the religions in terms of history and sociology, or lovingly to spell out Truth in them by the inspiration of the Spirit.

3. Within these religions, even if on occasion legalism has the upper hand, there are a number of privileged individuals who transcend the particular framework of religion, just as the life of the Spirit transcends the law. Our task is to discover, beyond all contingent signs and shapes, the profound intention of these spiritual men and then to relate their grasp of the divine to the object of our Christian hope. That is to say, we are to apply the apophatic method not only in talking of God among Christians, since all concepts of God are idols, but also in the ways of talking about God that are suggested by the non-Christian scriptures. Again, in our understanding of the man who holds to another faith, we are to be less concerned for purely descriptive knowledge than to be aware of him in his uniqueness — the other thus becoming for us a source of learning and a place of epiphany.

4. Without Communion there can be no communication. This is why

there can be no intercourse from the Christian side without a conversion which does away with any confessional pride and any feelings of cultural or historical superiority. This is a humility which requires that each be fulfilled in Christ by the other. A Christian community that is purified by the fire of the Spirit, dedicated to God and poor for the sake of God, will be able to lay itself open both to receive and to give in simplicity and vulnerability of the Gospel. She must accept challenging as brotherly correction; even in unbelief she must discover a bold rejection of the falsehoods that earlier Christians have not known how to overcome or have not wanted to.

5. It is in this spirit that communication will be possible. Christ will be offered from out of his lowliness, as what he really was in history and in what he said. The point is not to add new people to the Church. They will come by themselves when they there feel as if they were in their Father's house. What we are after is to discover the values that are of Christ in the other religions and thus to show forth Christ as their bond and his love as their extension. True mission laughs at missionary activity. Our only task is to follow the footsteps of Christ through the shadows of the religions.

> Night after night on my bed
> I have sought my true love.
> I have sought him but not found him.
> I said, "I will rise and go the rounds of the city,
>   through the streets and the squares,
>   seeking my true love."
> The watchman, going the rounds of the city,
>   met me and I asked, "Have you seen my true love?"
>
> (Song of Songs 3:1-3)

The task of the witness in a non-Christian milieu will be to give a name to him whom others have known as the Beloved. When they have become friends of the Bridegroom then it will be easy to name him. The whole missionary work of the Church will be to awaken the Christ who is asleep in the night of the religions. The Lord alone knows whether before the coming of the heavenly Jerusalem men will be able to celebrate together a truly glorious Paschal feast. What we can and do know now is that it is the beauty of Christ shining in our faces that is the promise of our ultimate reconciliation.

Raimundo Panikkar

The son of a Hindu father and a Spanish Catholic mother, Panikkar (b. 1918), who now lives in Barcelona, devoted much of his scholarly career as a Roman Catholic priest in India and the United States to defining the practical theological bases for authentic interreligious dialogue. In the following selection, from a provocative book exploring the true "meeting-place" for the Hindu-Christian encounter, Panikkar describes the encounter of religions as itself a *religious* act and envisions the *means* of salvation that God provides for non-Christians. Source: *The Unknown Christ of Hinduism: Towards an Ecumenical Christophany,* revised and enlarged ed. (Maryknoll: Orbis Books, 1981).

The Encounter between Christianity and Hinduism

The Christian encounter with Hinduism, as we have said, is essentially neither a doctrinal dialogue nor the mutual comprehension of two cultures. It is a historical encounter of religions in the concrete meeting of Men in society. This encounter can really take place, because it is an encounter in the Presence of the one who is already present in the hearts of those who *in good faith* belong to one or the other of the two religions.

Mutual understanding is absolutely necessary: it is an ineluctable condition. However, knowledge alone is not enough. It not only lacks the warmth necessary for a full human encounter, but it tends to produce reactions of an almost antagonistic sort, for human knowledge in fact always entails an egocentric movement. The "thing" known (doctrine, person) comes to *me*. I am at home, I am the host: I receive, welcome and assimilate the "things" that I know — I possess. I enrich myself.

Only an outgoing mutual love overcomes that egocentricity of knowledge. When I love, I go out, I give up, I am the guest, I am no more at home, I am received and possessed. Purely intellectual knowledge commits an offense against whatever it does not choose to assimilate, whatever is left behind. I may reach some synthesis in an intellectual victory over my opponent, but I bring only the spoils of the confrontation back to my system. Sankara [an important twelfth-century Hindu teacher], let us say, is overcome or "understood," but the Sankarites remain outside, unconvinced. This love requires from both sides an asceticism, a mystical life, a detachment from all categories and formulae, from both prejudices and critical judgments. This should not be taken as a denial of orthodoxy but as its implementation and integration into "orthopraxis" (right action).

An authentic Christian encounter with other religions requires a special asceticism: the stripping off of all externals, of "garb" and superficial form, and a lonely vigil with Christ, the naked Christ, dead *and* alive on the Cross, dead *and* alive in those Christians who dare to come to such an encounter with their brethren. This asceticism entails real mysticism, an immediate contact with Christ which carries the Christian beyond — not against — formulae and explanations. Only then is it possible to discover Christ where he is, for the moment, veiled; only then is it possible to help unveil or reveal the mystery hidden for long ages in God. Few indeed, except by some special grace, are capable of such a stripping, are able to remain with the naked Christ living within them, to perform this existential imitation of the incarnation of Christ. . . .

The meeting of religions should be a *religious* act, an act of incarnation and redemption, an encounter in *naked Faith,* in *pure Hope,* in *divine Love* — and not a conflict of formulae, in the expectation of "winning the others over" (— to what?). . . . This religious encounter is in reality much more than a meeting of two friends; it is a communion in being, in the one Being which is much more intimate to both than they are to themselves. It is communion not only *in* Christ but also *of* Christ. No condescension, no paternalism or superiority is to be found in the true encounter. Whether one's role is one of teaching or learning matters not at all in the unity of love. He who has the higher intensity, the richer knowledge of a certain area of spirituality will spontaneously dispense what he has, share it with the other, his neighbor. . . .

Theological Reflection

The superiority approach — and *a fortiori* that which views the relation between Christianity and Hinduism as one of opposition between two poles — is contradicted even by the principles of Christian theology.

Two propositions are universally accepted by Christian theology: one, salvation comes exclusively through Christ; and two, God does not condemn anybody. Now, this second proposition amounts to saying that God provides every Man coming into existence with the *means* of salvation.

We have mentioned God's universal will to save. Now if he created Men for union with him, then surely he also provided them with the means whereby to attain this end. If these means were exclusively in the visible Church or in "official" Christianity, other people could not be saved, but this, in fact, is not so. If it be true that "outside the Church there is no salvation," this "Church" should not be identified with a concrete organization, or even with adherence to Christianity. . . .

The ultimate reason for this universal idea of Christianity, an idea which makes possible the catholic embrace of every people and religion, lies in the Christian conception of Christ: he is not *only* the historical redeemer, but *also* the unique Son of God, the Second Person of the Trinity, the only ontological — temporal and eternal — link between God and the World.

However, when the mystical insight into the theandric nature of Christ weakens and is replaced by a merely historical understanding of the human actions of Jesus, then this Christian position appears untenable. When the myth of history begins to take hold of Western Christianity, Jesus Christ becomes the embodiment of the supreme Imperium. Incarnation becomes just a little slice of history and "evangelization" consists in "civilizing" others and incorporating them into one "Christian" (and post-Christian) world-order.

The theological problem that our question raises concerns the *means* of salvation that God provides for non-Christians, that is, in our case, for Hindus. Undoubtedly, salvation being a supernatural act (for it is union with God), it is always a gratuitous divine act, and there are no proportionate "natural" means here on earth for attaining participation in divine life. Yet the normal procedure of divine providence in dealing with the whole creation, not excluding Mankind, is not one of anarchical interference, but rather follows a pattern which is evidenced in what we call the physical and historical order. This happens in such a perfect way that very often it appears as though God's personal and individual care for each of his creatures is somehow left to cosmic or historical laws far removed from his concrete love for each of us, which even extends to the numbering of every hair on our head. In other words, his providence, even in the "supernatural" sphere, follows ordered and ordinary ways. And in this sense he provides normal, natural means for leading peoples and individuals to himself.

The normal and ordinary means within the Christian Church are the sacraments, which are different aspects, "signs," symbols, of the one and only sacrament of the New Testament, which is the Church as a whole and ultimately Christ himself. By virtue of their divine institution those sacraments, when received with the proper dispositions confer the divine grace that they symbolize.

I shall not linger on the doctrine of the "Cosmic Sacraments," but this much may be said in order to clarify my thesis. If we take the concept of sacrament not in the restricted sense used by the Church when she speaks of the sacraments of the New Law — to distinguish them from *other* sacraments — but in a more general sense, as applied by Christian Scholastics when speaking of the sacraments of the Old Testament and of the *sacramenta naturae* (sacraments of nature), then we may well say that *sacraments* are the ordinary means by which God leads the peoples of the earth towards himself.

No true sacrament is magical. Nevertheless the sacraments have a special causative strength because of their extrinsic connection with the will of God. Thus the efficacy of the Christian sacraments does not reside in themselves as isolated elements or actions, but depends in the action of Christ within them as instruments of grace. One may or may not assume that the same efficacy is conferred upon all other sacraments, *qua* sacraments. Yet it remains true that Christ may be active and at work in the human being who receives any sacrament, whether Christian or any other.

Further, because the human person is not just an individual, but also has a sociological, historical and cosmological dimension, salvation, though an inner and personal process, is prepared and normally carried out by external and visible means which we call sacraments. The good and *bona fide* Hindu as well as the good and *bona fide* Christian are saved by Christ

— not by Hinduism or Christianity *per se,* but through their sacraments and, ultimately, through the *mysterion* active within the two religions. This amounts to saying that Hinduism also has a place in the universal saving providence of God and cannot therefore be considered as negative in relation to Christianity.

As we have seen already, it is not just the Hindu's personal conscience that is concerned: the Hindu religion as such has also an important role to play, because only through its mediation can the Hindu attain his goal. In fact, in India, as in many other cultures of both past and present, the individual, i.e., the individual's separate consciousness such as is assumed in the West today, is hardly conceivable. Hence a private, personal relationship with God cannot be postulated as the normal and common way for everybody. This means that the hypothesis of *direct* and *immediate* action by Christ on an individual's conscience without a particular religion as a medium, i.e. without "sacraments," is, to say the least, psychologically very difficult and improbable in the majority of religions. The purely individualistic attitude of nineteenth century Europe is *still* unthinkable for the Indian people. . . .

The fact that Christ speaks to the whole Man means that he does not speak to an abstract and common nature, but to persons whose very being is intermingled with and inseparable from their beliefs, customs, ways of thinking, feeling, and so forth. Man is constitutively a historical and social being with cosmological dimensions, and Christ does not overlook this human dimension — he himself in his time walked and spoke as a Jew.

Individual conscience may be a purely historical evolution of Mankind, but the fact remains that if God looks after the salvation of the Hindu people, it cannot be through purely personal-individual action, which would have very little meaning; it has rather to be something collective, sociological and mythical. This again is the reason that Hinduism has a true place in the economy of salvation and cannot be equated with "sin," "falsehood" and the like.

My purpose is to recall and emphasize that, according to Christian doctrine, the Father in heaven makes his sun to rise on the good and on the evil, and sends rain on the just and on the unjust (Matt. 5:45), that Christ is the expectation of the peoples (Gen. 49:10), that his spirit is at work among non-believers (Rom. 15:21), that he is already found by those who did not seek him (Rom. 10:20), and that he is a hidden God (Isa. 45:15) who has sometimes hidden himself either in an unknown God (Acts 17:23) or in the hearts of Men of good will (Luke 2:14). Christians often need reminding that Christ himself taught Peter not to call profane or impure anything that God has made clean (Acts 10:15), for he already has other sheep which are not following the visible flock (John 10:16) and other disciples who work miracles and are not acknowledged by his visible followers (Mark 9:37). It was Christ also who sent a non-Jewish woman not to sow but actually to reap where others (non-Jews) had toiled, reminding his closest disciples of the meaning of this action (John 4:38). In ancient days God spoke to our fathers in many ways and by many means (Job 4:12, Jer. 49:7, etc.); now in recent times he has spoken to us through his Son (Heb. 1:1), in whom everything is summed up (Eph. 1:10), for he is the atonement not only for our sins, but for the defilement of the whole world (1 John 2:2). . . .

I venture to think that such an attempt as mine could find inspiration, illumination and justification in the famous encounter of St. Paul with the men of Athens (Acts 17:16-34). There, it will be recalled, there was a "pagan" shrine to an unknown and nameless God, and Paul said that he was proclaiming that very God whom they, without knowing it, were worshipping. Needless to say, it was not a zealous "strategy" which led Paul to utter such memorable words and to adopt such an attitude. Rather, unveiling a true face of God, he did not proclaim *another* God. After saying, further, that God was not far from any of his listeners, for "in him we live and move and are," he substantiated his bold statement with the saying of a Greek poet: "For we are also his off-spring." Here there comes to mind the refrain of the great cosmological hymn of the Rig-Veda: "What God shall we adore with our oblation?" One of the possible meanings of the text is the mysterious character of the Godhead, which can never be fully grasped and hence is only fittingly approached by an open interrogation. What on the Areopagus was a dedication in the dative is here a question in the dative: God is the "to whom?" of our search.

God is at work in all religions: the Christian *kerygma* does not proclaim a new God, but the *mirabilia* [wondrous things] of God, of which the Mystery of Christ hidden in God is the *alpha* and *omega*. This very expression in fact is declaring that Christ is not yet "finished," not "discovered," until the "last moment" or the "end" has come. The process itself is still open-ended.

In the wake of St. Paul we believe we may speak not only of the unknown God of the Greeks, but also of the *hidden Christ of Hinduism* — hidden and unknown and yet present and at work because he is not far from any one of us. St. Paul had to fight on two different fronts in order to defend the Christian position. On the one hand the Jews, even when converted, tended to make Christianity into a reformed sect of Judaism (cf. Rom. and Gal.). The Greeks, on the other hand, were inclined to absorb Christianity into a kind of gnosis or a variety of Greek wisdom (cf. 1 and 2 Cor.). In both cases the struggle was the same — against the attempt to minimize the figure of Christ and interpret it apart from the central mystery of the Trinity. Paul's reaction was to show how in Christ the mystery of God has been revealed, and how he — the *Pantocrator*, the cosmic redeemer, the beginning and end of all things, the only-begotten, the Logos — is at the same time Jesus, son of Mary, crucified by Men and risen from the dead so that he may sum up the whole of creation in himself and lead it back to God the Father, gathering together all the scattered pieces (cf. John 6:12) of wandering humanity, of a Mankind which remains full of expectancy, because the children of God are still to be made known (cf. Rom. 8:19).

Finally, I shall formulate a theological conclusion which is directly consequent upon this christological approach: the unity of Christ. Whatever God does *ad extra* happens through Christ. Thus, recognizing the presence of *God* in other religions is equivalent to proclaiming the presence of Christ in them, "for in him all things subsist" (Col. 1:17).

Hans Küng

A prolific Swiss Catholic scholar, Küng (b. 1928) for many years taught theology at the University of Tübingen, where he also served as director of its Institute for Ecumenical Research. Active in interreligious dialogue, Küng has published a number of works considering aspects of a Christian theology of religions. In the following selection, he succinctly outlines the foundations of his present stance in relation to four positions that he considers inadequate. Source: "Towards an Ecumenical Theology of Religions: Some Theses for Clarification," in *Christianity Among the World Religions*, ed. Hans Küng and Jürgen Moltmann (Nijmegen, Holland: Stichting Concilium; Edinburgh: T. & T. Clark Ltd., 1986).

Towards an Ecumenical Theology of Religions: Some Theses for Clarification

1. Four Inadequate Positions

a. The *atheist position:* no religion is true. Or else: all religions are equally untrue. Nevertheless our pure, theoretical reason is bound to this world and cannot reach far enough definitively to reject the question whether religion in reality corresponds to nothing or to an Absolute. To give one's assent to some ultimate ground, source or sense of the world and human

107

life such as is maintained in any of the great religions is not a matter of strict proof but of reasonable trust, which, however, reposes on good grounds.

b. The *absolutist position:* only one unique religion is true. Or else: all other religions are untrue. Nevertheless the dogma of the Fourth Lateran Council (1215) and of the Council of Florence (1442), "EXTRA ECCLE-SIAM NULLA SALUS," has no longer been held even by the Catholic Church since Vatican II, even though it is not often corrected. It is still being debated within the World Council of Churches, although it contradicts the will to universal salvation and the admittedly marginal but always percep-tible utterances about the heathen in Scripture, so that even the later Karl Barth was obliged to accept "other lights" besides the "one light."

c. The *relativistic position:* each religion is true. Or else: all religions are equally true. Nevertheless anybody who is really acquainted with the world religions can hardly maintain that they are all alike, especially when he or she thinks about the different basic types of mystical or prophetic religions. Even recourse to some supposedly overall similar religious (mys-tical) experience does not resolve the problem, because every religious experience is through and through an interpreted experience and so is penetrated by the relevant religious tradition and its various forms of expression.

d. The *inclusivist position:* one religion alone is the true one. Or else: all religions have a share in the truth of the one religion. Nevertheless, whether in the Indian variants (all religions represent only different levels of the one universal truth) or in the Christian variants (all religious people are anonymous Christians) the other religions are in fact relegated to a lower or a partial knowledge of the truth in such a way that one's own religion is from the outset raised to the status of a super-system. What seems to be tolerance proves in practice to be a sort of conquest by embrace, an integration through relativization and loss of identity.

2. The Critical Ecumenical Position

a. i. In place of an indifferentism for which everything is equally valid we need to posit something more in the nature of *indifference* towards alleged orthodoxy that sets itself up as the measure of the salvation or damnation of human beings and that sets out to enforce its claim to truth with power and means of compulsion.

ii. In place of a relativism, for which there is no Absolute, we need to posit something more in the nature of a sense of combined *relativity,* on the one hand, in the face of all human pretensions to absoluteness, which prevents a productive coexistence of the various religious, and, on the other, *relationality,* which enables one to see every religion as a web of connections.

iii. In place of a syncretism, in which everything imaginable and unimaginable is mixed together and fused, we need rather to posit something in the nature of a synthesis of all confessional and religious antagonisms, that still every day cost blood and tears, so that peace reigns between the religions instead of war, hate and strife.

b. i. We cannot have too much patience and religious freedom in the face of all religiously motivated impatience. No betrayal of *freedom* for the sake of freedom!

ii. The opposite is, however, also true: no betrayal of truth for the sake of freedom! The question of truth cannot be trivialized or sacrificed in the interests of some Utopia of future world unity and a religion of world unity. In the Third World, where people still remember the history of colonialism and the history of the missions bound up with it, such a Utopia is rightly seen as a threat to the culturo-religious identity of the rising nations.

iii. As Christians we are challenged, in the spirit of a *freedom* founded on Christ, to think afresh about the question of *truth.* For, unlike caprice, freedom is not simply freedom *from* all ties and duties, in any negative sense, but it is at the same time a freedom *for* a new responsibility: towards our fellow human beings, ourselves, the Absolute. True freedom is, therefore, freedom for truth.

c. i. The Christian possesses no monopoly of truth, and certainly has no right to invoke some pluralism of taste in order to renounce the *confession of truth;* dialogue and witness are not mutually exclusive. The witness to truth includes the courage to recognize and to articulate untruth.

ii. The boundaries between truth and untruth pass *through one's own present* religion. It follows that criticism of other positions is justifiable only on the basis of decisive self-criticism. This too is the only way in which integration of the values of other religions can be advocated. This means that not everything is equally true and good even in religions; there is false and bad in teaching about faith and morals, in religious rites and customs, institutions and authorities. Naturally this applies to Christianity too.

d. The need to discern between true (good) and false (bad) religion in all religions is what makes an interreligious criteriology an urgent task, the content of which can only be indicated:

e. i. In virtue of the general principle of ethics a religion is true and good when and to the extent that it is *humane* and that it protects and promotes rather than suppresses and destroys humanity.

ii. In virtue of the general criterion of religion, a religion is good and true when and to the extent that it remains true to its own *origin* or *canon* — its authentic being, the normative Scripture or pattern on which it bases its appeal.

iii. In virtue of the specific criterion of Christianity, a religion is true and good when and to the extent that it allows traces of Christ to be detected in its teaching and practice. This criterion can be applied *directly* only to Christianity — the self-critical question can be put whether and how far Christianity is in any way Christian. The same criterion can indeed also be applied to the other religions, but *indirectly* — and without arrogance: by way of clarifying the question whether and to what extent we can detect something of the spirit in other religions (especially in Judaism and Islam) that we characterize as Christian.

3. Outside and Inside Viewpoints

a. What is proclaimed today as "brand-new" teaching often proves to be the old teaching from the liberal Protestant stable. Such people do indeed hear God speaking through Jesus "as well" but have abandoned his normativity and "finality" (conclusiveness). They have put him on the level of other prophets alongside others (Christ together with other religions or other revealers, saviors, Christs) and so have lost all criteria for the discernment of spirits. Against such liberalism the protest of Karl Barth and "dialectical theology" (Rudolf Bultmann and Paul Tillich) was a necessary corrective. To go back in this direction is no progress.

b. Any theologian who is not prepared to give up this normativity and finality of Christ does so not because it is only through Christ as a critical catalyst that the other religions can "adapt themselves to our modern technology," but because otherwise he or she would be abandoning the central declaration of the Scriptures that go to make up the New Testament. For the whole of the New Testament — like it or not — Jesus is normative and definitive: he alone is the Christ of God (the oldest as well as the briefest confession of faith in the New Testament is just this: Jesous Kyrios), he is the "way, the truth and the life."

c. Holding fast to this two thousand years old conviction of truth —

without anguish or apologetic concern, but on good ground, in the way that Jews, Muslims, Hindus and Buddhists do to theirs — is, however, in no way identical with some theological "imperialism" and "neo-colonialism," which denies other religions their truth and rejects other prophets and seers. If one is to avoid the basic flaws in either the absolutist-exclusivist or the relativistic-inclusivist positions, one must distinguish the view from without and the view from within (or however else one cares to put it). This is the only way in which one can come to a nuanced answer to the question of the truth of religions.

d. Looked at from outside, observed as it were from the viewpoint of comparative religion, it goes without saying that there are *different true religions;* religions that, with all their ambivalence, correspond to at least certainly basically defined general (ethical and religious) criteria. There are different ways of salvation (with different ways of representing salvation) to the one goal, and these in part overlap and can in any case enrich each other. Yet the dialogue between these religions by no means demands the giving up of the standpoint of faith. For:

e. Looked at from inside, from the viewpoint of the believing Christian orienting him- or herself by the New Testament, therefore myself as an affected and challenged human being, there is a *true religion:* Christianity, in so far as it witnesses to one true God as he has declared himself in Jesus Christ. The one true religion in no ways excluded truth in the other religions but can let others be: as religions *true up to a point* ("conditionally" — or some such — true). So far as they do not directly contradict the Christian message, these religions can complete, correct and deepen the Christian religion.

4. Where Does a Dialogue without a Conviction of Faith Lead?

a. Anybody who renounces the normativity of his or her own tradition and takes as his or her point of departure the equal validity of the different "Christs" (Jesus, Moses, Muhammad, Gautama):

i. clearly presupposes as a result something that would not be unconditionally desirable even as the end-product of a long process of understanding — such a method seems to be *a prioristic:*

ii. requires of the other non-Christian parties what most of them reject, namely, that they should from the outset give up their belief in the normativity of their own message and their own bringers of salvation and take up the (typically Western and modern) standpoint of the basic equality of the various ways; such a way seems to be *unrealistic;*

iii. requires Christians themselves to demote Jesus Christ to the status of a provisional messiah and to give up the conviction of faith offered and demanded from the New Testament onwards (because springing from the normative and definitive Word of God given with Jesus) in favor of a leveling down of Jesus Christ to the other bearers of revelation and bringers of salvation ("Kyrios Jesous," on the same level as "Kyrios Kaísar" or "Kyrios Gautama"): such a stance would have to be characterized as *non-Christian* (and, it goes without saying, without any question of a heresy hunt);

iv. juxtaposes the various guiding figures as if they did not stand in a historical dependence on each other (whether Moses and Jesus, or Jesus and Muhammad) and were not honored in completely different ways within their own religions (as different as the position of Moses in Judaism, of Jesus in Christianity, or Muhammad in Islam or of Gautama in Buddhism): such a way of looking at things seems to be *unhistorical.*

b. The upshot of all this for practice is that anybody, whether as a Christian or not, who makes such a standpoint his or her own runs the risk of (willingly or unwillingly) distancing him- or herself from his or her own community of faith, indeed essentially of giving up his or her own religion. But the dialogue between the religions is not advanced by a few Western (or Eastern) intellectuals agreeing together. There is scarcely a need to engage in discussion if there is in the end nothing normative and definitive in any religion. Yet the Christian community of belief may allow itself to be persuaded to replace an ecclesio-centrism with a Christo-centrism or theo-centrism (which for Christians amount to the same thing!) but they are hardly likely to be persuaded to take up some vague soterio-centrism. Practice should not be made the norm of theory undialectically and social questions be expounded as the basis and center of the theology of religions.

5. Where Does a Dialogue on the Basis of a Conviction of Faith Lead?

a. Anybody who stands by the normativity of his or her own tradition and yet is open to other traditions:

i. starts off from the given and commits any final result and any agreement about the relationship of Jesus Christ and Muhammad (to take the Christian-Muslim dialogue as an example) wholly to the process of the dialogue and the understanding that emerges: a decidedly *a posteriori* approach;

ii. from the outset allows the partner in dialogue his or her stance of faith and first expects of him or her only unconditional readiness to hear and to learn, unrestricted openness that includes a transformation of both partners in the course of the process of mutual understanding; a *patiently realistic* way;

iii. acknowledges from the outset his or her own conviction of faith that for him or her Jesus is the Christ and so is normative and definitive, but he or she also takes very seriously the function of a Muhammad as an authentic (post-Christian) prophet and his "warning" about a declension from belief in one God in Christianity: a self-critically *Christian* standpoint;

iv. sees the various traditions, their origins and their bearers of salvation in their context and according to the standing they enjoy (Muhammad does not stand in the same place in Islam as Christ does in Christianity . . .), so that a nuanced view of the way in which the different traditions are interwoven becomes possible: a strongly *historical* way of looking at things even though it *is* anchored in the faith of all concerned;

b. the significance of this for *practice* is this: anybody who makes such a basic attitude his or her own, whether as a Christian or not, can combine commitment to faith and readiness to understand, religious loyalty and intellectual honesty. He or she has a critically reflective tie to his or her community and is trying simultaneously in regard to his or her as well as to the other community of faith not only to interpret something afresh but to change it — with a developing ecumenical community in view. It is in a similar spirit that for now going on for half a hundred years a few convinced Catholics and Protestants, rooted in their respective traditions and yet self-critical, have begun to speak with each other, and, precisely to the extent that they have remained true to their own communities of faith, have changed themselves and their partners — and, in due course, both church communities. What we can hope, therefore, is that some equivalent process will develop between the world religions, even if over a longer time-scale. . . .

Is this an entirely new task? By no means.

Is this not exactly what our forbears in the Church of antiquity did, the apologists and the Alexandrians Clement and Origen, when they encountered the neo-Platonic Stoic ways and worked out an ecumenically theological paradigm suitable to their age?

Did not Augustine and Thomas, confronted with a new Romano-German world, have to think theology through afresh in a process of transformation that was the way to a paradigm suitable for the Latin West?

Did not Luther and the Reformers have to allow themselves to be changed when in the great crisis of medieval theology and Church it became necessary to look back to the original gospel?

The Christian churches have lost a great deal of credibility in the course of encountering the world religions for the first time in the age of our modern paradigm, of belief in science and technology, colonialism and imperialism. This is the time — the time of our post-modern, post-colonial, polycentric age — to begin the dialogue with world religions afresh.

Paul F. Knitter

A former Divine Word missionary educated in Italy and West Germany, Paul F. Knitter is currently professor of theology at Xavier University, Cincinnati. In this essay, he attempts to show how a theology of liberation can aid a theology of religions. Source: *The Myth of Christian Uniqueness: Toward a Pluralistic Theology of Religions,* ed. John Hick and Paul F. Knitter (Maryknoll: Orbis Books, 1987).

Toward a Liberation Theology of Religions

There are three ways in which a liberation theology of religions can help theologians of dialogue maintain the richness of pluralism without allowing it to disintegrate into the pap of relativism.

1. Liberation theologians enter the hermeneutical circle — the process of trying to interpret and listen to the word of God — with a "hermeneutics of suspicion." They suspiciously remind themselves how easily — yes, how unavoidably — interpretations of scripture and formulations of doctrine become *ideology* — a means of promoting one's own interests at the expense of someone else's. All too often the truth that we propose as "God's will" or as divinely revealed is really our own disguised, subconscious will to maintain the status quo or to protect our own control of the situation or our own cultural-economic superiority. . . . Ideologized

doctrines and practices have first to be detected and revised before God's voice, in both the tradition and in the world, can really be heard. . . .

2. If the liberationists' hermeneutics of suspicion can help theologians of the religions clear away ideological obstacles to more effective dialogue, another foundation stone of liberation theology — the preferential option for (or the hermeneutical privilege of) the poor — can help, I suggest, resolve the complex and controversial questions concerning the presuppositions and procedures for interreligious dialogue. . . . The liberationists are telling us that without a commitment to and with the oppressed, our knowledge is deficient — our knowledge of self, others, the Ultimate. This is not to imply that we can know the truth *only* in such a commitment, but, rather, that without this option for the poor, the truth that we may know is, at best, incomplete, deficient, dangerous.

Because of its hermeneutical priority and potency, therefore, the preferential option for the oppressed (at least in the world as it exists today) serves as an effective condition for the possibility of dialogue — that which makes it possible for different religions to speak to and understand each other. If the religions of the world, in other words, can recognize poverty and oppression as a common problem, if they can share a common commitment (expressed in different forms) to remove such evils, they will have the basis for reaching across their incommensurabilities and differences in order to hear and understand each other and possibly be transformed in the process. . . .

Perhaps better than the monastery or the mystic's mountain, the struggle for justice can become the arena where Hindus and Muslims, Buddhists and Christians and Jews, can sense, and begin to speak about, that which unites them. What makes possible a *communication* in doctrine between believers from different paths is not only what Thomas Merton called a *communion of mystical-contemplative experience* but also and especially a communion of *liberative praxis*. . . .

If Christian attitudes have evolved from ecclesiocentrism to christocentrism to theocentrism, they must now move on to what in Christian symbols might be called "kingdom-centrism," or more universally, "soteriocentrism." For Christians, that which constitutes the basis and the goal for interreligious dialogue, that which makes mutual understanding and cooperation between the religions possible (the "condition of the possibility"), that which unites the religions in common discourse and praxis, is *not* how they are related to the church (invisibly through "baptism of desire"), or how they are related to Christ (anonymously [Rahner] or normatively [Küng]), nor even how they respond to and conceive of God, but rather, to what extent they are promoting *Soteria* (in Christian images, the *basileia*) — to what extent they are engaged in promoting human welfare and bringing about liberation with and for the poor and nonpersons.

A Christian liberation theology of religions, therefore, will propose as the "common" (though still "shaky") ground or starting point for religious encounter not *Theos,* the ineffable mystery of the divine, but rather, *Soteria,* the "ineffable mystery of salvation." Such a soteriocentric approach, it seems, is less prone to (though never fully immune from) ideological abuse, for it does not impose its own views of God or the Ultimate on other traditions; in this way it responds to Cobb's criticism of theocentrism. A soteriocentric approach to other faiths also seems to be more faithful to the data of comparative religions, for although the religions of the world contain a divergent variety of models for the Ultimate — theistic, metatheistic, polytheistic, and atheistic — "the common thrust, however, remains *soteriological,* the concern of most religions being *liberation (vimukti, moksa, nirvana)* rather than speculation about a hypothetical [divine] liberator."

3. So far, I have discussed how the different religions might *understand* each other. Is there any possibility that they might also be able to *judge* each other? . . . To call for such evaluative judgments is to rekindle fears of foundationalism, neocolonialism, and ideological abuse. Where are we to find criteria for judging or "grading" — criteria that have some inbuilt protection against being turned into exploitive tools and that can win general consensus in the academy and in the arena of interreligious encounter? Doctrinal criteria — concerning the qualities of the Ultimate, or the activity of a universal Logos, or the presence of an anonymous Christ or Buddha — prove too controversial and prone to ideology. Criteria from mystical experience — Merton's "communion before communication" or Panikkar's "Pneuma before Logos" — are helpful but often, in the end, hard to apply.

Might a soteriocentric basis for dialogue — the preferential option for the poor and nonpersons — provide general criteria that a variety of religions could agree to work with as a basis for grading themselves? . . . [Suggestions such as] "soteriological effectiveness," "a global ethic," the *humanum* need to be preferentially focused on the oppressed, the marginated, the powerless of our world, which means that these criteria have to be formulated and concretized in the actual praxis of liberation for the oppressed. Otherwise, such criteria run the risk of sinking into ineffectual theory or First World ideology. . . .

Soteriocentric criteria, therefore, serve as a *heuristic device* rather than as a defined basis. The criteria — what elements contribute to authentic, full liberation — can be known only in the actual praxis of struggling to overcome suffering and oppression, and only in the praxis of dialogue. What are the causes of suffering, of oppression? How best eliminate them? What kind of socio-cultural analysis is needed? What kind of personal transformation or alteration of consciousness is required? The preferential option for the poor does not provide prefabricated answers to such questions. And yet the starting point for struggling, together, toward answers is given in the fundamental option for and commitment to the oppressed. . . .

In holding up *Soteria* as the source of ethical criteria for interreligious dialogue, one need not be ideologically naive. Even though there may be general agreement about promoting justice and removing oppression, each religion or tradition will have its own understanding of what *Soteria* and liberation entail. Here, as Gavin D'Costa has pointed out in his criticism of my book [*No Other Name?*], every theocentric or soteriocentric approach remains, in a sense, inherently Christocentric (or Buddhacentric, Krishnacentric, Quranocentric). We all have our particular viewpoints, our perspectives, our different mediators. The criteria by which we understand what liberation means or what makes for authentic or deceptive salvation are provided by our particular mediators. The Universal, therefore, whether it be *theos* or *Soteria,* is always experienced, understood, and responded to via a particular symbol or mediator. In no way is Christ left behind; he remains the Christian's way, truth, and life.

But what makes the soteriocentric approach different from christocentrism or theocentrism is itself explicit recognition that before the mystery of *Soteria,* no mediator or symbol system is absolute. The perspective on *Soteria* given by any one mediator is always open to clarification, completion, perhaps correction by the viewpoints of other mediators. So again, the absolute, that which all else must serve and clarify, is not the church or Christ or even God — but rather, the kingdom and its justice. And although Christians understand and serve that kingdom *through* Christ, it is in seeking first the kingdom and its justice that all else will be added to them, including a clearer, perhaps corrected, understanding of that kingdom *and* of Christ. . . .

In order to avoid preestablished absolutist positions that prevent a genuinely pluralistic dialogue, Christians must, it seems, revamp or even reject their traditional understanding of Jesus Christ as God's final, definitive, normative voice. Can they do this and still call themselves Christians?

To show how a liberation theology of religions can help answer such christological quandaries, I offer the following four considerations.

1. As already mentioned, liberation theology insists that *praxis* is both the *origin* and the *confirmation* of theory or *doctrine*. All Christian beliefs and truth claims must grow out of and then be reconfirmed in the praxis or lived experience of these truths. According to liberation theology, one does not first know the truth and then apply it in praxis; it is in action, in doing, that truth is really known and validated. What this means for christology has been made clear by theologians such as Jon Sobrino and Leonardo Boff: we cannot begin to know who Jesus of Nazareth is unless we are following him, putting his message into the practice of our lives. This was the process by which the New Testament titles for Jesus came to be formulated; they were the fruit, the joyful kerygma, derived from the experience of following him. And because this experience varied according to the various communities and contexts of the early churches, the titles for Jesus proliferated.

Praxis, therefore, was the starting point of all christology. And it remains the criterion of all christology, for everything we know or say about Jesus must be continually confirmed, clarified, and perhaps corrected in the praxis of living his vision within the changing contexts of history. In this sense, therefore, as Boff tells us, nothing we say about Jesus is final. . . .

In other words, the Christian conviction and proclamation that Jesus is God's final and normative word for all religions cannot rest only on traditional doctrine *or* on personal, individual experience. We cannot know that Jesus is God's last or normative statement only on the basis of being told so or on the basis of having experienced him to be such in our own lives. Rather, the uniqueness of Jesus can be known and then affirmed only "in its concrete embodiment," only in the praxis of historical, social involvement. This means, concretely, that unless we are engaged in the *praxis of Christian dialogue* with other religions — following Christ, applying his message, within the dialogue with other believers — we cannot experience and confirm what the uniqueness and normativity of Christ mean. . . .

2. Another related ingredient in the theology of liberation — the *primacy of orthopraxis over orthodoxy* — assures Christians that if claims about the finality of Christ/Christianity are not presently possible, neither are they *necessary*. The primary concern of a soteriocentric liberation theology of religions is not "right belief" about the uniqueness of Christ, but the "right practice," with other religions, of furthering the kingdom and its *Soteria*. Clarity about whether and how Christ is one lord and savior, as

well as clarity about any other doctrine, may be important, but it is subordinate to carrying out the preferential option for the poor and nonpersons. Orthodoxy becomes a pressing concern only when it is necessary for orthopraxis — for carrying out the preferential option and promoting the kingdom. If orthodox clarity is not required for such purposes, it can wait.

I think it can wait. Christians do not *need* orthodox clarity and certainty concerning Jesus as the "only" or the "final" or the "universal" savior in order to experience and fully commit themselves to the liberating truth of his message. What Christians *do* know, on the basis of their praxis of following Jesus, is that his message *is* a sure means for bringing about liberation from injustice and oppression, that it *is* an effective, hope-filled, universally meaningful way of realizing *Soteria* and promoting God's kingdom. Not knowing whether Jesus is unique, whether he is the final or normative word of God for all times, does not interfere with commitment to the praxis of following him and working, with other religions, in building the kingdom. . . .

3. The possibilities, described earlier, of using the preferential option for the poor as a working criterion for "grading the religions" contain further christological implications. If liberating praxis with and for the poor and nonpersons is an indicator and measure of authentic revelation and religious experience, then Christians, whether they like it or not, have the means to discern not only whether but *how much* other religious beliefs and practices may be genuine "ways of salvation" — and further, whether and *how much* other religious figures may be genuine liberators and "saviors." In other words, the soteriocentric criteria for religious dialogue contained in the preferential option for the oppressed offer Christians the tools to critically examine and possibly revise the traditional understanding of the uniqueness of Christ.

Simply stated, from their ethical, soteriological fruits we shall know them — we shall be able to judge whether and how much other religious paths *and* their mediators are salvific. Judgments can go in different directions. In their academic and personal encounter with other believers and other paths, by applying the criteria of liberative praxis, Christian theologians may find that although there are other "saviors" in other traditions, still, Jesus the Nazarean appears to them — and perhaps to other believers too — as the unique and somehow special liberator — as he who unifies and fulfills all other efforts toward *Soteria. Or,* Christians may discover that other religions and religious figures offer a means and vision of liberation equal to that of Jesus, that it is impossible to "grade" saviors or enlightened beings in the sense of ranking them. . . . And yet, according to a soterio-centric liberation theology of religions, whether such discernments about uniqueness and finality are eventually made or not is, in the final analysis, not that important — as long as we, with all peoples and religions, are seeking first the kingdom and its justice (Matt. 6:33).

4. A liberation theology of religions offers help in dealing with another obstacle facing those who are exploring possibilities of a nonabsolutist or nondefinitive understanding of Christ. The final touchstone, it can be said, for the validity and appropriateness of a new understanding of Christ as "one among many," in a relationship of "complementary uniqueness" with others, is whether such a view will, eventually, be *received* by the faithful. . . .

The basic liberationist maxim that orthopraxis holds a primacy over orthodoxy is not only a challenging epistemological insight; it is also a workable pastoral tool for mediating the new nonabsolutist christologies to the *ecclesia*. By understanding and affirming the primacy of orthopraxis, the faithful can, I suggest, be helped to see that in "receiving" these new views of Jesus, they are not only remaining faithful to the witness of the New Testament and tradition, but are also being challenged to an even deeper commitment to Christ and his gospel. . . .

Those Christians who are challenged and enabled to make the link between their own experience, the gospel, and liberative praxis will agree, I am quite certain, that the essence of being a Christian is *doing* the will of the Father rather than knowing or insisting that Jesus is the one and only or the best of the bunch. In fact, the psychology of love and commitment would seem to suggest that the deeper and more secure one's commitment to a particular path or person is, the more one is open to the beauty or truth of other paths and persons. Christians can be led to see that neither their commitment to Jesus nor their ability to worship him (the *lex orandi*) need be jeopardized just because there may be others like him. Why, really, must something be "one and only" in order to merit our devotion and commitment? The Christian faithful will also grasp how much sound evangelical sense such a nonabsolutist approach to Christ makes: others will be much more readily convinced by Christians who give simple witness to how much their savior has actually done for them than by Christians who insist that "our savior is bigger than yours."

Recognition of the primacy of orthopraxis over orthodoxy can also be used pastorally to enable Christian believers to understand the nature of New Testament language and what it means to be faithful to this language. On the basis of their own experience of pondering and praying over

121

the scriptures, the faithful can readily grasp that the power and purpose of biblical language is first of all to call forth a way of life rather than a body of belief. . . .

It would be more accurate and pastorally effective, I think, to call the New Testament claims about Jesus "action language." He was called "one and only" or "only begotten" not *primarily* to give us definitive theologico-philosophical statements, and not *primarily* to exclude others, but rather to urge the action or practice of total commitment to his vision and way. . . . If recognizing the possibility of other saviors or mediators does not impede this praxis, then it is compatible with Christian identity and tradition.

In fact, it might be argued that today such a recognition of others is necessary for remaining faithful to the original witness about Jesus. Theologians who are exploring a pluralist theology of religions and a nonabsolutist christology are doing so not merely for the sake of novelty or for the sake of joining the excitement of a truly pluralist interreligious dialogue; rather, they do so because "the love of Christ urges them" (2 Cor. 5:14). They want to be faithful to the original message of the Nazarean — that to which Jesus always subordinated himself: the kingdom of love, unity, and justice.

Gavin D'Costa

An Indian-born Roman Catholic scholar, D'Costa is currently Senior Research Fellow at the West London Institute of Higher Education. He has served as a member of the British Council of Churches' Committee for Relations with People of Other Faiths and also a member of the Roman Catholic Committee for Other Faiths (England and Wales). In this selection, D'Costa argues for an inclusivist position which, grounded in the central Christian doctrine of the Trinity, rejects either a priori critical judgments or a priori positive affirmations of the world religions. Source: *Christian Uniqueness Reconsidered: The Myth of a Pluralistic Theology of Religions,* ed. Gavin D'Costa (Maryknoll: Orbis Books, 1990).

Christ, The Trinity, and Religious Plurality

The pluralists raise three factors that suggest a rethinking of traditional Christian approaches to other religions: relativity, mystery, and justice. Taking these issues seriously purportedly leads to a pluralist theology of religions, which broadly affirms the equal parity of all revelations. I wish to propose that this is not the case. The three sets of problems can be viewed differently from within a trinitarian perspective. The question of reconciling the historical particular with the universal, the question of *relativity*, is illuminated by the universal agency of God, based on the particularity of

123

the revelation of God in Christ. Christianity cannot therefore claim that its own particular revelation is the only important one, but rather that if the particularity of Christ discloses God then it must hold to the normativity (not exclusivity) of its own particular revelation, thereby maintaining its universal claims. A recognition of God's universal action cannot proceed without a normative Christology. Second, the question of the *mystery* of God and God's transcendence over and above every particular articulation is illuminated by the notion of the Holy Spirit, who constantly deepens and enlarges the Christian's understanding of God, the unfathomable mystery. Hence, Christians must be open to the workings of the Spirit in the world, in a manner that cannot be a priori specified, to be fully open to God. Finally, the question of promoting *justice,* the kingdom of God, cannot bypass the theological reflections which give a basis to such an approach. Hence, any liberation theology of religions requires a Christocentric trinitarianism to justify this focus on the new possible meeting points among the religions. . . .

Thesis One: A trinitarian Christology guards against exclusivism and pluralism by dialectically relating the universal and the particular.

The Trinity safeguards against an exclusivist particularism (Christo-monism) and a pluralist universalism (theocentricism) in that it stipulates against an *exclusive identification* of God and Jesus, as well as against a *non-identification* of God and Jesus. . . . Against an exclusivist Christo-monism, it must be stressed that "the Son is not the Father." Hence, although we come to know the Father through Jesus, we cannot turn Jesus into an idol and claim that the Father is exclusively known through him. It is through the Spirit *and* the Son that God is disclosed. Hence, any attempt to limit or monopolize God in terms solely of Jesus turns into a binitarianism or unitarianism, which fails to account for the fullness of the self-disclosure of God.

Against a pluralist theocentricism, it must also be stressed that "whatever is said of the Father is said of the Son." We cannot, as Christians, speak of the Father without the story of Jesus. The Father cannot be conjured up through speculation or abstractions, but is revealed in the particularities of history, in the story of the Son, understood and interpreted through the illumination of the Spirit. It is through constantly attending to the particularities of Jesus' story that we come to know who God is — which is the reason why the liturgy is at the heart of the Christian community. We cannot divorce our understanding of God from the story of Jesus and rend asunder the universal and particular. However, as we shall see shortly, the reading and enacting of the story of Jesus is transformed and challenged in the light of the world religions. . . .

Thesis Two: Pneumatology allows the particularity of Christ to be related to the universal activity of God in the history of humankind.

The doctrine of the Holy Spirit allows us theologically to relate the particularity of the Christ event to the entire history of humankind. One may note the biblical testimony to the creative, prophetic, and saving action of the Word and Spirit from the time of creation. The fact that this testimony is primarily related to the Jewish-Christian tradition should not blind us to the possible reality of God's creative, prophetic and saving activity elsewhere. (This, however, does not detract from the unique historical and theological relationship of Christianity to Judaism.) There are no good theological reasons to suggest that God's activity has stopped, but rather, given the universal salvific will of the Father revealed in Christ, we can have every expectation that God's activity in history is ongoing and certainly not historically limited to Christianity. The logical point I am making is this: *All* history, both past and to come, is potentially a particularity by which God's self-revelation is mediated. Chronologically and geographically there can be no preset limitations to this: "The Spirit blows where it will." Ecclesiologically this is affirmed in the condemnation of the Jansenist teaching that "outside the church no grace is granted." . . .

Thesis Three: A Christocentric trinitarianism discloses loving relationship as the proper mode of being. Hence love of neighbor (which includes Hindus, Buddhists, and others) is an imperative for all Christians.

God's self-disclosure in Christ shows that the proper mode of being is in *loving communion,* exemplified in the love between the Father and the Son, and correlatively the love between the three persons of the Trinity. Christians are called to reflect this reality, by which they are shaped, in their communion with others — in their Christian communities and more widely. Biblically, this is by our adoption as sons and daughters of God through our participation in the Sonship of Christ by the power of the Holy Spirit. Our mode of participation in Jesus' Sonship is by living the pattern of his crucified self-giving love and being empowered and guided by the Spirit to instantiate this pattern within our differing socio-historical contexts. It is through this modality of love that we are called into communion with God. Hence, *love of neighbor is co-essential with the love of God.* . . .

Thesis Four: The normativity of Christ involves the normativity of crucified self-giving love. Praxis and dialogue. . . .

The most radical clue to the meaning of love within our Christian story, which also acts as a criticism of our living out that story, is that mediated by Jesus' life, which finishes on the cross. The cross offers a pattern of self-giving and suffering love where vulnerability rather than worldly strength and success, suffering service rather than manipulation and coercion, and fidelity to God's will at whatever cost are important. Jesus concretizes these themes in his life. If we are to avoid the danger of allowing love of neighbor to turn into various forms of power, manipulation, and coercion over our neighbor, then we require the pattern and practice of suffering self-giving love. It is a pattern and practice encoded in the liturgical readings of the church. Through Jesus' story we are normatively shaped by the patterns of service and love encoded in his life and death, which are constantly recoded, to the extent of our participation in these patterns, by the power of the Spirit. We are called to a form of life that is oriented toward liberating humankind from the powers of evil, preaching the Good News to the poor, proclaiming release to captives, the recovery of sight to the blind, and setting at liberty those who are oppressed; all messianic *actions* heralding God's kingdom through suffering self-giving love and service rather than worldly strength, coercion, and manipulation.

In this sense, and it is only one sense, Christ's normativity is important for Christians in their relationship to other religions. It entails a form of discipleship which must actively seek to promote and herald the kingdom of God, and this will require working together with and sometimes against non-Christians. Christ's normativity correctly suggests that *working together with men and women from other religions for liberation from oppression* and suffering in all its many forms and, through this mutuality, discovering the many forms in which this oppression and suffering take place, is one proper mode of interreligious dialogue for Christians. . . .

In proportion to the promotion of the "kingdom" by people from other religions (in, for example, their facilitating justice, peace, love, and charity), Christians are radically questioned with regard to their own possibly restricted understanding of what the kingdom is, and also with regard to their recognition of the different ways in which God is working through the adherents of other religions. . . .

Thesis Five: The church stands under the judgment of the Holy Spirit, and if the Holy Spirit is active in the world religions, then the world religions are vital to Christian faithfulness. . . .

In John's Farewell Discourses, Jesus speaks of the Holy Spirit's relation to himself and the Father: "I have yet many things to say to you but you cannot bear them now. When the Spirit of truth comes, he will guide you into all truth; for he will not speak on his own authority, for whatever he hears he will speak, and he will declare to you the things that are to come. He will glorify me, for he will take what is mine and declare it to you. All that the Father has is mine; therefore I said that he will take what is mine and declare it to you" (John 16:12-15).

The full richness and depths of God are yet to be discovered even though in Christianity it is claimed that God has revealed himself definitively in Christ. "I have yet many things to say to you" is indicative of this recognition, which also poses this question: How is this deepening process of disclosure to take place? The answer given here is through the work of the Spirit, who will "guide" and "declare." What is interesting in this passage is the ongoing hermeneutical circle underpinning John's trinitarian theology. The process of guidance and declaration, or what we might call the ongoing disclosure of the fullness of revelation, is authorized and measured insomuch as it is in conformity to Christ ("He will glorify me, for he will take what is mine and declare it to you"). This conformity to Christ is itself only authorized because of his relationship to the Father ("All that the Father has is mine"). The riches of the mystery of God are disclosed by the Spirit and are measured and discerned by their conformity to and in their illumination of Christ. Insomuch as these riches are disclosed, Christ, the universal Logos, is more fully translated and universalized. In this sense, Jesus is the *normative* criteria for God, while not foreclosing the ongoing self-disclosure of God in history, through the Spirit.

The most important feature of this hermeneutical circle is the way in which Christ is both the norm for understanding God and yet not a static norm, but one that is being constantly transformed and enriched through the guiding/declaring/judging function of the Spirit. It also needs to be noted that this dialectical tension between Son and Spirit must necessarily remain unresolved until the eschaton, for only then will God be properly known face to face, so to speak. It is on the basis of these and other biblical passages that the teaching has evolved that the church stands under the constant judgment of the Holy Spirit and Christ if it is to be maintained in truth.

The significance of this trinitarian ecclesiology is that if we have good reasons to believe that the Spirit and Word are present and active in the religions of the world (in ways that cannot, a priori, be specified), then it is intrinsic to the vocation of the church to be attentive to the world religions. Otherwise, it willfully closes itself to the Spirit of truth, which it requires to maintain faithfulness to the truth and be guided more deeply into it. The doctrine of the Spirit thereby provides the narrative space in which the testimonies of people from the world religions, in their own words and lives, can unmask the false ideologies and distorted narrative practices within Christian communities. At the same time, it allows Christians to be aware of God's self-disclosure within the world's religions, and through this process of learning, enrich its own self-understanding. Without listening to this testimony, Christians cease to be faithful to their own calling as Christians, in being inattentive to God. . . .

Due to the narrative and paradigmatic form of Christianity, it is inevitable that in the [intraChristian] process of indigenization elements from another tradition will be adopted by Christianity according to its own narrative structure and according to its own paradigmatic rules and procedures. Such is the case with the use of the Hebrew Bible within the Christian canon, and with "sacerdotal vestments, the tonsure, the ring in marriage, turning to the East . . . the Kyrie Eleison" and many aspects within the evolving church. In this process of indigenization those elements rightly valued within other traditions are affirmed and employed within a new narrative structure, one that tells of a trinitarian God. If we can recall the words of St. John, all that is declared by the Spirit will glorify Christ, and thereby the Father. This is the key to the process of indigenization.

Elsewhere I have indicated the ways in which Indian Christians have tried to incorporate their Hindu and Indian heritage into their theology, worship, and practice. In the same way that Aquinas used Aristotle to articulate the depths of God's self-disclosure, some Indian Christians have used Sankara and Ramanuja. These transformations have affected every aspect of Christian life. If Christology has been rethought through Hindu categories, so has church dress and posture — to cite two liturgical examples. Rather than drawing on the civilian dress of the late Roman empire for its style of vestments, some Indian Christians have adopted the kavi robes of the Indian holy man. Similarly, rather than genuflection, deriving from the civil recognition of imperial officials in authority, some Indian Christians practice panchanga pranam (kneeling posture with forehead and both palms on the ground) on entering the consecrated grounds of the ashram-church.

The list is endless, as are the dangers attendant to the benefits in truly catholicizing Christianity and universalizing Christ. It is only through this attentive listening that Christianity is itself fulfilled in its deepening understanding of Christ and the ways of the Holy Spirit. This is counter to the notion of fulfillment often employed whereby Christianity is seen to fulfill other religions, implying its complete self-sufficiency. The unfinished task of indigenization is testimony to the incompleteness of Christianity and its own need of fulfillment.

Through my five theses I have tried to outline a possible direction for an inclusivist Christian theology of religions. The trinitarian Christology proposed has the virtue, as I see it, of reconciling both the exclusivist emphasis on the particularity of Christ and the pluralist emphasis on God's universal activity in history. In reconciling this polarity, such an approach further commends itself in its *committed* openness regarding the world religions. It is committed in its fidelity to the trinitarian God, upon which Christian hope, worship, and practice is based. It is committed in the measure by which the thoughts, words, and deeds of the Christian community testify to this hope that is within them and are open to the enrichment of their understanding and practice of this hope, which is seen now as through a "glass darkly" (1 Cor. 13:12).

CONTEMPORARY PROTESTANT VIEWS

Ernst Troeltsch

A German Protestant theologian and philosopher, Troeltsch (1865-1923) maintained broad interests in religio-historical and sociological studies of religion. Perhaps best known for his work *The Social Teachings of the Christian Churches,* he was particularly concerned with evaluating the impact of modern historical consciousness on Christian faith. In a lecture entitled "The Place of Christianity among the World Religions," written shortly before his death, he wrestled again with the problem that had occupied him in an earlier book, *The Absolute Validity of Christianity* (1902). In the following selection from that lecture, Troeltsch concludes that we can claim with certainty only Christianity's validity *for us.* Source: *Christian Thought: Its History and Application,* ed. Baron F. von Hügel (London: University of London Press, 1923).

The Place of Christianity among the World Religions

In my book on *The Absolute Validity of Christianity* I examined the means whereby theology is able to defend itself against these difficulties [posed by perceptions of historical relativity]. This of course involved an examination of the fundamental concepts of theology as such. I believed that I could here determine two such concepts, both of which claimed to establish the ultimate validity of the Christian revelation in opposition to the relativities revealed by the study of history.

The first of these concepts was the theory that the truth of Christianity is guaranteed by miracles. In our times we are no longer primarily concerned here with miracles in the external world, i.e. with the so-called "nature miracles," involving an infringement of natural law, but with the miracles of interior conversion and attainment of a higher quality of life through communion with Jesus and his community. In this connection, it is claimed, an entirely different type of causation comes into operation from that which is operative anywhere else in the world. . . .

The second fundamental concept of theology, which I have called the concept of evolution, presents a considerable contrast to the first. Its most important exponent is Hegel. According to this view Christianity is simply the perfected expression of religion as such. In the universal process of the unfolding Spirit, the fundamental impulse towards salvation and communion with God overcomes all the limitations of sense experience, of the natural order, of mythological form, until it attains perfect expression in Christianity, and enters into combination with the loftiest and most spiritual of all philosophies, namely that of Platonism. Christianity, it is maintained, is not *a particular* religion, it is *religion*. It is no isolated manifestation of Spirit, but the flower of spiritual life itself. . . . The whole history of religion and its obvious trend are thus a completely adequate proof of Christianity. . . .

I found myself obliged to dismiss both of these views as untenable. The former I rejected on the ground that an inward miracle, though it is indeed a powerful psychical upheaval, is not a miracle in the strict sense of the term. . . . Moreover, we should then be faced with the competition furnished by similar miracles in the non-Christian religions. . . .

If, however, we turn for this reason to the second view, we find the difficulties to be different, indeed, but no less formidable. The actual history of religion knows nothing of the common character of all religions, or of their natural upward trend towards Christianity. . . . Moreover, Christianity is itself a theoretical abstraction. It presents no historical uniformity, but displays a different character in every age, and is, besides, split up into many different denominations, hence it can in no wise be represented as the finally attained unity and explanation of all that has gone before, such as religious speculation suggests. . . .

What then is the solution? This is the question which I attempted to answer in my book. . . . It is quite possible, I maintained, that there is an element of truth in every religion, but that this is combined with innumerable transitory, individual features. This element of truth can only be disentangled through strife and disruption, and it should be our constant endeavour to assist in this process of disentanglement. The recognition of this truth is, however, an intuition which is born of deep personal experience and a pure consciousness. No strict proof of it is possible. . . . Such an intuition can only be confirmed retrospectively and indirectly by its practical fruits, and by the light that it sheds upon all the problems of life. . . .

We still require a broader foundation upon actual, objective facts. I believed that I had discovered such a foundation for Christianity in the terms in which its claim to ultimate validity finds instinctive and immediate expression; in other words, in its faith in revelation and in the kind of claim it makes to truth. . . . If we examine any of the great world religions we shall find that all of them, Judaism, Islam, Zoroastrianism, Buddhism, Christianity, even Confucianism, indeed claim absolute validity, but quite naively, and that in a very different manner in each case. . . . Judaism and Zoroastrianism were explicitly national religions, associated with a particular country and concerned with tasks presented by a particular type of civilization — in the case of the Jews primarily with questions of national loyalty and national aspiration. Islam, too, is at the bottom the national religion of the Arab peoples, compelling by the sword recognition of the prophetic claims of Muhammad in all the countries to which the Arab races have penetrated. . . . Confucianism and Buddhism again are rather philosophies than religions, and owe their claim to absolute validity more to the common character of thought than to belief in a specific religious revelation, whilst Confucianism is essentially a national movement and Buddhism is, as a matter of fact, bound to the conditions of life in tropical countries.

Now, the naive claim to absolute validity made by Christianity is of quite a different kind. All limitation to a particular race or nation is excluded on principle. . . . Moreover, it does not depend in any way upon human reflection or a laborious process of reasoning, but upon an overwhelming manifestation of God in the persons and lives of the great prophets. . . . Thus the naive claim to absolute validity of Christianity is as unique as its conception of God. . . . It possesses the highest claim to universality of all religions, for this its claim is based upon the deepest foundations, the nature of God and of man.

Such was the conclusion I reached in the book which I wrote some twenty years ago, and, from the practical standpoint at least, it contains nothing that I wish to withdraw. From the point of view of theory, on the other hand, there are a number of points which I should wish to modify today, and these modifications are, of course, not without practical effects.

My scruples arise from the fact that, whilst the significance for history of the concept of Individuality impresses me more forcibly every day, I can no longer believe this to be so easily reconcilable with that of supreme validity. The further investigations, especially into the history of Christianity . . . have shown me how thoroughly individual is historical Christianity after all, and how invariably its various phases and denominations have been due to varying circumstances and conditions of life. Whether you regard it as a whole or in its several forms, it is a purely historical, individual, relative phenomenon, which could, as we actually find it, only have arisen in the territory of the classical culture, and among the Latin and Germanic races. . . . On the other hand, a study of the non-Christian religions convinced me more and more that their naive claims to absolute validity are also genuinely such.

The subject to which I devoted most attention, however, was that of the relation of individual historical facts to standards of value within the entire domain of history in connection with the development of political, social, ethical, aesthetic, and scientific ideas. . . . I encountered the same difficulties in each of these provinces — they were not confined to religion. . . . What was really common to mankind, and universally valid for it, seemed, in spite of a general kinship and capacity for mutual understanding, to be at bottom exceedingly little, and to belong more to the province of material goods than to the ideal values of civilization.

The effect of these discoveries upon the conclusions reached in my earlier book was as follows.

The individual character of European civilization, and of the Christian religion which is intimately connected with it, receives now much greater emphasis, whilst the somewhat rationalistic concept of validity, and specifically of *supreme validity,* falls considerably into the background. . . . Our whole Christianity is indissolubly bound up with elements of the ancient and modern civilizations of Europe. From being a Jewish sect Christianity has become the religion of all Europe. It stands or falls with European civilization; whilst, on its own part, it has entirely lost its Oriental character and has become Hellenized and Westernized. . . .

Its primary claim to validity is thus the fact that only through it have we become what we are, and that only in it can we preserve the religious

136

forces that we need. . . . At the same time our life is a consistent compromise, as little unsatisfactory as we can manage, between its lofty spirituality and our practical everyday needs. . . . Thus we are, and thus we shall
remain, as long as we survive. We cannot live without a religion, yet the
only religion that we can endure is Christianity, for Christianity has grown
up with us and has become a part of our very being. . . .

Christianity could not be the religion of such a highly developed racial
group if it did not possess a mighty spiritual power and truth; in short, if
it were not, in some degree, a manifestation of the Divine Life itself. The
evidence we have for this remains essentially the same, whatever may be
our theory concerning absolute validity — it is the evidence of a profound
inner experience. This experience is undoubtedly the criterion of its validity,
but, be it noted, only of its validity *for us*. It is God's countenance as revealed
to us; it is the way in which, being what we are, we receive, and react to,
the revelation of God. It is binding upon us, and it brings us deliverance.
It is final and unconditional for us, because we have nothing else, and
because in what we have we can recognize the accents of the divine voice.

But this does not preclude the possibility that other racial groups,
living under entirely different cultural conditions, may experience their
contact with the Divine Life in quite a different way, and may themselves
also possess a religion which has grown up with them, and from which they
cannot sever themselves so long as they remain what they are. And they
may quite sincerely regard this as absolutely valid for them, and give expression to this absolute validity according to the demands of their own
religious feeling. We shall, of course, assume something of this kind only
among nations which have reached a relatively high stage of civilization,
and whose whole mental life has been intimately connected with their
religion through a long period of discipline. We shall not assume it among
the less developed races, where many religious cults are followed side by
side, nor in the simple animism of heathen tribes, which is so monotonous
in spite of its many variations. These territories are gradually conquered by
the great world religions which possess a real sense of their own absolute
validity. But among the great spiritual religions themselves the fundamental
spiritual positions which destiny has assigned to them persist in their dis-
tinctness. If we wish to determine their relative value, it is not the religions
alone that we must compare, but always only the civilizations of which the
religion in each case constitutes a part incapable of severance from the rest.
But who will presume to make a really final pronouncement here? Only
God himself, who has determined these differences, can do that. The various

racial groups can only seek to purify and enrich their experience, each within its own province and according to its own standards, and to win the weaker and less developed races for their own faith, always remembering that the religion thus adopted by another people will individualize itself anew.

The practical bearing of this new manner of thinking . . . brings to light one or two important consequences. In the first place, it has a considerable influence upon the question of foreign missions. . . . We have to maintain, in accordance with all our conclusions hitherto, that directly religious missionary enterprise must stand in quite a different relation to the great philosophical world religions from that in which it stands to the crude heathenism of smaller tribes. There can be always only a spiritual wrestling of missionary Christianity with the other world religions, possibly a certain contact with them. The heathen races, on the other hand, are being morally and spiritually disintegrated by the contact with European civilization; hence they demand a substitute from the higher religion and culture. We have a missionary duty towards these races, and our enterprise is likely to meet with success amongst them. . . . But in relation to the great world religions we need to recognize that they are expressions of the religious consciousness corresponding to certain definite types of culture, and that it is their duty to increase in depth and purity by means of their own interior impulses, a task in which the contact with Christianity may prove helpful, to them as to us, in such processes of development from within. . . . There can be no conversion or transformation of one into the other, but only a measure of agreement and of mutual understanding.

The second practical consequence of my new trend of thought concerns the inner development of Christianity itself. If my theory is correct, this development is closely related to the whole spiritual and cultural development of European civilization. . . . Christianity is drawn into the stream of spiritual development even within the churches, and still more outside and beyond them, in the free speculation of literature and philosophy. Moreover, it contains, like all the world religions, and perhaps more than any other world religion, the impulse and the power to a continual self-purification and self-deepening, for it has been assigned to that Spirit which shall lead men into all truth, and which seeks its fulfillment in the coming of the Kingdom of God; and again, because it has been bound up from the first with all the intellectual forces of Hellenism.

Under these circumstances the course of its development is unpredictable, for it is capable of assuming always new individualizations. A new era in the world's history is beginning for it at this moment. It has to ally itself anew to a new conception of nature, a new social order, and a profound interior transformation of the spiritual outlook, and has to bring to the suffering world a new peace and a new brotherhood. How this can be accomplished it is not for me to say here; indeed, the answer is as yet very far from clear. All that is certain is that Christianity is at a critical moment of its further development, and that very bold and far-reaching changes are necessary, transcending anything that has yet been achieved by any denomination. . . .

I only wish to emphasize now more strongly than I did then [in my earlier work] that this synthesis cannot as yet be already attained in any one of the historical religions, but that they all are tending in the same direction, and that all seem impelled by an inner force to strive upward towards some unknown final height, where alone the ultimate unity and the final objective validity can lie. And, as all religion has thus a common goal in the Unknown, the Future, perchance in the Beyond, so too it has a common ground in the Divine Spirit ever pressing the finite mind onward towards further light and fuller consciousness, a Spirit which indwells the finite spirit, and whose ultimate union with it is the purpose of the whole many-sided process.

Between these two poles, however — the divine Source and the divine Goal — lie all the individual differentiations of race and civilization, and, with them also, the individual differences of the great, comprehensive religions. There may be mutual understanding between them, if they are willing to renounce those sorry things, self-will and the spirit of violent domination. If each strives to fulfill its own highest potentialities, and allows itself to be influenced therein by the similar striving of the rest, they may approach and find contact with each other. . . . But, so far as human eye can penetrate into the future, it would seem probable that the great revelations to the various civilizations will remain distinct, in spite of a little shifting of their several territories at the fringes, and that the question of their several relative values will never be capable of objective determination, since every proof thereof will presuppose the special characteristics of the civilization in which it arises. . . .

This is what I wish to say in modification of my former theories. I hope you feel that I am not speaking in any spirit of scepticism or uncertainty. A truth which, in the first instance, is *a truth for us* does not cease, because of this, to be very truth and life. What we learn daily through our love for our fellow men, viz., that they are independent beings with standards of their own, we ought also to be able to learn through our love for mankind as a whole — that here too there exist autonomous civilizations with standards of their own. This does not exclude rivalry, but it must be a rivalry for the attainment of interior purity and clearness of vision. If each racial group strives to develop its own highest potentialities, we may hope to come nearer to one another. This applies to the great world religions, but it also applies to the various religious denominations, and to individuals in their intercourse with one another. In our earthly experience the Divine Life is not one, but many. But to apprehend the one in the many constitutes the special character of love.

Karl Barth

Reacting against the liberalism of his teachers, including Adolf von Harnack, Barth (1886-1968) became a leading figure following World War I in the emergence of a "dialectical" or "neo-orthodox" Protestant theology. Dismissed from his teaching post at the University of Bonn in 1935 because of his firm opposition to Nazi ideology, the Swiss theologian subsequently joined the faculty of the University of Basil. In the following selection, from his influential yet unfinished *Church Dogmatics*, Barth distinguishes between "religion" and "revelation" and explains in what sense Christianity may be responsibly referred to as the "true religion." Source: *Church Dogmatics*, vol. 1/2 (1932), trans. G. T. Thomson and H. Knight (Edinburgh: T. & T. Clark, 1956).

The Revelation of God as the Abolition of Religion

Religion as Unbelief

We begin by stating that religion is unbelief. It is a concern, indeed, we must say that it is the one great concern, of godless man. . . .

In the light of what we have already said, this proposition is not in any sense a negative value-judgment. It is not a judgment of religious science or philosophy based upon some prior negative judgment concerned with the nature of religion. It does not affect only other men with their religion. Above all it affects ourselves also as adherents of the Christian religion. It formulates the judgment of divine revelation upon all religion. . . .

To realize that religion is really unbelief, we have to consider it from the standpoint of the revelation attested in Holy Scripture. There are two elements in that revelation which make it unmistakably clear.

1. Revelation is God's self-offering and self-manifestation. Revelation encounters man on the presupposition and in confirmation of the fact that man's attempts to know God from his own standpoint are wholly and entirely futile; not because of any necessity in principle, but because of a practical necessity of fact. In revelation God tells man that He is God, and that as such He is his Lord. In telling him this, revelation tells him something utterly new, something which apart from revelation he does not know and cannot tell either himself or others. . . . This "coming to us" of the truth is revelation. It does not reach us in a neutral condition, but in an action which stands to it, as the coming of truth, in a very definite, indeed a determinate relationship. That is to say, it reaches us as religious men; i.e., it reaches us in the attempt to know God from our standpoint. It does not reach us, therefore, in the activity which corresponds to it. The activity which corresponds to revelation would have to be faith; the recognition of the self-offering and self-manifestation of God. We need to see that in view of God all our activity is in vain even in the best life; i.e., that of ourselves we are not in a position to apprehend the truth, to let God be God and our Lord. We need to renounce all attempts even to try to apprehend this truth. We need to be ready and resolved simply to let the truth be told us and therefore to be apprehended by it. But that is the very thing for which we are not resolved and ready. The man to whom the truth has really come will concede that he was not at all ready and resolved to let it speak to him. The genuine believer will not say that he came to faith from faith, but —. from unbelief, even though the attitude and activity with which he met revelation, and still meets it, is religion. For in faith, man's religion as such is shown by revelation to be resistance to it. From the standpoint of revelation religion is clearly seen to be a human attempt to anticipate what God in His revelation wills to do and does do. It is the attempted replacement of the divine work by a human manufacture. The divine reality offered and manifested to us in revelation is replaced by a concept of God arbitrarily and willfully evolved by man. . . .

From the standpoint of revelation, man's religion is simply an assumption and assertion of this kind, and as such it is an activity which contradicts revelation — contradicts it, because it is only through truth that truth can come to man. If man tries to grasp at truth of himself, he tries to grasp at it *a priori*. But in that case he does not do what he has to do when the truth comes to him. He does not believe. If he did, he would listen; but in religion he talks. If he did, he would accept a gift; but in religion he takes something for himself. If he did, he would let God Himself intercede for God: but in religion he ventures to grasp at God. Because it is a grasping, religion is the contradiction of revelation, the concentrated expression of human unbelief, i.e., an attitude and activity which is directly opposed to faith. . . .

2. As the self-offering and self-manifestation of God, revelation is the act by which in grace He reconciles man to Himself by grace. As a radical teaching about God, it is also the radical assistance of God which comes to us as those who are unrighteous and unholy, and as such damned and lost. . . . Jesus Christ does not fill out and improve all the different attempts of man to think of God and to represent Him according to his own standard. But as the self-offering and self-manifestation of God He replaces and completely outbids those attempts, putting them in the shadows to which they belong. Similarly, in so far as God reconciles the world to Himself in Him, He replaces all the different attempts of man to reconcile God to the world, all our human efforts at justification and sanctification, at conversion and salvation. The revelation of God in Jesus Christ maintains that our justification and sanctification, our conversion and salvation, have been brought about and achieved once and for all in Jesus Christ. And our faith in Jesus Christ consists in our recognizing and admitting and affirming and accepting the fact that everything has actually been done for us once and for all in Jesus Christ. He is the assistance that comes to us. He alone is the Word of God that is spoken to us. There is an exchange of status between Him and us; His righteousness and holiness are ours, our sin is His; He is lost for us, and we for His sake are saved. By this exchange (2 Cor. 5) revelation stands or falls. It would not be the active, redemptive self-offering and self-manifestation of God, if it were not centrally and decisively the *satisfactio* and *intercessio Jesu Christi*. . . .

True Religion

The preceding expositions have established the fact that we can speak of "true" religion only in the sense in which we speak of a "justified sinner."

Religion is never true in itself and as such. The revelation of God denies that any religion is true, i.e., that it is in truth the knowledge and worship of God and the reconciliation of man with God. For as the self-offering and self-manifestation of God, as the work of peace which God Himself has concluded between Himself and man, revelation is the truth beside which there is no other truth, over against which there is only lying and wrong. If by the concept of a "true religion" we mean truth which belongs to religion in itself and as such, it is just as unattainable as a "good man," if by goodness we mean something which man can achieve on his own initiative. No religion is true. It can only become true, i.e., according to that which it purports to be and for which it is upheld. And it can become true only in the way in which man is justified, from without; i.e., not of its own nature and being, but only in virtue of a reckoning and adopting and separating which are foreign to its own nature and being, which are quite inconceivable from its own standpoint, which come to it quite apart from any qualifications or merits. Like justified man, religion is a creature of grace. But grace is the revelation of God. No religion can stand before it as true religion. No man is righteous in its presence. It subjects us all to the judgment of death. But it can also call dead men to life and sinners to repentance. And similarly in the wider sphere where it shows all religion to be false it can also create true religion. The abolishing of religion by revelation need not mean only its negation: the judgment that religion is unbelief. Religion can just as well be exalted in revelation, even though the judgment still stands. It can be upheld by it and concealed in it. It can be justified by it, and — we must at once add — sanctified. Revelation can adopt religion and mark it off as true religion. And it not only can. How do we come to assert that it can, if it has not already done so? There is a true religion: just as there are justified sinners. If we abide strictly by that analogy — and we are dealing not merely with an analogy, but in a comprehensive sense with the thing itself — we need have no hesitation in saying that the Christian religion is the true religion. . . .

We can dare to state that the Christian religion is the true one only as we listen to the divine revelation. But a statement which we dare to make as we listen to the divine revelation can only be a statement of faith. And a statement of faith is necessarily a statement which is thought and expressed in faith and from faith, i.e., in recognition and respect of what we are told by revelation. Its explicit and implicit content is unreservedly conditioned by what we are told. But that is certainly not the case if we try to reach the statement that the Christian religion is the true religion by a

144

road which begins by leaving behind the judgment of revelation, that religion is unbelief, as a matter which does not apply to us Christians, but only to others, the non-Christians, thus enabling us to separate and differentiate ourselves from them with the help of this judgment. On the contrary, it is our business as Christians to apply this judgment first and most acutely to ourselves: and to others, the non-Christians, only in so far as we recognize ourselves in them, i.e., only as we see in them the truth of this judgment of revelation which concerns us, in the solidarity, therefore, in which, anticipating them in both repentance and hope, we accept this judgment to participate in the promise of revelation. At the end of the road we have to tread there is, of course, the promise to those who accept God's judgment, who let themselves be led beyond their unbelief. There is faith in this promise, and, in this faith, the presence and reality of the grace of God, which, of course, differentiates our religion, the Christian, from all others as the true religion. This exalted goal cannot be reached except by this humble road. . . .

To believe means, in the knowledge of our own sin to rely upon the righteousness of God which makes an infinite satisfaction for our sin. Concretely, it means, in the knowledge of our own contradiction against grace to cleave to the grace of God which infinitely contradicts this contradiction. In this knowledge of grace, in the knowledge that it is the justification of the ungodly, that it is grace for the enemies of grace, the Christian faith attains to its knowledge of the truth of the Christian religion. There can be no more question of any immanent rightness or holiness of this particular religion as the ground and content of the truth of it, than there can be of any other religion claiming to be the true religion in virtue of its inherent advantages. The Christian cannot avoid abandoning any such claim. He cannot avoid confessing that he is a sinner even in his best actions as a Christian. And that is not, of course, the ground, but the symptom of the truth of the Christian religion. The abandoning and confessing means that the Christian Church is the place where, confronted with the revelation, and grace of God, by grace men live by grace. If this were not so, how would they believe? And if they did not believe, how would they be capable of this abandoning and confessing? . . .

That there is a true religion is an event in the act of the grace of God in Jesus Christ. To be more precise, it is an event in the outpouring of the Holy Spirit. To be even more precise, it is an event in the existence of the Church and the children of God. The existence of the Church of God and the children of God means that true religion exists even in the world of human religion. In other words, there is a knowledge and worship of God and a corresponding human activity. We can only say of them that they are corrupt. They are an attempt both of lying and wrong and committed to futile means. And yet we have also to say of them that (in their corruption) they do reach their goal. In spite of the lying and wrong committed, in spite of the futility of the means applied, God is really known and worshipped, there is a genuine activity of man as reconciled to God. The Church and the children of God and therefore the bearers of true religion live by the grace of God. . . . That is what makes them what they are. That is what makes their religion true. That is what lifts it above the general level of religious history. . . . They are what they are, and their religion is the true religion, not because they recognize Him as such and act accordingly, not in virtue of their religion of grace, but in virtue of the fact that God has graciously intervened for them, in virtue of His mercy in spite of their apparent but equivocal religion of grace, in virtue of the good pleasure which He has in them, in virtue of His free election, of which this good pleasure is the only motive, in virtue of the Holy Spirit whom He willed to pour out upon them. . . . He, Jesus Christ, is the eternal Son of God and as such the eternal Object of the divine good pleasure. As the eternal Son of God He became man. The result is that in Him man has also become the object of the divine good pleasure, not by his own merit or deserving, but by the grace which assumed man to itself in the Son of God. In this One, the revelation of God among men and the reconciliation of man with God has been fulfilled once and for all. . . .

There is, of course, one fact which powerfully and decisively confirms the assertion, depriving it of its arbitrary character and giving to it a necessity which is absolute. But to discern this fact, our first task — and again and again we shall have to return to this "first" — must be to ignore the whole realm of "facts" which we and other human observers as such can discern and assess. For the fact about which we are speaking stands in the same relationship to this realm as does the sun to the earth. That the sun lights up this part of the earth and not that means for the earth no less than this, that day rules in the one part and night in the other. Yet the earth is the same in both places. In neither place is there anything in the earth itself to dispose it for the day. Apart from the sun it would everywhere be enwrapped in eternal night. The fact that it is partly in the day does not derive in any sense from the nature of the particular part as such. Now it is in exactly the same way that the light of the righteousness and judgment of God falls upon the world of man's religion, upon one part of that world,

146

upon the Christian religion, so that that religion is not in the night but in the day, it is not perverted but straight, it is not false religion but true. Taken by itself, it is still human religion and therefore unbelief, like all other religions. Neither in the root nor in the crown of this particular tree, neither at the source nor at the outflow of this particular stream, neither on the surface nor in the depth of this particular part of humanity can we point to anything that makes it suitable for the day of divine righteousness and judgment. If the Christian religion is the right and true religion, the reason for it does not reside in facts which might point to itself or its own adherents, but in the fact which as the righteousness and the judgment of God confronts it as it does all other religions, characterizing and differentiating it and not one of the others as the right and true religion. . . .

The one decisive question which confronts the Christian religion, or its adherents and representatives, in respect of its truth is this: who and what are they in their naked reality, as they stand before the all-piercing eye of God? Are they really His Church, His children, and therefore the adopted brethren of His eternal Son? If they are not, if their Christian religion is just a mask, then even if it is the most perfect and logical form of Christianity it is unbelief like all other heathen religions. It is falsehood and wrong and an abomination before God. But if they are, if they live by the grace of God, if they participate in the human nature of His eternal Son, if they are nourished by His body and His blood as earthly members of His earthly body in communion with Him as their heavenly Head: then for the sake of this fellowship their sins are forgiven, even the sin of their religion is rightly pardoned. Their Christian religion is the justified religion and therefore the right and true religion. Beyond all dialectic and to the exclusion of all discussion the divine fact of the name of Jesus Christ confirms what no other fact does or can confirm: the creation and election of this religion to be the one and only true religion. Of course, the one decisive question can never be spared the Christian religion and its adherents and representatives. It can never become irrelevant. It can never be regarded as settled. Whenever Christianity confronts other religions, or a Christian the adherent of another religion, this question stands over them like a sword. From that standpoint we can and must say that, in the world of religions, the Christian religion is in a position of greater danger and defenselessness and impotence than any other religion. It has its justification either in the name of Jesus Christ, or not at all. And this justification must be achieved in the actuality of life, of the Church and the children of God. But the achieving of this life is grace, the grace of the Word which begets faith, and the Church and children of the Word, according to its free and inconceivable compassion. The possibility of a negative answer to that question is the abyss on the fringe of which the truth of the Christian religion is decided. A positive decision means a positive answer to the question. It means that the Christian religion is snatched from the world of religions and the judgment and sentence pronounced upon it, like a brand from the burning. It is not that some men are vindicated as opposed to others, or one part of humanity as opposed to other parts of the same humanity. It is that God Himself is vindicated as opposed to and on behalf of all men and all humanity. That it can receive and accept this is the advantage and preeminence of Christianity, and the light and glory in which its religion stands. And as it does not have this light and glory of itself, no one can take it away from it. And it alone has the commission and the authority to be a missionary religion, i.e., to confront the world of religions as the one true religion, with absolute self-confidence to invite and challenge it to abandon its ways and to start on the Christian way.

Hendrik Kraemer

A well-known Dutch theologian, phenomenologist, and missiologist, Hendrik Kraemer (1888-1965) served as the first director of the Ecumenical Institute at Bossey, Switzerland. In his most influential work, *The Christian Message in a Non-Christian World*, commissioned for study and discussion at the historic 1938 World Missionary Conference of the International Missionary Council at Tambaram (Madras), India, Kraemer developed a position he called "biblical realism," a position heavily influenced but not uncritical of Karl Barth's theology. The following excerpt is taken from *Why Christianity of All Religions?* (Philadelphia: Westminster Press, 1962).

Is Christianity an "Absolute"?

No one sufficiently alert to read between the lines will have failed to observe that I have aimed not a few shafts of criticism at Christianity; and thus no one will be unduly surprised at my answering the question placed at the head of this chapter with a decided "No." . . .

My resounding "No" to the question whether or not Christianity is an "absolute" follows from what I have said again and again in the foregoing pages about "Christianity," considered as a concrete, historical phenomenon, standing on the same footing as the rest in its character as one of the major religions. When one looks at it from that point of view, it makes no sense to say that Christianity, as opposed to all the "other" religions, is the "true" one. If we take the word in the absolute sense invariably ascribed to it in ordinary usage, then *there is no true religion.* If one looks at the thing honestly, there are only religions which present, though no doubt in various ways, interwoven threads of truth and error which it is impossible to disentangle. One must bear this firmly in mind, *a propos* especially of the conspicuous tendency at the present time for many "progressive" Christians and even more for those "modern" people who are estranged from Christianity and the Church to jump to remarkable and singular conclusions and to say, as though the matter were settled beyond all possibility of dispute: Don't try to tell me there is only one religion that is true; all religions are true. People talk like this because they feel that some slur is cast on their intellectual standing and their "modernity" by the notion that the only proper "Christian" standpoint should be held to be that Christianity is the one true — uniquely true — religion. It just goes to show how necessary it is to take up the question whether Christianity is an "absolute." . . .

What do people actually mean by "absolute"? They mean: unsurpassable, unimpeachable, valid; something which affords a standard of reference and is fully authoritative. That is what they mean when they speak of "absolute truth" or of "the absolute" as the *terminus ad quem* of all thought, which yet transcends all thought.

There is therefore a point beyond which there is nothing further to be said. There is in man the obstinate and persistent need for "something absolute," even if it is simply that he must call everything in question. It would seem that he cannot get along without some impregnable "fixed point," a "something to go by." But then we discover what a bundle of inconsistency he is. If he particularly wants to be certain about something, he must then go and find irrefutable proof. Take for instance the proofs intended to demonstrate beyond all further rational argument the existence of God. They have been weighed and found wanting, though of course they can be of help to us mortals as we grope and feel our way along, and thus perform a very useful service. As *proofs,* however, they are worthless. By thus "proving" the absolute men land themselves in a fresh impasse, because all they have shown is that the absolute gets its absoluteness from some more ultimate point of reference by virtue of which it is "proved," so that the whole absoluteness of the absolute falls completely to the ground. And what might this superior point of reference be? It is, after all, the rational judgment of man; Reason, that is, with a capital R; and as that pertains to man in his relative condition it cannot be absolute, the more so since in the rational judgment of different men the voice of Reason not infrequently says different and contradictory things.

But this is a matter we cannot go further into here. If we did, I should find myself fairly and squarely having to take to pieces all the great systems of thought of both hemispheres! The little that I have said is simply meant to drive home the point that man is, so to speak, riding on a merry-go-round. He hungers after the absolute. He cannot do otherwise; and if he loses that hunger, then there is something very seriously wrong with him. In that hunger and in the desire to hold on to it and more especially to make sure once and for all that it will last he satisfies and disposes of it. Small wonder then that he seeks a remedy in making "absolutes" for himself. The Bible, in its blunt way, calls them "idols." The many "myths" and "ideologies," the whole host of "unassailable principles" which are at such a high premium and are so much talked about today are examples of such *manufactured* "absolutes," are "pseudo-absolutes," that is to say, or still better: idols. Yet behind all this there is an obstinate and restless religious impulse. Christianity as a religion which has unfolded in an historical setting is just like other religions in being a body of human ideas and institutions which is "passing away," as all things human do, and so cannot possibly be absolute.

The transient, non-absolute character of everything, including civilizations and religions, does not mean that nothing of eternal value can happen within them. But of course the only man who can rightly and reasonably say that is one for whom no principles or products of human achievement, however splendid, nor Reason nor Chance nor Progress, constitute the highest values — the man who believes in the Eternal God and in His Judgment. And it is precisely that which makes him realize the relative nature of all things human, not excluding religions.

Nevertheless, in the light of our criterion a distinction really does have to be drawn between Christianity, as one among the religions, and the "other" religions. Christianity as one of the religions is to be distinguished from the other religions, that is, for this cardinal reason: that although it enjoys its full share of human frailty, Christianity does arise out of the Revelation of God in the Person of Jesus Christ.

Christianity Not Absolute

Christianity as a religion can and must be continually taking its bearings from that Revelation and must allow itself to be drawn away from the paths of error and into the true way. More often than not it sets about the task in such a half-hearted fashion that it calls down upon its own head the criticism which it so thoroughly deserves and gets from people inside and outside the fold. There is however an extremely important and salient point to notice about the special position of Christianity, not primarily as a form of religion and culture, but *qua* Christian Church, in that the Church is under the rule and authority of her Lord, Jesus Christ; she has the promise of God's Holy Spirit as her Guide and Comforter; and she can always receive light from the Word which is God's gift to her in the Bible. How much like the children of Israel, how hardened and disobedient she can often be despite these privileges, is only too apparent from the many shameful blots which stain her past and disfigure her even today. Yet these favors are real and remain real by God's grace; and they function still.

Christianity is therefore not absolute. It is not even in all respects the "best" religion, if by that we mean the religion which has found, comparatively speaking, the "best" and noblest way of expressing religious truth and experience. During those parts of my life spent amidst other religions it has struck me many a time that certain religious attitudes and emotions are more finely expressed in those religions than in Christianity. That is plain for any fair-minded man to see; and one has a duty to say so and to give honor where honor is due. Here are a few instances of the case in point.

If one moves in the Muslim world and sees there, for example, with what tremendous conviction the Muslim gives expression to the idea of Allah's sovereign majesty and reality in the *"Allahu Akbar"* (God alone is great), one can look in vain for any parallel in Christianity, even in the most splendid liturgies (the core of which is to be found in Isaiah 6), which goes further and deeper than the absolute Omnipotence and Sublime Excellence of Allah. If one travels through India, one can meet with groups of pilgrims possessed by so deep and passionate a yearning after religious truth that one is reduced to silence by it and has to admit that one has never come across anything like it in "Christian" countries. As a Christian, one feels oneself in contact here with a craving for God awakened by the Holy Spirit. . . .

Yet nothing of this ought for one moment to shake our conviction that Christianity is the religion for us; because it is not a matter of clinging to Christianity but of clinging to Jesus Christ, to whom Christianity is attached by indissoluble ties. Certainly it should make us more humble and more respectful of others. What is absolute then is not Christianity but the Revelation of God in Jesus Christ. He has no need of our proofs. He simply reigns from the cross, even were no one to recognize the fact. . . .

152

The fact that Christianity and the Christian Church are abidingly concerned and involved on this very score of the Revelation of God in Jesus Christ explains why their history, compared with that of the other religions, has been the most stirring and dramatic, the most tremendous in its lapses and aberrations, the most movingly impressive in the depths and heights of the unselfish service of God and neighbor. For that Revelation of God in Jesus Christ has been effective and vital in every age. So often the Church has kicked against it as "against the pricks"; yet it has always been the source of her life.

Thus the Revelation of God in Jesus Christ is alone absolute, alone unmovable, sure and to be trusted. Precisely there is our touchstone for the truth. Jesus Christ and His Kingdom are the hidden center and goal of history. . . .

In saying all this I make no attempt at all to prove or demonstrate the truth of Jesus Christ. That one can only experience by acting upon it for oneself, by taking the Man of the New Testament at His word and laying oneself open before Him. What one does for oneself is to surrender. What one can and must do, of course, is to give testimony to Him; a very different matter from providing or demonstrating something. . . .

What attitude ought "Christians" to adopt nowadays in the new encounter with the other great religions, and not least in their personal contacts with representatives of those religions, which are certain to be always on the increase in the future? . . .

Are we to be stuck with vagueness and uncertainty and simply turn back after all to what is of immediate concern to us at the moment, just leaving the whole thing to look after itself? Are we to form an organized opposition, keep up a barrage of protest and issue manifestoes about basic "Christian" principles? . . .

The new task which thus faces us as Christians is to be both firm and forbearing and at the same time to combine this with loyalty to the truth, in love. If that is going to come about, it will not be without its ups and downs; and it will not even be possible except as the conviction dawns upon us that the power to accomplish it is not primarily a matter of knowledge, indispensable as that may often be, nor of an ability to draw sharp and clear distinctions between this and that; *rather is it a matter of living in a deeper, more real communion with Jesus Christ.* He alone is able to show us how to combine a firm determination with truth and love. . . .

Far better that way than to flounder in confusion, embarrassment or anxiety. As we deepen our cognizance of Christianity thus, we shall find ourselves, as a direct consequence, waking up to the vital need for a renewal of the Church; and that means throwing ourselves wholeheartedly into the Ecumenical Movement and the business of recovering the Church's unity.

I mean here a renewal of the Church which will not merely argue for, but actually demonstrate through what we practice and profess, the truth that the knowledge of our Lord Jesus Christ "excels all things," as Paul says so impressively and at some length in Philippians 3:4-9. To put the knowledge of Jesus Christ as the vital, renovating power above all else, as Paul does there — and to set it first and foremost over and above all our "churchly," theological and other standpoints — is the only true way, the only true answer, that can be offered to the other religions and to those who profess them. One way only will command respect and have power to persuade: and that is the Church's manner of *being*, the way she *is*, as she lives by the renewing power of Christ, for all to feel and see. I firmly believe that, without knowing it, this is what the world is waiting for.

Paul Tillich

One of the most important philosophical theologians of twentieth-century Protestantism, Tillich (1886-1965) argued that Christianity should be interpreted in the context of the history of religions. In the first selection, Tillich asserts that, although it cannot be that there is no salvation apart from Jesus as the Christ, he *is* the ultimate criterion of every healing and saving process. In the second selection from his last public lecture, Tillich speaks of the dynamic character of the history of religions as related to its *telos:* the "Religion of the Concrete Spirit." Sources: *Systematic Theology,* vol. 2 (Chicago: University of Chicago Press, 1957); *The Future of Religions,* ed. Jerald C. Brauer (New York: Harper & Row, 1966).

I: The New Being in Jesus as the Christ as the Power of Salvation

The universal significance of Jesus as the Christ, which is expressed in the symbols of subjection to existence and of victory over existence, can also be expressed in the term "salvation." He himself is called the Savior, the Mediator, or the Redeemer. . . .

With respect to both the original meaning of salvation (from *salvus,* "healed") and our present situation, it may be adequate to interpret salvation as "healing." It corresponds to the state of estrangement as the main

155

characteristic of existence. In this sense, healing means reuniting that which is estranged, giving a center to what is split, overcoming the split between God and man, man and his world, man and himself. Out of this interpretation of salvation, the concept of the New Being has grown. Salvation is reclaiming from the old and transferring into the New Being. This understanding includes the elements of salvation which were emphasized in other periods; it includes, above all, the fulfillment of the ultimate meaning of one's existence, but it sees this in a special perspective, that of making *salvus*, of "healing."

If Christianity derives salvation from the appearance of Jesus as the Christ, it does not separate salvation through the Christ from the processes of salvation, i.e., of healing, which occur throughout all history. . . . There is a history of concrete revelatory events in all periods in which man exists as man. It would be wrong to call that history itself the history of revelation (with some theological humanists). But it would be equally wrong to deny that revelatory events occur anywhere besides the appearance of Jesus as the Christ. There is a history of revelation, the center of which is the event of Jesus the Christ; but the center is not without a line which leads to it (preparatory revelation) and a line which leads from it (receiving revelation). Further, we have asserted that where there is revelation, there is salvation. Revelation is not information about divine things; it is the ecstatic manifestation of the Ground of Being in events, persons, and things. Such manifestations have shaking, transforming, and healing power. They are saving events in which the power of the New Being is present. It is present in a preparatory way, fragmentarily, and is open to demonic distortion. But it is present and heals where it is seriously accepted. On these healing forces the life of mankind always depends; they prevent the self-destructive structures of existence from plunging mankind into complete annihilation. This is true of individuals as well as of groups and is the basis for a positive evolution of the religions and cultures of mankind. . . .

This view of the history of salvation excludes an unbiblical but nevertheless ecclesiastical view of salvation. It is the belief that salvation is either total or non-existent. Total salvation, in this view, is identical with being taken into the state of ultimate blessedness and is the opposite of total condemnation to everlasting pain or eternal death. If, then, the salvation to eternal life is made dependent upon the encounter with Jesus as the Christ and the acceptance of his saving power, only a small number of human beings will ever reach salvation. The others, either through a divine decree or through the destiny which came upon them from Adam's Fall or through their own guilt, are condemned to exclusion from eternal life. Theologies of universalism always tried to escape this absurd and demonic idea, but it is difficult to do so, once the absolute alternative between salvation and condemnation is presupposed. Only if salvation is understood as healing and saving power through the New Being in all history is the problem put on another level. In some degree all men participate in the healing power of the New Being. Otherwise, they would have no being. The self-destructive consequences of estrangement would have destroyed them. But no men are totally healed, not even those who have encountered the healing power as it appears in Jesus as the Christ. Here the concept of salvation drives us to the eschatological symbolism and its interpretation. It drives us to the symbol of cosmic healing and to the question of the relation of the eternal to the temporal with respect to the future.

What, then, is the peculiar character of the healing through the New Being in Jesus as the Christ? If he is accepted as the Savior, what does salvation through him mean? The answer cannot be that there is no saving power apart from him but that he is the ultimate criterion of every healing and saving process. We said before that even those who have encountered him are only fragmentarily healed. But now we must say that in him the healing quality is complete and unlimited. The Christian remains in the state of relativity with respect to salvation; the New Being in the Christ transcends every relativity in its quality and power of healing. It is just this that makes him the Christ. Therefore, wherever there is saving power in mankind, it must be judged by the saving power in Jesus as the Christ.

II: The Significance of the History of Religions for the Systematic Theologian

A theologian who accepts the subject, "The Significance of the History of Religions for the Systematic Theologian," and takes this subject seriously, has already made, explicitly or implicitly, two basic decisions. On the one hand he has separated himself from a theology which rejects all religions other than that of which he is a theologian. On the other hand if one accepts this subject affirmatively and seriously, he has rejected the paradox of a religion of non-religion, or a theology without theos, also called a theology of the secular.

Both of these attitudes have a long history. The former has been renewed in our century by Karl Barth. The latter is now most sharply expressed in the so-called theology-without-God language. . . .

In order to reject both this old and new orthodox attitude, one must accept the following systematic presuppositions. First, one must say that revelatory experiences are universally human. Religions are based on something that is given to a man wherever he lives. He is given a revelation, a particular kind of experience which always implies saving powers. One never can separate revelation and salvation. There are revealing and saving powers in all religions. God has not left himself unwitnessed. This is the first presupposition.

The second assumption states that revelation is received by man in terms of his finite human situation. Man is biologically, psychologically, and sociologically limited. Revelation is received under the conditions of man's estranged character. It is received always in a distorted form, especially if religion is used as a means to an end and not as an end in itself.

There is a third presupposition that one must accept. When systematic theologians assume the significance of the history of religions, it involves the belief that there are not only particular revelatory experiences throughout human history, but that there is a revelatory process in which the limits of adaptation and the failures of distortion are subjected to criticism. Such criticism takes three forms: the mystical, the prophetic, and the secular.

A fourth assumption is that there may be — and I stress this, there *may* be — a central event in the history of religions which unites the positive results of those critical developments in the history of religion in and under which revelatory experiences are going on — an event which, therefore, makes possible a concrete theology that has universalistic significance.

There is also a fifth presupposition. The history of religions in its essential nature does not exist alongside the history of culture. The sacred does not lie beside the secular, but it is its depths. The sacred is the creative ground and at the same time a critical judgment of the secular. But the religious can be this only if it is at the same time a judgment on itself, a judgment which must use the secular as a tool of one's own religious self-criticism. . . .

The first question confronting a theology of the history of Israel and of the Christian Church is the history of salvation, but the history of salvation is something within the history. It is expressed in great symbolic moments, in *kairoi* such as the various efforts at reform in the history of the Church. In the same way, nobody would identify history of religions and history of salvation, or revelation, but one searches for symbolic moments. If the history of religions is taken seriously, are there *kairoi* in the general history of religions? Attempts have been made to find such *kairoi*. There was the enlightenment of the eighteenth century. Everything for these theologians was a preparation for the great *kairos*, the great moment, in which mature reason is reached in mankind. There are still religious elements in this reason: God, freedom, immortality. Kant developed it in his famous book, *Religion Within the Limits of Pure Reason.*

Another attempt was the romanticist understanding of history which led to Hegel's famous effort. From his point of view, there is a progressive history of religion. It progresses according to the basic philosophical categories which give the structure of all reality. Christianity is the highest and last point, and it is called "revealed religion," but this Christianity is philosophically demythologized. Such a view is a combination of Kantian philosophy and the message of the New Testament.

All earlier religions in Hegel's construction of the history of religions are *aufgehoben*, which can only be translated by two English words, namely, "taken in" and "removed." In this way, therefore, that which is past in the history of religion has lost its meaning. It is only an element in the later development. This means, for instance, that for Hegel the Indian religions are long, long past, long ago finished, and have no contemporary meaning. They belong to an early stage of history. Hegel's attempt to develop a theology of the history of religion resulted in the experiential theology which was very strong in America about thirty years ago. It was based on the idea of remaining open to new experiences of religious character in the future. Today men like Toynbee point in this direction — or perhaps look for that in religious experience which leads to a union of the great religions. In any case, it is a post-Christian era that is looking for such a construction.

It is necessary to mention also Teilhard de Chardin who stresses the development of a universal, divine-centered consciousness which is basically Christian. Christianity takes in all spiritual elements of the future. I am dissatisfied with such an attempt. I am also dissatisfied with my own, but I will give it in order to induce you to try yourself because that is what one should do if he takes the history of religions seriously.

My approach is dynamic-typological. There is no progressive development which goes on and on, but there are elements in the experience of the Holy which are always there, if the Holy is experienced. These elements, if they are predominant in one religion create a particular religious type. It is necessary to go into greater depth, but I will only mention a tentative scheme which would appear this way. The universal religious basis is the experience of the Holy within the finite. Universally in everything finite and particular, or in this and that finite, the Holy appears in a special way. I could call this the sacramental basis of all religions — the Holy here and now which can be seen, heard, dealt with, in spite of its mysterious character. We still have remnants of this in the highest religions, in their sacraments, and I believe that without it, a religious group would become an association of moral clubs, as much of Protestantism is, because it has lost the sacramental basis.

Then, there is a second element, namely a critical movement against the demonization of the sacramental, making it into an object which can be handled. This element is embodied in various critical ways. The first of these critical movements is mystical. This mystical movement means that one is not satisfied with any of the concrete expressions of the Ultimate, of the Holy. One goes beyond them. Man goes to the one beyond any manifoldness. The Holy as the Ultimate lies beyond any of its embodiments. The embodiments are justified. They are accepted but they are secondary. One must go beyond them in order to reach the highest, the Ultimate itself. The particular is denied for the Ultimate One. The concrete is devaluated.

Another element, or the third element in the religious experience, is the element of "ought to be." This is the ethical or prophetic element. Here the sacramental is criticized because of demonic consequences like the denial of justice in the name of holiness. This is the whole fight of the Jewish prophets against sacramental religion. In some of the words of Amos and Hosea this is carried so far that the whole cult is abrogated. This criticism of the sacramental basis is decisive for Judaism and is one element in Christianity. But again I would say, if this is without the sacramental and mystical element, then it becomes moralistic and finally secular.

I would like to describe the unity of these three elements in a religion which one could call — I hesitate to do so, but I don't know a better word — "The Religion of the Concrete Spirit." And it might well be that one can say the inner *telos*, which means the inner aim of a thing, such as the *telos* of the acorn is to become a tree — the inner aim of the history of religions is to become a Religion of the Concrete Spirit. But we cannot identify this Religion of the Concrete Spirit with any actual religion, not even Christianity as a religion. But I would dare to say, of course, dare as a Protestant theologian, that I believe that there is no higher expression for what I call the synthesis of these three elements than in Paul's doctrine of the Spirit. There we have the two fundamental elements: the ecstatic and the rational element united. There is ecstasy but the highest creation of the ecstasy is love in the sense of *agape*. There is ecstasy but the other creation of ecstasy

160

is *gnosis,* the knowledge of God. It is knowledge, and it is not disorder and chaos.

The positive and negative relation of these elements or motives now gives the history of religions its dynamic character. The inner *telos* of which I spoke, the Religion of the Concrete Spirit, is so to speak, that toward which everything drives. But we cannot say that this is a merely futuristic expectation. It appears everywhere in the struggle against the demonic resistance of the sacramental basis and the demonic and secularistic distortion of the critics of the sacramental basis. It appears in a fragmentary way in many moments in the history of religions. Therefore, we have to absorb the past history of religions, and annihilate it in this way, but we have a genuine living tradition consisting in the moments in which this great synthesis became, in a fragmentary way, reality. We can see the whole history of religions in this sense as a fight for the Religion of the Concrete Spirit, a fight of God against religion within religion. And this phrase, the fight of God within religion against religion, could become the key for understanding the otherwise extremely chaotic, or at least seemingly chaotic, history of religions.

Now as Christians we see in the appearance of Jesus as the Christ the decisive victory in this struggle. There is an old symbol for the Christ, Christus Victor, and this can be used again in this view of the history of religions. And so it is already connected in the New Testament with the victory over the demonic powers and the astrological forces. It points to the victory on the cross as a negation of any demonic claim. And I believe we see here immediately that this can give us a Christological approach which could liberate us from many of the dead ends into which the discussion of the Christological dogma has led the Christian churches from the very beginning. In this way, the continuation of critical moments in history, of moments of *kairoi* in which the Religion of the Concrete Spirit is actualized fragmentarily can happen here and there.

The criterion for us as Christians is the event of the cross. That which has happened there in a symbolic way, which gives the criterion, also happens fragmentarily in other places, in other moments, has happened and will happen even though they are not historically or empirically connected with the cross.

John Hick

Danforth Professor of the Philosophy of Religion and director of the Blaisdell Programs in World Religions and Cultures at the Claremont Graduate School, Hick (b. 1922) has been a provocative advocate, through numerous publications, for a pluralistic theological perspective. In the first selection, he argues for a "Copernican revolution" in a Christian theology of religions; in the second, he suggests the need to rethink the doctrine of the Incarnation. Sources: *Problems of Religious Pluralism* (New York: St. Martin's Press, 1985); *God Has Many Names* (Philadelphia: Westminster Press, 1982).

I. Religious Pluralism and Absolute Claims

In one sense the absoluteness of, say, Christianity means the salvific sufficiency of its gospel and its way for Christians — that is, for those whose religious life is determined by that gospel and way. In this sense the absoluteness of Christianity is compatible with the absoluteness of Islam, or again of Hinduism, or Buddhism or Judaism, salvifically sufficient as these different messages and ways are for those who have been spiritually formed by them. But, since "absolute" so strongly suggests uniqueness, and the impossibility of being surpassed or even equalled, it seems inappropriate to apply it to this pluralistic conception. And in fact this plural sense is the polar opposite of the religious absolutism that I want to discuss here. Let me approach it, however, through this opposite, namely religious pluralism.

By this I mean the view that the great world faiths embody different perceptions and conceptions of, and correspondingly different responses to, the Real or the Ultimate from within the major variant cultural ways of being human; and that within each of them the transformation of human existence from self-centeredness to Reality-centeredness is manifestly taking place — and taking place, so far as human observation can tell, to much the same extent. Thus the great religious traditions are to be regarded as alternative soteriological "spaces" within which, or "ways" along which, men and women can find salvation/liberation/fulfillment.

From this point of view, the proper understanding of one's own religious faith and commitment in comparison with others' can be well expressed by adapting a phrase of Rosemary Ruether's. She speaks of her own commitment as a Roman Catholic, rather than as some other kind of Christian, as a matter of "ecclesial ethnicity" rather than as involving a judgement that her church is superior to others. [See *Theologians in Transitions,* ed. James M. Wall, p. 163.] Extending the idea, we may say that one's being a Muslim, or a Christian, or a Hindu, or whatever, is normally a matter of "religious ethnicity." That is to say, Christianity, or Buddhism, or Islam, or whatever, is the religious community into which one was born, into whose norms and insights one has been inducted, and within which (usually at least) one can therefore most satisfactorily live and grow. There are of course spiritual immigrants; but they are very few in comparison with the vast populations through which each religious tradition is transmitted from generation to generation. And having been born into, say, the Christian religious world one does not have to be able to prove (even to one's own satisfaction) that it is superior to the other religious worlds in order for it to be right and proper for one to be wholeheartedly a Christian. Realistically viewed, one's religious commitment is usually a matter of "religious ethnicity" rather than of deliberate comparative judgement and choice.

But nevertheless each of the great traditions has long since developed a self-understanding which at some point jars, or even positively clashes, with this conception of religious pluralism.

Thus in the Hindu tradition one believes that one has access to the *sanatana Dharma,* the eternal truth, incarnated in human language in the Vedas. There is a general tolerance of other ways, often however combined with the assumption that sooner or later everyone in his or her own time

— and if not in the present life then in another — will come to the fullness of the Vedic understanding. . . . In the Hebrew tradition it is held that the Jews are God's "chosen people," partners in a special covenant, so that they may be God's means of revelation to all mankind. Thus, whilst to be a Jew has often involved special burdens and sufferings, sometimes of the most extreme and appalling kind, yet to be a Jew is also, from the Jewish point of view, to stand in an unique relationship to God. . . . In the Buddhist tradition it is held that the true appreciation of our human situation occurs most clearly and effectively in the teachings of Gautama Buddha; and that any doctrine which denies the ceaselessly changing and insubstantial character of human life, or the possibility of attaining to the 'further shore' of *nirvana,* is not conducive to liberation from the pervasive unsatisfactoriness of ordinary human existence. . . . In Islam there is the firm belief that Muhammad was 'the seal of the prophets' and that through the Qur'an God has revealed to mankind the true religion, taking up into itself and fulfilling all previous revelations. . . . And in the Christian tradition there is a powerful inbuilt basis for the sense of the unique superiority of the Christian faith in the doctrine that Jesus Christ, the founder and focus of the religion, was God himself — or more precisely, the Second Person of the divine Trinity — in human form. . . .

Psychologically, then, the sense of the unique superiority of one's own religious tradition may be simply a natural form of pride in and ingrained preference for one's own familiar group and its ways. And thus far it is to be accepted and taken into account as an inevitable feature of human life; though it must not be allowed to inhibit the spiritual travel which has been called the imaginative 'passing-over' into another religious world and then coming back with new insight to one's own.

But natural pride, despite its positive contribution to human life, becomes harmful when it is elevated to the level of absolute truth and built into the belief system of a religious community. This happens when its sense of its own validity and worth is expressed in doctrines implying an exclusive or a decisively superior access to the truth or the power to save. A natural human tribal preference thereby receives the stamp of divine approval or the aura of a privileged relationship to the Divine. The resulting sense of a special status has in turn, in some cases, either spontaneously motivated or been manipulated to motivate policies of persecution, coercion, repression, conquest and exploitation, or a sense that others cannot be left to follow their own faith or insight but must be converted to one's own gospel. It is at this point, at which the sense of the superiority of one's own tradition is enshrined in formal doctrines, as an essential article of faith, that the idea of religious pluralism is felt as a challenge and may be resisted as a threat. It is also at this point however that the acceptance of religious pluralism can lead to creative doctrinal development.

It is for the adherents of each of the great traditions to look critically at their own dogmas in the light of their new experience within a religiously plural world. . . . The clear trend of mainline Catholic and Protestant attitudes is away from the absolutism of the past. But it is easier for this to happen at the level of practice than at the level of theological theory. For there can be no doubt that traditional Christian belief, as expressed in the scriptures, the ecumenical creeds, and the major dogmatic pronouncements and confessions, has been understood as embodying an absolute claim for the Christian Gospel and the Christian way of salvation. According to this system of belief, the historical Jesus was God the Son, the Second Person of the divine Trinity, living a human life; and by his death on the cross he has atoned for human sin, so that by responding to him in genuine repentance and faith, and gratefully accepting the benefits of his sacrifice, we may be reconciled to God and so become part of Christ's Church and heirs of eternal life.

Probably the majority of Christian theologians today want to remain loyal to the heart, at least, of this traditional teaching, centering upon the unique significance of Christ as God incarnate and as the source of human salvation, whilst however at the same time renouncing the old Christian absolutism. And so it has become common to give the old doctrines a universal rather than a restrictive meaning. It is taught that the salvation won by Christ is available to all mankind; though whenever and wherever it occurs it has been made possible only by his atoning death. His sacrifice on the cross is thus the necessary condition of human salvation; but its benefits may nevertheless be enjoyed by people who know nothing of him, or even who consciously reject the Christian interpretation of his life and death. Again, the divine Logos which became personally incarnate within the Jewish stream of religious life as Jesus of Nazareth has also been at work within other streams of religious life, inspiring spiritual leaders and thus being actively present (though no doubt in varying degrees) in Hinduism, Buddhism, Islam, and so on. Consequently there may well be significant religious lessons which Christians can learn from the people of these other traditions.

But I want to suggest that these moves, whilst admirably ecumenical in intent, only amount to epicycles added to a fundamentally absolutist structure of theory in order to obscure its incompatibility with the observed facts. In analogy with the old Ptolemaic picture of the universe, with our earth at its center, traditional Christian theology sees the religious universe as centered in the person of Christ and his Gospel. In the history of astronomy, when new observations of the movements of the planets seemed to conflict with the Ptolemaic scheme smaller circles were added to the theory, centering on the original circles, to complicate the projected planetary paths and bring them nearer to what was observed; and these epicycles enabled the old picture to be retained for a while longer. Analogously, the Ptolemaic theology, with Christianity at the center, is now being complicated by epicycles of theory to make it more compatible with our observations of the other great world faiths.

Purely theoretically, these moves can succeed. Further epicycles can be added indefinitely, as required, and the abandonment of the old scheme thereby indefinitely postponed. The problem is one not of logical possibility but of psychological plausibility. Natural human candidness sooner or later finds it unprofitable, and even perhaps undignified, to go on investing intellectual energy in defence of a dogma which seems to clash with the facts. And so when a simpler and more realistic model emerges there is liable to be a paradigm-shift such as took place in the Copernican revolution from the earth-centered to the helio-centric conception of the universe. In the theology of religions a comparably simpler and more realistic model is today available in the theocentric or, better, Reality-centered, conception with its pluralistic implications. Here the religious universe centers upon the divine Reality; and Christianity is seen as one of a number of worlds of faith which circle around and reflect that Reality.

A wholehearted shift to religious pluralism would mean abandoning not only the older and cruder Ptolemaic theology but also the more sophisticated versions with their new epicycles. For to hold that divine grace reaches the other worlds of faith via our own (i.e. via the person and cross of Christ) would be like holding that the light of the sun can only fall upon the other planets by being first reflected from the earth. To take a different analogy, it is as though there were a life-saving medicine the true chemical name of which is Christ. This medicine is available in its pure form only under the brand name of Christianity. But there are other products which, unknown to their purveyors, also contain Christ, though diluted with other elements and marketed under other names. In these circumstances a knowledgeable pharmacist would always recommend Christianity if it is available. However, there may be places where it is not available; and there, for the time being at least, another product will serve as an adequate second-best. This, I would suggest, is essentially the theology of religions created by the currently favoured theological epicycles.

But, once these epicycles are seen for what they are, it is I think clear that a Christian acceptance of religious pluralism must involve the kind of rethinking of the doctrine of the Incarnation that has in fact been taking place during the last fifty years or so. . . .

II. By Whatever Path . . .

Let me first ask the question that is so important to us as Christians, namely, what does all this imply concerning the person of our Lord? What about the uniqueness of Christ, the belief that Jesus was God incarnate, the second Person of the holy Trinity become man, the eternal Logos made flesh? Did he not say, "I and the Father are one," and "No one comes to the Father, but by me"? Here, unfortunately, we have to enter the realm of New Testament criticism: and I say "unfortunately" because of the notorious uncertainties of this realm. There are powerful schools of thought, following fashions which tend to change from generation to generation, but no consensus either across the years or across the schools. But this at least can be said: that whereas until some three or four generations ago it was generally accepted among biblical scholars that Jesus claimed to be God the Son, with a unique consciousness of divinity, so that the doctrine of the incarnation was believed to be firmly based in the consciousness and teaching of Jesus himself, today this is no longer generally held and is indeed very widely thought not to be the case. I am not going to enter into a detailed discussion of the New Testament evidence: I am neither competent to do this, nor is there space. I will only quote some summarizing words of Wolfhart Pannenberg in his massive work *Jesus — God and Man* (Westminster Press, 1968), where he says: "After D. F. Strauss and F. C. Baur, John's Gospel could no longer be claimed uncritically as a historical source of authentic words of Jesus. Consequently, other concepts and titles that were more indirectly connected with Jesus' relation to God came into the foreground of the question of Jesus' 'Messianic self-consciousness.' However, the transfer of these titles to Jesus . . . has been demonstrated with growing certainty by critical study of the Gospels to be the work of the post-Easter community. Today it must be taken as all but certain that the pre-Easter Jesus neither designated himself as Messiah (or Son of God) nor accepted such a confession to him from others" (p. 237). Not all New Testament scholars would endorse Pannenberg's words. But certainly one can no longer regard it as a fact proved out of the New Testament that Jesus thought of himself as God incarnate. On the contrary, this now seems to be very unlikely. And certainly we cannot rest anything on the assumption that the great Christological sayings of the Fourth Gospel (such as "I and my Father are one") were ever spoken, in sober historical fact, by the Jesus who walked the hills and villages of Galilee. It seems altogether more probable that they reflect the developing theology of the church toward the end of the first century.

Now if Jesus himself did not think of himself as God incarnate, one might well ask whether his disciples ought to do so. But instead of pursuing that question directly, it seems more profitable to accept that the Son-of-God and God-incarnate language has become deeply entrenched in the discourse of Christian thought and piety, and to ask what *kind* of language it is. Is the statement that Jesus was God incarnate, or the Son of God, or God the Son, a statement of literal fact; and if so, what precisely is the fact? Or is it a poetic, or symbolic, or mythological statement? It can, I think, only be the latter. It can hardly be a literal, factual statement since after nearly two thousand years of Christian reflection no factual content has been discerned in it — unless, that is, we give it factual content in terms of the idea of Jesus' virgin birth. We could then say that his being the Son of God means that the Holy Spirit fulfilled the role of the male parent in his conception. But he would then be a divine-human figure such as is familiar from Greek mythology; as, for example, Hercules, whose father was the god Jupiter and whose mother was a human woman. However, this has never seriously been regarded as the real meaning of the doctrine of the incarnation. What then is its real meaning? Whenever in the history of Christian thought theologians have tried to spell out its meaning in literal, factual terms the result has been heretical. A classic example would be Apollinaris's theory that Jesus' body and soul were human but that his spirit was the eternal divine Logos. This was rejected as heresy because it implied that Jesus was not genuinely human. And all attempts to treat the incarnation as a factual hypothesis have likewise been rejected by the church because they have failed to do justice either to Jesus' full humanity or to his full deity. Indeed one may say that the fundamental heresy is precisely to treat the incarnation as a factual hypothesis! For the reason that it has never been possible to state a literal meaning for the idea of the incarnation is simply that it has no literal meaning. It is a mythological idea, a figure of speech, a piece of poetic imagery. It is a way of saying that Jesus is our living contact with the transcendent God. In his presence we find that we are brought into the presence of God. We believe that he is so truly God's servant that in living as his disciples we are living according to the divine purpose. And as our sufficient and saving point of contact with God there is for us something absolute about him which justifies the absolute language which Christianity has developed. Thus reality is being expressed mythologically when we say that Jesus is the Son of God, God incarnate, the Logos made flesh.

When we see the incarnation as a mythological idea applied to Jesus to express the experienced fact that he is our sufficient, effective, and saving point of contact with God, we no longer have to draw the negative conclusion that he is man's one and only effective point of contact with God. We can revere Christ as the one through whom we have found salvation, without having to deny other points of reported saving contact between God and man. We can say that there is salvation in Christ without having to say that there is no salvation other than in Christ.

John B. Cobb Jr.

A leading American "process" theologian born to Methodist missionary parents in Japan, Cobb (b. 1925) has consistently argued for a pluralist perspective that yet remains christocentric. In the first selection, Cobb attempts to delineate a Christian path through dialogue and beyond, distinguishing his approach from that of John Hick, Paul Knitter, and W. C. Smith. In the second, he proposes "the Way of creative transformation as The Way which is Christ." Sources: *Beyond Dialogue: Toward a Mutual Transformation of Christianity and Buddhism* (Philadelphia: Fortress Press, 1982); "Is Christianity a Religion?" in *What Is Religion? An Inquiry for Christian Theology,* ed. Mircea Eliade and David Tracy (Nijmegen, Holland: Stichting Concilium; Edinburgh: T. & T. Clark Ltd.; New York: Seabury Press, 1980).

I. The Road through Dialogue and Beyond

Insistence on a purely transcendent God as the common ground of religion [by scholars such as John Hick, Paul Knitter, and W. C. Smith] has negative consequences . . . for Christian self-understanding. Believing that God is common to the religious traditions and that Christ is particular to Christianity, all three theologians hold that Christians will participate in dialogue more openly if we shift from Christocentrism to theocentrism. Since what is thought to be common to the religious Ways is what is more radically transcendent, along with Christology all concern for divine immanence is downplayed. God is spoken of as the Transcendent or the Absolute. Hick is particularly critical of the doctrines of Trinity and incarnation through which Christians historically have checked the tendency to a one-sided transcendence.

In their moves away from Christocentrism both Knitter and Hick identify it with the idea that Jesus is absolute. There are certainly problems with that view. It seems to deny the full humanity of Jesus or at least his fully personal humanity, and from my perspective such a doctrine deserves rejection quite apart from interest in dialogue with others. But Knitter himself well describes another Christology which he then neglects. "The totality of Jesus is the Christ, the cosmo-theandric principle, the universal revealing and saving presence of God; but the totality of the Christ is not Jesus and cannot be contained in and limited to him" ["Christianity as Religion: True and Absolute? A Roman Catholic Perspective," in *What Is Religion?: An Inquiry for Christian Theology*]. This doctrine has strong grounds in the Christian tradition, and it is this Christ that is central to the faith of many Christians. It is the Christ to whom John Paul II's encyclical *Redemptor Humanis* bears witness.

Our critics could reply that this Christ is God, so that this kind of Christocentrism is really theocentrism after all. This is true. For Christian orthodoxy, Christ is God! But there is a profound religious difference between centering our concern on the revealing and saving presence of God in ourselves and in our world and centering our attention on the noumenal Absolute and its conditioned appearances. In the former case we focus attention on what is happening in the world. In the latter, religion calls us away from this world toward another sphere which alone "has absolute reality and value" [John Hick, "Toward a Philosophy of Religious Pluralism," *Neue Zeitschrift für systematische Theologie* 22, no. 2 (1980):147]. To sacrifice belief in the incarnation for the sake of dialogue would not only impoverish us but would also take from us our most precious potential gift to the dialogue partner. . . .

Although dialogue has its place in all human relationships, the most important dialogues will be those with communities which are most impressive in their attainment of understanding, insight, distinctive experience, community life, or character. It is these from which Christians have most to learn, whether they are religious or not and regardless of how different they are from Christianity. It is these also toward which traditional forms of witness are least likely to be effective. And, indeed, conversion of members of these communities, if it involves their abandonment of those virtues which are distinctive to them, is a doubtful gain. If the conversion of all Jews to Christianity meant the obliteration of Judaism, the world would be a poorer place.

Dialogue with representatives of such groups would be first and foremost for our own sake as Christians. We would hope to enrich our lives and purify our faith by learning from them. We would of course also offer what we believed to be true and valuable in our own tradition. It would be important to us to display its importance in such a way as to challenge our dialogue partners to grow.

But this dialogue, if it succeeds, passes quickly beyond dialogue. It realizes what is sometimes spoken of as the "risk" of dialogue. That risk is that in the process of listening one will be forced to change in a more than superficial way. Christian dialogue theory is ambiguous with respect to its desire to impose that risk on the partner. It denies the intention to convert, and yet witnesses to Christian truth with the intention that it be heard in all its transformative power. Official dialogue theory has thus far had almost nothing to say about the desirability of fundamental change on the part of the Christian participants, although as we have seen, participants in dialogue are moving vigorously to change this situation.

Beyond dialogue, I suggest, lies the aim of mutual transformation. One may, if one wishes, speak of this as simply another stage of dialogue. However, once a Christian has learned something of first importance from the partner, much of the work of internalizing and integrating this new understanding may better be done in solitude or with other Christians rather than in further conversation. Only when some significant progress has been made in this work will it be important to meet again to take up the dialogue at that new place to which the participants have come.

There is an acute question as to whether one can play a representative role and also allow oneself to be significantly transformed through dialogue. The transformation that happens to the individuals involved may raise keen suspicions among those whom they initially represented. But changes among leaders, if they are truly leaders, can and do at times affect the communities which they lead. Changes in Catholic and Jewish leaders resulting from dialogue can alter Catholic-Jewish relations at many levels over a period of time. If Christian dialogue with Jews alters the formulations of Christology by those Christians who participate, and if this is truly a representative and influential group of Christians, the implicit anti-Judaism of much of our Christological work may be overcome, and in time preaching and Christian education may be affected. This is a legitimate goal for dialogue and for what lies beyond dialogue.

The emphasis thus far is upon the transformation of Christians and, through Christian individuals, of Christianity. To follow the previous example, it is not clear that Christians can offer much to Jews except apologies until Christianity has been freed of its anti-Judaism. Sensitization to the manifold dimensions and depths of anti-Judaism can be gained by Christians through dialogue with Jews, but the transformation of Christian teaching and practice must be the work of Christians beyond dialogue. The Christianity that would emerge from such a transformation could approach Jews in a quite new way. Its witness to Jesus as the Christ might even be convincing! Perhaps Jews could some day be encouraged to reintegrate into their own history the story of Jesus, and perhaps that would prove an event of transforming significance in the inner history of Judaism. But Christians are not in a position to speak thus to Jews until our own transformation has advanced a long way. The Christian purpose in the dialogue with Jews must be to change Christianity. . . .

This emphasis on the transformation of Christianity is the first way in which the purpose of authentic dialogue leads beyond dialogue. But the Christian purpose cannot be only the enrichment and purification of Christianity (and even this must be for the sake of the other as well). Dialogue has a missional goal. That Christians hope to make a difference in others through dialogue should not be concealed.

The difference between dialogue and more conventional forms of witness, it is now clear, is that dialogue is associated with making a contribution to religious communities as communities rather than with the conversion of individual members of the community to Christianity. At least on the Catholic side this has now entered to some extent into official policy. The debate has moved on to the next stage. It is between those who see the history of salvation as bringing all the religions finally to Christianity and those who see them as enduring to the end with their separate and valid contributions.

This issue is too sharply posed, chiefly because the transformations of Christianity through dialogue have been too little considered. A Christianity that has genuinely encompassed the history of the Jews in its effective memory and a Judaism which has integrated Jesus into its history will not become one, but the present sharp lines of distinction between them will blur. From such a Judaism Christianity will have much to learn, and from a Christianity which has in this way been re-Judaized, Jews too will have something to learn. The resultant new stage of the dialogue will again reduce the remaining oppositions. This convergence can be interpreted neither as the movement of Judaism into Christianity nor as simply helping Jews to be better Jews as that is usually understood. We who believe in Christ cannot but believe that becoming better Jews will involve Jews with a new appropriation of Jesus, and by whatever name, a deeper faith in what we know as Christ. But none of this can have present meaning, for we in our conscious and unconscious participation in the long history of Christian anti-Judaism have hardly begun the process of our own purgation and transformation. For that we need the help of Jews. . . .

But in this book I wish to treat a more difficult example, that of Mahayana Buddhism. I believe the pattern here should be similar. At present we are not in a position to offer much to thoughtful Buddhists. The reason is different. Anti-Buddhism is not built into our traditions, and our crimes against Buddhists are not comparable to those against Jews. But Buddhists have a depth of insight into the nature of reality which we lack. As long as a Buddhist's becoming a Christian entails abandoning that insight, conversion is not a serious possibility, and it is certainly not a desirable goal of the Christian mission. Until we can share that insight and transform our understanding of our own faith through it, we will have little to say that can or should command Buddhist attention. Hence our present need is to learn through dialogue, and then beyond to rethink our beliefs. But our purpose in all this cannot be only our own edification and improvement. It must be also to help Buddhists.

We may quite properly say that our concern for the Buddhists is that they become better Buddhists. But as in the preceding case, that can easily be misunderstood. We believe that Buddhists lack something of supreme importance when they do not incorporate Jesus Christ into their Buddhism. We believe they will be better Buddhists when they have done so.

To think of the transformation of Christianity by Buddhism must involve, as in the case of Judaism, the incorporation into our effective memories of Buddhist history. That process has begun. Gautama, at least, is a figure of human history revered also by many Christians. But that is just a beginning. The story of the Buddhist saints and the expansion of Buddhism throughout East Asia is not yet a part of the effective memory of Christians. If Buddhism and Christianity are to grow together, both must cultivate a global memory. Since both understand themselves as universal religious traditions, this must be at the same time the road to their own inner fulfillment. . . .

II. Pluralism and the Christian Claim

Now we can assert that Christianity is that Way which affirms that Jesus Christ is The Way. Of course Christianity as it concretely exists is only one Way among many ways, and this fact is a profound inner problem for Christian faith and theology. We have already noted some of the efforts to deal with this problem. We can summarize and briefly evaluate five unsatisfactory options.

(a) Rejection: Some affirm that, in spite of the obvious fact that many people find great meaning in other ways, they are all fundamentally wrong. The harshness of this judgement comports poorly with Christian love and humility.

(b) Identity: Some claim that behind the apparent diversity of ways what is important is truly the same. But no satisfactory formulation of the identity has been offered.

(c) Paths up the same mountain: Since the evidence is too strong against the identity of all ways, others argue that there are diverse ways to the same destination. The problem is that this seems false. The goals of unity with Brahman and of bringing justice to human society are not the same.

(d) Relativism: We can take the given pluralism of ways as indication that in fact there is no standard by which to evaluate their relative merits. They are all different and all to be respected equally. This sanctions even the most naive and vicious proposals. It leads quickly to indifference to all ways.

(e) Syncretism: We can piece together from all the ways that we like best and establish a new way. However, in the process we are likely to lose much of what is most valuable in all. Our new religion will have no more depth than we are now prepared to give it, and that is not much.

As an alternative to these I propose the Way of creative transformation as The Way which is Christ. The emphasis here is that to follow this Way is not to commit ourselves to a fixed body of beliefs, attitudes, and actions. Christian faith is confidence in The Way even though we cannot discern where it is leading. It is readiness to expose the security of established patterns to new challenges. Strange beliefs, attitudes, and practices which have some appearance of truth and goodness are among the most important of these challenges. When we confront them we can try to retreat along the Way we have come to some point that is safer, but that is not faith. We can argue against them and try to show that their apparent truth and goodness is entirely false in so far as they differ from what we have already learned. But that does not express faith either. Alternatively, we can open ourselves to learn from them. If we are impressed by what we hear and depressed by the problems we have encountered in our own Way, we may convert to the other way, but that, too, shows a lack of faith. If in learning from others we simply add new information to old, leaving the old unchanged, that is still not faith, for The Way is always a binding together of the old and the new. But if we are genuinely open to the new, allowing it to transform the old, not destroying but fulfilling it, that is faith. This is the Way of creative transformation.

If we understand The Way which is Christ in this fashion, then we need not be disturbed that factually Christianity is one Way among others. That recognition no longer leads to relativism. If the ways simply lie alongside one another so that one must choose between them, and if there are no criteria by which to choose, then relativism results. But if the way which is Christ is The Way of being creatively transformed by all those other ways which have something of worth to teach us, then the way that is Christ can indeed be for us The Way. It is not for us to claim that Christianity is The Way which already possesses all truth and goodness. It is enough to affirm that Christ is The Way which is open to all truth and goodness. Our claim is not that we have arrived. It is that we are on The Way.

But our pluralistic conscience requires that we ask whether other ways cannot equally claim to be The Way. That question is not to be answered *a priori* either by a generous "of course" or by insistence on Christian uniqueness. Every claimant requires honest and open examination. We cannot avoid our Christian biases in the process of such examination, and we should acknowledge them and discount our own judgments accordingly. But we should not blind ourselves thereby to what is great and distinctive in The Way that is Christ.

The Christian claim depends upon an eschatological orientation of the Christian way which distinguishes it from many other ways. Christian faith involves openness to the new, whereas religious ways that believe that the perfect is the primordial do not have the same reason to be open to other traditions for what is different in them. It seems that the eschatological can include the primordial in a sense in which the primordial cannot include the eschatological. On the other side, the non-traditional and less religious ways are almost always limited to something less than totality. They are defined by commitments which inevitably exclude as well as include.

Even if there are reasons to think that many other ways do not have the some potentiality to be The Way as does the Christian way, we are called to remain open. The Christian witness is not that no other way has the possibility of being The Way. It is enough to know that Christ is The Way.

Choan-Seng Song

Professor of theology and Asian cultures at the Pacific School of Religion, Berkeley, and regional professor of theology at the South East Asia Graduate School, C.-S. Song formerly served as associate director of the Department of Faith and Order of the World Council of Churches and president of Tainan Theological College and Seminary, Taiwan. In the following selection, he defines love as "the art of the impossible" and calls for "dialogical conversion" through believing in others. Source: *Tell Us Our Names: Story Theology from an Asian Perspective* (Maryknoll: Orbis Books, 1984).

More Love Affair Than Truth Affair

Do you remember how Tertullian (ca. 160-225), the father of Latin theology, answered his own rhetorical question: What has Jerusalem to do with Athens? "Nothing!" was his reply. . . . Christian piety and secular impiety must part company. There is no bridging the two. The affair between Christianity and other religions, between Christian culture and pagan culture, between Christians and non-Christians, is a "truth affair."

Christian mission has been very much a truth affair of Christians with the world. . . . Truth is a universal claim. Being a universal claim, it cannot tolerate other truth claims. It has no accommodation to make, much less compromise. All in all, a truth affair is a judgmental affair. It judges, and is not to be judged. It conquers, and is not to be conquered. Union of contradictions, opposites, and polarities is not its particular interest. . . .

If truth is the art of the possible, then love is the art of the impossible. . . . Truth, despite its lofty claims, is limited in its power to unite the "ununitable"; love, despite its humble and soft appearance, is unlimited in its power to unite the "ununitable." Perhaps this is one of the most important lessons divided churches still have to learn in their ecumenical efforts. It is also one of the deepest facts that this conflict-ridden world of ours needs to take to heart if it wants to avoid a nuclear catastrophe of an apocalyptic magnitude. . . .

What, then, is Christian mission? How are we to understand it? Christian mission . . . should be, first and foremost, a love affair. If it is a love affair, it mainly has to do with persons, not principles. Principle is what a truth affair likes to talk about. In the case of Christian mission, there is a principle that God's revelation is fully and totally given in the Christian faith. . . . If the full revelation of God is lodged in Christianity, then it will not be found in other religions. . . . If God's full revelation is not to be found elsewhere, then there is nothing divinely good in what those outside the Christian church believe and do. This third principle leads to a rather controversial conclusion: those who have not had the gospel preached to them are unreached by God. . . .

If Christian mission proceeds on such principles, it assumes that there are hundreds of millions of persons unreached by God. But fortunately for those "unreached" millions, God seems to have no special liking for the kind of principles just mentioned. God knows that when it comes to persons, not abstract concepts, what matters most is love. God is love, and love does not make persons into principles. . . . Above all, it does not divide persons into the "reached" and the "unreached." The whole creation is the arena of God's love. . . . History is the time and space of God's engagement in the work of redemption. To assert that some histories — in fact most histories — are unreached by God is to put limits to the redeeming power of God's love that gives hope to those in despair. . . . Christian mission in essence should be a love affair of the church with other human beings with whom God has already fallen in love. It is Christians seeking union with them in God. It is Christian believers building with them a community in the power of God's love. If this is what Christian mission is, then Christian mission is God's mission; it is also a person-centered mission. . . .

178

Dialogical Conversion

We must admit that Christians have much stronger critical views of other religions than do Hindus and Buddhists, if not Muslims and Jews. We think that these other religions represent human revolt against God. At best we concede them to be aberrations of the true way of God. When it comes to salvation, we Christians have a very definite view: as long as persons of other faiths do not believe in Jesus Christ, the door of God's salvation is closed to them.

But in our humbler moments we may realize that things are not necessarily dictated by the way our strong views want to have us believe. Jesus tells us that "not everyone who calls me 'Lord, Lord' will enter the kingdom of heaven, but only those who do the will of my heavenly Father" (Matt. 7:21). When we enter the room filled with believers of other religions, we shall not meet many who call Jesus "Lord," but we may meet quite a few who do the will of his "heavenly Father." The history of each nation in Asia, for instance, relates many examples of persons, great and small, who have dedicated themselves to the cause of peace, justice, and love. Are they saved or not? This is an impudent question. It is almost a blasphemous question. . . .

We have been ignorant about them [persons of other religious traditions] and have misunderstood them. But let us not be upset by this. To become aware of one's ignorance is to be initiated into interfaith dialogue. Can we not call it "blessed ignorance"? Without such an initiation rite, painful though it may be, dialogue cannot take place. In that initiation rite we must confess that we have not really understood persons of other faiths. Such confession leads to an enlightenment. It enables us to see others and ourselves in a new light. It compels us to look at others and ourselves from different perspectives. And out of the heart of all this may arise a conviction: that we and they, together, are to be guided into a deeper truth, to be led to a truer light, and to be embraced by the all-loving God. . . .

What can make interfaith dialogue possible, honest, and constructive is nothing else but this faith-bargain: I believe in you and you believe in me. This sounds so simple, yet is difficult. It is not often that we hear Christians say to Buddhists, "we believe in you." It is not common for Muslims to say to Hindus, "we believe in you." But without this faith-bargain, interfaith dialogue is bound to fail.

Words that come from the heart bear the mark of truth. This is another point to emphasize. Believers are quick — all too quick, it seems to me — to raise the question of truth. No compromise on the truth! The warning is serious and carries an echo of threat. Yes, truth must threaten the accused murderer in court; it will prove the crime of murder. Truth here is the result of a thorough investigation. Truth must also be the standard of measurement applied to the physical world. Here truth is scientific objectivity. No one can reject that one and one is two, unless a mathematical principle is proven false. In cases such as these, truth has to do more with knowing than with believing. . . .

Truth in religion is something indispensable. After all, some believers will even die for the truth of their faith. This kind of truth has to do more with believing than with knowing. I *believe* in God, although I cannot produce a scientific, objective proof of God's existence. I believe Jesus died for me on the cross, although his death took place two thousand years ago and there is an enormous space-time gap between him and me. Truth of religion, in short, is the truth of the heart. It is at the heart level that Christians should be able to say they believe in Buddhists. Interfaith dialogue is the place where we may learn to say such a thing. It is not the place where we outdo each other with intricate formulations of our doctrines and conduct vehement defense of our traditions. . . .

But our world community is divided into many hostile communities. The rich do not live in the dream of the poor. Ideological rightists do not share the vision of ideological leftists. Oppressors and oppressed exclude each other from their respective political goals. Humankind has constructed a dangerous world community. Our world community is one in which communities divided on account of race, sex, or creed are poised for fatal showdowns.

Religions have contributed their share to this divided world community. They have torn hearts apart with their truth claims and their religious absolutism. Believers who have the spiritual power and resources to forestall an apocalyptic day of destruction seem to have hastened it. This world community needs to be saved and renewed. But how?

I have no illusion that a fragile thing such as interfaith dialogue can work the miracle of saving and renewing our world community. But it could at least do something to keep the foundations of world community from eroding away yet further. Nothing less than dialogical conversion is needed for such a gigantic task. . . .

On the strength of this bargain (to believe in each other), a new spiritual force may be generated from religious communities, enabling human communities to strive for an undivided world community. Buddhism, for example, has a cosmological vision of nirvana that is "based on egolessness and is not anthropocentric but rather cosmological. . . . Salvation . . . [is] emancipation from the cycle of birth and death which is part of the transience of the universe."

Can Christians, Muslims, or Hindus share this vision? As we know, scientists and theologians of diverse religious persuasions today are forced to reevaluate the concepts and interrelationships of God, humanity, and nature. A renewed appreciation of the wholeness of creation on the part of Christian theologians ought to prompt them to explore cosmological aspects of Buddhist life and faith.

Examples such as this can be multiplied. The point is that persons of different religions have the capacity to live in each other's dreams and visions — Buddhists in Christians', Hindus in Muslims', or Christians in Confucianists'. I call this "dialogical conversion." As such conversion takes place, truth — the utmost concern of some believers — will perhaps authenticate itself in ways beyond our theological imagination. Our experience of God may be greater, richer, deeper, and higher than we have understood God to be in our own separate religious compartments. But most of all, we may discover that God is far more directly, far more deeply, and far more painfully involved in the agonies and hopes of humanity. We may finally come to learn that God has little liking for dogmatism and exclusivism.

Who says dialogue with persons of other faiths must not have a hidden purpose of conversion? All those who take part in interfaith dialogue — Hindus, Christians, Buddhists, Jews, Muslims — say so. This is a ground rule of the exercise. When dialogue is used as a secret weapon to convert others to a different religion, the very spirit of dialogue is violated. There will be no listening to, sharing of, and penetrating into the most profound thing in life — the experience of the divine in the midst of the human.

But there is another kind of conversion: turning away *(metanoia)* from using dialogue as a means to convert others and turning toward stepping into the life of one's dialogue partners. There is such a thing as "dialogical conversion." Short of such conversion, interfaith dialogue remains an academic exercise that does not enrich, expand, and deepen the vision of a spiritual community. Believers of living faiths must be dedicated to such a vision.

Marjorie Hewitt Suchocki

Ingraham Professor of Theology at the School of Theology at Claremont, Suchocki (b. 1933) formerly served as academic dean of Wesley Theological Seminary. In the following selection, she offers a feminist perspective on religious pluralism, arguing that *justice* should be the fundamental criterion of value in the dialogue among religions. Source: *The Myth of Christian Uniqueness: Toward a Pluralistic Theology of Religions*, ed. John Hick and Paul F. Knitter (Maryknoll: Orbis Books, 1987).

In Search of Justice: Religious Pluralism from a Feminist Perspective

Liberation theology has pointed to the invidious effects that follow when one mode of humanity is made normative for others. Such normativeness, combined with power, allows and invites exploitation of all those falling outside the norm. Furthermore, it distorts the perspective of those counted as falling within the norm, leading to problems in adequately knowing either self or others. As liberation theologians — whether feminist, black, or Third World — have dealt with this theme, they have focused on universalized norms in the realm of social, political, and personal structures of existence. The thesis of this essay is that the principle holds for religion as well: universalizing one religion such that it is taken as the norm whereby all other religions are judged and valued leads to oppression, and hence falls short of the norm that liberationists consider ultimate — the normative justice that creates well-being in the world community.

A feminist perspective, therefore, suggests that one must radically affirm religious pluralism, but not without bringing a critical consciousness of well-being in human community to interreligious and intrareligious discussion. Justice is thus to be the fundamental criterion of value and the focus of dialogue and action among religions.

To develop and hold such a position raises interesting problems. First, is it not the case that establishing justice as a norm whereby all religions are judged simply introduces one universal for another, and hence continues the pattern of oppression? Secondly, and closely related to this, who defines "well-being"? Justice is a concept closely aligned to religious convictions, and each concept of justice reflects the religious sensitivities and suppositions of the culture that gave it birth. Thirdly, if the first and second problems cannot be answered adequately, then we must face the situation of religious relativism, which would follow were there no acceptable norms of discernment to be applied to religious positions.

Such relativism involves the supposition that each religion is governed by norms and perceptions uniquely conditioned by the cultural and historical situation of the religion. The only authentic critique of a religion would therefore be an internal critique, developed within the parameters of the normative system or systems within the religion itself. There would be no "meta" view whereby the truth or values of the religion could be judged. An interreligious stance, therefore, would revolve around an open dialogue with no judgments formed as to the truth or value of the religions.

My feminist rejection of absolutizing one religion as the norm for all others accepts the uniqueness and self-naming quality of each religion. I reject, however, the possibility of entering into dialogue with no judgments whatsoever. We are not creatures suspended from some skyhook, impartially surveying the human scene; we are part and parcel of its buzzing confusion, and enter into dialogue value-laden and value-projecting. What is called for is not a nonjudgmental dialogue with other religions in light of the relativism of belief systems, but a shift of judgment from ideological ground to ethical ground, along with an open recognition of the conditioned nature of the norm of justice we bring, and commitment to critical exploration of the norm in the very dialogue wherein it is brought to bear. . . .

Absolutizing one religion, such that it becomes normative for all others, is a dynamic with clear parallels to sexism, whereby one gender is established as the norm for human existence. Therefore the critique of sexism can be extended as a critique of religious imperialism.

The feminist critique of sexism and its effect upon women takes two routes. First, feminists point to the sense in which masculine experience has been universalized in defining all that is fully human. Under such a guise, women's experience is either nonexistent, or subsumed under masculinity. . . . The second route is not to subsume and therefore erase women's experience under the so-called universal norms developed by men, but to assign to women those characteristics that men consider problematic in human existence. Traditionally, these characteristics have been dependence, emotionality, sensuality, and weakness. . . . In both cases women are silenced, save for their ability to echo the dominant voice of man. The consequence of the absolutized masculine norm is oppression of women in all areas of life: public and private, social and spiritual. . . . Just as the universalization of male experience functions either to absorb women within the masculine norm or to ascribe to women those characteristics that men are not willing to name clearly as belonging to themselves, even so the universalization of one religion leads to similar distortions.

I take as an illustration an enormously popular book in Christian theology, Hans Küng's *On Being a Christian*. The book is particularly pertinent: its clear intent, from page 1 through 602, is to demonstrate the superiority of Christianity over against other modes of being human, whether secular or religious. On page 1, Küng acknowledges the challenge of the "great world religions." He asks, "is Christianity something essentially different, really something special?" His answer on page 602 summarizes the argument of the book:

> The Christian element therefore is neither a superstructure nor a substructure of the human. It is an elevation or — better — a transfiguration of the human, at once preserving, canceling, surpassing the human. Being Christian therefore means that the other humanisms are transfigured: they are affirmed to the extent that they affirm the human reality; they are rejected to the extent that they reject the Christian reality, Christ himself; they are surpassed to the extent that being Christian can fully incorporate the human, all-too-human even in all its negativity.

Parallels with sexism can be drawn in that the norm of Christ is applied to other religions regardless of norms that may be generated from within those religions. Just as the norm of masculinity is applied to women regardless of women's protestations that their own experience of humanity is sufficient to generate their own norms, even so Christian norms are projected uncritically upon non-Christian religions. Such inclusivist stances toward other religions violate their integrity. Also, just as women are measured and judged by masculine experience, even so Küng measures and judges other religions by Christian experience. Further, the form of sexism that separates reprehensible qualities from men and projects them upon women is also operative in Küng's treatment. The qualities which he specifically names as negative in other religions have parallels within Christianity. These parallels are not acknowledged. Rather, they are rendered invisible in Christianity by projecting them as somehow appropriately descriptive of other religions. Here the exclusivist attitude toward women finds its echo in an exclusivist attitude toward other religions.

The consequences of this negation of the value of the other are familiar to women. There is indeed a "superiority-inferiority" syndrome, whether the superiority be deemed cheap or virtuous. This works against the mutuality necessary for full dialogue. There is also exploitation. For women, their labor is devalued and their possibilities are denied. For other religions, their contributions to Christianity are secondary to Christianity's contributions to them. Possibilities for their continuing development are valued not in accordance with their own history, but in accordance with their transformation into closer alignment with Christianity. Measurement against an absolute norm, whether sex or religion, renders invisible or secondary all those in whom the norm is not found. . . .

The same dynamics that promote sexism with repercussions against men as well as women apply with regard to the absolutizing of one religion vis-à-vis all others. Distortions in knowledge and exploitation in relationships follow.

If no religion can set itself up as a norm for all others, do we find ourselves in a situation of unrelieved relativism? Is there no transcendence of our particularity that allows us to determine what is a valid stance toward self and others in the world? I suggest that the norm championed by feminists and other liberation theologians is also a norm for reflection on the world religions. That norm is justice. . . .

The justice applied normatively by liberation theologians centers upon inclusiveness of well-being. . . . Valuation in a concrete mode of justice would begin with fundamental, physical well-being. Food, water, shelter, work, and community are primary, constituting as they do needs fundamental to all human existence. Building upon these values is a second level of justice in terms of human dignity and recognition in the human community. This level involves a self-naming, an appreciation of self and others. A third level of justice is openness to self-development and self-determination within the context of community. The levels are successive, each building upon the other, and each moving toward a multiplicity of forms. The first level, physical well-being, is relatively uniform although . . . even here there can be divergent interpretations. The second level of self-naming and dignity in community invites diversity as an essential component of community. The third level carries this openness to diversity further still, indicating not only a diversity of individuals, but of communities. Thus if the forms of justice are actualized in human community, there will be recognition of multiple modes of being human, with this multiplicity valued positively. . . .

The ultimate test of justice is precisely the degree to which it knows no boundaries to well-being. A justice that establishes well-being within the context of its own community and ignores the well-being of those outside that community is to that degree unjust. Likewise, a community that establishes its own well-being through exploitation of the well-being of those outside the community is to that degree unjust. A supposition underlying this statement is that the world is a network of interrelationship and interdependence. Thus a value of concrete forms of justice implicitly and explicitly pushes toward an affirmation of pluralism. It provides, however, not only an affirmation of pluralism, but a criterion for judging the forms of pluralism that it engenders. . . .

Religions will . . . have different valuations of what constitutes the justice of physical well-being in society, and these valuations may well have their source in the historical development of the religion within its society. Thus agreement concerning physical well-being and even wider understandings of justice should not be sought within the religious interpretations of society. Insofar as they are, then any norm of justice might well be criticized for being as imperialistic as Küng's employment of the norm of Christ, for it takes the notion of physical well-being developed in a culture-specific context and applies it evaluatively to all cultures and religions.

I suggest, however, that there is another base of contact among the religions that allows a nonimperialistic criterion of justice. Oddly enough, the contact puts us back again in the ideological realm we supposedly left behind in calling for justice rather than doctrine as the basis of dialogue. If it is the case that interpretations of well-being are rooted in the salvific interaction of religion with ordinary and extraordinary problems of existence, then it is possible that each religion's deepest valuation of what physical existence should be lies, not in its coping with the exigencies of history, but in its projection of the ideal. By looking at each religion's vision of the ultimately perfect mode of existence for its saints or holy ones, whether that vision be otherworldly or not, we might find some echo of unanimity on the value of freedom from suffering.

My point is that justice is not given a universally acceptable content, not even with regard to physical well-being. Some of the variances in definition may be traceable to the ways in which religions have interpreted and dealt with negative factors in existence. We must be sensitive to these variances, but they do not require a full relativization of justice such that it is rendered useless as a norm to judge that which is of greater or lesser value in and among religions. On the contrary, we must look to the heart of justice in each religion as that which renders life meaningful in light of a vision of what existence should be. Using justice as a norm means that the primary visions within each religion of what societal life should be in a "perfect" world is a source of judgment that can be used internally within each religion to judge its present societal forms of justice. Dialogue among the religions can likewise proceed from the development of mutual concerns for justice that can lead to concerted actions for justice in the world. Justice is a dynamic and transformative notion, capable of being used even to judge itself. . . .

What is necessary, then, in looking for a nonimperialistic mode of justice is to look at ultimate rather than penultimate visions of justice. The determinate mode of justice must be drawn from the vision of the termination of adversity, or the ideal form of human existence envisioned in each religion. This vision is far more likely to yield agreement on the value of at least the basic forms of justice dealing with physical existence. If so, then the criterion of justice in that minimal mode can appeal to an internal norm within each religion. This mitigates the charge that the norm of justice as a basis for making value judgments concerning religions is as imperialistic as doctrinal norms.

The situation remains, however, that the second and third levels of justice have an inherent diversity within them such that interreligious dialogues of exploration concerning these diversities can be only that: listening and learning in openness to the other, which ultimately is self-enriching. Paradoxically, the one employing the norm that affirms diversity must expect to encounter — and affirm — systems that, containing no valuation of diversity, reject or devalue one's norm and the system it reflects. An absolutist, by definition, cannot affirm the pluralist, whereas the pluralist is bound, likewise by definition, to affirm the alternative of absolutism so long as it promotes well-being. . . .

Affirming religious pluralism within the context of justice shifts the focus of dialogue to the concreteness of human well-being. The very exploration of human well-being, however, inevitably directs our attention to questions concerning how we determine what constitutes well-being, or into the heart of the ideological nature of the religions. Interreligious dialogue focused on justice promotes intrareligious dialogue concerning ultimate and penultimate values. The pluralism among religions then finds itself calling attention to the pluralism within each religion; dialogue engenders dialogues. Affirming one another's diversity may grant us the privilege of "listening in" to the internal dialogues, in the hope of understanding and mutual transformations. One vision of justice can temper, criticize, and deepen another, and through dialogue each vision might grow richer in understanding and implementation.

Diana L. Eck

Professor of comparative religion and Indian studies at Harvard University, Eck has served as moderator of the World Council of Churches' Subunit on Dialogue with People of Living Faiths and Ideologies. The following selection was taken from a 1988 address in Tambaram (Madras), India, celebrating the historic 1938 conference sponsored by the International Missionary Council on the same site fifty years earlier. Eck considers the question of revelation, critiques the theological method of Barth and Kraemer, and emphasizes the Christian's responsibility of discernment through dialogue. Source: *International Review of Mission* 78, no. 307 (July 1988).

The Religions and Tambaram: 1938 and 1988

As D. G. Moses, professor of philosophy from Nagpur, put it, fifty years ago in this hall, "Time was when each thought his own religion superior.... But . . . with the ever-increasing means of communication and transportation and the growing study of comparative religion, the old attitude has been made impossible. We know too much of the religions of the world today to assume naively the unquestioned superiority and validity of one's own faith."

What Moses expressed here at Tambaram is even more true today. The tremendous growth in the study and understanding of religion, the translation of sacred texts of Hindus, Buddhists, and Muslims, the deeper

189

understanding of their traditions of faith, *has* made the old attitude impossible. We can say, as we do, that God's incarnation in Jesus Christ is unique. As Bishop Newbigin said in his sermon: there is nothing to put beside that revelation; it is central in our lives and in the life of the church. At the same time we know that our Muslim brothers and sisters will affirm the uniqueness, the centrality, and the finality of God's revelation in the Word, the holy Qur'an. And we know that when the Buddhist speaks of insight, *vipassana,* seeing deeply into the nature of life and death and suffering, he or she is not speaking of a narrow truth that is only for Buddhists, but a universal truth which they invite us all to see.

People of other faiths also witness to the truth, the transcendence, the universality, the uniqueness of what they have seen. It is not weak-hearted relativism to recognize this as a fact, nor is it a betrayal of our faith in Christ. The question posed by this fact is an urgent one. How does our knowledge of and life with people of other faiths — be they neighbours, colleagues, friends, or even members of our own families — recast our understanding of ourselves as Christians and our understanding of the task and mission of the church? . . .

My grandmother had never met a Hindu, had never read the *Bhagavad Gita,* and perhaps had never heard of it. She had no contact whatsoever with the thinking, the devotion and the communities of faith that are Hindu. In no meaningful sense did she share a world with Hindus. On the other hand, I do. I have read the *Bhagavad Gita* and studied its commentaries. On my bookshelves are well-worn copies of the *Upanishads,* the *Shiva Purana,* the *Narayaniyam* and the *Tiruvacakam.* My question is: What does this fact, which moves me into a wider *oikoumene* than my grandmother knew, mean for my life and thinking as a Christian? After all, one cannot isolate the understandings and questions that have emerged from such readings in a closet of the mind, and then go about one's spiritual business as a Christian as if one had not been touched and challenged and changed by them. This is a serious question of life and of theology for our time. . . .

"Dialogue" is very much on our minds in the church today. Sometimes, by dialogue, we mean something formal, something arranged: Christians, Muslims and Hindus coming together to share and discuss. But more broadly and deeply, more meaningfully, the source of dialogue is . . . the process of mutual understanding and mutual questioning, I of my Hindu friend, my Hindu friend of me. In dialogue we invite our neighbors to tell us who they are. We do not talk *about* them. We talk *with* them. We do not define their identity, but listen to their self-understanding. We have questions for them, they for us. Our goal is not to agree, but to understand, to replace prejudice and stereotype with relationship. Some of the dialogue takes place in our own minds as we struggle to understand what we have learned from our neighbours. Dialogue is a process of openness and mutuality. In dialogue we do not settle for one-way proclamation, announcement and witness, but also invite the testimony and witness of those with whom we share a world. To turn away from such mutuality and dialogue is to settle for a totalitarian regime of faith, untested and unquestioned by the voices and the commitments of others.

I do not stand here alone, for the churches are filled with people whose own contexts have raised such questions. Perhaps more aptly, in some places, the churches are emptied of people with such questions, for the churches have often evaded these questions, unable to respond to them seriously. . . .

Hendrik Kraemer's name is closely identified with Tambaram. In preparation for the meeting, Kraemer, who had been a Dutch missionary in Indonesia and who, in 1937, returned to Leiden to take Brede Kristensen's chair in Comparative Religion, was asked to write a book discussing "the evangelical approach to the great non-Christian faiths." Because it is so well-known, that book, *The Christian Message in a Non-Christian World*, has in a sense become not simply the preparatory volume, but the final report of Tambaram. It is important for us to remember, however, that there were many other voices in the Tambaram debate, some of which radically disagreed with Kraemer, and whose collected accountings are given in the volume of the Tambaram report called *The Authority of the Faith*.

Let me select just one issue that brings to light the nature of the Tambaram discussion on world religions: the question of revelation. Kraemer raised the issue himself in the form of a question: "From the standpoint of the Christian revelation, what answer can be given to the question: Does God — and if so, how and where does God — reveal Himself in the religious life as present in the non-Christian religions?" [*The Christian Message in a Non-Christian World*, p. 111].

This is a question with which many of us have struggled. What has God been doing, what *is* God doing, in the diverse, rich, and on the whole generative religious life of humankind? How has God, the God we know in Christ, been involved? The question is important, but equally important is how we will go about finding an answer. Who will we ask? With whom will we discuss this question? To what authority will we turn?

From one perspective, if we want to know what God has been doing in the religious life of Muslims, or what God has revealed of God's self to Hindus, it would seem imperative to ask a Muslim, or a Hindu, "What have you discovered? What have you seen, or what has been shown to you? What is your struggle?"

But Kraemer does not go about grappling with his question in this way. Although he lived for years in Muslim Indonesia, there are no Muslim voices in his approach. He talks *about* Islam, as about other traditions, but the voices of Muslims do not enter in. In discussing this particular question, there is no dialogue with Muslims. There are no questions posed *to us* by Muslims. Rather, his method for answering the question, "Does and, if so, how and where does God reveal himself to Muslims?" is to consult Christian revelation, Christian scripture and Christian theology. Christian scripture, however, does not address itself to the question of what God has been doing for Muslims. It bears witness to what God has done for us. . . .

Following Karl Barth, Kraemer makes a radical distinction between "revelation," by which he means Christian revelation, and the "religions." Religions, Christianity included, are human efforts. Revelation is the self-disclosure of the transcendent God. Christianity as a religion is at least guided by God's revelation in Christ. Again and again, in referring to other religious traditions, Kraemer speaks of them as "worldviews," as "human efforts to apprehend the totality of existence," as the "vast and desperate effort of mankind to get somehow an apprehension of the totality of existence" [*The Christian Message in a Non-Christian World*, p. 135].

On the matter of religion, there should be no argument that religious traditions are the human side of the encounter with the divine. I would rather say, however, that they are human achievements, not "vast and desperate" human efforts. Nonetheless, religions are not dropped from on high, for no one would claim that God is in the business of revealing religions. God reveals God's self.

As for revelation, on the other hand, I would disagree with Kraemer. He interprets revelation in a very specific, and, what some at Tambaram felt to be, a very narrow way. He does not sanction the idea of "general revelation," or of "progressive revelation." It is to his credit that he did not want to see Christian revelation as somehow the flower of progressive revelation, the fulfillment of lesser revelations to other people in history. But Kraemer makes this point not to press for the integrity or the mystery of God's revealing to people of other faiths. Not at all. For Kraemer, revelation was uniquely and fully in Jesus Christ and in Christian scripture.

There is a serious problem here, however. Given the way in which Kraemer has approached the question of what God might have been doing in the religious life of non-Christian religions, he simply cannot respond

192

to it in a way that is illuminating or useful to the crisis of our times. In fact, he responds to it by defining the question out of existence as a real question. To rephrase the question in his own terms: from the standpoint of Christian revelation, given the fact that revelation is defined by Christ, that Christ is constitutive of revelation, how does God reveal himself in non-Christian religions? In these terms, he does not, according to Kraemer.

Kraemer does not say it quite so bluntly. There are lines here and there upon which one can seize for a more open interpretation. God "shines revealingly" through the religious traditions of humankind. But all in all, "it is undiscerning to dub religious and moral achievements because they impress us as sublime and lofty, revelations of the same quality as the revelation in Christ . . ." [*The Christian Message in a Non-Christian World*, p. 122].

I do not believe that I, or any of us, ought to be in the business of "dubbing" the claims of our Shri Vaisnava or Shaiva Siddhantin neighbors "revelations" or "not revelations." As a Christian, I can bear witness to what God has done for me, for the people of my family of faith, for those of us who call ourselves Christians, and indeed for all people. But I cannot make claims as to what God has *not* done. I cannot say what God has not done for the Hindu or for the Muslim. For the affirmation of the Hindu or Muslim as to God's revealing, I must listen to the witness of the Hindu or Muslim and seek to understand what he or she has to say. Kraemer's response to his own question as to what God might be revealing in the "non-Christian" religions is strictly a formal and doctrinal response. It does not seem to come from a living context of people, with real voices and real questions, such as the Muslims among whom he lived in Indonesia, who witness daily to God's oneness and God's revealing word in the holy Qur'an. In the end, Kraemer's response to the important question of God's revelation in other traditions is as dry and doctrinaire as Barth's answer to someone who is said to have asked how he was so sure Hindus could not be saved if he had never met a Hindu. Barth is said to have replied, "*A priori.*" And *a priori* is simply not an adequate answer for the world in which we now live. . . .

Another voice (at Tambaram in 1938) was that of A. G. Hogg, principal of Madras Christian College, who (in opposition to Kraemer) put forth the idea, later developed so carefully by Wilfred Cantwell Smith, that the adherents of other religions are people of faith. They direct their hearts and minds to God, they pray and meditate and submit themselves to the discipline of spiritual life. They seek God. They find God. As Hogg put it:

Is it not indispensable for a right attitude in missionary approach that

193

one should be expectant of finding, among genuine adherents of other religions, men of God for whose non-Christian faith one should feel not mere respect, not even merely admiration as for a fine product of human culture, but religious reverence? Is there any such thing as a religious faith which in quality or texture is definitely not Christian, but in the approach to which one ought to put the shoes off the feet, recognizing that one is on the holy ground of a two-sided commerce between God and man? In non-Christian faith may we meet with something that is not merely a seeking but in real measure a finding, and a finding by contact with which a Christian may be helped to make fresh discoveries in his own finding of God in Christ?" [*The Authority of the Faith*, 94-95].

Hogg's statement here is remarkable. Not only did he reject Kraemer's negative assessment of other religions as merely human phenomena; he saw adherents of these traditions as people of faith, from whom one might discover afresh our own finding of God in Christ. . . .

Revelation is not, as T. C. Chao put it (at the 1938 conference), a "quick thrust into the furnace" by the divine saviour, but an event that goes on happening as each person sees, turns, believes and takes into his or her heart the love of God. W. C. Smith makes a similar point in *Toward a World Theology*. . . . The good news, as Smith puts it, is not only that God did something in first century Palestine that we have described as the fullness of God's revelation, but the good news is that God goes on doing something. "The locus of revelation is always the present, and always the person. The channel of revelation in the Christian case, Christ, is a figure in history. But history, I have insisted, moves forward, and is the process by which He comes to us; it is not something to be studied backwards, as the process by which we try to recapture him" [*Toward a World Theology*, 174].

I would agree with Bishop Lesslie Newbigin's sermon affirmation that in the revelation of Jesus Christ we are talking about a real historical event, with a date and a place. But I would insist with W. C. Smith that the date and place of God's revelation to us in Christ is not only in first century Palestine, but in each century, in each decade, on each continent. Indeed it is here at Tambaram in 1988. If the locus of revelation is the present, we in the present time have the responsibility of discerning and responding to what God may be doing today. God reveals God's self, not simply "truths about God's self" that we can put in our pockets and possess.

Let us turn, with this responsibility of discernment, to Kraemer's question of God's revealing in the religious life of other traditions of faith.

If we really are to wrestle with this question, we can do so only by attentive listening to what other people of faith have said, verbally and symbolically, about the revelation of the divine. . . .

By sharing a world with Hindus (for example) and by attending alertly to common Hindu rites, we come to understand something of Hindu faith. I would go farther, however, and say that in this encounter with Hindus, different as their ways of faith may be from ours, we might also come to understand and confess our own faith more deeply. Let me . . . offer some examples.

I understand the power and mystery of the incarnation more deeply in my own faith for having lived for several years in the Hindu holy city of Banaras, where pilgrims come to pray in and bathe in the river Ganga, and where pilgrims also come to die and be cremated on the banks of the Ganga. Having struggled to understand this place where life and death, this shore and the far shore, are juxtaposed and interrelated, I have seen more clearly the terrible and transcendent fact of Christ's incarnation, death and resurrection. Banaras challenged me to struggle with the agony, as well as the glory, of God's revealing.

And in the worship of Krishna, I have seen something of the humility and vulnerability of God's incarnation in the person of Jesus. Krishna is the adopted baby, the mischievous child, the lovely youth who came to live among the most rustic of rural folk. I discovered something of the sweetness and tenderness of faith, having seen Vaishnavas about the business of the loving care of Krishna in his many temples — offering him milk and sweets, tops and toys, flower garlands and a pillow for his head, the love offerings of people whose greatest gift to the divine child is love.

I would insist that such understandings and discoveries do not lead to the relativization or domestication of Jesus . . . but rather unleash the incarnate One from domestication in first century Palestine into a world of life and death, diversity and struggle, today. . . .

Many have suggested on this anniversary occasion that one of the great discoveries of Tambaram in 1938 was the discovery of the worldwide family of the Christian church, the *oikoumene,* for at that meeting, for the first time, over half of the participants were from the "younger churches" of what we now refer to as the "third world." May the discovery and challenge of Tambaram in 1988 be that this *oikoumene,* this world house, is indeed the *whole* inhabited earth, not just that part of it that is Christian. It is to this *oikoumene* that we are called in our time to respond.

195

Lesslie Newbigin

A theologian and missionary who served in India for almost forty years, much of it as a bishop of the Church of South India, Lesslie Newbigin (b. 1909) was the last general secretary of the International Missionary Council and the first director of the Division of World Mission and Evangelism of the World Council of Churches. In the following selection, Newbigin strongly affirms the uniqueness of Jesus Christ while he rejects the extreme position that all non-Christians are eternally separated from God. Source: *The Gospel in a Pluralist Society* (Grand Rapids: Eerdmans, 1989).

The Gospel and the Religions

We must look first at the strictly exclusivist view which holds that all who do not accept Jesus as Lord and Savior are eternally lost. We shall later look at the question whether this is in fact what fidelity to Scripture requires us to hold. There are several reasons which make it difficult for me to believe this. If it were true, then it would be not only permissible but obligatory to use any means available, all the modern techniques of brainwashing included, to rescue others from this appalling fate. And since it is God alone who knows the heart of every person, how are we to judge whether or not another person truly has the faith which is acceptable to him? If we hold this view, it is absolutely necessary to know who is saved and who is not, and we are then led into making the kind of judgments against which Scripture warns us. We are in the business of erecting barriers: Has she been baptized? Has he been confirmed by a bishop in the historic succession? Or has she had a recognizable conversion and can she name the day and the hour when it happened? We are bound to become judges of that which God alone knows. . . .

An important group of writers who reject both this exclusivism on the one hand and a total pluralism on the other, take an inclusivist position which acknowledges Christ as the only Savior but affirm that his saving work extends beyond the bounds of the visible church. Probably the most influential exponent of this view has been Karl Rahner with his conception of anonymous Christianity. It is important to note here that Rahner is not merely affirming that individual non-Christians can be saved — certainly no new doctrine — but that the non-Christian religions as such have a salvific role. . . . While Rahner's idea of "anonymous Christianity" has not proved widely acceptable, the idea that the non-Christian religions as such are to be understood as vehicles of salvation is widely accepted. It has indeed become a sort of orthodoxy and those who are not willing to accept it are dismissed as simply out-of-date. . . .

I believe that we must begin with the great reality made known to us in Jesus Christ, that God — the creator and sustainer of all that exists — is in his own triune being an ocean of infinite love overflowing to all his works in all creation and to all human beings. I believe that when we see Jesus eagerly welcoming the signs of faith among men and women outside the house of Israel; when we see him lovingly welcoming those whom others cast out; when we see him on the cross with arms outstretched to embrace the whole world and when we hear his whispered words, "Father, forgive them; they know not what they do"; we are seeing the most fundamental of all realities, namely a grace and mercy and loving-kindness which reaches out to every creature. I believe that no person, of whatever kind or creed, is without some witness of God's grace in heart and conscience and reason, and none in whom that grace does not evoke some response — however feeble, fitful, and flawed. . . .

All true thinking about this, as about every matter, must be held within the magnetic field set up between these two poles: the amazing grace of God and the appalling sin of the world. To live in this magnetic field is to live in an atmosphere which is charged with power, tingling, as it were, with electricity. One is always in the (humanly speaking) impossible position of knowing that one is — along with all others — at the same time the enemy of God and the beloved child of God. To live in this charged field of force is always at the same time supremely demanding and supremely affirming. But we are always tempted to slacken the tension by drawing away from one or the other of the two poles. Nowhere is this more clear than in the attitude we take to people outside the household of faith. We can opt for a solution which relies wholly on the universality and omnipotence of grace and move toward some form of universalism. Here the sharpness of the issue which God's action in Christ raises for every human soul is blunted. There is no life-or-death decision to be made. We can relax and be assured that everything will be all right for everybody in the end. Over much theological writing about the gospel and the world's religions one is tempted to write the famous words of Anselm: "Nondum considerasti quanti ponderis sit peccatum" — "You have not yet taken full account of sin." Or, on the other hand, the Christian may be so conscious of the abyss of sin from which only the grace of God in Jesus Christ could rescue him that he is unwilling to believe that the same grace can operate in ways beyond his own experience and understanding. His relation to the man or woman outside the Church, or outside the particular embodiment of Christianity to which he adheres, can only be that of the saved to the lost. In both cases genuine dialogue is impossible. In the first case there is no real dialogue because nothing vital is at stake; it is merely a sharing of varied experiences of the same reality. In the second case dialogue is simply inappropriate. The person in the lifeboat and the person drowning in the sea do not have a dialogue. The one rescues the other; the time to share their experiences will come only afterward.

If we are to avoid these two dangers, if we are to live faithfully in this spiritual magnetic field between the amazing grace of God and the appalling sin of the world, how are we to regard the other commitments, faiths, worldviews to which the people around us and with whom we live and move adhere? I believe that the debate about this question has been fatally flawed by the fact that it has been conducted around the question, "Who can be saved?" It has been taken for granted that the only question was, "Can the good non-Christian be saved?" and by that question what was meant was not, "Can the non-Christian live a good and useful life and play a good and useful role in the life of society?" The question was, "Where will she go when she dies?" I am putting this crudely because I want to make the issue as clear as possible. The quest for truth always requires that we ask the right questions. If we ask the wrong questions we shall get only silence or confusion. In the debate about Christianity and the world's religions it is fair to say that there has been an almost unquestioned assumption that the only question is, "What happens to the non-Christian after death?" I want to affirm that this is the wrong question and that as long as it remains the central question we shall never come to the truth. And this is for three reasons:

a. First, and simply, it is the wrong question because it is a question to which God alone has the right to give the answer. I confess that I am astounded at the arrogance of theologians who seem to think that we are authorized, in our capacity as Christians, to inform the rest of the world about who is to be vindicated and who is to be condemned at the last judgment. . . . Hans Küng (*On Being a Christian,* p. 99) is scathing in his contempt for Protestant theologians who say that we must leave the question of the ultimate fate of non-Christians in the hands of God. Rahner is equally sure that it is the duty of Christian theologians to tell the faithful adherents of a non-Christian religion that he can be saved but that he will have a better chance of salvation if he becomes a Christian and no chance at all if he refuses this invitation. And Wesley Ariarajah rebukes Visser 't Hooft for what he calls a "theology of neutrality" because the latter said, "I don't know whether a Hindu is saved: I only know that salvation comes in Jesus Christ" (*International Review of Mission,* July 1988, pp. 419-20). I find this way of thinking among Christians astonishing in view of the emphatic warnings of Jesus against these kinds of judgments which claim to preempt the final judgment of God. . . .

b. The second reason for rejecting this way of putting the question is that it is based on an abstraction. By concentrating on the fate of the individual soul after death, it abstracts the soul from the full reality of the human person as an actor and sufferer in the ongoing history of the world. Once again we have to insist that the human person is not, essentially, a soul which can be understood in abstraction from the whole story of the person's life. This reductionist move is as misleading as the corresponding move of the materialists and behaviorists who want to explain the human person simply as a bundle of physical activities. If we refuse both these forms of reductionism, then the question we have to ask is not, "What will happen to this person's soul after death?" but "What is the end which gives meaning to this person's story as part of God's whole story?" It has often been pointed out that the verb "to save" is used in the New Testament in three tenses — past, present, and future. We were saved, we are being saved, and we look forward for salvation. By common consent it is agreed that to understand the word we must begin from its eschatological sense, from the end to which it all looks. Salvation in this sense is the completion of God's whole work in creation and redemption, the summing up of all things with Christ as head (Eph. 1:10), the reconciling of all things in heaven and earth through the blood of the cross (Col. 1:20), the subjecting of all hostile powers under the feet of Christ (1 Cor. 15:24-28). The other uses of the verb (we have been saved, we are being saved) must be understood in the light of the end to which they look. The question of salvation is wrongly posed if it is posed in respect to the human soul abstracted from God's history of salvation, abstracted therefore from the question, "How do we understand the human story?" Being saved has to do with the part we are playing now in God's story and therefore with the question whether we have understood the story rightly. It follows that our dialogue with people of other faiths must be about what is happening in the world now and about how we understand it and take our part in it. It cannot be only, or even mainly, about our destiny as individual souls after death. Insofar as the debate has concentrated on this latter question, it has been flawed.

c. The third reason for rejecting this way of putting the question is the most fundamental: it is that the question starts with the individual and his or her need to be assured of ultimate happiness, and not with God and his glory. All human beings have a longing for ultimate happiness, and the many worldviews, religious or otherwise, have as part of their power some promise of satisfying that longing. We must believe that this longing is something implanted in us by God. He has so made us that we have infinite desires beyond the satisfaction of our biological necessities, desires which only God himself can satisfy. Our hearts are restless till they find rest in him. On our journey he gives us good things which whet our appetite but do not finally satisfy, for they are always corrupted by the selfishness that desires to have them as our own possession. The gospel, the story of the astonishing act of God himself in coming down to be part of our alienated world, to endure the full horror of our rebellion against love, to take the whole burden of our guilt and shame, and to lift us up into communion and fellowship with himself, breaks into this self-centered search for our own happiness, shifts the center from the self and its desires to God and his glory. It is true, God forgive us, that Christians have turned this event into something that they thought they could possess for themselves; that they have privatized this mighty work of grace and talked as if the whole cosmic drama of salvation culminated in the words "For me; for me"; as if the one question is "How can I be saved?" But this is a perversion of the gospel. For anyone who has understood what God did for us all in Jesus

Christ, the one question is: "How shall God be glorified? How shall his amazing grace be known and celebrated and adored? . . ."

What are the practical consequences of taking this as the starting point in our relation to people of other faiths? I suggest four immediate implications:

1. The first is this: we shall expect, look for, and welcome all the signs of the grace of God at work in the lives of those who do not know Jesus as Lord. In this, of course, we shall be following the example of Jesus, who was so eager to welcome the evidences of faith in those outside the household of Israel. This kind of expectancy and welcome is an implication of the greatness of God's grace as it has been shown to us in Jesus. For Jesus is the personal presence of that creative word by which all that exists was made and is sustained in being. He comes to the world as no stranger but as the source of the world's life. He is the true light of the world, and that light shines into every corner of the world in spite of all that seeks to shut it out. . . .

2. The second consequence of the approach I suggest is that the Christian will be eager to cooperate with people of all faiths and ideologies in all projects which are in line with the Christian's understanding of God's purpose in history. . . . There are struggles for justice and for freedom in which we can and should join hands with those of other faiths and ideologies to achieve specific goals, even though we know that the ultimate goal is Christ and his coming in glory and not what our collaborators imagine.

3. Third, it is precisely in this kind of shared commitment to the business of the world that the context for true dialogue is provided. As we work together with people of other commitments, we shall discover the places where our ways must separate. Here is where real dialogue may begin. . . . If we are doing what we ought to be doing as Christians, the dialogue will be initiated by our partners, not by ourselves. They will be aware of the fact that, while we share with them in commitment to some immediate project, our action is set in a different context from theirs. It has a different motivation. It looks to a different goal. . . . They will discover that we are guided by something both more ultimate and more immediate than the success of the project in hand. And they will discover that we have resources for coping with failure, defeat, and humiliation, because we understand human history from this side of the resurrection of the crucified Lord. It is — or it ought to be — the presence of these realities which prompts the questions and begins the dialogue. And, once again, the dialogue will not be about who is going to be saved. It will be about the

question, "What is the meaning and goal of this common human story in which we are all, Christians and others together, participants?"

4. Therefore, the essential contribution of the Christian to the dialogue will simply be the telling of the story, the story of Jesus, the story of the Bible. The story is itself, as Paul says, the power of God for salvation. The Christian must tell it, not because she lacks respect for the many excellencies of her companions — many of whom may be better, more godly, more worthy of respect than she is. She tells it simply as one who has been chosen and called by God to be part of the company which is entrusted with the story. . . . She will seek faithfully both to tell the story and — as part of a Christian congregation — so conduct her life as to embody the truth of the story. But she will not imagine that it is her responsibility to insure that the other is persuaded. That is in God's hands.

It has become customary to classify views on the relation of Christianity to the world religions as either pluralist, exclusivist, or inclusivist, the three positions being typically represented by John Hick, Hendrik Kraemer, and Karl Rahner. The position which I have outlined is exclusivist in the sense that it affirms the unique truth of the revelation in Jesus Christ, but it is not exclusivist in the sense of denying the possibility of the salvation of the non-Christian. It is inclusivist in the sense that it refuses to limit the saving grace of God to the members of the Christian Church, but it rejects the inclusivism which regards the non-Christian religions as vehicles of salvation. It is pluralist in the sense of acknowledging the gracious work of God in the lives of all human beings, but it rejects a pluralism which denies the uniqueness and decisiveness of what God has done in Jesus Christ. Arguments for pluralism and inclusivism usually begin from the paramount need for human unity, a need hugely increased by the threats of nuclear and ecological disaster. We must surely recognize that need. But the recognition of the need provides no clue as to how it is to be met, and certainly does not justify the assertion that religion is the means by which human unity is to be achieved. The question of truth must be faced. C.-S. Song is one of those who wishes to play down the role of truth because, as he says, truth judges, polarizes, divides. Truth, he says, cannot unite the ununitable; only love can. So the Christian mission must be an affair of love, not an affair of truth (*Tell Us Our Names*, Orbis Books, 1984, pp. 105ff.). But it is not love which encourages people to believe a lie. As a human race we are on a journey and we need to know the road. It is not true that all roads lead to the top of the same mountain. There are roads which lead over the precipice. In Christ we have been shown the road. We cannot treat that knowledge as a private matter for ourselves. It concerns the whole human family. We do presume to limit the might and the mercy of God for the ultimate salvation of all people, but the same costly act of revelation and reconciliation which gives us that assurance also requires us to share with our fellow pilgrims the vision that God has given us the route we must follow and the goal to which we must press forward.

James A. Borland

Borland is professor of New Testament and theology at Liberty Baptist Theological Seminary in Lynchburg, Virginia. The following selection is excerpted from his 1989 presidential address at the annual meeting of the Evangelical Theological Society, entitled "A Theologian Looks at the Gospel and World Religions." In the first part of his address, Borland seeks to demonstrate how the world religions are in total antithesis to Christian doctrine with regard to God's attributes, the human condition, Christology, and soteriology. In the second part, included here, he proceeds to answer the question of the possibility of salvation for persons outside the church of Jesus Christ by reviewing relevant New Testament texts. Source: Journal of the Evangelical Theological Society 33, no. 1 (March 1990).

Everyone Must Hear and Believe the Gospel to Be Saved

Is it possible to be saved apart from believing the gospel of Christ? Can Christ save a good Hindu through his Hinduism? Are there "ascended masters" from all religions in heaven today? Can other religions be termed "saving structures" because they in some way direct people to the "cosmic Christ," as Raymond Panikkar teaches [cf. *The Unknown Christ of Hinduism*, 54]? Is Cantwell Smith wrong to claim that the non-Christian religions are "channels through which God Himself comes into touch with these His children" and that "both within and without the Church, so far as we can see, God does somehow enter into men's hearts" [cf. *The Faith of Other Men*, 136, 140]?

Norman Anderson states: "I have no doubt whatever that the presentation of the gospel, by voice or writing, is the normal way by which people are reached and won." But is he correct when he continues by saying that "I do not believe that we have any biblical warrant to assert that this is the *only* way"? He further claims: "On the contrary, I believe there is much, in the Bible and experience, to point to the fact that God *can,* and sometimes does, work directly in men's hearts to convict them of sin, and prompt them to throw themselves on his mercy." [cf. *Christianity and World Religions: The Challenge of Pluralism*, 175.]

Robert Brow, who agrees with Anderson, summarizes: "Anderson argues that humble repentance and faith indicate a true work of God in the heart, and that to those who have this kind of faith, Christ's sacrifice is applied, whether before or after the crucifixion. We need not deny, therefore, that there could be a saving work of God among men who have not heard the preaching of Christ crucified" [R. Brow, review of N. Anderson, *The World's Religions*, in *Christianity Today*, 2 July 1971, 25-26].

At this juncture I must register my dissent from Anderson's viewpoint. I find nothing in the Bible to support his contentions. In fact, God's Word continuously presents many disclaimers. Jesus was fairly emphatic about the absolute impossibility of reaching heaven apart from himself. The English translation of John 14:6 preserves the precise original word order with its usual emphases: "I am the way, the truth, and the life. No one comes to the Father except through me."

The apostles of Christ are not evasive in this regard either. The apostle Peter, said to be filled with the Holy Spirit, boldly stated: "There is no salvation by anyone else, for no one else in all the wide world has been appointed among men as our only medium by which to be saved" (Acts 4:12).

The apostle Paul declared: "For no other foundation can anyone lay than that which is laid, which is Jesus Christ" (1 Cor 3:11). Again he stated: "For there is one God and one Mediator between God and men, the Man Christ Jesus" (1 Tim. 2:5).

The apostle John plainly said, "This life is in his Son. He who has the Son has life; he who does not have the Son of God does not have life" (1 John 5:11b-12). John's Gospel contains equally plain and strong statements as seen below.

Christ and the apostles taught that in order for one to appropriate the provision of Christ personal faith or belief was a necessity. Furthermore faith cannot be nebulous but must have an object — a correct object if one aspires to a certain goal. The ultimate provision for salvation has always been the death of Jesus Christ. The means of securing salvation has always been faith. But the actual content of faith — that is, what must be believed — has changed with the progressive nature of God's revelation.

Abel's faith, for example, was exhibited in that he "offered *the God-appointed sacrifice*" [A. Saphir, *The Epistle to the Hebrews,* 7th ed., 738]. The content of Abraham's justifying faith, as stated in Genesis 15:6, was that God would fulfill his promise of many descendants.

Since Calvary, the unchanging required content of one's faith is the gospel. Nothing else saves, while all else damns. No substitutions, additions or imitations are permitted. Any other gospel is not another that can save. It only brings with it an anathema (Gal. 1:6-9).

I take issue with Anderson's idea that it is "through the basic fact of God's general revelation, vouchsafed in nature and in all that is true (including, of course, the truth there is in other religions), and the equally fundamental facts of our common humanity, that the Spirit of God, or the 'cosmic Christ,' brings home to men and women something of their need" [Anderson, *The World's Religions,* 236]. Anderson's suggestion is that this conviction may be enough enlightenment to result in salvation apart from ever naming the name of Christ.

Is this possible? If it were, then it seems strange for Paul, who understood so much about general revelation in Romans 1–2, to insist several chapters later that men cannot "call on him in whom they have not believed. . . . And how shall they believe in him of whom they have not heard? And how shall they hear without a preacher? And how shall they preach unless they are sent?" (10:14-15a). Indeed Paul declared: "So then, faith comes by hearing, and hearing by the word of God" (10:17).

Christianity's founder and writing apostles unanimously state the absolute dictum that faith during this dispensation must be placed in none other than Jesus Christ and his finished work on Calvary.

Several examples of cross-cultural conversion in our dispensation are recorded in the New Testament. Each demonstrates hearing this special revelation of the gospel and placing faith in Christ, not a nebulous repentance and faith based on general revelation.

Philip traveled to Samaria, "preached Christ unto them" (Acts 8:5), and "when they believed the things concerning . . . the name of Jesus Christ,

206

they were baptized" (8:12). If they could have been saved without hearing the gospel, why was Philip so concerned to go there? Later an educated court official from Ethiopia was reading Isaiah, perhaps in Hebrew or Aramaic. An angel directed Philip to Gaza. Once he arrived there, the Holy Spirit had him join the inquiring Ethiopian. Philip "preached unto him Jesus" (8:35). This man's conviction and desire to know prompted God to send a prepared messenger to announce the gospel content necessary for salvation.

Cornelius's story in Acts 10 is similar. A Roman centurion, he was a devout and just man who feared God and even prayed to God. The text also makes it clear that he was lost. Yet God would not save him apart from his hearing and believing the gospel. In a vision an angel instructed Cornelius to send for Peter "to hear words" (v. 22), and Cornelius later recalled: "When he comes, he will speak to you" (v. 32). Peter in Acts 11:13-14 recounts concerning Cornelius: "And he told us how he had seen an angel standing in his house, who said to him, 'Send men to Joppa, and call for Simon whose surname is Peter, who will tell you words by which you and all your household will be saved.'"

What were Peter's words? After proclaiming the gospel he exhorted "that, through his name, whoever believes in him will receive remission of sins. While Peter was still speaking these words, the Holy Spirit fell upon all those who heard the word" (10:43b-44).

Every heathen who has ever gotten saved has had to believe that same gospel. The eunuch was saved that way. Cornelius was saved that way. The jailer at Philippi was saved that way. I was saved that way, and so were you if you name the name of Christ. And I do not believe we have any warrant to claim that God is doing things differently today, no matter how frequently it may be surmised.

The New Testament makes it abundantly clear that saving faith must be focused on the person and work of Jesus Christ. Ponder some of Jesus' own words in John's Gospel: "Whoever believes in him should not perish but have eternal life" (3:15). "Whoever drinks the water that I shall give him will never thirst" (4:14). "You are not willing to come to me that you may have life" (5:40). "This is the work of God, that you believe in him whom he sent" (6:29). "I am the bread of life. He who comes to me shall never hunger, and he who believes in me shall never thirst" (6:35). "Everyone who sees the Son and believes in him may have everlasting life" (6:40). "He who believes in me has everlasting life" (6:47). "Unless you eat the flesh of the Son of Man and drink his blood, you have no life in you" (6:53).

"He who believes in me" (7:38). "I am the light of the world. He who follows me shall not walk in darkness but have the light of life" (8:12).

"If you do not believe that I am he, you will die in your sins" (8:24). "I am the door. If anyone enters by me, he will be saved" (10:9). "I am the resurrection and the life. He who believes in me, though he may die, he shall live. And whoever lives and believes in me shall never die" (11:25-26). "I am the way, the truth, and the life. No one comes to the Father except through me" (14:6). "And when he has come, he will convict the world of sin, and of righteousness, and of judgment: of sin, because they do not believe in me" (16:8-9).

Jesus' final words on the necessity of faith being directed in him are in his high-priestly prayer: "I do not pray for these alone, but also for those who will believe in me through their word; that they all may be one, as you, Father, are in me, and I in you; that they also may be one in us, that the world may believe that you sent me" (17:20-21). Notice carefully how Jesus looks down across the centuries with the same plan of salvation in view. No changes are contemplated.

The apostles never moved away from the precept that saving faith can only be in Christ. Paul again and again proclaimed faith in Christ as the only way of salvation. In Galatians, one of Paul's earliest writings, he said, "Knowing that a man is not justified by the works of the law but by faith in Jesus Christ, even we have believed in Christ Jesus, that we might be justified by faith in Christ" (Gal. 2:16). [See also Gal. 2:20; 3:22, 26; Phil. 1:29; Rom. 10:9-13]. John, who penned the last books of the New Testament, said, "But these are written that you may believe that Jesus is the Christ, the Son of God, and that believing you may have life in his name" (John 20:31). "He who has the Son has life; he who does not have the Son of God does not have life" (1 John 5:12). "He who believes in him is not condemned; but he who does not believe is condemned already, because he has not believed in the name of the only begotten Son of God" (John 3:18).

Were the apostles a bit too idealistic to hold that all are condemned who do not personally name Jesus on their lips and believe his gospel? Not at all. They were simply following orders, Jesus' marching orders for the Church as found in the great commission. It was Jesus who said, "Make disciples of all the nations" (Matt. 28:19). It was Jesus who said, "Go into all the world and preach the gospel to every creature. He who believes and is baptized will be saved; but he who does not believe will be condemned" (Mark 16:15-16). It was Jesus who said, "It was necessary for the Christ to suffer and to rise from the dead the third day, and that repentance and remission of sins should be preached in his name to all nations, beginning at Jerusalem" (Luke 24:46-47).

Conclusion

If it was necessary to go then, why not now? If preaching the gospel is required to reach those who are near at hand, why should it not be required to reach those in far-flung lands? Let me pose the question in reverse: If God can save people in faraway places without their hearing and believing the gospel, why can he not accomplish the same everywhere? If taking the gospel to every creature was a concern of Christ's two thousand years ago, why should his *modus operandi* be abandoned now, especially without a word from him to that effect?

Are we more enlightened than our Master? Do we know something that Jesus failed to understand? Our methods can be improved, but our message never. Our methods can change, but our mission is unchanging. To hold out the possibility of any other way of salvation does not add to God's greatness but depreciates his Word and the work of the Church through the ages. To teach any other way of salvation for the heathen diminishes missionary zeal and leaves the helpless hopeless.

Don A. Pittman

Formerly on the faculties of the University of Chicago and Texas Christian University, Pittman currently teaches history of religions and interreligious dialogue at Tainan Theological College and Seminary, Tainan, Taiwan. A specialist in Chinese religions and Buddhist studies, he has been an active participant in interreligious dialogue. In the following selection, from an essay entitled "Testing a Two-Eyed Truth," in reference to John A. T. Robinson's book, *Truth is Two-Eyed*, he proposes four criteria for evaluating truth in inter-traditional dialogue. Source: *Encounter* 53, no. 4 (autumn 1992).

The Dialogical Matrix for Truth Seeking

If a dialogical method for testing truth concerning ultimacy is affirmed, rejected are two commonly adopted parameters for the endeavor. That is, first, many persons wish to limit truth-seeking to inner-personal dialogue. What is determinative in the agent's testing and committal process is his or her own *personal* experience, no matter finally what others may testify about their similar or different experiences. That which is affirmed and valued is that which conforms to the individual's sense of truth. Indeed, for many persons, despite possible appearances of a willingness to entertain perspectival enhancement or correction from others, or an actual willingness for others to live out their own rather different sense of truth — as long as quality of life infringement does not thereby occur — truth is simply "what *I* believe."

Many more persons, however, recognizing the potent dangers in such an individualistic limitation on truth-seeking, extend the parameters of the endeavor to intra-traditional dialogue. That is, to a greater or lesser degree, they are willing to accept that their own personal experience is insufficient as a measure of truth, that they need the confessions of others within their own perspectival community to enhance, correct, and complete their own sense of visionary and ethical truth. Formal criteria for truth may be identified and utilized by the community as a plumb line for all expressions of "truth" within and outside of the particular tradition, past, present, and future. Criteriological precision and deviational limitation become important matters for intra-traditional debate. In this process, use of accepted criteria may permit some persons to observe and celebrate the fact that elements of the truth are affirmed by persons outside the tradition, or even to acknowledge elements of truth in the witness of persons outside the tradition that are not incompatible with the accepted criteria but not fully developed within their own heritage. However, the criteria for truth discernment are fundamentally known and truth is essentially "what *my tradition* believes."

An increasing number of persons today, recognizing the dangers and unfortunate limitations of both inner-personal and intra-traditional parameters for truth-seeking, have advocated the need for inter-traditional, or inter-perspectival dialogue on the broadest scale. The suggested expansion of dialogical horizons is not itself without dangers. The axial issue, of course, is the identification of criteria for truth, criteria that cannot be imposed *prior to the dialogue.* Some certainly argue that to propose transcending tradition-specific criteria is to propose relativism, for in such a dialogue there are no foundational events or persons or texts to serve as an absolute canon for discernment. Syncretism is also often mentioned as a danger, seen either as a sometimes arrogant human attempt to create an unwarranted new heritage from disparate, unconnected, and incompatible elements, and/or the rigid imposition of criteria constructed artificially for a specified end.

The problem is how to *sustain* meaningful inter-traditional dialogue without, perhaps even unconsciously, moving toward relativism — at which point the discussion ends for a lack of interest — or toward a new form of syncretistic exclusivism — at which point the discussion ends for a lack of purpose. The challenge is to find a way to talk seriously and openly with persons from all perspectives about our common life together, about what we understand to be true, extending to them the same expectation for the possibility of learning that we hope they extend to us. That requires a willingness to extend the parameters of truth-seeking beyond inner-personal dialogue (my *personal* experience), intra-traditional dialogue (my *tradition's* experience), to inter-traditional dialogue (our *human* experience).

Some will question, beyond the desirability of such an extension, the practical viability of maintaining a fundamental tension between a particular perspectival commitment (to a form of Christianity, Buddhism, etc.) and a perspectival openness to alternative commitments that requires continual testing. Some have argued that they affirm both the resolute application of tradition-specific criteria for truth and the practice of inter-traditional dialogue. However, the valuing of inter-traditional dialogue in such a case may represent only an attempt to speak respectfully to persons known to be fundamentally mistaken concerning ultimate truth; it may represent a search for elements of confirmation for accepted visionary and ethical truth claims (certainly no extra-traditional grounds would be admitted for disconfirmation); it may involve at most, for some, the theoretical possibility of a modest augmentation of truth through an acceptance of claims not fully recognized or developed in one's own heritage but wholly in consonance with its central tenets. Yet, this does not essentially move beyond the *a priori* declaration that truth is what *my tradition* believes, failing, therefore, to extend fully to what I am describing as inter-traditional or inter-perspectival dialogue.

For the most fragile, expansive form of global dialogue concerning ultimacy, it will be necessary for each participant initially to offer for consideration tentative proposals concerning criteria for visionary and ethical truth. In so doing, tradition-specific criteria need not, indeed cannot, be abandoned. To reiterate, all persons enter into the dialogue with commitments, however ambiguously held. Strategically, it must only be agreed that such tradition-specific criteria function *dialectically* with inter-traditional (tradition-transcending) criteria. Historically Jewish, Christian, Hindu, or Islamic criteria, for example, will be offered for consideration *in relation to* proposed criteriological frameworks for broad inter-traditional dialogue. That is, such articulations of tradition-specific criteria may neither be given immediate primacy in the dialogue nor discounted. They are to be valued for what they represent: important, diverse interpretations of holy revelations, insights, and commitments of human beings who, through them,

212

hope to come closer to the full realization of truth. References, for example, to particular scriptural passages (Vedic, Qur'anic, Biblical, etc.) in inter-traditional discussions of human rights issues, medical ethics, or ecological concerns are important. However, since their canonical authority will not be recognized immediately by all discussants, their claims will require interpretation in relation to tradition-transcending criteria. . . .

Participants must recognize that inter-traditional criteria may not be utilized rigidly in an authoritarian manner, which would rightly justify the criticism that one inter-traditional universal has simply replaced another personal or intra-traditional universal imperialistically. Indeed, it is rather to be contended that proposals for inter-traditional criteria for truth serve to evoke dialogue, public evaluation rather than silent indifference or intolerant condemnation, precisely because they are not explicitly grounded *as such* in the devotional discourse of particular perspectival communities. While admittedly *artificial,* in the sense of representing an artful, crafted stratagem, they should not be judged, prior to careful consideration of their usefulness, as totally *arbitrary,* because the most adequate inter-tradition criteria should resonate with and be suggested by intuitions — in some cases more central, in some cases more peripheral — that are common to a great many perspectival traditions. Moreover, while they may be "artificial," or if one insists "arbitrary" to that extent, they may not be applied *arbitrarily,* i.e., in an insensitive authoritarian manner. A common criticism of efforts to consider inter-traditional criteria is that while a global dialogue concerning beliefs and values may be energetically engaged and relationships facilitated between persons of widely differing commitments to visionary and ethical images and ideals for our life together, no absolute verities are uncompromisingly proclaimed, verities around which the life of all persons must revolve and through which ultimate transformation occurs. This criticism unnecessarily polarizes the options and may reflect a lack of faith in the power of one's visionary and ethical truths to claim through the dialogical process the lives of all people. . . .

Four primary inter-traditional criteria, I would suggest, should initially be explored in testing truth claims: rationality, inclusivity, relationality, and creativity.

By rationality, I mean whether or not a truth claim functions within its structure of signification and more generally in such a way that consistent, critical thought is not obviated. By this I intend not to suggest an unnecessary diminution of reference to ultimate mystery, religious paradox, or faith, or to validate a specifically Western style of philosophical reasoning.

What I wish to propose is that perspectives on truth which open one to the public forum, to the global discussion on significant issues, rather than isolate one in an uncritically accepted worldview, are perspectives more likely to express ultimate truth. A position that is presented as inaccessible to questioning and unnecessary to defend with compelling evidence of any kind is less likely to represent truth.

By inclusivity, I refer appreciatively to Robinson's valuation of "two-eyedness." That is, that which is more likely to be true ultimately is that which appreciates and appropriates diversity. That which is less likely to be true is that which sharply rejects all alternate perspectives or co-opts them via unilateral assimilation. As Paul Knitter has asserted, in arguing for a new model for truth, "what is true will reveal itself mainly by its ability to *relate* to other expressions of truth and to *grow* through these relationships — truth defined not by exclusion but by relation" [*No Other Name?* 219]. This criteria should not be used to support the relativist's position that all perspectives on transformational truth are equally valid or equally false, thus discouraging the very enlivened debate concerning truth discernment that is its aim. Rather, it should be used to identify positions which may be more holistically responsive than others to the range of human experiences and values which deserve a hearing in the public arena.

This second criteria leads naturally to the third, relationality, for that which is most likely to be true is that which is ultimately productive of well-being (wholeness) for all things which constitute the cosmic reality as we know it. Hans Küng has acknowledged the importance of this element with his description of a "general ethical criterion" [*Theology for the Third Millennium*, 240ff.]. Marjorie Suchocki, moreover, has argued, as a feminist, that justice, or well-being, should be the fundamental criterion of value ["In Search of Justice," in *The Myth of Christian Uniqueness*, ed. J. Hick and P. Knitter, 149ff.]. "Well-being," of course, is a polyvalent term which, as Suchocki remarks, can refer to physical and psychological, individual and communal forms. Definitional disagreements at any level of meaning can be significant. Moreover, very different understandings, conditioned by one's context, may exist concerning penultimately destructive choices made for the sake of ultimately productive outcomes. Yet, the criterion is useful in pressing participants in dialogue to attempt to define well-being and to interrelate explicitly visionary and ethical truths. That which is less likely to be true is that which is presented as impervious to such practical demands for the promotion of healthy human relationships and cosmic well-being.

By creativity I intend to suggest as a criterion for transformational truth a future orientation. That is, that which is more likely to be true is that which directs one's attention not only to past verities that require conservation, but to the possibilities for new verities that emerge at the margins of human understanding. Past verities provide the foundation for new insights. Yet, that which is more likely to be false is that which is so concerned with protecting the interpretations of the valued past that there is no freedom for creative insight, no provision or protection for those who labor at the limits of acceptable diversity to quest for greater truth. Creativity links past and present with the future.

It may be objected that these four inter-traditional criteria are not immediately decisive for the resolution of conflicting truth claims. For some, their generality renders them practically useless in contrast to specific inner-personal or intra-traditional criteria. Yet, in response, it is to be argued that the purpose of such criteria is not to serve directly — and one might just as well say imperialistically — as a final canon for truth discernment but *to help to set an agenda for dialogue.* The purpose of this type of proposal for inter-traditional criteria is precisely the promotion of foundational questions, not the provision of final answers. The purpose is to suggest that participation in a global, multi-perspectival, confessional, and truth-seeking discourse on transformational truth is both possible and necessary.

The test of a two-eyed truth, or in our pluralistic culture of any claim concerning what is true ultimately, may *begin* most effectively in dialogue with an inter-traditional exploration of criteria for commitment, a consideration of the range of meanings and applicability of potentially useful criteria such as rationality, inclusivity, relationality, and creativity. Confession *qua confession* of tradition-specific norms and ideals will, of course, in such an exploratory dialogue, be appropriate and necessary in dialectical relation to tradition-transcending norms and ideals. It may even be argued that by *beginning* inter-perspectival dialogue with reflections on useful tradition-transcending criteria for the discernment of truth, tradition-specific criteria, as described by each participant in the midst of dialogue, may receive a more serious consideration than would be the case if they were simply asserted initially. Indeed, it is likely that only by maintaining a reflective process that intentionally appeals to and sensitively relates visionary and ethical insights at all three levels of discourse — the inner-personal, intra-traditional, and inter-traditional — may any of us be said to have opened ourselves to the truth, the complete truth, which shall finally make us free.

A Christian Postscript

Historically, Christians have believed that amidst the vagaries and ambiguities of life the triune God, through the Holy Spirit, remains present with us and will guide us into all truth (John 16:13). While the church is multiform because of divergent *interpretations of* the Christ, the Logos incarnate, the church is fundamentally one because of *trust in* the Christ. Jesus was, we proclaim, decisively disclosive of the Ultimate, though we have never claimed that the Ultimate was, thereby, totally disclosed. God is greater than we have been able to comprehend. Our fundamental commitment, then, is to God and not to our current images of God. We have more to learn about the creative power that sustains all things and relates to all beings than we have thus far understood. This affirmation does not diminish the significance of the witness to truth represented in the voices of scripture and tradition. Yet, it does remind us that the Ultimate draws us into the future to a beatific vision the full dimensions of which we cannot know. Faithfulness, therefore, proceeds not simply by constrictive reiterations of past perceptions but often by expansive interpretations relating our historically dynamic religious heritage to potentially new discernments of God's saving presence among all peoples.

SECTION II

MISSION AND MINISTRY

Global Mission Today:
Seven Key Questions

As our global connectedness becomes an increasingly more prominent reality for the church and a concern for theological education worldwide, three facets of this phenomenon affect most directly the practice of mission and evangelization.

First, since globalization means that world cultures are drawing closer and closer together, the impact of a missions practice in one part of the world is no longer localized to that part of the world. It now affects the whole Christian church.

In the globalization of its mission, the church is not only responding to an essential aspect of its nature, but is also following trends within other spheres of contemporary life. At one time, it seemed as if the only functional global community in the world was the scientific community, in which technology served as the universal language. Within the last three decades, however, a second facet of human culture has also become more and more internationalized: the economic sphere. The state of the total global economy is becoming an important concern for businesses, banks, and securities markets everywhere. Local and regional economies interact within the framework of larger international economic relationships. For example, if the price of oil in the Middle East rises dramatically it affects the vitality of the entire global economy. If the Japanese securities exchange weakens, the whole financial world becomes enervated to some extent. Were the Russian economy completely to collapse, the shock waves would soon be felt around the world, with potentially serious consequences far beyond the borders of the country. Moreover, within the last decade, a third related facet of human culture has become increasingly globalized: the political realm. The important endeavors of the United Nations have never been so diversified. The breakup of the Soviet Union and the decline of communism in Eastern Europe, despite spawning regional conflicts and ethnic strife, have signaled a step forward toward global democracy. Democratic pluralisms are becoming a standard goal or realized feature of a growing majority of world governments.

In addition to these elements of our growing sense of connectedness, an awareness of "world Christianity" is quickly becoming a fourth dimension of the globalization that members of the church are experiencing. In fact, it is becoming increasingly difficult to talk about churches in North America, East Asia, Africa, or anywhere else, acting unilaterally on any issue. Actions in the United States have effects on churches in Romania and Egypt. Christian communities in India and Brazil make decisions that change the way British and Australian Christians understand and seek to make their witness known. This means that Christian mission and evangelism are becoming global in a way never seen before in the history of the church.

Second, Christianity's extraordinary missionary successes are having an unanticipated effect on the Western Christian church. As the gospel becomes indigenous to cultures far different from those of Europe and North America, theologians from other continents are sending the Good News back to the West in diverse and fascinating forms.

Missions has clearly become a two-way cultural street. For example, while North Americans have engaged in mission work in Korea, Korean churches are now sending missionaries to the United States to engage in evangelization within our rather secularized society. Asian and African theologians have not only studied the theological classics of the Western church, but are now writing theologies being studied by Western Christians that reflect not only the truth of the gospel but the realities of their local cultures. Furthermore, while Western churches have raised moneys to support multidimensional mission endeavors in Asia, the Korean Christian Church, in the wake of the Los Angeles riots in 1992, sent $100,000 in relief money to L.A. churches to help with the rebuilding, and more recently additional moneys to help with the earthquake disaster in southern California.

These examples, which could be multiplied, highlight the loss of a center of the modern missionary movement as it was identified in the "Great Century of Missions," often dated 1815-1914. Christianity began, of course, as a small Jewish sect in Palestine. Yet, by the mid-fourth century it had emerged as the official religion of the Roman Empire, through the patronage of Constantine and his three sons. After the Empire's collapse, and especially after the rise of Islam in the Middle East, the religion's heartland was centered in Europe. As modern Europe became more secularized during the nineteenth and twentieth centuries, and as the churches in the former American colonies flourished with religious freedoms, in many respects the church's missionary center, especially for Protestantism, shifted to the United States. However, since World War II, in view of challenges to all imperialistic attitudes and actions, and encouraged by the growth of Christian ecumenism, the sense of mutuality within the global church has developed to the point where it is clearly more difficult now to identify Christianity's missionary center. Worldwide Christianity, with all the mutual exchanges, interactions, and influences within a global church which that implies, is becoming — some say has already become — a definite reality.

Third, globalization presents the missionaries of the world with unparalleled opportunities and dangers.

Closer ecumenical contacts within the church, more diverse cultural influences within society, and critical eco-justice challenges that affect the entire created order make today's Christian missionary effort an exciting endeavor in which to be involved. How the church responds to its challenges and opportunities in this axial period in history will thoroughly test its integrity in discipleship. Access to satellite communications means that it is now feasible to perceive more vividly many aspects of the world's woundedness and to share more freely those perceptions with almost all Christians worldwide as we wrestle with our calling. Advances in transportation technologies mean that missionaries are increasingly mobile and can quickly respond to situations where needed. A greater number of democratic governments means fewer and fewer societies are closed to the church's mission work. In such a context, the global church is presented with new opportunities for ministries of word and deed.

Yet every opportunity has inherent within it seeds of danger. Unique opportunities may be squandered while committees are formed and debates continue concerning appropriate responses. New forms of imperialism and domination may emerge when differences cannot be quickly resolved. Some new strategies for mission may be ineffective or counterproductive. Accordingly, questions about the definition of Christian mission, the methodologies of missionaries, and even questions about the ends of mission itself are being raised with a renewed intensity in the light of globalization.

The edited readings by missiologists and missionaries that follow in this second section of the book address many of these fundamental questions concerning mission and ministry. The selections call attention to the seismic shifts taking place in missions circles today and a number of the patterns that have emerged through practical theological reflection on the nature of the church's discipleship. In fact, all of the readings address one or more of *seven key questions of missions:*

1. What is mission?

The question of definition is an extremely important one today because many Christians obviously disagree over what misson means. Of course, professional missiologists within the church constantly develop different definitions and theoretical models in relation to different understandings of scripture and history; thus, scholarly theological inquiry in the church and the academy proceeds by and thrives on criticism in dialectical movements between tradition and innovation. Yet key terms such as mission, evangelism, and witness are not merely technical theological terms about which scholars may form judgments without caution. Why? Because many Christians who are not technical scholars use them and are quite sure of what they mean. That is, these terms have common, everyday usages in the life of congregations. For a great many Christians, mission means what missionaries go overseas to do; evangelism is telling the gospel story so that people who have not heard it or do not believe it come to believe it. Witness is telling other people what Jesus Christ means to one's life. The *American Heritage Dictionary,* for example, reflecting the weight of Christian tradition, defines mission as "a body of persons sent to do religious work overseas"; evangelism is defined as "the zealous preaching and dissemination of the gospel"; witness is defined as "to testify to."

In the last century in particular, some missiologists have raised serious questions about the appropriateness of these commonsense definitions, have wondered aloud whether in our time Christians should be zealous about mission (when it refers strictly to going overseas) to do evangelism (when it means solely encouraging people to change the way they believe) by witnessing (when it merely entails expressing to others verbally what Jesus Christ means to them). As we in the church have learned more about other great religions and cultures, and have come to appreciate more manifestly the unique gifts and strengths of each, some missiologists have suggested that Christians in mission are not called simply to reshape other cultures or to negate other religions. Mission, some have argued, ought primarily to mean being resolutely but sensitively Christian in the presence of others; evangelism ought basically to mean responding, when asked, why Christians believe and act as they do; witnessing ought most fundamentally to mean the living of a compassionate Christian life. Among the authors included in our selection, Alexandre Ganoczy falls in this category.

Other missiologists, like Donald McGavran, reject attempts to move away from what they take to be the commonsense meanings of such key terms. In view of the fact that most people in the church already know what mission, evangelism, and witness mean, such scholars assert, these meanings should be retained. If new understandings are ventured concerning how and where God is at work and what God is calling us as individuals and as a church to do in relation to people who are not Christian, then let different terminology be developed that is clear and distinctive. Christians will still not all agree on priorities in global ministry. Yet at least we will be able to avoid confusion as we prayerfully debate those issues. As Paulos Mar Gregorios, for example, remarks in his essay, "The Witness of the Churches," "The modern Christian use of the term 'witness' seems to imply a meaning somewhat different from what ordinary usage ascribes to it. . . . Theologians . . . find it quite difficult to distinguish adequately between witness, mission and evangelism if the terms are defined in an all-inclusive manner. The confusion that now prevails in the ecumenical jargon can only be described as monumental."[1]

Similar confusion today surrounds many key words like "salvation," "uniqueness," and "absoluteness." As we have seen, the question of who is saved and who is not saved is an extremely controversial theological issue today. Are only those who explicitly name the name of Jesus in faith saved? Are only sincere and compassionate religious seekers saved, whether Christian or not? Is everyone saved? Is it even proper to ask a question to which only God has the answer, or to talk about individual salvation without in the same breath talking about the "salvation," or "transformative healing" of larger cultural, economic, and political systems? Increasingly, in theological discourse Christians are forced to define clearly what they mean when they employ the term "salvation."

The related question of what the "uniqueness" of Christianity might

1. Paulos Mar Gregorios, "The Witness of the Churches: Ecumenical Statements on Mission and Evangelism," *The Ecumenical Review,* July 1988.

mean is similarly being raised. In essays included here, for example, Michael Amaladoss argues that a new, more inclusive paradigm concerning God's activity in the world is needed to frame an understanding of Christianity's uniqueness, while Lesslie Newbigin asserts that the more traditional and exclusive view, with some modifications, will serve us just fine. Amaladoss wishes to describe the particular identity of Christians in relation to the larger reality of God's universal saving will that is present and active everywhere through various ways. "It is a plan progressively realized in history," he states. "It leads to the unification of all things till God is all in all." Newbigin disagrees with this approach, which tends to diminish the radical newness of God's revelation in Jesus Christ, and he laments the fact that many Christians today "are less ready to affirm the uniqueness, the centrality, the decisiveness of Jesus Christ as universal Lord and Savior, the Way by following whom the world is to find its true goal, the Truth by which every other claim to truth is to be tested, the Life in whom alone life in its fullness is to be found."

A related question regards the "absoluteness" of the Christian claims. Some in the church, while willing to affirm Christianity's *uniqueness* — in the sense that there is no other religion that makes the exact same claims — stop short of endorsing its *absoluteness* — in the sense that it and it alone describes Ultimate Truth. Ganoczy, who represents this theological trend, writes, in fact: "What then is the relationship between Christianity . . . and the other religions? Whenever they are experienced seriously and sincerely by men of good will, they are relative seeds of an absolute plant." Again, many Christians disagree with this stance because for them the Christian religion, in so far as it attends to God's once and for all revelation in Jesus Christ, is both unique and absolute.

This question of definitions and the related practical missiological issues are, of course, complex. Yet many Christians would support Gregorios's call for attention to terminological clarity. At least they would urge that unnecessary ambiguities be avoided in order for interpretive options to stand forth for critical scrutiny in relation to attempts to envision where God is leading the church in ministry.

2. Why do mission?

Like the definition of mission, the goal of mission is hotly debated in churches today. One answer that remains compelling for many is that we engage in mission in order to save souls. In their statement, "To the Ends of the Earth: A Pastoral Statement on World Mission," the National Conference of Catholic Bishops in the U.S.A. explicitly affirms this view. They declare forthrightly that "Conversion [is] the goal of mission. Though dialogue is a vital characteristic of mission, it is not the goal of missionary proclamation." Pope John Paul II is similarly clear about conversion in "Redemptoris Missio." McGavran, writing from an evangelical Protestant Christian point of view, is equally specific: "The primary mission of the church is to tell everyone everywhere of God's provision for salvation and to enroll in the ark of salvation — the church of Jesus Christ — as many as believe." Some church leaders would even argue that the sole criterion for determining success in mission is whether new Christian converts are being baptized.

Many Christians, however, also recognize the need to provide in mission for the material welfare of other human beings who are in need, i.e., for the hungry, the thirsty, the stranger, the naked, the sick, and the imprisoned. As even McGavran, who emphasizes the eternal salvation of souls, puts it, "Christians believe and the Scriptures teach that it is God's purpose in salvation that the whole individual be benefited. The Scriptures say, 'Seek first the kingdom of God, and his righteousness,' and clothes, food and other material blessings will be added unto you (Matt. 6:33). Reconciled people live better in this world than do the unreconciled. The church, made up of saved sinners, is a community whose members obey God's laws and care for each other." Of course, especially within the ecumenically minded Protestant churches, there are those who give principal emphasis to this understanding of the goal of mission.

A third and strongly argued goal is peace and justice. Mortimer Arias, for example, talking about missions to Latin America, says that "there is a converging thrust to recover the whole Gospel, for the whole person, and for the whole of Latin American society." For Arias and others, the whole of society means not just the religious part but the political and the economic parts. Politics and economics are too often characterized by injustice and evil. It is part of the church's mission to address these injustices and evils, helping the oppressed to confront and forgive their oppressors, while helping the oppressors to repent of their sins and to work actively toward reconciliation and reciprocity.

A fourth goal often articulated for the church's mission is for the provision of spiritual encouragement for peoples everywhere. Grant McClung, speaking from a Pentecostal perspective, notes that "for pentecostals, the Holy Spirit is personally active, living in and directing its servants. The Holy Spirit is not just a force or influence but personally and powerfully potent on the frontiers of mission." By focusing on the spiritual dimension, some missiologists find it easier to talk about the cross-cultural dimensions of Christianity and its relationship to other ethnic, racial, and religious groups. The goal is to tap into that common spiritual heritage and give it a specifically Christian meaning.

A fifth goal for mission is to plant the church. Traditionally it has been the Roman Catholic Church that has emphasized this goal. One does not have to read far in "Redemptoris Missio" to sense the importance of church planting as a goal of Roman Catholic missions. However, other Christian traditions also stress the importance of church planting. As McClung puts it, "Pentecostals have seen the planting of responsible, reproducing congregations as the abiding fruit of world evangelism and have often measured their progress, as Robert Bryant Mitchell has said, 'by the development of mature congregations and the buildings which they erect.' "

All of these goals play an important part in missions, as many have affirmed. The pope, Michael Amaladoss, and James Engel specifically mention the importance of using a wide variety of mission methodologies and of recognizing the several goals that the New Testament seems to delineate as proper aims of witness. Some Christian leaders continue to lament the confusion that has resulted from different perspectives on the goal of mission. Others cite the inefficiency that overlapping mission efforts have created in some contexts — the disparity between the large number of competing missionaries, for example, sent to impoverished countries like Haiti and the relative lack of missionaries sent to the growing number of secularized, industrialized megacities of the world. Still others argue for a variety of approaches for practical as well as theological reasons, noting that different mission problems require flexibility in approach. Political conditions, for example, sometimes mean that certain strategies (e.g., public preaching) may become inadvisable or illegal and that other methods are needed.

3. Who are the missionaries?

The traditional model of the missionary may be summarily stated in the following way: "A 'Western' Christian, trained in a Bible College in Europe or the United States, and sent to either Africa or Asia for an extended period of time to evangelize a tribal group in a remote part of the countryside."

Although other missionary models have emerged, it is probable that if you surveyed the average church member in the West and presented a kind of free association test with the word "missionary," this basic paradigm would be found to persist.

In fact, however, this stereotypical image is no longer the dominant one. Because of the globalization trends we have already noted, significant changes have taken place in the identity of missionaries. Four of the more significant changes include the move from foreign to indigenous missionaries, from professional to lay missionaries, from career to short-term missionaries, and from Western to Eastern and Southern missionaries.

From foreign to indigenous. This change is not particularly new in its conception, but in terms of practical implementation it is just coming into its own. It has long been recognized that persons reared within a particular culture have a better chance of explaining religious concepts to people of that culture than those outside and ignorant of the culture. Their chances of being effective witnesses are greatly increased by experiential knowledge of language, thought-forms, and sociological structure.

The argument, however, goes far beyond one of effectiveness. Some missiologists have stressed the danger of a monocultural approach to mission in which the essence of Christianity is effectively identified with one culture (i.e., Western), which becomes an inevitable associate of the gospel. Arias expresses it this way: "[We must] see missionaries as indigenous agents [rather] than as historical transmitters. Another way of putting it is to say that the missionary became a figure of cross-cultural significance rather than one of determined foreign domination."

This helpful recognition of the dangers of cultural imperialism on the part of the sending church, however, should not, emphasize some missiologists, lead to an idealization and romanticization of indigenous target cultures at the expense of the universal truth of the Christian gospel. Truth ought not be sacrificed at the altar of cross-cultural sensitivity. When this has happened, the result has been either a cultural objectification in reverse or a kind of cultural relativism where any cultural expression of Christianity is judged to be as valid and good as any other, with little regard for a kind of enduring spiritual truth that supersedes culture. Recognition of this cultural overreaction has led some to argue provocatively concerning cross-cultural mission that while the various cultural manifestations of Christianity are lacking in important respects, each should also be seen as having valuable insights into the essence of the faith. Lamin Sanneh has written most convincingly on this exciting dynamic.

From professional to lay. The globalization of mission, paradoxically, entails the localization or contextualization of mission. Increasingly, the Christian mission field is no longer envisaged to be strictly overseas somewhere; it is equally to be engaged within our unique local neighborhoods, which are globally interrelated. In view of the large number of our neighbors whose lives are largely shaped by secular values, and in light of the growing missionary endeavors of many other religions in our pluralistic societies, the mission field begins right at our doorsteps. In fact, more than ever now the church is growing in its self-understanding toward a "missionhood of the believer." Everyone is in fact a missionary.

In addition, again in contrast to predominant stereotypes, missionaries are no longer strictly ordained professionals, Christians called and set apart, specially trained in theology and languages, and sent overseas for an extended period of time to preach the gospel. Although many such people continue to engage in ministries in countries other than that of their origin, lay missionaries with a variety of gifts for proclamation and service play an increasingly important role in the work of the church universal.

From career to short-term. The sending out of witnesses to the gospel (the root meaning of the word mission) often continues to be at the initiation of a single church or church-related organization which determines needs in another setting and develops strategic plans to address them. Yet, in many cases today, missionaries are appointed only in response to direct requests for a specific kind of assistance for a limited time from partner churches overseas. While this is intended to recognize the significance of mutuality in the extension and acceptance of invitations, and of the practical abilities of indigenous churches to discern where God is leading them and where they need help, some critics charge that this practice poses unnecessary delimitations on sending churches.

This approach is not unrelated to the concept of the short-term versus the career missionary. Short-term missionaries are those who are sent out with defined responsibilities for a specified length of time, often with no intention of repeating the experience. Short-term missions may last from a few days spent helping to erect a church building in another country, to three months solving something like a water problem in a village, to perhaps a year establishing a church-related hospital somewhere. Many factors have made the short-term mission feasible: the ease of travel, the technology to solve difficult technical problems relatively quickly, and the project orientation of many baby-boomer achievers.

From Western missionaries to Eastern and Southern missionaries. Perhaps the most significant development in missions — at least for those who have been inspired by the image of the sacrificial Western Christian missionary commissioned to live among the non-Christian peoples of the East and South — is that the formerly non-Christian Eastern and Southern Hemispheres are now sending missionaries to the West. Japanese and Korean missionaries, for example, abound in Europe and the United States, trying to offer a word of salvation to people in an anti-spiritual, materialist culture that is grounded in a dangerous overemphasis on individual freedoms. On the one hand, some understand this continuing trend in "reverse mission" as a great compliment to the Western church, as a sign of the success of its mission to Asia, Africa, and South America, as well as a sign of maturity of the younger mission churches which look beyond their own welfare to engage in global mission elsewhere in the world. On the other hand, some westerners still find it difficult for whatever reason to receive Christian missionaries from other countries.

4. Who are the missionized?

There is no more contentious question in all of missiology than that which seeks to identify just who it is that Christians should be missionizing. The traditional answer, of course, is that all persons who do not claim Jesus Christ as their personal Lord and Savior are the proper objects of mission. In this respect, the stance of Christianity has parallels to other great world religions. The articles by Swami Palami, Frank Whaling, and Isma'il al-Faruqi, regarding Hindu, Buddhist, and Islamic mission respectively, have been included to emphasize this common religious outlook. Al-Faruqi remarks, for example: "The Muslim is to never give up that God may guide his fellow-man to the truth. The example of his own life, his commitment to the values he professes, his engagement, constitute his final argument. If the non-Muslim is still not convinced, the Muslim is to rest his case with God."

Yet decisions concerning who actually needs to be brought into the fold are important. Some within the church think that those individuals who appear to have a deep faith in another one of the great world religions and are leading compassionate lives of service surely must have some kind of relationship with the triune God in the interiority of their souls. Therefore, it is sometimes maintained that Christian missionaries need not be so concerned with such persons. Sincere religious followers from all traditions should concentrate their energies less on fruitless spiritual competi-tion with one another and more on those whose lives are informed by secular non-religious and anti-religious ideologies. A few in the church are even willing to claim further that no one needs missionizing. God will eventually save the elect — whether that be all humankind or a few — in spite of their best attempts to rebel, so Christians need to concentrate more on the faithfulness of their own spiritual journey in relationship with God through Christ. The issue of universalism has in particular become one of the great battlegrounds in the church.

An interesting middle position has developed in Christian as well as other missionary traditions. It is typified by a further comment made by al-Faruqi regarding Muslim missions. "Da'wah (evangelism) in Islam," he writes, "has never been thought of as exclusively addressed to the non-Muslims. All men stand under the obligation to actualize the divine pattern in space and time. This task is never complete for any individual." A parallel Christian emphasis on mission as something that everyone needs appears to blur the distinction between evangelism and discipleship. As a result, many think that this is less than helpful. Others argue, however, that it may beneficially reduce the unhealthy, arrogant triumphalism that has often accompanied missions efforts in the past. If we Christians will only realize, they charge, that we need to be constantly growing in our own faith, it may appropriately reduce whatever inclinations we may have to view ourselves as spiritually superior to non-Christians.

5. Where do we do mission?

There seem to be three answers to this question. The first is "to the ends of the earth." Again, this is the traditional answer, and Newbigin reminds us that the call to go everywhere has not been vitiated by the globalizing factors within our contemporary world.

The second answer is that we need to engage in mission only within the local context. We cannot effectively do mission in cultures of which we are not a part. The gaps are too great, and we must trust the Holy Spirit of God to work in all cultures in ways that for those of us in other cultures can only be described as mysterious.

The third answer is that we should engage in mission only where we are specifically invited by indigenous partner churches. While some may object to the characterization, an analogous relation has been suggested between this position and the "Prime Directive" of the popular television series, *Star Trek: The Next Generation:* i.e., to serve respectfully within another social setting only where and to the extent permitted by the existing rules of local culture.

Interestingly, these three positions on the context of mission are not precisely correlated with various theological positions. Many conservative missiologists can be found advocating a more limited, home-looking missiological context, particularly given the growing secularization of Western culture. Craig Van Gelder writes eloquently about the needs of America as a mission field, while, on the contrary, many theologically liberal missiologists still see the whole world as the context of mission.

6. How do we do mission?

There have never been more methodologies available to Christian missionaries. This is in large part due to the tremendous technological sophistication of the modern world. Satellite hook-ups, high-speed printing presses, computerized market targeting, and mass distribution capabilities mean that the gospel can be told, written, and marketed in literally thousands of different forms and locales.

Yet the question of methodology has been heightened in recent years because there is a growing willingness to use diverse missiological methods in relation to the varying demands of the particular cultural context. Formerly, most missiological agencies tended to see themselves as specialists in a particular methodological approach. More and more, however, they are using a wider variety of approaches in order to meet more effectively the needs of different cultures. Questions surrounding methods employed have thus become crucial, particularly in cases where some see the essence of the gospel story being distorted by the medium. Yet these enduring mission questions have been joined by new ones:

(a) Questions of power: Can the gospel, the story of strength through weakness, be truthfully told when there is such a power disparity between sending and receiving agencies in today's mission market? Arias raises this issue in his analysis of the historic problems in Latin American missions, where the gospel has too often been paired with the power of Western marketing techniques and too little identified with the needs of the poor. How can the strong help the weak when the real resources of the gospel teach servanthood and love?

(b) Questions of money: Jonathan Bonk raises some extremely important questions regarding the lifestyle of Western missionaries when compared with the poorer cultures to which they are often sent. The disparities between a gospel that counsels satisfaction with little and current lifestyles that constantly demand more are sometimes so sharp that the whole purpose of mission seems to be lost — or worse, transformed into a message of economic growth. Yet many find an answer to this real dilemma in responsible and sacrificial stewardship and in forms of self-imposed poverty.

(c) Questions of technology: Technology has succeeded in making life longer, easier, and more convenient. However, significant questions can be raised about whether technology has made life more profound, meaningful, and joyous. Thus, when technology is applied to missions, some question whether we risk the danger of achieving the bigger and better at the expense of the truer and the more spiritual. The technological revolution cannot be rolled back, of course, even in the area of missions. The real question is whether it can be made compatible with the Good News.

7. What is the nature of the competition?

In one sense the nature of the "competition" to the story of Jesus Christ should be seen as inconsequential. Jesus himself said that if you are for God, it does not matter who lines up on the other side. The truth that Jesus taught is an all-encompassing, positive, accepting, loving message. However, the question of competition endures.

The question continues to be raised, in part, because there is no shortage of self-proclaimed competitors to the story of Jesus. The articles by Palami, Whaling, and al-Faruqi make clear that Hindus, Buddhists, and Muslims understand their traditions as valid alternatives to the Christian tradition. Sometimes spiritual competition is seen as friendly and cooperative, sometimes as hostile. Yet however congenial interreligious relations might be in particular times and places, other religious communities, many of which share with the church certain beliefs and values, ultimately do not interpret the meaning of life in the same way as Christians.

For some in the church the primary opposition to Christian efforts is interpreted as coming from Satan; the principalities and powers are seen to be aligned against the Christian community as they have never been before. As McGavran notes, our problems originated with humankind being "tempted by Satan," and Satan continues to harass us. Missions must never underestimate the power of that harassment, nor be lulled into seeing opposition as lying solely within some penultimate power (social institutions, political systems, religious traditions, etc.) when it can ultimately be traced to its root cause, the "father of all lies." For still other Christians, the ultimate root cause is secularism, the neglect of the spiritual realm altogether. We live in a day and age where it is unfashionable to be too explicit about one's spiritual leanings, and it is this apathy toward anything that cannot be measured, counted, touched, or banked that forms the real opposition to the Christian message.

These seven key questions may be found woven into the fabric of the collection of readings that follow. The selections are intended to exemplify the different forms of piety and sometimes sharply conflicting theological perspectives that shape the life of the church today. It is crucial that Christians everywhere grapple with each of these seven questions and come to some conclusions about them for themselves. Only by each of us taking that kind of personal responsibility for the mission of the church, entering into dialogue with God and one another about the difficult issues involved, will the mission of the church continue to prosper.

Discussion Questions:

1. How has the mission task changed in the twentieth century?

2. What do you see as the principal mission challenges of the twenty-first century?

3. What do you understand to be the proper goals of Christian mission? How do you prioritize the multiple legitimate goals of mission?

4. How has the increasing interaction between the religions of the world affected the Christian mission effort?

5. What role does culture play in the mission endeavors?

6. What are the potential dangers of the various cultural expressions of Christianity? Can you cite an example?

7. What are the potential benefits of the various cultural expressions of Christianity? Can you cite an example?

8. How can the issues of economic and power disparities between missionaries and the people whom they come to serve be addressed?

9. Are there guidelines for using modern "technologies" that can lessen the dangers of mission mediums distorting the mission message?

For Further Reading:

Barrett, David. *World Christian Encyclopedia.* Nairobi: Oxford University Press, 1982.

Bosch, David. *Transforming Mission: Paradigm Shifts in Theology of Mission.* Maryknoll: Orbis Books, 1991.

Douglas, J. D., ed. *Let the Earth Hear His Voice.* Minneapolis: World Wide Publications, 1975.

DuBose, Francis. *Classics of Christian Missions.* Nashville: Broadman Press, 1979.

Griffiths, Paul J. *Christianity through Non-Christian Eyes.* Maryknoll: Orbis Books, 1990.

Hutchison, William. *Errand to the World: American Protestant Thought and Foreign Missions.* Chicago: University of Chicago Press, 1987.

Kraemer, Hendrik. *The Christian Message in a Non-Christian World.* London: Edinburgh House Press, 1937.

Latourette, Kenneth. *A History of the Expansion of Christianity.* 7 vols. New York: Harper, 1937-45.

Mott, John R. *The Evangelization of the World in This Generation.* London: Student Volunteer Movement, 1902.

Neill, Stephen. *A History of Christian Missions.* New York: Penguin Books, 1986.

FOUR VIEWS OF MISSION

Redemptoris Missio

Pope John Paul II

To commemorate the twenty-fifth anniversary of Vatican II's Decree on Missionary Activity, John Paul II published his eighth encyclical, entitled *Redemptoris Missio.* The Latin title of the council document, *Ad Gentes* ("to all peoples"), is the major theme of the encyclical: the pope distinguishes sharply among missionary activity, pastoral care, and the reevangelization of people "who no longer consider themselves members of the church and live a life far removed from Christ and his Gospel" (#33). Only the mission *ad gentes* is missionary activity proper; missionary activity consists in proclaiming Christ as the only Savior (#4) and working toward the establishment of the church in all parts of the world. . . . We have reprinted several important parts of the two hundred-page encyclical: the first section reprints the christocentric sections of the document, along with its treatment of the reign (kingdom) of God. Also included are the pope's important reflections on the new kinds of Areopagus that today's world presents to evangelizers and his cautious appraisal of interreligious dialogue. Source: *New Directions in Mission and Evangelization: Basic Statements 1: 1974-1991,* ed. James Scherer and Stephan Bevans (Maryknoll: Orbis Books, 1992), 169-76.

The church's universal mission is born of faith in Jesus Christ as is stated in our Trinitarian profession of faith: "I believe in one Lord, Jesus Christ,

237

the only Son of God, eternally begotten of the Father. . . . For us men and for our salvation he came down from heaven: By the power of the Holy Spirit he was born of the Virgin Mary and became man." The redemption event brings salvation to all, "for each one is included in the mystery of the redemption and with each one Christ has united himself forever through this mystery." It is only in faith that the church's mission can be understood and only in faith that it can find its basis.

Nevertheless, also as a result of the changes which have taken place in modern times and the spread of new theological ideas, some people wonder: Is missionary work among non-Christians still relevant? Has it not been replaced by interreligious dialogue? Is not human development an adequate goal of the church's mission? Does not respect for conscience and for freedom exclude all efforts at conversion? Is it not possible to attain salvation in any religion? Why then should there be missionary activity?

"No One Comes to the Father but by Me" (John 14:6)

5. If we go back to the beginnings of the church, we find a clear affirmation that Christ is the one savior of all, the only one able to reveal God and lead to God. In reply to the Jewish religious authorities who question the apostles about the healing of the lame man, Peter says: "By the name of Jesus Christ of Nazareth whom you crucified, whom God raised from the dead, by him this man is standing before you well. . . . And there is salvation in no one else, for there is no other name under heaven given among men by which we must be saved" (Acts 4:10, 12). This statement, which was made to the Sanhedrin, has a universal value, since for all people — Jews and Gentiles alike — salvation can only come from Jesus Christ. . . .

Thus, although it is legitimate and helpful to consider the various aspects of the mystery of Christ, we must never lose sight of its unity. In the process of discovering and appreciating the manifold gifts — especially the spiritual treasures — that God has bestowed on every people, we cannot separate those gifts from Jesus Christ, who is at the center of God's plan of salvation. Just as "by his incarnation the Son of God united himself in some sense with every human being," so too "we are obliged to hold that the Holy Spirit offers everyone the possibility of sharing in the paschal mystery in a matter known only to God. God's plan is "to unite all things in Christ, things in heaven and things on earth" (Eph. 1:10). . . .

238

The Kingdom in Relation to Christ and the Church

17. Nowadays the kingdom is much spoken of, but not always in a way consonant with the thinking of the church. In fact, there are ideas about salvation and mission which can be called *anthropocentric* in the reductive sense of the word inasmuch as they are focused on man's earthly needs. In this view, the kingdom tends to become something completely human and secularized; what counts are programs and struggles for a liberation which is socioeconomic, political and even cultural, but within a horizon that is closed to the transcendent. Without denying that on this level too there are values to be promoted, such a notion nevertheless remains within the confines of a kingdom of man, deprived of its authentic and profound dimensions. Such a view easily translates into one more ideology of purely earthly progress. The kingdom of God, however, "is not of this world . . . is not from the world" (John 18:36).

There are also conceptions which deliberately emphasize the kingdom and which describe themselves as "kingdom centered." They stress the image of a church which is not concerned about herself, but which is totally concerned with bearing witness to and serving the kingdom. It is a "church for others" just as Christ is the "man for others." The church's task is described as though it had to proceed in two directions: on the one hand promoting such "values of the kingdom" as peace, justice, freedom, brother-hood, etc., while on the other hand fostering dialogue between peoples, cultures and religions so that through a mutual enrichment they might help the world to be renewed and to journey ever closer toward the kingdom.

Together with positive aspects, these conceptions often reveal negative aspects as well. First, they are silent about Christ: The kingdom of which they speak is "theocentrically" based, since, according to them, Christ cannot be understood by those who lack Christian faith, whereas different peoples, cultures and religions are capable of finding common ground in the one divine reality, by whatever name it is called. For the same reason they put great stress on the mystery of creation, which is reflected in the diversity of cultures and beliefs, but they keep silent about the mystery of redemption. Furthermore, the kingdom, as they understand it, ends up either leaving very little room for the church or undervaluing the church in reaction to a presumed "ecclesiocentrism" of the past and because they consider the church herself only a sign, for that matter a sign not without ambiguity.

239

18. This is not the kingdom of God as we know it from revelation. The kingdom cannot be detached either from Christ or from the church.

Mission *Ad Gentes* Retains Its Value

33. The fact that there is a diversity of activities in the church's one mission is not intrinsic to that mission, but arises from the variety of circumstances in which that mission is carried out. Looking at today's world from the viewpoint of evangelization, we can distinguish three situations.

First, there is the situation which the church's missionary activity addresses: peoples, groups and sociocultural contexts in which Christ and his Gospel are not known or which lack Christian communities sufficiently mature to be able to incarnate the faith in their own environment and proclaim it to other groups. This is mission *ad gentes* in the proper sense of the term.

Second, there are Christian communities with adequate and solid ecclesial structures. They are fervent in their faith and in Christian living. They bear witness to the Gospel in their surroundings and have a sense of commitment to the universal mission. In these communities the church carries out her activity and pastoral care.

Third, there is an intermediate situation, particularly in countries with ancient Christian roots and occasionally in the younger churches as well, where entire groups of the baptized have lost a living sense of the faith or even no longer consider themselves members of the church and live a life far removed from Christ and his Gospel. In this case what is needed is a "new evangelization" or a "re-evangelization." . . .

34. Missionary activity proper, namely the mission *ad gentes*, is directed to "peoples or groups who do not yet believe in Christ," in whom the church "has not yet taken root" and whose culture has not yet been influenced by the Gospel. It is distinct from other ecclesial activities inasmuch as it is addressed to groups and settings which are non-Christian, because the preaching of the Gospel and the presence of the church are either absent or insufficient. It can thus be characterized as the work of proclaiming Christ and his Gospel, building up the local church and promoting the values of the kingdom. The specific nature of this mission *ad gentes* consists in its being addressed to "non-Christians." It is therefore necessary to ensure that this specifically "missionary work that Jesus entrusted and still entrusts each day to his church" does not become an

indistinguishable part of the overall mission of the whole people of God and as a result become neglected or forgotten.

On the other hand, the boundaries between pastoral care of the faithful, new evangelization and specific missionary activity are not clearly definable, and it is unthinkable to create barriers between them or to put them into watertight compartments. Nevertheless, there must be no lessening of the impetus to preach the Gospel and to establish new churches among peoples or communities where they do not yet exist, for this is the first task of the church, which has been sent forth to all peoples and to the very ends of the earth. Without the mission *ad gentes,* the church's very missionary dimension would be deprived of its essential meaning and of the very activity that exemplifies it.

Also to be noted is the real and growing interdependence which exists between these various saving activities of the church. Each of them influences, stimulates and assists the others. The missionary thrust fosters exchanges between the churches and directs them toward the larger world, with positive influences in every direction. The churches in traditionally Christian countries, for example, involved as they are in the challenging task of new evangelization, are coming to understand more clearly that they cannot be missionaries to non-Christians in other countries and continents unless they are seriously concerned about the non-Christians at home. Hence missionary activity *ad intra* is a credible sign and a stimulus for missionary activity *ad extra* and vice versa. . . .

Parameters of the Church's Mission *Ad Gentes*

37. By virtue of Christ's universal mandate, the mission *ad gentes* knows no boundaries. Still, it is possible to determine certain parameters within which that mission is exercised in order to pin a real grasp of the situation.

(a) *Territorial limits.* Missionary activity has normally been defined in terms of specific territories. The Second Vatican Council acknowledged the territorial dimension of the mission *ad gentes* dimension which even today remains important for determining responsibilities, competencies and the geographical limits of missionary activity. Certainly a universal mission implies a universal perspective. Indeed, the church refuses to allow her missionary presence to be hindered by geographical boundaries or political barriers. But it is also true that missionary activity *ad gentes,* being different from the pastoral care of the faithful and the new evangelization of the non-practicing, is exercised within well-defined territories and groups of people.

The growth in the number of new churches in recent times should not deceive us. Within the territories entrusted to these churches — particularly in Asia, but also in Africa, Latin America and Oceania — there remain vast regions still to be evangelized. In many nations entire peoples and cultural areas of great importance have not yet been reached by the proclamation of the Gospel and the presence of the local church. Even in traditionally Christian countries there are regions that are under the special structures of the mission *ad gentes,* with groups and areas not yet evangelized. Thus, in these countries too there is a need not only for a new evangelization, but also, in some cases, for an initial evangelization.

Situations are not, however, the same everywhere. While acknowledging that statements about the missionary responsibility of the church are not credible unless they are backed up by a serious commitment to a new evangelization in the traditionally Christian countries, it does not seem justified to regard as identical the situation of a people which has never known Jesus Christ and that of a people which has known him, accepted him and then rejected him while continuing to live in a culture which in a large part has absorbed Gospel principles and values. These are two basically different situations with regard to the faith.

Thus the criterion of geography, although somewhat imprecise and always provisional, is still a valid indicator of the frontiers toward which missionary activity must be directed. There are countries and geographical and cultural areas which lack indigenous Christian communities. In other places, these communities are so small as not to be a clear sign of a Christian presence, or they lack the dynamism to evangelize their societies or belong to a minority population not integrated into the dominant culture of the nation. Particularly in Asia, toward which the church's mission *ad gentes* ought to be chiefly directed, Christians are a small minority even though sometimes there are significant numbers of converts and outstanding examples of Christian presence.

(b) *New worlds and new social phenomena.* The rapid and profound transformations which characterize today's world, especially in the Southern Hemisphere, are having a powerful effect on the overall missionary picture. Where before there were stable human and social situations, today everything is in flux. One thinks, for example, of urbanization and the massive growth of cities, especially where demographic pressure is greatest. In not a few countries, over half the population already lives in a few "megalopolises," where human problems are often aggravated by the feeling of anonymity experienced by masses of people.

In the modern age, missionary activity has been carried out especially in isolated regions which are far from centers of civilization and which are hard to penetrate because of difficulties of communication, language or climate. Today the image of mission *ad gentes* is perhaps changing: Efforts should be concentrated on the big cities, where new customs and styles of living arise together with new forms of culture and communication, which then influence the wider population. It is true that the "option for the neediest" means that we should not overlook the most abandoned and isolated human groups, but it is also true that individuals or small groups cannot be evangelized if we neglect the centers where a new humanity, so to speak, is emerging and where new models of development are taking shape. The future of the younger nations is being shaped in the cities.

Speaking of the future, we cannot forget the young, who in many countries comprise more than half the population. How do we bring the message of Christ to non-Christian young people, who represent the future of entire continents? Clearly, the ordinary means of pastoral work are not sufficient: What are needed are associations, institutions, special centers and groups, and cultural and social initiatives for young people. This is a field where modern ecclesial movements have ample room for involvement.

Among the great changes taking place in the contemporary world, migration has produced a new phenomenon: Non-Christians are becoming very numerous in traditionally Christian countries, creating fresh opportunities for contacts and cultural exchanges, and calling the church to hospitality, dialogue, assistance and, in a word, fraternity. Among migrants, refugees occupy a very special place and deserve the greatest attention. Today there are many millions of refugees in the world and their number is constantly increasing. They have fled from conditions of political oppression and inhuman misery, from famine and drought of catastrophic proportions. The church must make them part of her overall apostolic concern.

Finally, we may mention the situations of poverty — often on an intolerable scale — which have been created in not a few countries and which are often the cause of mass migration. The community of believers in Christ is challenged by these inhuman situations: the proclamation of Christ and the kingdom of God must become the means for restoring the human dignity of these people.

(c) *Cultural sectors: the modern equivalents of the Areopagus.* After preaching in a number of places, St. Paul arrived in Athens, where he went to the Areopagus and proclaimed the Gospel in language appropriate to and understandable in those surroundings (cf. Acts 17:22-31). At that time the Areopagus represented the cultural center of the learned people of Athens, and today it can be taken as a symbol of the new sectors in which the Gospel must be proclaimed.

The first Areopagus of the modern age is the world of communications, which is unifying humanity and turning it into what is known as a "global village." The means of social communication have become so important as to be for many the chief means of information and education, of guidance and inspiration in their behavior as individuals, families and within society at large. In particular, the younger generation is growing up in a world conditioned by the mass media. To some degree perhaps this Areopagus has been neglected. Generally, preference has been given to other means of preaching the Gospel and of Christian education, while the mass media are left to the initiative of individuals or small groups and enter into pastoral planning only in a secondary way. Involvement in the mass media, however, is not meant merely to strengthen the preaching of the Gospel. There is a deeper reality involved here: since the very evangelization of modern culture depends to a great extent on the influence of the media, it is not enough to use the media simply to spread the Christian message and the church's authentic teaching. It is also necessary to integrate the message into the "new culture" created by modern communications. This is a complex issue, since the "new culture" originates not just from whatever context is eventually expressed, but from the very fact that there exist new ways of communicating, with new languages, new techniques and a new psychology. Pope Paul VI said that "the split between the Gospel and culture is undoubtedly the tragedy of our time," and the field of communications fully confirms this judgement.

There are many other forms of the "Areopagus" in the modern world toward which the church's missionary activity ought to be directed; for example, commitment to peace, development and the liberation of peoples; the rights of individuals and peoples, especially those of minorities; the advancement of women and children; safeguarding the created world. These too are areas which need to be illuminated with the light of the Gospel.

We must also mention the important "Areopagus" of culture, scientific research and international relations which promote dialogue and open up new possibilities. We would do well to be attentive to these modern areas of activity and to be involved in them. People sense that they are, as it were, travelling together across life's sea and that they are called to ever greater unity and solidarity. Solutions to pressing problems must be studied, discussed and worked out with the involvement of all. That is why international organizations and meetings are proving increasingly important in many sectors of human life, from culture to politics, from the economy to research. Christians who live and work in this international sphere must always remember their duty to bear witness to the Gospel.

38. Our times are both momentous and fascinating. While on the one hand people seem to be pursuing material prosperity and to be sinking ever deeper into consumerism and materialism, on the other hand we are witnessing a desperate search for meaning, the need for an inner life and a desire to learn new forms and methods of meditation and prayer. Not only in cultures with strong religious elements, but also in secularized societies the spiritual dimension of life is being sought after as an antidote to dehumanization. This phenomenon — the so-called "religious revival" — is not without ambiguity, but it also represents an opportunity. The church has an immense spiritual patrimony to offer mankind, a heritage in Christ, who called himself "the way, and the truth and the life" (John 14:6): It is the Christian path to meeting God, to prayer, to asceticism and to the search for life's meaning. Here too there is an "Areopagus" to be evangelized. . . .

Dialogue with Our Brothers and Sisters of Other Religions

55. Interreligious dialogue is a part of the church's evangelizing mission. Understood as a method and means of mutual knowledge and enrichment, dialogue is not in opposition to the mission *ad gentes;* indeed it has special links with that mission and is one of its expressions. This mission, in fact, is addressed to those who do not know Christ and his Gospel, and who belong for the most part to other religions. In Christ, God calls all peoples to himself, and he wishes to share with them the fullness of his revelation and love. He does not fail to make himself present in many ways, not only to individuals but also to entire peoples through their spiritual riches, of which their religions are the main and essential expression even when they contain "gaps, insufficiencies and errors." All of this has been given ample emphasis by the council and the subsequent magisterium, without detracting in any way from the fact that salvation comes from Christ and that dialogue does not dispense from evangelization.

In the light of the economy of salvation, the church sees no conflict between proclaiming Christ and engaging in interreligious dialogue. Instead, she feels the need to link the two in the context of her mission *ad gentes.* These two elements must maintain both their intimate connection and their distinctiveness; therefore they should not be confused, manipulated or regarded as identical as though they were interchangeable.

I recently wrote to the bishops of Asia: "Although the church gladly acknowledges whatever is true and holy in the religious traditions of Buddhism, Hinduism and Islam as a reflection of that truth which enlightens all men, this does not lessen her duty and resolve to proclaim without fail Jesus Christ, who is 'the way and the truth and the life.' . . . The fact that the followers of other religions can receive God's grace and be saved by Christ apart from the ordinary means which he has established does not thereby cancel the call to faith and baptism which God wills for all people" [*L'Osservatore Romano,* July 18, 1990]. Indeed, Christ himself, "while expressly insisting on the need for faith and baptism, at the same time confirmed the need for the church, into which people enter through baptism as through a door." Dialogue should be conducted and implemented with the conviction that the church is the ordinary means of salvation and that she alone possesses the fullness of the means of salvation.

Contemporary Evangelical Theology of Mission

Donald A. McGavran

Donald McGavran was the driving force behind the large, well-respected School of World Mission of Fuller Theological Seminary. For evangelicals the key to mission is individual salvation. The planting of the church is important, but only as a means toward the end of personal decisions for Christ. Source: Arthur F. Glasser and Donald A. McGavran, *Contemporary Theologies of Mission* (Grand Rapids: Baker, 1983).

Our portrayal of the evangelical theology of mission will not exactly suit all the many branches of the Christian church. Lutheran evangelicals will, in this chapter, miss some distinctive Lutheran stresses. Methodist evangelicals will miss some of the wordings they treasure. Calvinists would have phrased some of these doctrines differently. Indeed the phrasings we have used have been chosen, not because they represent our exact thought on the subject, but rather because we believe they represent common evangelical theological positions. Every evangelical church has its own wordings designed to fit both its understanding of the central teachings of the Bible and those contemporary issues of particular importance in its place of labor. We hope the following wordings of the main doctrines of the evangelical theology of mission will be accepted by evangelicals as substantially the truth set forth in the Bible. . . .

The Main Doctrines or Axioms

1. *The Absolute Inspiration and Authority of the Bible.* God has not left men and women to wonder and speculate concerning the eternal verities about Himself, humankind, sin, salvation, eternal lostness, eternal life, ethical conduct, freedom of will, the worship of idols, and the deification of human ideals, whether of power, sex, or money. On all these and other matters of enormous interest to human beings, God has given a clear revelation of His will. This is called special revelation. It is contained in the Bible, which is God's Word, His deliberate disclosure of His holy will through inspired writers. . . .

2. *The Doctrine of the Soul and of Eternal Life.* Each individual is an immortal soul in a physical body. When one believes on Jesus Christ, one's sins are forgiven. Now saved, the individual has become a new creation and entered on eternal life. He or she starts to live as a member of God's household, part of the body of Christ. After the death of the physical body, both body and soul, in God's good time, are raised to eternal life. 1 Corinthians 15:52 says, "The dead will be raised imperishable and we shall be changed." The whole passage, verses 50 to 56, is a clear statement of this doctrine. . . .

3. *The Doctrine of the Lostness of the Human Race and of Eternal Salvation.* God, by His Word and His glory, freely created the world out of nothing. He made Adam and Eve in His own image as the crown of creation, that they might have fellowship with Him. Tempted by Satan they rebelled against God. They were estranged from their Maker, yet responsible to Him. Therefore, apart from grace, we humans are incapable of returning to God. We are fallen beings. Unless we turn in faith to the Redeemer, we are lost. Through faith in Jesus Christ and His atoning death, we are justified by God, our sins are forgiven, we receive eternal life. We become part of the chosen race, the royal priesthood. This is eternal salvation. Eternal salvation is not gained by living a moral life or accepting one of the humanly devised ideologies or religions. It comes only through faith in Jesus Christ and His redemptive work for us. The evangelical theology of mission rejects universalism — the teaching that all will be saved — on the grounds that it is not part of the biblical revelation.

4. *The Doctrine of Christ, the Only Mediator.* The only Mediator between God and the human race is Christ Jesus our Lord, God's eternal Son, who, being conceived by the Holy Spirit, was born of the virgin Mary. He fully shared and fulfilled our humanity by His life of perfect obedience. By His death in our

stead, He revealed the divine love and upheld divine justice, removing our guilt and reconciling us to God. There is therefore no way to be reconciled to God other than by believing and trusting in the atonement He has wrought by Christ. Since Jesus Christ is the only Mediator, it is by Him alone that we can come to God. There is no other name by which we can be saved. Only as people of every race, culture, language, condition, and economic status believe on Jesus Christ is it possible for them to be reconciled to God.

Evangelicals are well aware of the problem which this doctrine raises concerning those many millions who through no fault of their own do not know the gospel of Christ or are not in touch with His church. Yet evangelicals cannot believe that God will save such men and women, counting their belief in Baal, Ashtaroth, modern civilization, Rama, Krishna, Gautama, Marx, or money as sufficient to win them salvation. Rather evangelicals believe that, according to the teaching of the Bible, those who do not believe in Christ are lost. Evangelicals also believe that God is sovereign. Should He so choose, He can bring those who know nothing of Jesus Christ back into fellowship with Himself. But the means by which He might do this (and whether in point of fact He ever does do it) remain hidden. God has not chosen to reveal this in Scripture.

In consequence of this doctrine, an inescapable responsibility rests on Christians to proclaim the gospel and tell men and women everywhere of the only Mediator between God and them, and the only way of salvation, the cross of Christ.

5. *The Doctrine of the Church as Christ's Body, the Household of God.* God by His Word and Spirit creates the one holy and universal and apostolic church, calling sinners of the whole human race into the fellowship of Christ's body. By the same Word and Spirit, He guides and preserves for eternity the new redeemed humanity, the church of Jesus Christ, which (no matter what their tribe, caste, clan, class, culture, or economic condition) is spiritually one with the people of God in all ages and constitutes the church of Christ on earth. . . .

6. *Evangelization and the End Time.* The Bible repeatedly tells us of the last day, the day of judgment, the end of this world and the beginning of God's perfect rule in a new heaven and a new earth. The twenty-fourth chapter of Matthew is only one of several passages which portray the ingathering of God's people from among the Gentile nations as preparatory to the end of the age. The present world will pass away. The signs of the last day are the beginnings of the birth pangs of the new world — the perfect kingdom of God. It is coming. Nothing can stop it. Before it comes,

however, the world must be evangelized. "This gospel of the kingdom will be preached in the whole world as a testimony to all nations, and *then* the end will come" (Matt. 24:14, NIV, emphasis added). . . .

7. *The Primary Mission of the Church.* God has given the church many tasks to perform. The church must evangelize the world and assemble Christians for worship, adoration of God, and systematic instruction in His Word. The church must rear its children in the fear and admonition of the Lord, and apply Christ's teaching on individual and corporate levels, so that all areas of life, whether the family, neighborhood, city, state, or world, will gradually be transformed till God's will rules them all. Jesus came preaching this kingdom of God.

Among these various tasks, the primary mission of the church is to tell everyone everywhere of God's provision for salvation and to enroll in the ark of salvation — the church of Jesus Christ — as many as believe. The church is both the body of Christ (and thus has eternal value in and of itself) and God's instrument for the propagation of the gospel and the spread of His kingdom. Evangelicals reject the false doctrine that the only valid goal is a Christian social order, and that the church is only a temporary expedient, an instrument toward this end. To be sure, the church is God's instrument. Our great Head does use His body toward His ends. But the church is also the bride of Christ and has an absolute value completely separate from the achievement of a transformed society or an evangelized world. . . .

8. *The Doctrine of the Holy Spirit.* The Holy Spirit, the third person of the Trinity, who empowers believers to lead holy and righteous lives, also impels them to fervent, intelligent evangelism of *panta ta ethne*. Evangelism, whether of nominal Christians in the neighborhood or of persons in nearby and faraway lands who have never heard, is carried out under the direction of the Holy Spirit. Evangelism is not initiated by humans. We would never evangelize on our own. The nominal fringe of the church has no interest in winning others to life in Christ. The whole missionary movement is inspired, guided, directed, and brought to fruition by the Holy Spirit. . . .

Doctrines Speaking to Current Issues

1. *Biblical Truth Applied to Non-Christian Religions.* The day when Christians and non-Christians were separated by vast distances and Christians knew little or nothing of non-Christian religions has passed. Today, knowledge of non-Christian religions and ideologies is widely available. Courses

in Communism, Hinduism, Buddhism, humanism, and the like are taught in every university. Many of the teachers of these courses believe that all religions are merely what various people have thought about God, human freedom, the soul, life after death, and similar subjects. Consequently one system is just as likely as another to voice at least some truth. Relativism pervades the intellectual climate of today. It holds that the Bible is not especially revealed by God, but (like other religious books) is a compilation of what humans have thought. Literary and historical criticism of the Bible, when applied on the presupposition that it is merely a human creation, encourages the growth of relativism.

Let us see what the evangelical doctrine of revelation and the Bible has to say to this modern condition. God has made evident to men and women what is to be believed about Himself. His attributes, eternal power, and divine nature have from the beginning been clearly seen. But men and women, even though they knew God, did not honor Him as God, but became futile in their speculations and exchanged the glory of the incorruptible God for images in the form of corruptible humans, birds, beasts, and crawling creatures. They exchanged the truth of God for a lie (Rom. 1:18-23). Some of the religious systems and ideologies formed by humans are sublime, some reasonable, some fanciful, and some are gross distortions of God and of the human race. As Christians study non-Christian religions (whether these be Marxist, humanist, Hindu, Muslim, Buddhist, or others), they rejoice in all true insights which human beings, using their God-given reason, have been able to form; but Christians measure truth always by the revealed Word of God. Evangelicals do not believe that men and women by their own unaided wisdom can perceive and frame religious truths which are superior to those given by God through His prophets and His Son. Evangelicals, however, teach that by observing the excellencies of some parts of non-Christian ideologies and systems, Christians may be stimulated to a fresh study of the Bible and find there truths of which they have been insufficiently aware.

2. *Biblical Truth Applied to Dialogue.* With the collapse of European empires, many European Christians suddenly realized that if they met their former subjects at all, they would meet them as equals. Consequently the Europeans asked, "How does one preach Christ to one's equals?" Certainly not, they thought, by proclaiming the truth. That would alienate the non-Christian. It is far better to talk as equals. To listen as well as speak. Respectfully to lay before the other what one believes to be the truth. Monologue — a superior telling an inferior of truth the latter does not know — must give place to dialogue or a joint search for truth.

What biblical truth does the evangelical apply to this demand for dialogue? God has commanded that the gospel be proclaimed to the ends of the earth, and that Christians bear witness to Jesus Christ everywhere and disciple all the *ethne* in the world. An essential part of this doctrine is that men and women are saved as they hear the gospel and believe on Jesus Christ. The Christian is an ambassador beseeching all to be reconciled to God through belief in Christ. Proclamation may be by word or deed, and must be unabashedly intentional. Of course, some aspects of Christian life are so winsome that without intentional proclamation outsiders may be attracted to the gospel, but the Christian who does not intend proclamation cannot lay claim to fulfilling God's command. Intentional witness and intentional proclamation are the duty of Christians and churches.

Dialogue with people of other faiths (and of no faith), listening to them and engaging them in discourse about ethics, religions, rites, ceremonies, and sacred books, and, in the process, telling them of Christ, is obviously one method by which the Christian discharges the Lord's command to spread the gospel. In dialogue, one can proclaim. One can also proclaim the gospel by distributing tracts, reading the Bible aloud, showing films, broadcasting by radio, teaching Scripture in schools, taking some sort of social action, treating patients in Christ's name, and many other ways. Dialogue is one of these. Christians may use dialogue as a method.

However, the Christian cannot use dialogue as philosophy. That is, in dialogue with a non-Christian one is not to agree in advance that what both of them believe are equally true. One cannot say, "Both of us have part of the truth. Let us pool what we know and come to a greater understanding of the truth." Such dialogue denies the authority of the Bible and is inadmissible in any sound theology of mission. The Bible tells us what God has revealed about Himself, the human race, eternal life, sin, salvation, and the like. No human knowledge, whether of Christians or non-Christians, can successfully contravene that authority. A Christian may properly engage in dialogue, provided he or she holds firmly to the final authority of the Bible. . . .

3. *Biblical Truth Applied to Holistic Evangelism.* We live in a world where Marxism has ridiculed all thought of the future life as "pie in the sky by and by." Communists have set out to give to peasants and factory laborers the food, comfort, health, education, and housing which formerly were available only to the wealthy. The northern fourth of the human race lives in affluence. The southern three-fourths live in poverty. Remembering our Lord's ministry to the poor and goaded by Marxist teachings and ridicule, some Christians are loudly proclaiming that any evangelism which so much

as mentions eternal life is a detriment to the Christian cause. Instead, they say, we need an evangelism which spends all its efforts fighting for temporal this-worldly improvements for the poor in every land. Facing today's conditions, this is "holistic evangelism."

What Christian truth does the evangelical bring to bear on this cry for holistic evangelism? Christians believe and the Scriptures teach that it is God's purpose in salvation that the whole individual be benefited. The Scriptures say, "Seek ye first the kingdom of God, and his righteousness," and clothes, food and other material blessings will be added unto you (Matt. 6:33, KJV). Reconciled people live better in this world than do the unreconciled. The church, made up of saved sinners, is a community whose members obey God's laws and care for each other. Thus they, by God's grace, achieve a better life than do non-Christians. It is serious error to believe that becoming a Christian confers a benefit recognizable only after death. The salvation of Christ influences all aspects of human life, making them sweeter, more just, more harmonious, more peaceful, and more abundant. Eternal life is a reality and so is abundant temporal life.

In accordance with this doctrine, Christian missions through the ages have engaged in education, medicine, agriculture, development, and reconciliation of groups at enmity with each other. Many forms of social action and uplift have been carried on. A large part of the budget of most missionary societies has been spent on acts of humanization. Evangelicals repudiate the lie that they have neglected serving the present life of men and women. They point to whole populations delivered from disease, to famines alleviated, to school systems spread throughout entire nations, and to consciences pricked concerning the evils of untouchability in India, slavery in Africa, and other inhuman conditions in other lands. Christian mission, more than any other factor, has been responsible for the rise and spread of the movement to Christian unity. Holistic evangelism is — and has been — an essential part of Christian mission as revealed by the Bible.

However, in framing the doctrine of holistic evangelism we must take seriously our Lord's words in Mark 8:36, "What does it profit a man to gain the whole world, and forfeit his soul?" (NASB). When to these words we add those recorded in Mark 9:43-48, it becomes clear that no this-worldly good can compare with eternal salvation. Our Lord said, "If your eye causes you to stumble, cast it out; it is better for you to enter the kingdom of God with one eye, than having two eyes, to be cast into hell, where their worm does not die, and the fire is not quenched" (NASB).

253

Mission and Evangelism —
An Ecumenical Affirmation

WCC Central Committee

The *Ecumenical Affirmation* which follows may be the single most important ecumenical statement on mission in the last two decades. In 1976, following the Fifth Assembly of the World Council of Churches at Nairobi (1975), the WCC Central Committee asked the CWME to prepare a document containing the basic convictions of the ecumenical movement on mission and evangelism. In July 1982 the Central Committee gave its approval to the document which was then sent to member churches for their study, inspiration, and guidance. The document has been warmly acclaimed in both conciliar and nonconciliar circles as a statement of convergence. The key to the document's favorable reception lies in its simple, nontechnical, biblical language and in its selection of seven "basic convictions" on mission and evangelism. Source: *New Directions in Mission and Evangelization 1: Basic Statements 1974-1991*, ed. James Scherer and Stephan Bevans (Maryknoll: Orbis Books, 1992), 36-51.

Preface

The biblical promise of a new earth and a new heaven where love, peace and justice will prevail (Ps. 85:7-13; Isa. 32:17-18, 65:17-25 and Rev. 21:1-2)

254

invites our actions as Christians in history. The contrast of that vision with the reality of today reveals the monstrosity of human sin, the evil unleashed by the rejection of God's liberating will for humankind. Sin, alienating persons from God, neighbour and nature, is found both in individual and corporate forms, both in slavery of the human will and in social, political and economic structures of domination and dependence.

The Church is sent into the world to call people and nations to repentance, to announce forgiveness of sin and a new beginning in relations with God and with neighbours through Jesus Christ. This evangelistic calling has a new urgency today. In a world where the number of people who have no opportunity to know the story of Jesus is growing steadily, *how necessary it is to multiply the witnessing vocation of the church!* . . .

The Call to Mission

The present ecumenical movement came into being out of the conviction of the churches that the division of Christians is a scandal and an impediment to the witness of the Church. There is a growing awareness among the churches today of the inextricable relationship between Christian unity and missionary calling, between ecumenism and evangelization. "Evangelization is the test of our ecumenical vocation." . . .

The Call to Proclamation and Witness

The mission of the Church ensues from the nature of the Church as the Body of Christ, sharing in the ministry of Christ as Mediator between God and His Creation. This mission of mediation in Christ involves two integrally related movements — one from God to Creation, and the other from Creation to God. The Church manifests God's love for the world in Christ — through word and deed, in identification with all humanity, in loving service and joyful proclamation; the Church, in that same identification with all humanity, lifts up to God its pain and suffering, hope and aspiration, joy and thanksgiving in intercessory prayer and eucharistic worship. Any imbalance between these two directions of the mediatory movement adversely affects our ministry and mission in the world.

Only a Church fully aware of how people in the world live and feel and think can adequately fulfill either aspect of this mediatory mission. It

255

is at this point that the Church recognizes the validity and significance of the ministry of others to the Church, in order that the Church may better understand and be in closer solidarity with the world, knowing and sharing its pains and yearnings. Only by responding attentively to others can we remove our ignorance and misunderstanding of others, and be better able to minister to them.

At the very heart of the Church's vocation in the world is the proclamation of the kingdom of God inaugurated in Jesus the Lord, crucified and risen. Though its internal life of eucharistic worship, thanksgiving, intercessory prayer, through planning for mission and evangelism, through a daily lifestyle of solidarity with the poor, through advocacy even to confrontation with the powers that oppress human beings, the churches are trying to fulfill this evangelistic vocation.

The starting point of our proclamation is Christ and Christ crucified. "We preach Christ crucified, a stumbling block to Jews and folly to Gentiles" (1 Cor. 1:23). The Good News handed on to the Church is that God's grace was in Jesus Christ, who "though he was rich, yet for your sake he became poor, so that by his poverty you might become rich" (2 Cor. 8:9). . . .

It is this Jesus that the Church proclaims as the very life of the world because on the cross he gave his own life for all that all may live. In him misery, sin and death are defeated once and forever. They cannot be accepted as having final power over human life. In him there is abundant life, life eternal. The Church proclaims Jesus, risen from the dead. Through the resurrection, God vindicates Jesus, and opens up a new period of missionary obedience until he comes again (Acts 1:11). The power of the risen and crucified Christ is now released. It is the new birth to a new life, because as he took our predicament on the cross, he also took us into a new life in his resurrection. "When anyone is united to Christ, there is a new creation; the old has passed away, behold, the new has come" (2 Cor. 5:17).

Evangelism calls people to look towards that Jesus and commit their life to him, to enter into the kingdom whose king has come in the powerless child of Bethlehem, in the murdered one on the cross.

Ecumenical Convictions

In the ecumenical discussions and experience, churches with their diverse confessions and traditions and in their various expressions as parishes, monastic communities, religious orders, etc., have learned to recognize each other as participants in the one worldwide missionary movement. *Thus, together, they can affirm an ecumenical perception of Christian mission expressed in the following convictions under which they covenant to work for the kingdom of God.*

1. Conversion

The proclamation of the Gospel includes an invitation to recognize and accept in a personal decision the saving lordship of Christ. It is the announcement of a personal encounter, mediated by the Holy Spirit, with the living Christ, receiving his forgiveness and making a personal acceptance of the call to discipleship and a life of service. God addresses himself specifically to each of his children, as well as to the whole human race. Each person is entitled to hear the Good News. Many social forces today press for conformity and passivity. Masses of poor people have been deprived of their right to decide about their lives and the life of their society. While anonymity and marginalization seem to reduce the possibilities for personal decisions to a minimum, God as Father knows each one of his children and calls each of them to make a fundamental personal act of allegiance to him and his kingdom in the fellowship of his people.

While the basic experience of conversion is the same, the awareness of an encounter with God revealed in Christ, the concrete occasion of this experience and the actual shape of the same differs in terms of our personal situation. The calling is to specific changes, to renounce evidences of the domination of sin in our lives and to accept responsibilities in terms of God's love for our neighbour. John the Baptist said very specifically to the soldiers what they should do; Jesus did not hesitate to indicate to the young ruler that his wealth was the obstacle to his discipleship.

Conversion happens in the midst of our historical reality and incorporates the totality of our life, because God's love is concerned with that totality. Jesus' call is an invitation to follow him joyfully, to participate in his servant body, to share with him in the struggle to overcome sin, poverty and death. . . .

2. The Gospel to All Realms of Life

In the Bible, religious life was never limited to the temple or isolated from daily life (Hos. 6:4-6; Isa. 58:6-7). The teaching of Jesus on the kingdom of God is a clear reference to God's loving lordship over all human history. We cannot limit our witness to a supposedly private area of life. The lordship of Christ is to be proclaimed to all realms of life. In the Great Commission, Jesus said to his disciples: "All authority in heaven and on earth has been given to me. Go, therefore, and make disciples of all nations, baptizing them in the name of the Father and of the Son and of the Holy Spirit, teaching them to obey all that I have commanded you. And lo, I am with you always, to the close of the age" (Matt. 28:19-20). The Good News of the kingdom is a challenge to the structures of society (Eph. 3:9-10; 6:12) as well as a call to individuals to repent. "If salvation from sin through divine forgiveness is to be truly and fully personal, it must express itself in the renewal of these relations and structures. Such renewal is not merely a consequence but an essential element of the conversion of whole human beings."

"The Evangelistic Witness is directed towards all of the *ktisis* (creation) which groans and travails in search of adoption and redemption. . . . The transfiguring power of the Holy Trinity is meant to reach into every nook and cranny of our national life. . . . The Evangelistic Witness will also speak to the structures of this world; its economic, political, and societal institutions. . . . We must re-learn the patristic lesson that the Church is the mouth and voice of the poor and the oppressed in the presence of the powers that be. In our own way we must learn once again 'how to speak to the ear of the King, on the people's behalf. . . . Christ was sent for no lesser purpose than bringing the world into the life of God." . . .

3. The Church and Its Unity in God's Mission

To receive the message of the kingdom of God is to be incorporated into the body of Christ, the Church, the author and sustainer of which is the Holy Spirit. The churches are to be a sign for the world. They are to intercede as he did, to serve as he did. Thus Christian mission is the action of the body of Christ in the history of humankind — a continuation of Pentecost. Those who through conversion and baptism accept the Gospel of Jesus partake in the life of the body of Christ and participate in an historical tradition. Sadly there are many betrayals of this high calling in the history of the churches. Many who are attracted to the vision of the kingdom find it difficult to be attracted to the concrete reality of the Church. They are invited to join in a continual process of renewal of the churches. "The challenge facing the churches is not that the modern world is unconcerned about their evangelistic message, but rather whether they are so renewed in their life and thought that they become a living witness to the integrity of the Gospel. The evangelizing churches need themselves to receive the Good News and to let the Holy Spirit remake their life when and how he wills."

The celebration of the eucharist is the place for the renewal of the missionary conviction at the heart of every congregation. According to the Apostle Paul, the celebration of the eucharist is in itself a "proclamation of the death of the Lord until he comes" (1 Cor. 11:26). "In such ways God feeds his people as they celebrate the mystery of the Eucharist so that they may confess in word and deed that Jesus Christ is Lord, to the glory of God the Father."

The eucharist is bread for a missionary people. We acknowledge with deep sorrow the fact that Christians do not join together at the Lord's table. This contradicts God's will and impoverishes the body of Christ. The credibility of our Christian witness is at stake.

Christians are called to work for the renewal and transformation of the churches. Today there are many signs of the work of the Holy Spirit in such a renewal. *The house gatherings of the Church in China or the Basic Ecclesial Communities in Latin America, the liturgical renewal, biblical renewal, the revival of the monastic vocation, the charismatic movement, are indications of the renewal possibilities of the Church of Jesus Christ.*

In the announcement to the world of the reconciliation in Jesus Christ, churches are called to unite. Faced with the challenge and threat of the world, the churches often unite to defend common positions. But common witness should be the natural consequence of their unity with Christ in his mission. . . .

4. Mission in Christ's Way

"As the Father has sent me, even so I send you" (John 20:21). The self-emptying of the servant who lived among the people, sharing in their hopes and sufferings, giving his life on the cross for all humanity — this was

Christ's way of proclaiming the Good News, and as disciples we are summoned to follow the same way. "A servant is not greater than his master; nor is he who is sent greater than he who sent him" (John 13:16).

Our obedience in mission should be patterned on the ministry and teaching of Jesus. He gave his love and his time to all people. He praised the widow who gave her last coin to the temple; he received Nicodemus during the night; he called Matthew to the apostolate; he visited Zacchaeus in his home; he gave himself in a special way to the poor, consoling, affirming and challenging them. He spent long hours in prayer and lived in dependence on and willing obedience to God's will.

An imperialistic crusader's spirit was foreign to him. Churches are free to choose the ways they consider best to announce the Gospel to different people in different circumstances. But these options are never neutral. Every methodology illustrates or betrays the Gospel we announce. In all communications of the Gospel, power must be subordinate to love.

Our societies are undergoing a significant and rapid change under the impact of new communication technologies and their applications. We are entering the age of the information society, characterized by an ever increasing media presence in all relationships, both interpersonal and intersocial. Christians need to re-think critically their responsibility for all communication processes and re-define the values of Christian communications. In the use of all new media options, the communicating church must ensure that these instruments of communication are not masters, but servants in the proclaiming of the kingdom of God and its values. As servants, the new media options, kept within their own limits, will help to liberate societies from communication bondage and will place tools in the hands of communities for witnessing to Jesus Christ.

5. Good News to the Poor

There is a new awareness of the growing gap between wealth and poverty among the nations and inside each nation. It is a cruel reality that the number of people who do not reach the material level for a normal human life is growing steadily. An increasing number of people find themselves marginalized, second-class citizens unable to control their own destiny and unable to understand what is happening around them. Racism, powerlessness, solitude, breaking of family and community ties are new evidences of the marginalization that comes under the category of poverty.

There is also a tragic coincidence that most of the world's poor have not heard the Good News of the Gospel of Jesus Christ; or they could not receive it, because it was not recognized as Good News in the way in which it was brought. This is a double injustice: they are victims of the oppression of an unjust economic order or an unjust political distribution of power, and at the same time they are deprived of the knowledge of God's special care for them. To announce the Good News to the poor is to begin to render the justice due to them. The Church of Jesus Christ is called to preach the Good News to the poor following the example of its Lord who was incarnated as poor, who lived as one among them and gave to them the promise of the kingdom of God. Jesus looked at the multitudes with compassion. He recognized the poor as those who were sinned against, victims of both personal and structural sin.

Out of this deep awareness came both his solidarity and his calling to them (Matt. 11:28). His calling was a personalized one. He invited them to come to him, to receive forgiveness of sins and to assume a task. He called them to follow him, because his love incorporated his respect for them as people created by God with freedom to respond. He called them to exercise this responsibility towards God, neighbours and their own lives. The proclamation of the Gospel among the poor is a sign of the messianic kingdom and a priority criterion by which to judge the validity of our missionary engagement today. . . .

A growing consensus among Christians today speaks of God's preferential option for the poor. We have there a valid yardstick to apply to our lives as individual Christians, local congregations and as missionary people of God in the world. . . .

6. Mission in and to Six Continents

Everywhere the churches are in missionary situations. Even in countries where the churches have been active for centuries we see life organized today without reference to Christian values, a growth of secularism understood as the absence of any final meaning. The churches have lost vital contact with the workers and the youth and many others. This situation is so urgent that it commands priority attention of the ecumenical movement. The movement of migrants and political refugees brings the missionary frontier to the doorstep of every parish. The Christian affirmations on the worldwide missionary responsibility of the Church will be credible if they are authenticated by a serious missionary engagement at home. As the world becomes smaller, it is possible even for Christians living far away to be aware of and inspired by faithful missionary engagement in a local situation. Of special importance today is the expression of solidarity among the churches crossing political frontiers and the symbolic actions of obedience of one part of the body of Christ that enhance the missionary work of other sectors of the Church. So, for example, while programmes related to the elimination of racism may be seen as problems for some churches, such programmes have become, for other churches, a sign of solidarity, an opportunity for witness and a test of Christian authenticity. Every local congregation needs the awareness of its catholicity which comes from its participation in the mission of the Church of Jesus Christ in other parts of the world. Through its witnessing stance in its own situation, its prayers of intercession for churches in other parts of the world, and its sharing of persons and resources, it participates fully in the world mission of the Christian Church.

This concern for mission everywhere has been tested with the call for a moratorium, a halt — at least for a time — to sending and receiving missionaries and resources across national boundaries, in order to encourage the recovery and affirmation of the identity of every church, the concentration on mission in its own place and the freedom to reconsider traditional relations. The Lausanne Covenant noted that "the reduction of foreign missionaries and money in an evangelized country may sometimes be necessary to facilitate the national church's growth and self-reliance and to release resources for unevangelized areas." Moratorium does not mean the end of the missionary vocation nor of the duty to provide resources for missionary work, but it does mean freedom to reconsider present engagements and to see whether a continuation of what we have been doing for so long is the right style of mission in our day.

Moratorium has to be understood *inside* a concern for world mission. It is faithfulness of commitment to Christ in each national situation which makes missionary concern in other parts of the world authentic. There can never be a moratorium of mission, but it will always be possible, and sometimes necessary, to have a moratorium for the sake of better mission. . . .

7. Witness among People of Living Faiths

Christians owe the message of God's salvation in Jesus Christ to every person and to every people. Christians make their witness in the context

NOT DIALOGUE BUT MISSION OR TRUE WITNESS

of neighbours who live by other religious convictions and ideological persuasions. True witness follows Jesus Christ in respecting and affirming the unique new freedom of others. We confess as Christians that we have often looked for the worst in others and have passed negative judgment upon other religions. We hope as Christians to be learning to witness to our neighbours in a humble, repentant and joyful spirit.

The Word is at work in every human life. In Jesus of Nazareth the Word became a human being. The wonder of his ministry of love persuades Christians to testify to people of every religious and nonreligious persuasion of this decisive presence of God in Christ. In him is our salvation. Among Christians there are still differences of understanding as to how this salvation in Christ is available to people of diverse religious persuasions. But all agree that witness should be rendered to all.

Such an attitude springs from the assurance that God is the creator of the whole universe and that he has not left himself without witness at any time or any place. The Spirit of God is constantly at work in ways that pass human understanding and in places that to us are least expected. In entering into a relationship of dialogue with others, therefore, Christians seek to discern the unsearchable riches of God and the way he deals with humanity. For Christians who come from cultures shaped by another faith, an even more intimate interior dialogue takes place as they seek to establish the connection in their lives between their cultural heritage and the deep convictions of their Christian faith.

Christians should use every opportunity to join hands with their neighbours, to work together to be communities of freedom, peace and mutual respect. In some places, state legislation hinders the freedom of conscience and the real exercise of religious freedom. Christian churches as well as communities of other faiths cannot be faithful to their vocation without the freedom and right to maintain their institutional form and confessional identity in a society and to transmit their faith from one generation to another. In those difficult situations, Christians should find a way, along with others, to enter into dialogue with the civil authorities in order to reach a common definition of religious freedom. With that freedom comes the responsibility to defend through common actions all human rights in those societies.

Life with people of other faiths and ideologies is an encounter of commitments. Witness cannot be a one-way process, but of necessity is two-way; in it Christians become aware of some of the deepest convictions of their neighbours. It is also the time in which, within a spirit of openness and truth Christians are able to bear authentic witness, giving an account of their commitment to the Christ, who calls all persons to himself.

Looking toward the Future

Whether among the *secularized masses of industrial societies, the emerging new ideologies* around which societies are organized, the *resurging religions* which people embrace, the *movements of workers and political refugees, the people's search for liberation and justice, the uncertain pilgrimage of the younger generation* into a future both full of promise and overshadowed by nuclear confrontation — the Church is called to be present and to articulate the meaning of God's love in Jesus Christ for every person and for every situation.

The missionary vocation of the Church and its evangelistic calling will not resist the confrontation with the hard realities of daily life if it is not sustained by faith, *a faith supported by prayer, contemplation and adoration.* "Gathering and dispersing, receiving and giving, praise and work, prayer and struggle — this is the true rhythm of Christian engagement in the world." Christians must bring their hearts, minds and wills to the altar of God, knowing that from worship comes wisdom, from prayer comes strength, and from fellowship comes endurance. "To be incorporated into Christ through the work of the Holy Spirit is the greatest blessing of the kingdom, and the only abiding ground of our missionary activity in the world." The same Lord who sends his people to cross all frontiers and to enter into the most unknown territories in his name, is the one who assures: "I am with you always, to the close of the age."

Theology and Strategy
of Pentecostal Missions

L. Grant McClung

McClung, a former missionary to Europe, teaches mission and
church growth at the Church of God School of Theology in
Cleveland, Tennessee. Note the emphasis on the role of the
Holy Spirit in the Pentecostal view of missions. Source: *International Bulletin of Missionary Research*, January 1988, 2-6.

What do pentecostals believe? Why do they grow? In a nutshell, these seem
to be two of the bottom-line questions raised when missiologists consider
the theology and strategy of pentecostal mission. . . . In this introductory
review, I . . . attempt a summarization of pentecostal church-growth factors
from my perspective. I recognize the risk in asking an insider to critique
his own heritage. Without attempting to be laudatory, allow me to suggest
forthrightly answers to three questions: (1) What do we believe? (2) Whom
do we employ? (3) How do we get the job done?

What Do We Believe?

In scanning the field of pentecostal literature, I have found a number of
major theological themes as they relate to mission. I shall briefly note only
five of them.

1. *A Literal Biblicism.* Pentecostals have been marked by their exactness in following a literal interpretation of Scripture, so much that they have been characterized as "people of 'the Book.'" For pentecostals, the issue of biblical authority is non-negotiable and is *the* beginning point for missions theology and strategy. Every major pentecostal group has strong statements regarding the authority of Scripture.

2. *An Experiential Christianity.* Pentecostal pioneer David J. du Plessis called it "truth on fire." In spite of accusations of shallow hermeneutics and subjectivity, pentecostals have remained insistent that God is to be personally experienced through the Holy Spirit. For us, there need not be any polarization between doctrine and experience.

3. *The Personality and Power of the Holy Spirit.* For pentecostals, the Holy Spirit is personally active, living in and directing its servants. The Holy Spirit is not just a force or influence but personally and powerfully potent on the frontiers of mission. Prudencio Damboriena observed in Latin American pentecostalism that pentecostal beliefs and practices cannot be understood until one grasps

> ... the centrality of the Third Person of the Trinity in their theology and in their lives. To them Pentecost is not a mere historical event that took place almost two thousand years ago, but an always renewed presence of the Spirit in the world. The Holy Spirit is now, as then, the "creator" and the "vivifier" of men.

Pentecostals understand the experience of the baptism of the Holy Spirit as an indispensable endowment of power for service (Luke 24:49; Acts 1:8) and insist that it is normative and expected for each believer to seek for a "personal Pentecost."

4. *A Strong Christology.* Since the baptism of the Holy Spirit and the accompanying evidence of speaking in tongues have been central to pentecostal experience, the movement has been criticized for too much emphasis upon one person of the Godhead, namely, the Holy Spirit. Early pentecostal writings reveal the opposite. Pentecostal literature is replete with a strong Christology. For pentecostals, Jesus is personally present in the experience of empowerment as the Baptizer in the Holy Spirit (Matt. 3:11; Mark 1:8; Luke 3:16; John 1:33). They believe in the ministry of the Holy Spirit, which lifts up Jesus Christ (John 15:26; 16:14-15).

5. *An Urgent Missiology.* Eschatological urgency is at the heart of understanding the missionary fervor of early pentecostalism. Eschatology

"belongs to the essence of Pentecostalism." Pentecostal missiology cannot be rightly understood apart from its roots found in premillennialism, dispensationalism, and the belief in the imminent return of Christ.

Whom Do We Employ?

1. *Supernatural Recruitment.* A better way to ask this question would be, "By whom are we deployed?" The pentecostal tradition has placed high value on being sent by the Holy Spirit. Philip's assignment from the Holy Spirit (Acts 8) would make good preaching material for most pentecostals who have held dreams, visions, prophecy, tongues and interpretations, words and inner impressions, and even the audible voice of God in high regard as means of supernatural recruitment and guidance.

One interesting point on supernatural deployment is the oft-recorded experience of persons being in prayer, "hearing" the name of a place that they had never heard of before, and later having to find the place on a map. Recently, in discussing intercession for "hidden peoples," Foursquare pastor Jack Hayford said, "One man I know was given the name of a province in China which he had never heard of. He had to find it on the map to verify it existed, yet the Holy Spirit had whispered it to his heart while he prayed."

2. *A Lay Movement.* Sociological and historical studies have reflected upon the humble social origins of the pentecostals. Without a long history of formal theological training for "the ministry" (as a class set apart), the pentecostal tradition has emphasized that all the body are ministers and everyone a preacher. By and large, this is yet true. On the North American and European scene, however, there are signs of institutionalism and clear distinctions between a "professional clergy" and a lay ministry.

3. *Your Daughters Shall Prophesy.* A large part of the dynamic growth of the pentecostal movement is due to its ability since its inception to mobilize and effectively deploy women into missionary service. Many pentecostal organizations have designations for "Lady Ministers" or "Lady Evangelists" and provide for their licensing. Interestingly, seven of the twelve members of the Azusa Street Credential Committee were women. This committee selected and proved candidates for licensing. Much of today's pentecostal growth, especially outside North America, is due to the energy, courage, and leadership of committed women. Paul Yonggi Cho has espoused this as a key ingredient in the success of his 500,000-member pentecostal church in Seoul, Korea.

How Do We Get the Job Done?

A potpourri of practices could be suggested. Broadly speaking, pentecostal mission practices have been characterized by supernatural power, biblical pragmatism, committed personnel, and systematic propagation. Enough has been said about the first three of those factors. Let me discuss the element of "systematic propagation" as something sometimes overlooked by outside observers of pentecostal practices.

In emphasizing the leading of the Holy Spirit, pentecostals have been misunderstood to have a "sitting where they sit and letting God happen" kind of attitude.

Though pentecostals are characterized by a "spontaneous strategy of the Spirit," they have not been without a plan. As pioneer pentecostal missiologist Melvin L. Hodges has said: "This prominence given to the role of the Holy Spirit should not lead us to believe that the human role is one of complete passivity. There is need for the engaging of all our mental, physical, material, and spiritual powers in the planning and execution of God's work."

As with theological motivations, there are numerous issues, elements, and practices associated with pentecostal methodology and strategy. I shall briefly highlight five common practices: indigenous churches, church planting, urban strategies, literature distribution/publishing, and missions stewardship.

1. *Indigenous Churches.* Pentecostal missions have sought from the outset to develop indigenous churches. In many overseas situations the national pentecostal churches have expanded rapidly, eventually absorbing and controlling the parent mission's organization or denomination. One of the pentecostal observers most responsible for this emphasis in the last forty years is Melvin L. Hodges, whose book *The Indigenous Church* [Springfield, Mo.: Gospel Publishing House, 1953] has become the standard work on the subject. A sequel, *The Indigenous Church and the Missionary,* was published by William Carey Library in 1978.

2. *Church Planting.* After he returned from researching pentecostals in Brazil, William R. Read wrote, "This is not merely rapid growth, but a new kind of growth. The Pentecostals are engaged almost wholly in church planting." Pentecostals have seen the planting of responsible, reproducing congregations as the abiding fruit of world evangelism and have often measured their progress, as Robert Bryant Mitchell has said, "by the development of mature congregations and the buildings which they erect."

3. *Urban Strategies.* The twentieth-century pentecostal movement began (in a wider sense) in a city and has continued to be at home in urban areas, particularly in the non-Western world where pentecostal growth and urbanization have seemed to develop side by side. Read concluded that in Latin America the pentecostal strength was in the city. McGavran's research from 1978 in India also found that pentecostals were taking advantage of the migration from villages to cities. His conclusion was that they were "buying up urban opportunities."

4. *Literature Distribution/Publishing.* Among some fifteen "Causes for the Initial Success of Pentecostalism," John Thomas Nichol has given strong emphasis to tabloid-sized newspapers and other early publications that became the "means of disseminating the message of Pentecostalism to the far-flung corners of the globe." He has documented no less than thirty-four pentecostal periodicals that came into existence between 1900 and 1908. In more recent times, Read has attributed a massive literature program as one of the elements in the phenomenal growth of the Assemblies of God in Brazil.

By and large it may be true, as C. Peter Wagner claims, the "pentecostals have majored in being *doers* of the Word, much more than just *hearers* of the Word or even *writers* of the Word." The first generation of pentecostals did not major in analytical and systematized theologies (only in the last three decades has this type of scholarly work begun to emerge), but they were not silent when it came to popular literature read by the ordinary person. For this reason, the movement flourished among the winnable masses.

Today, publishing ministries remain high on the list for all major pentecostal groupings. Major denominations publish a variety of papers and journals, and an International Pentecostal Press Association has been formed. Pentecostal missiology is still young as a field and there is no specific journal for this discipline, though pentecostals are now being regularly asked to contribute to standing missiological journals.

5. *Missions Stewardship.* Pentecostals have traditionally, since their inception, given generously to the cause of missions. In capturing the urgency of their times, Horace McCracken recounts the early years between 1906 and 1908 when "whole families volunteered for the Word, sold their possessions, and started for the field. They were possessed with a passion to go to the ends of the earth for their Lord, and no sacrifice seemed too great for them that the gospel might be proclaimed and the coming of the Lord might be hastened."

In the classical pentecostal denominations of North America, missions budgets continue to receive the largest share of donations. In the Assemblies of God alone, for example, foreign-missions giving increased from $339,111 in 1939 to more than $48 million forty-three years later, in 1982. Pentecostals are doing the job because they put their money where their heart is and God blesses their missions stewardship.

In Retrospect

What do we believe? Out of a literal biblicism there is a strong emphasis upon experiencing God through the power of the Holy Spirit, a stated belief in the supremacy and centrality of Jesus Christ, and an urgent missiology born out of premillennial eschatology. Whom do we employ? With a high regard for supernatural recruitment, pentecostals emphasize the ministry of the laity, including the leadership of women. How do we get the job done? Among other church-growth methodologies, pentecostals emphasize indigenous church planting in urban settings, widely disseminate their teachings and practices through publishing, and place missions as the number-one priority for financial support.

MISSION IN NON-CHRISTIAN RELIGIONS

Mission-Minded Hindus Going Global

Swami Palimi

Hinduism is often thought to be a nonmissionary religion. Such is not the case for all Hindus. The rationale for mission, and the form it takes, however, is quite different from that of Western religions. Source: *Pulse,* 8 February 1991, 2-3.

We send greetings and the rainbowed aloha from Hawaii to you . . . our friends at the *Evangelical Missions Quarterly.* You have asked us to reflect on the "growing missionary spirit in Hinduism" with special reference to the reason behind it, the extent of its influence and what the future holds. When I opened your letter, I thought the subject too vast and the time too short. A proper response would require months of research, not to mention the days of crystal-ball work you threw in. Then I realized that every worthy enterprise in history began with someone's rash and unruly theory and suddenly felt a new sense of competence in undertaking the task you set.

There are many who will tell you that Hinduism has no missionary dimension at all. Zip. They have witnessed the devastating social and personal effects of unethical missionary effort over several centuries, and this impels them to repudiate the missionary spirit. If by the word *missionary* we mean the attitudes and strategies of aggressive world proselytism, then they are right. Hindus find such an approach to be spirituality repellent, not spiritual at all, but more akin to the ways of door-to-door encyclopedia salesmen. To a Hindu, spirituality is ever humble, loving, serene, introspective, all-embracing. The corollary is that anything which is arrogant, dis-

273

dainful, anxious, externalized and especially intolerant is not spiritual. And right or wrong, Hindus view most (by no means all) missionaries as possessing the latter qualities in healthy measure.

On the other hand, if by the word *missionary* we mean an eagerness to share our beloved faith with those who want to know of it, then these people are dead wrong and Hinduism is a veteran of the missionary tradition. Adi Shankara was a missionary of this type, so were compelling bhaktars (votaries of God) like Chaitanya and Appar. Hindu philosopher and ex-president of India, Dr. S. Radhakrishnan (1988-1975), wrote in *The Hindu View of Life:* "In a sense, Hinduism may be regarded as the first example in the world of a missionary religion. Only its missionary spirit is different from that associated with the proselytizing creeds. It did not regard as its mission to convert humanity to any one opinion. For what counts is conduct, not belief."

I think you are right that Hinduism's missionary sense is growing. Witness the internationalization of dozens of Hindu institutions locked for centuries inside India. Consider the successful and controversial ISKCON [International Society for Krishna Consciousness], or Hare Krishna movement, with an artistic and well-funded publications program distributing millions of books in dozens of languages each year. The rapidly growing Radhasoami and Sai Baba movements have made vigorous efforts to move onto the global stage. There is the Brahma Kumari sect, strong in education and the peace movement, working effectively in the United Nations. Their millenarian concepts (unusual in the Hindu world), feminist emphasis, disciplined ways and ecumenical meditations make them a force to contend with.

The real action is not in the big movements, it's in a million villages from Georgetown to Montreal, from Durban to Chicago. Hindus everywhere are becoming stronger and more assertive. You have asked why. I offer six possible reasons.

There has been an unprecedented influx of talent and money from the West in the past thirty years, giving these groups the ability to reach out. When a Hindu moves into a U.S. boardroom or an American truth seeker joins a rural ashram in Kentucky, suddenly members have access to new resources, to Wall Street and Madison Avenue, to computers and communications facilities. The group's message is the same, but the means to promote it has been amplified several magnitudes.

The West is clearly open to the Hindu message, ready to hear about yoga, meditation, mysticism, healing and the ancient ways. Such "products" were too sophisticated for public consumption thirty years ago, but today they're the hottest item on the shelf. Not a small part of this phenomenon is related, indirectly, to the coming of the New Age movement.

The new rules of world spirituality are a reason. As once-believing nations bury communism's failed effort to conquer the world, so a large part of the non-Christian/non-Muslim world is laying to rest the conquest-driven, one-way-only concept of religion. They are replacing it with views of the Divine which they perceive to be more healing, more focused on the individual's reach for enlightenment, more naturally devotional, richer in technique and less authoritarian. A related trend is the wholesale rejection of the concepts of hell, sin and Satan. A 1990 *San Francisco Chronicle* poll showed that 35 percent of the local residents practice yoga or meditation and 25 percent believe in reincarnation. Hindu institutions find they have answers when people ask about chakras, inner light or consciousness. They have methods when people want to calm the mind and "go within." This knowledge is the stock-in-trade of any Hindu teacher.

The dual support which science and the Green Movement have inadvertently aligned with human and animal rights, with strict nonviolence, with an awareness, indeed a reverence, of nature [is a reason].

The remarkable discovery made by the human family of late, that ethnic and native cultures possess value and must, like species, be preserved from further extinction. This rediscovery of identity and resurgence of ancient heritages nearly destroyed can be seen among the Hawaiians, the Eskimos, the Native Americans, the tribals of Africa, Japan, Australia — virtually everywhere! Hinduism, with a culture older than them all, has benefited from, and supported, this ethnic renaissance.

A backlash among certain Hindus who feel they have for too long been abused by succeeding waves of missionaries: Dutch, Portuguese, Muslim, British, and American. They seem to have reached their limit to forebear, preferring now to express defiance, to wield power instead of wisdom, and ultimately to abandon the central Hindu ethic which inspired Mahatma Gandhi and Martin Luther King — non-injury to others. Unfortunately, this decidedly violent and un-Hindu response is burgeoning.

That is the why of it all. Now to what the future may hold. I suspect that Hinduism will have a surprisingly sophisticated network around the globe in another twenty years. You will see the first Hindu encyclopedia and far more publications from Hindus, and people will embrace their lack of unbending dogma as a new wisdom. There will be no TV evangelism, no mass meetings in football stadiums. That does not fit the Hindu's way.

It will be small, intimate, grass roots. You will see the unusual missionary style of the Transcendental Meditation movement proliferate — a button-down, quasi-scientific validation of the ancient Vedic tradition. You will see alliances from among Hindus and Christians (probably Episcopalians at first, not the Assembly of God). International conclaves, notably the peace and ecumenical movements, will be deeply affected by Hindus. A small army of yoga missionaries — hatha, raja, siddha and kundalini — beauti-fully trained in the last ten years, is about to set upon the Western world. They may not call themselves Hindu, but Hindus know where yoga came from and where it goes.

As you know, Hindus represent one-sixth of the human family, nearly a billion souls. How Hindus and Christians (and Muslims) define their roles as missionaries in the twenty-first century is obviously critical to the maturing global reality of religious pluralism, where cooperation must replace competition, where learning from each other must replace domi-nation, where love must replace suspicion.

We hope these musings prove useful to you and close with a quote from Swami Vivekananda, Hinduism's greatest modern missionary, spoken in January of 1895, "What I now want is a band of fiery missionaries." It's a hundred years late, but it appears he's going to get his wish.

A Comparative Religious Study of Missionary Transplantation in Buddhism, Christianity, and Islam

Frank Whaling

Frank Whaling is a member of the divinity faculty at New College in the University of Edinburgh, Scotland, where he is coordinator of religious studies degrees and the religious studies unit. In this article he analyzes methods used by the world religions to compare themselves with one another and then, adapting one of those methods, compares three forms of mission. The following excerpt is from his section on Buddhist missions. Source: *International Review of Mission*, October 1981, 314-33.

The Buddhist spread from India into China is one of the most impressive missionary exploits in the history of religion. The hypothetical problems were formidable. China had an antipathy to foreign intrusions. The Buddhists were certainly foreign, they were also radically different from indigenous Chinese elements. There were differences of language; Sanskrit had nothing in common with Chinese. There were sociological differences; the Buddhist Sangha (order of monks) sat lightly to the family whereas the Chinese stressed the family and filial piety. There were philosophical differences; the Buddhists recognized the law of *karma* and the wheel of rebirth whereas the Chinese had little interest in the afterlife except for the ancestor tradition. There were mythological differences; the Buddhists recognized a pantheon of deities although denying them ultimate significance whereas the Chinese almost uniquely were uninterested in deities. There were political differences; the Sangha was an extraordinary norm bestriding politics and society whereas the Chinese indigenous religions, even the Taoist, were essentially attempts to solve political and social tensions. The Buddhist task was, therefore, the formidable one of overstepping boundaries not merely of geography but also of worldview.

The necessary preliminary to the Buddhist advance from India into China was the establishment of communications between the two areas. This was accomplished through the medium of the Silk Route which consisted of a linking system of trade routes connecting the central Asian oases. The possibility of inter-travel was further strengthened by the rise of expanding empires at either end of the main route, the Han Empire in China, and the Kushan Empire in northeast India. The fact that the Kushan Empire under leaders such as Kaniska became a stronghold of the Mahayana form of Buddhism was also significant in that it was mainly Mahayana Buddhism that eventually prevailed in China. The mere fact of the possibility of Buddhist advance would have been purely notional without a desire to cross into China and the skill effectively to achieve this. The desire of the Sangha to preach the goal of Nirvana through the Dharma and the Buddha to other cultures dated back at least to the great Indian emperor Asoka himself and originated in germ in the Buddha's own refusal to wallow in his enlightenment because of the need to communicate to others the answer to the problem of *dukkha* that he himself had found. The skill to preach effectively also originated in germ in the skill in means whereby the Buddha had spoken to the condition of particular people in particular situations. However the Buddha's talks within his own culture had been relatively easy compared with that facing the Buddhist missionaries into China. In describing how they succeeded in their task we have time only to sketch the main features.

In the first place there was a time of initial contact by Buddhist missionaries from the Kushan Empire with the Central Asian oases of Khotan, Kucha, Turfan, and Tun-huang which were under the hegemony of the Han Empire. From there they gradually seeped down into China itself and by the middle of the first century were present in the capital Lo-yang and at P'eng-ch'eng monastery to the east. By the second century they were present in other centers and great missionary translators such as An Shih-kao had begun their epic translating work. Until the end of the second century progress was relatively slow because of the cohesive political and philosophical strength of the Han Empire, but after its demise in 220 the Buddhist appeal was more obvious at a time of social and philosophical disintegration. The collapse of Han Confucianism opened the way for the deepening of Buddhist influence. Neo-Taoist philosophy grew in importance at this time and provided a sort of bridge whereby Buddhism was able to become more sinicized. The Buddhists matched their own concepts with neo-Taoists or other concepts already present in China. The Buddhist *dharma* or *bodhi* were translated as *Tao;* the Buddhist *Arhat* (saint) was translated as the Taoist *chen-jen* (immortal); *Nirvana* became the Taoist *wu-wei;* the Buddhist *sila* (morality) became the Confucian *hsia-hsun* (filial submission); the Buddhist *Mahabhutas* (four elements) were matched with the Chinese Five Elements; the five Buddhist lay ethical precepts were matched with the five Confucian normative virtues. Although translations and *ko-i* (matching concepts) were still rudimentary, nevertheless they were important; for example the matching of karma with the neo-Taoist view of Tao introduced into Chinese thought the notions of the moral implication of behavior, emptiness, and the continuity of life after death. In addition to this, Chinese scholars who saw the point of the Taoist ideal of retiring from the world at this time of political confusion began to gravitate towards the Sangha which increasingly developed not merely as a center of learning but also as a means of social advancement of the lesser gentry. Through the medium of the gentry the Buddhists were poised to influence other parts of society. By 320 the Buddhists had made a strong initial contact with the Chinese world, they had become implanted in China and had begun the task of indigenizing their worldview in China.

In 320 China was effectively split into two sections, north and south. Buddhist advance in the north, now controlled by the barbarians, took a different form from its spread in the south where there was greater continuity with the traditions of ancient Chinese civilization. In south China, the Buddhists increasingly penetrated into all levels of society. The translation of the scriptures became increasingly sophisticated, and contacts with the imperial court helped to spread Buddhist concepts among the educated class. Political fragmentation from 346 to 403 facilitated the rise of new Buddhist centers away from the court in the country areas, the homelands of the gentry. Missionaries such as Hui-yüan of Lu Shan worked not just among the gentry but also among the laity, and Hui-yüan it was who founded a cult of Amitabha in 402 which foreshadowed the popular devotionalism of Pure Land Buddhism. By the end of the fourth century

Buddhist influence was such that it was attacked by opponents as being foreign, anti-social, anti-state, and of no practical use — a sure sign of its growing penetration. During the fifth and early sixth centuries Buddhist influence became virtually supreme in south China. Prince Ching-ling and Emperor Wu gave active support to the extent of ransoming themselves to gain money for the Buddhists. Three important philosophical schools arose in the south, namely the Nirvanasutra School, the Satyasiddha School, and the San-lun School. Translation work continued to grow in volume and quality. Moreover the peasantry were now influenced by the vivid narratives, the promise of salvation, and the dramatic acts of the Buddhist missionaries who were now mainly Chinese rather than Indian in personnel. By 589 the Buddhist tradition was predominant in the south.

In the north the story was different. As in western Europe barbarians flooded into northern China and divisions arose among them as well as between them and the Chinese populace. Accordingly the Buddhist penetration of northern China was different. It did not rely so much upon the patient translation of Buddhist scriptures or the sophisticated communication of Buddhist concepts. The pioneer missionary from Kucha in Central Asia, Fo-tu-t'eng, was typical of the alternative approach. His approach was more shamanistic than conceptual or spiritual. His aim was mass conversion of the people by the use of magic to impress the barbarian rulers. Buddhism, he claimed, could help towards victory, provide better crops, cure disease. Additional advantages from the ruler's viewpoint were the Buddhist tradition's universal ethical system which could provide a uniting value system to undergird their power, and its usefulness as a counter weight to Confucian influence at court. Fo-tu-t'eng succeeded, with the result that there was no prolonged period of gradual penetration as in the south. It was a case of rapid mass conversion. The corollary was that Buddhists became allied to the state to whose fate they became linked. Within this context of state patronage and mass conversion, the Buddhists attempted to deepen the understanding of their tradition within a nominally converted society. The northern Wei dynasty encouraged the work of Kumarajiva, one of the greatest translators in the history of religion. The great cave sculptures at Lung-men provided aesthetic inspiration not only for China but also for Korea and Japan, which were shortly to be missionized from China as China had been from India. The Buddhists accommodated their approach with the Confucian stress upon filial piety by introducing prayers for the welfare of ancestors and departed family members, and they adapted to folk religion by means of a thoroughgoing syncretism. The popularity of the cult of Maitreya and the growing interest in Mahayana devotionalism gave further aesthetic and emotional stimulus to the peasantry. By 589 the northern Buddhist tradition had great social and political influence; it had popular support; and its willingness to adapt to local situations meant that it supplemented or complemented rather than supplanted indigenous religions.

What are the tentative conclusions that we may draw from this rapid survey of the spread of Buddhism from India into China? In the first place, the desire for mission must be there, as also must be the possibility of communication and transport from one culture into another. In other words, there must be the internal motivation to undertake mission, and the external conditions to allow of its propagation. In the Buddhist case, the first was hers by birthright; the second was provided by the Silk Route and the Han and Kushan Empires.

In the second place, the opportunity for a breakthrough in the Buddhist mission in China was provided by the collapse of a strong empire and the uncertain situation produced by the fall of Han Confucianism. Mission thrived when the old political structure and the old certainties disappeared.

In the third place, there was the need for a bridge to enable the Buddhist tradition to enter into Chinese culture. It could not translate or explicate its alien ideas in their pristine Indian form. Hermeneutics and linguistic dexterity were necessary. The hermeneutical bridge was provided by the neo-Taoists; the translation work was provided by superb translators ranging from An Shih-kao to Kumarajiva and beyond.

In the fourth place, mission advanced in China in two different ways, by slow penetration in the south and by rapid penetration in the north. In the south, a premium was placed upon accurate translation of the scriptures and the awakening of philosophical understanding among the literate class. This led to the quickening of interest among the rulers, and finally more popular methods were used to appeal to the peasantry. In the north, Fo-tu-t'eng converted the barbarian rulers and through them there was a mass conversion of the peasantry. This was followed by a process of religious education among the peasantry and the elite. Although more swift, the process of rapid penetration was also more brittle in that Buddhist fortunes were mortgaged to those of the state.

In the fifth place, the Buddhist mission into China passed through a number of linked though separate stages. At the start there was a period of contact and implantation when Buddhist missionaries entered China and established a Buddhist minority presence. They began the work of explaining the Buddhist Dharma to the Chinese by means of translations and ko-i (matching concepts). This period lasted for anything up to three hundred years according to when we date the Buddhist entry into China. It was the necessary preparation for the Chinese acceptance of Buddhist teaching. This is true not only of the south, but also of the north where the barbarian rulers already belonged to the Chinese cultural orbit which by now contained a Buddhist element. The second main stage was that of acceptance and penetration when the Buddhist tradition became more than a presence in Chinese life. As we have seen, Buddhist penetration in the south was slow and it proceeded from the gentry to the rulers and peasantry. In the north it was rapid proceeding from the rulers to the peasantry and gentry. At this point the Buddhists had achieved a firm position in Chinese society. In the third and final stage, the Buddhist tradition was not merely an accepted element in Chinese culture but a flourishing, expanding, and increasingly dominant element. Buddhist art arose; Buddhist emperors appeared; Buddhist missionaries went from China to Korea and Japan; opposition to the Buddhists became vocal, politically in the north and religiously through the Taoist Hua-hu theory in the south; the Buddhist tradition became indigenized in regard to language, in regard to personnel, and in regard to Chinese adaptations of the Buddha's message in indigenous forms such as Pure Land; Buddhist influence spread within all levels of society from top to bottom.

In the sixth place, once the Buddhists had established a presence in China the following factors had to be resolved for significant expansion to be achieved. The contradictions between Buddhist and Chinese values (especially those separating the Buddhist Sangha ideal from the Chinese family ideal of filial piety) had to be overcome; it was necessary for the ruling elite to establish a tolerant acceptance of the Buddhist intellectual position; Chinese translations of Buddhist sutras were needed and adequate matching concepts had to be formulated; a modus vivendi had to be found with indigenous religious elements either by attraction (in the case of neo-Taoism) or defense (against later Taoist and Confucian charges); and favorable political conditions were needed either negatively through the fall of the Han dynasty or positively through the conversion of the barbarian rulers or the support of a Ching-ling.

Finally, there is the paradox that as the Buddhist tradition flourished in China, so it began to wane in India, the land of its birth. As in India, the Buddhists did not seek to annihilate other religious forces but to work with them in a complementary fashion. As the Buddhist tradition declined before the renascent Hindus in India, it grew to be one of the San Chiao, the three ways of China — a dominant but not monolithic way. . . .

On the Nature of Islamic Da'wah

Isma'il al-Faruqi

Isma'il al-Faruqi (d. 1986) was professor of Islamics at Temple University in Philadelphia. In this article he defines Islamic mission, da'wah, discusses the methodology that the Qur'an prescribes for da'wah, and outlines the content of da'wah. Internal citations are to passages in the Qur'an. Source: *International Review of Mission,* October 1976, 391-409.

Allah, *subhanahu wa ta'ala,* has commanded the Muslim: "Call men unto the path of your Lord by wisdom and goodly counsel. Present the cause to them through argument yet more sound" (Qur'an 16:125). Da'wah is the fulfillment of this commandment "to call men unto the path of Allah." Besides, it is the effort by the Muslim to enable other men to share and benefit from the supreme vision, the religious truth, which he has appropriated. In this respect it is rationally necessary, for truth wants to be known. It exerts pressure on the knower to share his vision of it with his peers. Since religious truth is not only theoretical, but also axiological and practical, the man of religion is doubly urged to take his discovery to other men. His piety, his virtue and charity impose upon him the obligation to make common the good which has befallen him.

Da'wah Methodology

Da'wah is not coercive. "Calling" is certainly not coercing. Allah (s.w.t.) has commanded, "No coercion in religion" (2:256). It is an invitation whose objective can be fulfilled only with the free consent of the called. . . . If they are not convinced, they must be left alone (5:108; 3:176-177; 47:32). Certainly, the Muslim is to try again and never give up that God may guide his fellow-man to the truth. The example of his own life, his commitment to the values he professes, his engagement, constitute his final argument. If the non-Muslim is still not convinced, the Muslim is to rest his case with God. . . . From this it follows that the societal order desired by Islam is one where men are free to present and argue their religious causes with one another. It is a kind of academic seminary on a large scale where he who knows better is free to tell and to convince, and the others are free to listen and be convinced. Islam puts its trust in man's rational power to discriminate between the true and the false. . . .

Da'wah is directed to Muslims as well as non-Muslims. It follows from the divine commandment that da'wah must be the end product of a critical process of intellection. Its content cannot be the only content known, the only content presented. For there is no judgment without consideration of alternatives, without comparison and contrast, without tests of inner consistency, of general consistency with all other knowledge, without tests of correspondence with reality. . . . That is why da'wah in Islam has never been thought of as exclusively addressed to the non-Muslims. It is as much intended for the benefit of Muslims as of non-Muslims. . . . All men stand under the obligation to actualize the divine pattern in space and time. This task is never complete for any individual. The Muslim is supposedly the person who, having accepted the burden, has set himself on the road of actualization. The non-Muslim still has to accept the charge. Hence, da'wah is necessarily addressed to both, to the Muslim to press forward toward actualization and to the non-Muslim to join the ranks of those who make the pursuit of God's pattern supreme. . . .

Da'wah is anamnesis. In commanding the Muslim to call men to the path of Allah (s.w.t.), He did not ask him to call men to anything new, to something which is foreign or unknown to them. Islam is *din al-fitrah* (natural religion) which is already present in its fullness in man by nature. It is innate, as it were, a natural constituent of humanity. The man who is not *homo religiosus,* and hence *homo Islamicus,* is not a man. This is Allah's branding of His creation, namely, that He has endowed all men as His creatures, with a *sensus numinus,* a *fitrah,* with which to recognize Him as

Allah (God), Transcendent Creator, Ultimate Master, and One. It is history which confirms this natural faculty with its primeval perceptions and intellections, cultivates and enriches it or warps it and diverts it from its natural goal. . . . Da'wah is based upon the Islamic assertion that primeval religion or monotheism is found in every man, and that all he needs is to be reminded of it. . . .

Da'wah is ecumenical. Islam's discovery of *din al-fitrah* and its vision of it as base of all historical religion is a breakthrough of tremendous importance in interreligious relations. For the first time it has become possible to hold adherents of all other religions as equal members of a universal religious brotherhood. All religious traditions are *de jure,* for they have all issued from and are based upon a common source, the religion of God which He has implanted equally in all men, upon *din al-fitrah.* The problem is to find out how far the religious traditions agree with *din al-fitrah,* the original and first religion; the problem is to trace the historical development of religions and determine precisely how and when and where each has followed and fulfilled, or transcended and deviated from *din al-fitrah.* . . . Da'wah is ecumenical par excellence because it regards any kind of intercourse between the Muslim and the non-Muslim as a domestic relationship between kin. The Muslim comes to the non-Muslim and says, "We are one; we are one family under Allah, and Allah has given you the truth not only inside yourself but inside your religious tradition which is *de jure* because its source is in God." The task of dialogue, or mission, is thus transformed into one of sifting the history of the religion in question. Da'wah thus becomes an ecumenical cooperative critique of the other religion rather than its invasion by a new truth.

Da'wah Content

Islam's essence is critically knowable. It is not the subject of "paradox" nor of "continuing revelation" nor the object of construction or reconstruction by Muslims. It is crystallized in the Holy Qur'an for all men to read. It is as clearly comprehensible to the man of today as it was to that of Arabia of the Prophet's day (570-632 C.E.) because the categories of grammar, lexicography, syntax, and redaction of the Qur'anic text . . . have not changed through the centuries. . . . Arabic has remained the same for nearly two millennia, the last fourteen centuries of which being certainly due to the Holy Qur'an. . . .

The essence of Islam is *tawhid* or the witnessing that there is no god but God. Brief as it is, this witness packs into itself four principles which constitute the whole essence and ultimate foundation of the religion:

First, that there is no god but God means that reality is dual. [Reality consists] of a natural realm, the realm of creation, and a transcendent realm, the Creator. This principle distinguishes Islam from trinitarian Christianity where the dualism of creator and creature is maintained but where it is combined with a divine immanentism in human nature in justification of the incarnation. Tawhid requires that neither nature be apotheosized nor transcendent God be objectified, the two realities ever remaining ontologically disparate.

Second, tawhid means that God is related to what is not God as its God. God is creator, ultimate cause, master, ultimate end. Creator and creature . . . are relevant to each other regardless of their ontological disparateness which is not affected by the relation. . . . The divine will is commandment and law, the "ought" of all that is, knowable by the direct means of revelation, or the indirect means of rational and/or empirical analysis of what is. Without a knowable content, the divine will would not be normative or imperative, and hence would not be the final end of the natural. . . .

Thirdly, tawhid means that man is capable of action. . . . [Creation] is malleable or capable of receiving man's action, and that human action on malleable nature . . . is the purpose of religion. Contrary to the claims of other religions, nature is neither fallen or evil, nor a sort of *Untergang* of the absolute, nor is the absolute an apotheosis of it. Both are real, and both are good — the Creator being the *summum bonum* and the creature being intrinsically good and potentially better as it is transformed by human action into the pattern the Creator has willed for it.

Fourthly, tawhid means that man, alone among all the creatures, is capable of action as well as free to act or not to act. This freedom vests him with a distinguishing quality, namely responsibility. It casts upon his action its moral character; for the moral is precisely that which is done in freedom, i.e., done by an agent who is capable of doing, as well as of not doing it. . . . It is of the nature of moral action that its fulfillment be not equivalent to its non-fulfillment, that man's exercise of his freedom in actualizing the divine imperative be not without difference. Hence, another principle is necessary, whereby successful moral action would meet with happiness and its opposite with unhappiness. . . . This is what "The Day of Judgment" and "Paradise and Hell" are meant to express in religious language.

Fifthly, tawhid means the commitment of man to enter into the nexus of nature and history, there to actualize the divine will. It understands that will as pro-world and pro-life and hence, it mobilizes all human energies in the service of culture and civilization. . . . Islamic *da'wah* is not based upon a condemnation of the world. . . . In this, as in the preceding aspects, Islamic *da'wah* differs from that of Christianity. . . . Islam holds man to be not in need of any salvation. Instead of assuming him to be religiously and ethically fallen, Islamic *da'wah* acclaims him as the *khalifah* of Allah, perfect in form, and endowed with all that is necessary to fulfill the divine will. . . . "Salvation" is hence not in the vocabulary of Islam. *"Falah,"* or positive achievement in space and time of the divine will, is the Islamic counterpart of Christian "deliverance" and "redemption."

Sixthly, tawhid restores to man a dignity which some religions have denied by their representation of him as "fallen," as existentially miserable. By calling him to exercise his God-given prerogatives, Islamic *da'wah* rehabilitates him and reestablishes his sanity, innocence, and dignity. His moral vocation is the road to his *falah.* Certainly the Muslim is called to a new theocentrism; but it is one in which man's cosmic dignity is applauded by Allah and His Angels. Christianity calls man to respond with faith to the salvific act of God and seeks to rehabilitate man by convincing him that it is he for whom God has shed His own blood. Man, it asserts, is certainly great because he is God's partner whom God would not allow to destroy himself. This is indeed greatness, but it is the greatness of a helpless puppet. Islam understands itself as man's assumption of his cosmic role as the one for whose sake creation was created. He is its innocent, perfect and moral master; and every part of it is his to have and to enjoy. He is called to obey, i.e., to fulfill the will of Allah. But this fulfillment is in and of space and time precisely because Allah is the source of space and time and the moral law.

SECTION II READINGS

ISSUES IN MISSION

The Absolute Claim of Christianity:
The Justification of Evangelization
or an Obstacle to It?

Alexandre Ganoczy

One problem that plagues modern missions theorists is how to evaluate Christianity's claim to absolute truth. Ganoczy suggests that if the claim is made philosophically, it actually hurts missions. If the claim is made theologically, however, it can be seen as part of a humanity-wide search for religious truth, and be a positive part of the missions effort. Source: *Evangelization in the World Today,* ed. Norbert Greinacher and Alois Müller, Concilium Series, no. 114 (New York: Seabury Press, 1979), 19-28.

The Problem

Christian theologians claim that Christianity has received absolute religious truth from God in Jesus Christ. My question here is: Can this claim be regarded as an essential precondition for active evangelization on the part of the churches? Does this claim to absolute truth really promote God's cause, which the churches have to represent in the world? Or does it have the opposite effect and act as an obstacle to the furtherance of that cause? . . .

These questions can only be answered if the two basic concepts on which they are based are examined more closely. I shall therefore look more

291

closely at the theological status of these two concepts — the absolute claim and evangelization — and their interrelationship.

The Absolute Claim

"Absolute" is, of course, above all a philosophical concept. Something is absolute if it "is in every respect in itself and through itself and therefore in no respect dependent." The truth is absolute for the thinker, good is absolute for the man who acts, and being is absolute for the man who exists. In philosophy, certain qualities are recognized as belonging to the absolute: universality, which sustains the individual, independence, on which everything else is dependent, necessity, which asserts itself against chance, and an unconditioned nature that conditions everything else. It is obvious that philosophy has always had good reasons for attributing these and other absolute qualities to the one God, although it was not until a relatively late date — probably in the writings of Nicholas of Cusa — that the noun "Absolute" was used as a philosophical name for God. The specifically theological names for God have always, throughout the whole of Christian history, been predominantly biblical. (Examples of such names are Lord, Creator, Redeemer, and so on.) In these names, it was not so much a metaphysical position seen, as it were, at the top of the hierarchy and occupied by a being existing in himself and above all other beings that was stressed, as the personal relationship between a God who was active in human history and man. . . .

What, then, is the relationship between Christianity, understood in this way, and the other religions (which Rahner only considers generally)? Whenever they are experienced seriously and sincerely by men of good will, they are relative seeds of an absolute plant. Rahner himself has commented in this context: "The seed has no right not to want to become a plant." The seed, then, has to be brought out of its state as a seed and into its fully developed state as a plant. This is the essential task of the Christian mission. According to Wilhelm Thusing, "Mission is . . . necessary because implicit Christianity must become explicit and in this way come to itself."

Evangelization

The task of evangelization, then, clearly has an essential part to play in this transcendental theology of the school of Rahner, as it obviously does not in the dialectical philosophy of religion of Hegel. According to Rahner, evangelization forms an essential part of the Christian claim to absolute religious truth. It is only in the light of that absolute claim that evangelization can really be understood. At this point, however, a certain doubt arises: Is this necessarily the case? Does the Christian religion have to insist on this absolute claim, based on either philosophical or theological argument, in order to justify the need for mission? Is the situation not very different in the normative sources of Christian faith?

If we consider the proclamation and indeed the whole attitude of Jesus of Nazareth that can be recognized behind the New Testament witness, we cannot say that it contains any appeal to one reality for salvation that was previously given and only has to be made explicit. On the contrary, everything is determined by the radical newness of the kingdom of God that is eminent and voluntarily brought about. If anything can be called "absolute," it is surely the coming of the kingdom of God, that cannot be produced by any anthropological or historical development, or either forced or prevented by any human power. Only the future reality of the *basileia* has sovereign universal, independent and unconditioned qualities. Jesus himself makes himself relative with regard to the *basileia* of his Father. He wanted to show only the *basileia*, only to be its herald and to anticipate only it. He did not emphasize his own title of Messiah, which might have expressed his unique and absolute quality with regard to the kingdom that was to come. He acted in a messianic way and probably lived consciously as the Messiah, but he certainly did not strive after the name of Messiah. Jesus' evangelizing and kerygmatic way of speaking always points away from himself and toward God alone and his practical aim was the welfare and salvation of the poor, the captives and the sinners (see, for example, Mark 1:14; Luke 4:18; 8:1) of his own environment. To this end he devoted his full power in the task of spreading his eschatological message and his prophecy and promise for the future. His work of evangelization was essentially a theocentricity that was radically anthropocentric in practice and in no sense a sublime egocentricity. . . .

Evangelization has the following characteristics: There is a consciousness of the radical newness and irreducibility of the saving message of the risen Christ. This leads to a memory for the living example of Jesus and a deep theocentricity that is at the same time concentrated on the welfare, happiness and salvation of one's fellow men and is therefore a concretely soteriologically-oriented theocentricity. There is also a consciousness in the task of evangelization of man's eschatological relationship with the future

293

and consequently of the temporary nature of all forms of mediation carried out by the Church. Finally, the only absolute aim for the evangelizing *ekklesia* is the *basileia* that is to come.

One important consequence of my summary of the essential characteristics of evangelization is that it is necessary to evangelize actively. It is unfortunately very common in missiology to shorten the New Testament perspective by quoting the commandment given by Jesus to be missionaries to the world. This decisionistic view of the situation in fact obscures the really decisive aspect, which is that the people of God of the new covenant are led to evangelize because of the very nature of Christian faith itself. This faith is a faith in the God of Jesus Christ who makes himself public and manifest. Hegel was right in perceiving in Christianity the "revealed religion" through which the spirit at the same time expresses and empties itself and also comes to itself. The New Testament, however, goes far beyond Hegel by presenting Christianity with the four characteristics of message, mission, assembly and *ekklesia* of the sacraments. Because Christians are placed in the imitation of Christ as the messenger, the one sent, the one who assembles from God and the one who is truly present, it is therefore "natural" for them to be active as missionaries.

On the other hand, the view has to be criticized on the basis of the New Testament witness that the Church "saves" by its missions those who would otherwise fall victims to definitive disaster. The Church is not a redeemer, not an "only ark of salvation," outside which there are no real "elements of truth and sanctification." The Church would therefore be wrongly advised if it were to construct its theory and praxis of the mission on a modernized variant of the Johannine contrast of light and darkness. Only God can save. He alone can know infallibly who is to be redeemed and by whom. It is also reserved to him alone to determine how much darkness and how much light there is to be both outside and inside the churches. According to the New Testament, it is the task of those churches to be the sent people of God at the service of the one who sends and the place and organ of the one who saves and to carry out this task in freedom and knowledge.

Evangelization and the Absolute Claim

The relationship between evangelization and the absolute claim of Christianity can be approached in the following way. In the first place, the Church and theologians would be well-advised to consider seriously the problem of language. The fact that there was no talk of an absolute claim in the evangelizing work of the early Christian community is very significant. A verbal claim to absolute truth made by the missionary is open to many interpretations. To what, for example, does this claim apply? What or who is "absolute"? The Church? Christianity as the religion of "fullness"? Christian faith as an absolute certainty of the truth of the revelation of Christ? God, apart from whom there can be no mediation of salvation for any religion at all? Finally, we may also ask whether the philosophical term "absolute" is really suitable as a name for the God of the Old and New Testaments who was so personally involved in man's history.

In the second place, the problem of history should also be considered by asking the following question: What advantages and disadvantages resulted in the past when the claim to absolute truth was made systematically by those responsible for the Christian missions? I cannot unfortunately give a detailed answer containing many subtle distinctions to this question because of lack of space. We can, however, accept the opinion of many critics of the history of the Christian missions — both Christian and non-Christian — that more harm than good has been caused by the absolute claim. This opinion is not in the first place based on the frequently criticized association between those working in the mission field and the representatives of the colonial powers. On the contrary, it is a view resulting from an examination of the missionary attitude that the Christian possesses full religious truth and has therefore, on the basis of this possession, only to give, admonish and teach or to purify, save and liberate. What is forgotten in this attitude is that Christianity is always fragmentary and provisional at any given stage of history and that its present historical form always looks forward to the future. Its existence is, in other words, always eschatological and this means that the Christian — and the Christian mission — is often placed in a situation of "not yet" rather than "already." It is therefore advisable for Christian missionaries to be extremely cautious in what they say about possessing absolute truth. Only benefit can result from refraining to speak about such a possession in the dialogue with people of other religions and cultures. . . .

Can the absolute claim of Christianity ever be meaningful in the task of proclaiming the Gospel to non-Christians and within the framework for non-Christian cultures? It can, I think, be meaningful only if it is regarded as a demand which the missionary makes of himself. This demand is that he should live his own Christianity to the maximum and optimum degree himself, that he should be a total witness to faith. It is in the fulfillment of this demand to bear living witness that this superlative claim (the verbal form of what "absolute" ought to mean) has a real place. Bearing witness to faith can never be sufficiently convincing or convinced. Only the "absolutely" convinced believer can convince others of the truth of his faith. Only a Christian who confesses without conditions and the unconditioned saving value of Jesus Christ as the possibility and the offer of salvation for all man can have the right attitude towards non-Christians, an attitude that involves a readiness to exchange in dialogue, to learn and to teach.

In conclusion, we may say that the service of evangelization is really a service performed for the one absolute God or, to express this biblically, it is a preparation of oneself and the world for the reception of the kingdom of God that is to come. Faith in Christ results in a maximum imitation of Jesus himself, who evangelized, but never preached himself. This faith also leads to a tireless bearing of witness to the fact that the fulfillment of all mortal mankind has become a promise in the resurrection of the crucified Jesus by God. This coming of God and his kingdom is prepared by the work of evangelization. We bear witness to the coming of the God, who is more than the absolute one in that he comes, in the relative and fragmentary experience of our historical situation of being on the way to the kingdom.

Dialogue and Mission:
Conflict or Convergence?

Michael Amaladoss

Amaladoss serves as an assistant to the superior general of the
Society of Jesus in Rome and is a former editor of the theological
journal *Vidajyoti*. Recent Roman Catholic Church documents
talk about the role of other religions in salvation. For Christians,
this raises the question "Why evangelize?" Amaladoss accepts
the hypothesis and suggests an answer to the question. Source:
International Review of Mission, July 1986, 222-41.

There is a widespread feeling today in the church that its traditional missionary dynamism is growing weaker. This phenomenon is being blamed
on an emerging theology of religions on the one hand and, on the other,
on a broadening of the focus of mission effort. Proclamation leading to
conversion is seen as only one aspect of evangelization, the other aspects
being dialogue, liberation and inculturation. Increasing secularization and
dechristianization have made the whole world the field of mission so that
one speaks of the mission to six continents. The other religions are seen in
a more positive light as "ways of salvation" calling for inter-religious dialogue. Some theologians have not only moved from christocentrism to
theocentrism, but even propose the possibility of many incarnations. Are
we finding facile solutions to the problem of religious pluralism, sacrificing
in the process the identity of the church and of Christ? In this atmosphere

the dialectical relationship between mission and dialogue becomes radical-ized into an opposition, with the result that a variety of middle positions that try to hold on to both poles of the dialectic tend to get overlooked. I think that mission and dialogue are in a convergent rather than conflictual relationship. . . .

A Positive View of Other Religions

The Second Vatican Council declared in its *Constitution on the Church:*

> Those also can attain to everlasting salvation who, through no fault of their own, do not know the Gospel of Christ or His Church, yet sincerely seek God and, moved by grace, strive by their deeds to do His will as it is known to them through the dictates of conscience.

This text reaffirms traditional doctrine. It might, however, seem to limit itself to the interior, personal relationship between God and an in-dividual in the secrecy of his or her conscience. . . .

The Pluralism of Religions

As soon as one speaks of many ways to salvation one will be accused of relativism. Is it not like saying: "all religions are the same," "all religions are true," "all religions lead to God as all rivers lead to the sea?" *The Document on Religious Freedom* of the Second Vatican Council states very clearly:

> The highest norm of human life is the divine law — eternal, objective, and universal — whereby God orders, directs and governs the entire universe and all the ways of the human community, by a plan conceived in wisdom and love. Man has been made by God to participate in this law. . . . Hence every man has the duty, and therefore the right, to seek the truth in matters religious. . . . Truth, however, is to be sought after in a manner proper to the dignity of the human person and his social nature. The inquiry is to be free, carried on with the aid of teaching or instruction, communication, and dialogue. . . . In all his activity a man is bound to follow his conscience faithfully. . . . Of its very nature, the exercise of religion consists before all else in those internal, voluntary, and free acts whereby man sets the course of his life directly toward

God. . . . However, the social nature of man itself requires that he should give external expression to his internal acts of religion; that he should participate with others in matters religious; that he should profess his religion in community.

In matters of religion and faith, the guidance of conscience is decisive. It is not religions that give salvation; they are only ways. It is God who offers freely salvation to humankind who responds in freedom. . . .

The Church and Other Religions

What is the self-awareness of the church in the midst of the religions? I think we can say that after the Second Vatican Council no one would think of the church and other religions in terms of presence/absence of salvation or light/darkness. There would, however, be some who would still think in terms of divine/human, supernatural/natural. Apart from the fact that such dichotomies are no longer current in theology today, such an attitude is untenable after the repeated affirmations of God's universal salvific will and of a common divine plan for the world. Terms like implicit/explicit, partial/full are more common today. One sees the history for salvation as a straight line that moves from the cosmic to the mosaic and the Christian covenant. The process is one of explication and fulfillment. While we cannot deny the special significance of the short period of history between Moses and Jesus it would not be fair to narrow down salvation history to that small section. A special call finds its meaning only in relation to the whole. So we cannot understand the significance of this brief period of history without setting it back in the context of the universal history of humankind, which is also a salvation history, because God has willed and planned to save all. . . .

The Uniqueness of Christ

To say that the fullness is in the future may still upset some. Is not Christ our fullness? Do we not have everything with Christ? Is he not the unique savior? Has he not saved all by dying for all? So we come to the christological problem.

We profess our faith "Christ died for all." What is the meaning of this statement? There is a spectrum of theological opinions varying from the purely juridical to the organic. Some would say that Christ has made satisfaction for all. The graces he had amassed by his infinite sacrifice are given to all who sincerely repent. The other extreme would be that Christ has saved the whole of humanity by the very act of uniting himself to it; this happens already at the incarnation. Some would speak of a corporate personality: Christ does not die and rise again instead of us, but all of us die and rise with him. Some others would stress the risen Christ: in future of his passion and death Christ is now established with power before the throne of God as Lord and Savior. Karl Rahner proposes the theory of real-symbol causality: it is real because it is a definitive commitment that unites both the yes's of God and humankind in one person; it is of universal significance because it expresses both God's will to save all people and Jesus' solidarity with every person; it is symbolic, because it is a prototype of every divine-human encounter. Whatever the theory we prefer, we have to safeguard a certain number of things; that the freedom and historicity of every person's response is respected; that this possibility of response is available to people not only after Jesus but also before him; that the possibility is not tied to an explicit profession of faith in Jesus in the church.

We are faced here with an event in history that has a transcendent significance. Those who wish to point to the centrality of Jesus and the church in a narrow manner harp on the historical aspect of the matter and speak of the scandal of particularity. Yet it would seem to me that only insofar as we liberate the mystery from its historical particularity without severing the link, can we realize its universal significance. As a matter of record, in the New Testament, the progressive realization of the universal significance of the death and resurrection of Jesus is accompanied by the realization of the universal outreach of his personality as the cosmic Christ of St. Paul and the Logos of St. John.

A New Paradigm

The new paradigm, which has already been evoked a number of times earlier, could be outlined in three points. God's universal saving will is present and active everywhere through various ways. It is a plan progressively realized in history. It leads to the unification of all things till God is all in all. The three high points that structure the process and therefore have a special universal significance are creation, the paschal mystery and the final fulfillment. In this historical process the paschal mystery is a definitive moment of irrevocable commitment in which God's free offer and humankind's free acceptance of divine self-communication meet in a single act — a single person. The church is a continuing sacramental (symbolic) re-presentation of this definitive divine-human encounter, called by its very being to witness to and to promote the plan of God — the mystery — which it does not identify with itself. The church has no exclusive claims on the mystery, except that of being its witness and servant, both in life and proclamation. It does not offer easier or fuller salvation. God alone is the savior present and active in the world in ways often unknown to us. Because of the universal salvific will of God and the socio-historical character of the human person the salvific divine-human encounter is also taking place through other religions and their symbolic structures: scriptures, codes of conduct and rituals. . . .

Integral Evangelization

The primary task of evangelization is the advancement of the mystery of God's plan for the world — the promotion of the kingdom. The building up of a local witnessing community is certainly an element in this task; but not an exclusive element. The kind of activity that we actually have in a given place would depend on the concrete circumstances, needs and possibilities. We have to read the signs of the times and discern the Lord's call in a given situation, rather than go with an abstract list of priorities. The signs of the times include, for instance, the urgency of a particular need such as poverty, oppression, inter-religious strife, etc., or the readiness of a given group of people to listen to the good news.

Living in Asia in multi-religious societies, in the task of promoting common human and evangelical values, we are called to collaborate with the members of other religions toward providing a common religious and moral foundation to our developing societies. Speaking to Muslim and Hindu representatives in Nairobi, John Paul II said:

> The close bonds linking our respective religions — our worship of God and the spiritual values we hold in esteem — motivate us to become fraternal allies in service to the human family. . . . We are all children of God, members of the great family of man. And our religions have a special role to fulfill in curbing these evils and in forging bonds of trust and fellowship. God's will is that those who worship him, even if not

united in the same worship, would nevertheless be united in brotherhood and in common service for the good of all.

Whatever may be their absolute faith positions, the different religions can and do find a common perspective in the area of human and religious values. Differences in their historico-cultural roots also make their approaches complementary towards the promotion of integral humanism. An awareness of the church's own limitations in standing up for humankind in the past and of the contemporary record of countries that Asians identify as Christian would help us to remain humble.

Why Proclamation?

If other religions too are ways of salvation why proclaim the gospel and seek to baptize people? The need of other people for salvation motivated missionaries in former times. We today do not share their anxiety. Should that anxiety be an essential element in our enthusiasm in proclaiming the good news? The motivation to proclaim the good news is a combination of an internal urge and a call. I have discovered and experienced the good news, and the joy of this experience drives me to share it with others. This internal drive is confirmed and strengthened by the call of Christ to go out into the whole world and be a witness to the good news. I also feel the urge to proclaim the good news because I am convinced that it has something essential and specific to contribute, according to the plan of God, to the growth of the new humanity. The cross and resurrection, the new commandment, the commitment to a new humanity to be progressively built up in history are perspectives that give a new kind of meaning to human experience. The good news can hardly play its role effectively in the world unless it is visibly and socially present in culture as local church, indigenous and inculturated. To build up such a witnessing church is also a task of mission.

Why Dialogue?

As soon as one no longer sees the relationship of Christianity to other religions as presence/absence or superior/inferior or full/partial, etc., dialogue becomes the context in which even proclamation has to take place. For even when proclaiming the good news with assurance one has to do it with great respect for the freedom of God who is acting, the freedom of the other who is responding and the church's own limitations as a witness. It is quite proper then that the Asian bishops characterized evangelization itself as a dialogue with various Asian realities: cultures, religions and the poor.

When faith encounters faith no other way but dialogue is possible, if one respects the other's convictions. When a developed metacosmic religion meets a simple cosmic one, the relationship may not be equal culturally. But when one metacosmic religion meets another, dialogue seems the only possible way. Besides, one cannot hold on to an absolute commitment of faith without relativizing the other from one's own point of view. Karl Rahner, in a rare moment, tells us the following story:

> Nishitani, the well-known Japanese philosopher, the head of the Kyoto school, who is familiar with the notion of the anonymous Christian, once asked me: what would you say to my treating you as an anonymous Zen Buddhist? I replied: Certainly you may and should do so from your point of view; I feel myself honored by such an interpretation, even if I am obliged to regard you as being in error or if I assume that, correctly understood, to be a genuine Zen Buddhist is identical with being a genuine Christian, in the sense directly and properly intended by such statement. Of course in terms of objective social awareness it is indeed clear that the Buddhist is not a Christian and the Christian is not a Buddhist.

A faith commitment gives an absolute value not only to the absolute, but also to the real-symbol that mediates that absolute. Two believers who meet each other, even when they realize that the absolute to which they are both committed is the same, do not on that account relativize the mediating real-symbols. That is why a sort of super-theology that would reconcile in a higher synthesis two absolute commitments is not possible, though it would always remain a rational temptation. One can escape this predicament only at the level of interpersonal relationship that not only respects each other's freedom and the sovereign freedom of God, but also enters into a convergent movement through mutual sharing of experiences leading to mutual challenge and mutual growth.

Proclamation and dialogue are relationships between persons. In the last analysis, the plurality of free persons is the basis of a pluralistic world. Plurality demands dialogue and community. It abhors system. Plurality, freedom, dialogue and community should pose no problem for people who contemplate the trinity.

We Are the World

James Engel

James Engel teaches missions at Eastern Baptist College. He suggests that the current Christian missions effort is foundering on two very practical problems: finances and motivation. He suggests that baby boomers have the money, but are turned on and tuned in to missions in very different ways from their parents. Source: *Christianity Today,* 24 September 1990, 32-34.

Unless radical changes are made by mission agencies and local churches, Christian baby boomers will not provide the human and financial resources needed for accelerated evangelism in the 1990s.

"Evangelize the World by AD 2000!" is a heady and contagious rallying cry. It is heard worldwide from such diverse sources as the Lausanne Movement, Roman Catholics, Anglicans, Southern Baptists, mission agencies, and the Bible societies. And there are nearly 100 worldwide "megaplans" calling for a drastic increase in human financial resources in this decade.

While vision soars, few have addressed the sobering issue of where needed resources will come from. It is somehow assumed that the American church will carry the lion's share, as it has done for many decades. Unfortunately, this is nothing more than fanciful, wishful thinking that ignores the reality that missionary vision and support is eroding, not increasing.

A generation of American Christians have supported the cause of world evangelization by giving their time and money obediently and generously. Unfortunately, they have aged and are mostly beyond 55. And this aging (and shrinking) resource base is stretched to the limit and unable to expand to meet any new demands.

We are at a time when the resource burden should be shifting to the pivotal generation born between 1946 and 1964 — the baby boomers. But there is real doubt that they will meet the challenge, because boomer priorities and interests diverge sharply from that of traditional missionary enterprise. They will be the missing link in the resource chain that could doom AD 2000 visions unless churches and mission agencies radically change present resource mobilization strategies.

Marching to a Different Drum

Boomers, as a generation, differ sharply from their elders. There is greater tolerance for diversity and ready acceptance of formerly taboo lifestyles. They are motivated by economic well-being, good personal relationships, and a comfortable family life. The international arena is not a primary part of their worldview.

In another sense, however, boomers have an outlook that favors activism. There is a prevailing entrepreneurial spirit and desire for immediate gratification. While distrust of traditional institutions is common, boomers view themselves as problem solvers who, if given an appropriate challenge, are likely to rise to meet it.

In fact, there is a surprising willingness to contribute both time and money to worthy causes. Social researcher Daniel Yankelovich explains it this way:

> This generation has the ability to look reality in the eye; they won't follow old, outmoded ideas out of sentiment. . . . Their generation does not have a sentimental attachment to the old days. If there are new realities, they will face them.

While they can be mobilized to attack world and societal needs if a cause is seen as worthy, most Christian boomers are largely immune to the cause of world missions as it has traditionally been practiced and presented.

The most recent in a series of studies of Christian baby boomers undertaken at the Wheaton College Graduate School disclosed that only 10 percent from a cross section of evangelical churches place a high priority on spreading the gospel overseas. When asked which causes they would support financially if they had the resources, they ranked traditional mission activities such as church planting, evangelism, short-wave broadcasts, and Bible schools dead last.

Why is this the case? This generation has drawn in on itself. The idealism fanned by John F. Kennedy's challenge to sacrifice died in the ashes of the Vietnam War, and the disappointing international programs and sloganeering calling for American-led evangelistic initiatives fall largely on deaf ears. No amount of gut-wrenching, high-powered appeal to sacrifice will change this outlook.

Do not assume, however, that this generation of Christians is characterized by indifference. Boomers are interested in local causes that affect life right where they live. But they express equal interest in training and equipping nationals (as opposed to sending expatriates). Underlying everything is a heart commitment to holistic ministries encompassing economic development and social justice.

Furthermore, boomers are willing to commit time and funds when they own the cause. This means that they will come aboard full steam when their entrepreneurial spirit can be channeled into direct, hands-on strategy development. They will not buy into someone else's program unless they have a hand in shaping it.

Career missionary service is unattractive to the majority, however, largely because of the disruptions it can bring to family life. Boomers are, therefore, not likely to meet the burgeoning needs for full-time missionaries. Short-term service is quite another matter, especially among singles.

Restoring the Missing Link

Let's face it — Christians are too often viewed as customers for high-powered, mission-marketing efforts by agencies and denominations. Boomers, however, are giving a clear negative vote by saying, "We want a different product." I, for one, think they are right.

The boomers' entrepreneurial outlook says, "Let me be a part of the process. Let me see and feel the need and work as a partner with those on the scene to find the solutions. Otherwise I'm not interested in your grand megaplans, in *your* program."

If international vision is to be expanded, direct exposure and involvement overseas is an absolute necessity; *short-term service is the key to the problem.* Our data from the Wheaton Graduate School study clearly demonstrate that those who come for a brief visit have significantly greater awareness of the commitment to world evangelization.

Churches all over the United States are finding that returned short-termers are the catalysts who can spark vital missions programs. The Church on the Way in Van Nuys, California, is just one that has seen a true transformation. Pastor Jim Tolle says short-termers "come back and tell friends, and they are never the same again. They see people in their poverty, and they see them sacrifice everything for the kingdom of God. They come back to their stereo systems and new cars, and something changes in their mentality."

Returned short-termers become effective opinion leaders. Missions indifference can yield, thus leading to a marked increase in involvement at both the local-church and agency levels.

Although most boomers are not open to career service at this stage of life, our survey shows that almost half will consider short-term involvement. This high level of interest is confirmed by the fact that 43 percent of all missionaries serving overseas in 1988 were sent for short terms (between 2 and 11 months), compared with 36 percent in 1985. The proportion is expected to reach 50 percent by 1993.

Unfortunately, too many mission boards have failed to capitalize on the potential of short-term ministry. Seventy percent of short-termers in 1988 served with only two agencies: the Southern Baptist Foreign Mission Board and Youth With a Mission. Even more disturbing is the fact that two-thirds of all agencies report no short-termers whatsoever. Unless this short-sighted policy is remedied, missions executives must face the fact that boomers will fail to respond. The inevitable result will be a decline in funds and personnel.

Creative Partnership

"The cities of Latin America must be reached — thousands are perishing daily." This appeal might motivate elders, but it will leave most boomers cold — unless they are shown how they can make a difference by direct participation. If it becomes clear that a contribution of $8,000 from a local church will support a national evangelist who will plant two new churches, each serving people he has led to Christ, quite a different response will be found. Interest jumps all the more if creative ways can be found for church members to participate on site.

Agencies who view the local church as only a pass-through source for funds and human resources will increasingly find boomers remaining on the sideline. Creative partnership links will become a necessity.

The first challenge is to the local church. If your congregation is passive, you face an uphill struggle in building a vital missions program among boomers. The Wheaton Graduate School research shows a direct correlation between active involvement in local outreach and interest in mission. Where there is little outreach, boomers will be indifferent to the world scene.

Mission agencies, in turn, must face the growing reality that career service is only one way to attract the necessary personnel. Major adjustments will be required in field strategies to use short-termers creatively. The time has come to view short-term service as the essential beginning stage of lifetime involvement, which can lead to catalytic mobilization of others and eventual full-time service (following retirement or the arrival of the empty nest).

Here are some other requirements for stimulating boomer interest and involvement:

1. End the all-too-common dichotomy between evangelism and social action. Boomers readily embrace an understanding of the kingdom of God that affirms the lordship of Jesus Christ over all phases of life.

2. Do not feed the polarization of the body of Christ into such camps as liberal/evangelical or charismatic/noncharismatic. Boomers do not respond to such labels and will look to the more central issue of commitment to biblical fundamentals.

3. Do not focus on denominational agency loyalty, because these are largely irrelevant to boomers. What you stand for and do is what counts.

4. Unleash boomers' entrepreneurial spirit by encouraging new ideas and strategies. They are forced to innovate in the secular world and expect a similar openness to change in Christian service.

5. Stress the importance of training and equipping nationals. Boomers know that the greatest challenge lies in building disciples who can shoulder their own burden.

As one who is well past boomer age, I am mightily encouraged that this generation is compelling us to rethink our premises. Boomers, when properly motivated, can bring a greatly needed shot of vitality into the missions enterprise.

Mission and Mammon: Six Theses

Jonathan J. Bonk

Jonathan J. Bonk, a Mennonite, is chairperson of the Mission Studies Department, Winnipeg Theological Seminary, Otterburne, Manitoba, Canada. The son of missionary parents, he grew up in Ethiopia, later returning there to work with the Relief and Rehabilitation arm of SIM International from 1974-76. The themes in this essay are developed further in his book, *Money and Missions: The Role of Affluence in the Christian Missionary Enterprise from the West* (Herald Press, 1992). Source: *International Bulletin of Missionary Research*, October 1989, 174-81.

The missionary expression of the Western churches is deeply affected by the press and pull of a social ethos that, if examined closely, is seen to be shaped, inspired, and driven by consumerism — the deep conviction that life consists in the abundance of possessions, especially more, better, up-to-date possessions. . . .

The price missionaries must pay for their participation in affluence has never been higher. In exchange for the comforts and efficiencies of personal affluence, Western missionaries sacrifice a measure of apostolic effectiveness and credibility. But this pound of flesh is a mere scratch beside the loss of personal integrity that rich missionaries — as personal representatives of a Lord who became poor for our sakes — must inevitably suffer. This "hidden" cost may be expressed by means of six theses:

1. *Possession of wealth makes Western missionary insulation not only*

possible, but highly probable. A primary advantage of wealth is its capacity to provide those who possess it with goods and services that serve to cushion them from the harsh realities of life. . . . That insularity, which the privileged accept as their entitlement, manifests itself in virtually every facet of a Western missionary's life. Comfortable, well-furnished residences; closets with several changes of clothing; cupboards stocked with a great variety of nutritious foods; medicine cabinets brimming with efficacious prophylactics and drugs of various kinds; medical plans to deal with a child's crooked teeth or a parent's failing kidney; insurance policies providing for the well-being of loved ones in the event of an untimely emergency; registered retirement savings plans that, by taking careful thought of the morrow, are calculated to assist the aged missionary in the final transition between this life and the next; the costly mobility — by means of personal motor vehicles — to which every Westerner feels entitled; resources sufficient for expensive local and international flights to whisk a family away from danger or to take a family on a much-needed furlough; educational opportunities unmatched anywhere in the world for children; fun-filled, expensive vacations for the family; an abundance of ingenious technological aids of various kinds, each device promising and sometimes delivering efficiency in accomplishing personal and professional ends. Such derivatives of personal affluence constitute the "nonconducting material" of which missionary insulation from the "heat" and "sound" of poverty is fashioned.

2. *The insular affluence of Western missionaries makes independence possible, segregation necessary, and isolation from the poor unavoidable.* . . . The fierce love of personal independence is not left behind when Western missionaries travel abroad. The independence to which Westerners are accustomed is costly to maintain in other parts of the world. Only the person of considerable means can hope to afford it; conversely, the person wishing to live in an American way must have access to wealth.

Independence is even more costly in nonmonetary terms, however. Not surprisingly, Western missionary communities have from the beginning been marked by a de facto racial segregation, since membership is based upon economic criteria that can generally be met only by Western Christians. This is not to say that all contact with impoverished nonwhites is avoided. On the contrary, it is often the plight of such poor that has figured most prominently in Western missionary journeys to the ends of the earth. But such contacts have tended — particularly in places where there are large concentrations of missionaries among even larger numbers of the poor — to accentuate the missionaries' absolute independence of and segregation from the poor. This is isolation. There is something both ironic and tragic in the specter of a supremely relational gospel being proclaimed by an isolated community of segregated whites. . . . Since biblical faith is, above all, a relational faith, it is not only sad, but sinful, when personal possessions and privileges prevent, distort, or destroy the relationships of Christ's followers with the poor. But this appears to be an almost inevitable consequence of personal affluence.

3. *The independence, segregation, and isolation that come with wealth translate into an unbridgeable social gulf between rich and poor.* This social gulf makes genuine fraternal friendship so awkward as to be virtually impossible. . . . Between families of widely disparate means and standards of living, friendship is extremely unlikely. With whom does a missionary naturally choose to spend leisure time? With whom is a vacation comfortably shared? Who is likely to listen comprehendingly, sympathetically, understandingly to a couple as they pour out the peculiar frustrations, burdens, and perplexities of missionary parenting? With whom is a Western missionary likely to go shopping for family birthday or Christmas gifts? Who is able to commiserate with the missionary on the inadequacy of his or her support level? From whom will a missionary likely seek advice on personal financial matters — investment, banking, saving? In every case, it is very doubtful that the poor would have any part in these aspects of a missionary's life. The social rapport required must obviously be reserved for social and economic peers. The presence of the poor in such situations would be an embarrassment to any missionary of even moderate sensitivity.

The staggeringly high relational price that Western missionaries must pay for their affluence could perhaps be overlooked, or at least endured, were it not for its insidious effects upon the communication process. For medium and message are both significantly affected by the relationship of the missionary to the convert or would-be convert. If the message of the cross consisted simply of a series of theologically correct propositions about God, humankind, and salvation, then the obligation to preach the gospel could be fulfilled by means of public announcement over the radio. But the Word must always be made flesh, and dwell among humanity. And the Way has always best been shown by those who can be accompanied by would-be pilgrims. Missionaries are above all Way-showers, whose lives must be imitatable by their converts. Missionaries are not simply voice boxes, but pilgrims who invite others to join them on the narrow way. . . .

4. *Personal affluence in the context of poverty raises legitimate doubts concerning a missionary's willingness to obey and ability to teach the whole*

311

counsel of God regarding mammon. . . . If "greed" be defined as the desire for more than enough in a social context in which some have less than enough, then most who journey from North American shores must accept the fact that most of the world so considers them. Among the most awkward challenges faced by Western missionaries abroad is the necessity of explaining to the truly needy why Westerners not only need to be staggeringly wealthy by the standards of all but a few, but will doubtless need even more next year. In the eyes of the poor even the ordinary missionary must seem to incarnate many of those qualities, which, by Paul's standards, disqualified a person from office in a church: a lover of money (1 Tim. 3:30), one who has not fled from but, rather embraced great gain (1 Tim. 6:5-11). According to Paul, the children of darkness are characterized by self-indulgence of every kind, and by "a continual lust for more" (Eph 4:19). "But among you," Paul continues, "there must not be even a *hint* (italics added) of . . . greed. . . . For of this you can be sure: No . . . such person . . . has any inheritance in the kingdom of Christ and of God" (Eph. 5:3-5). These are sobering words to those of us who — despite being surrounded by the truly needy — have come to expect as our due steady improvement in our already high standard of living, even if it must be at the expense of those who barely subsist.

Sadly, a strong case can be made in support of the proposition that Western missionaries — true sons and daughters of their churches back home — show no great willingness to lose all things for the sake of Jesus Christ. Far from being, in Paul's words, "rubbish" (Phil. 3:7-8), their material symbols of affluence have become absolutely essential for the continuation of mission from the West. Christ's teaching on the abundance of possessions cannot be taught — because it will not be practiced — by most Western Christians.

5. *The money- and power-based strategies generated by the institutional and personal affluence of Western missionaries contradict principles that are at the very heart of Christian mission as prescribed in the New Testament. . . .* The affluence-based mission of the Western church — in contrast to the incarnation-based mission of its Lord — most naturally serves as an ecclesiastical springboard for moving up, not down; its independently secure missionaries find lording both more natural and more immediately effective than serving, although many have convinced themselves that domination is service. The great marvel of living in the technological age is that one's mission can speed up, rather than — as in the case of Christ — slow down and finally come to a complete halt on the cross. We have discovered

— to our great relief — that prolonging one's abundant life is not only personally gratifying; it is a demonstrably superior way of marketing the good news than is, say, dying. And thus the gospel is reduced to the peddling of ideas about the One who was rich but for our sakes became poor, and who personally demonstrated what has proved to be true ever since: spiritual vitality comes to full potency only through weakness (2 Cor. 12:9-10).

The affluent church — by abandoning the incarnation as a model for its own life and mission — has demonstrated its fundamental spiritual impotence. For as theologian Trevor Verryn reminds us, "Only the truly strong are able to lay aside their power in an act of self-emptying and assume a position of powerlessness." The strategy of the cross that has ever marked the true servant of God is nowhere more accurately or inadvertently summed up than in the words of the ridicule of the religiously powerful who, satisfied that they had saved themselves no end of trouble by at last disposing of Jesus, chuckled among themselves, "He saved others, but he can't save himself!" Alas for religious teachers of that day and this! In trying to save themselves, they cannot save others. . . .

6. *Both the motives and the message of affluent missionaries are suspect, and biblical teaching on wealth and poverty, the rich and the poor, must necessarily be truncated when conveyed via an affluent channel.* Missionaries cannot challenge converts to a way of life that they themselves are unwilling to live. This is a centuries-old problem that recurs wherever missionaries from the West have gone to do their work among materially poorer societies.

Can the secure and infinitely better-off missionaries teach those who barely subsist about sacrifice, about simplicity, about costly discipleship? Can they demonstrate their personal faith in the truth that godliness with contentment is great gain (1 Tim. 6:6-19)? How can the Western missionary teach poor Christians not to become engrossed in the things of this world because they are all passing away — when the missionary's own lifestyle suggests a preoccupation with possessions (1 Cor. 7:30-31)? Is it possible for affluent missionaries to claim honestly, in the midst of their plenty, that they consider everything as rubbish compared to the surpassing greatness of knowing Christ Jesus their Lord, for whose sake they have lost all things (Phil. 3:8)? Is it possible that missionaries from the West so reflect the values of the West that such things can only be "taught," not demonstrated? Honest answers to questions such as these indicate that both the credibility and the integrity of missionary endeavors from the wealthy nations are in jeopardy. In summary, Western missionary affluence is the human culture in which profoundly theological, relational, and ethical problems most naturally thrive: preoccupation with possessions; an exclusive dependence upon power-based statuses and strategies; and ethical double standards.

Western Christians rightly regard the poverty of fellow human beings as a gigantic problem about which we seem able to do very little; we have proved less willing to view our personal affluence as a spiritual — hence even greater — problem. . . .

What can be done? Is it really true, as Ivan Illich insisted, in 1970, that "There is no exit from a way of life built on $5000-plus per year . . ."? The Western missionary experience of the 1980s seems to support his pessimism; but are change, repentance, conversion — the stock-in-trade of missionary preaching — possible only for nonmissionaries?

The possibility of the Christian mission being carried out without vast financial resources or an elite corps of highly paid professional Western missionaries is not merely a theoretical possibility. For the major part of the church's existence it has been a necessity, and as the twentieth century draws to a close, it is increasingly clear that most missionary endeavor has been, is being, and must continue to be undertaken by missionaries for the poorer churches. One of the most difficult lessons the Western church will one day be compelled to learn is, according to theologian David Bosch, "how to become again what it originally was and was always supposed to be: the church without privileges, the church of the catacombs rather than of the halls of fame and power and wealth." . . .

Among the richly varied theological motifs running through the pages of the New Testament, three are of such broad significance as to touch upon every other facet of Christian faith and practice: the incarnation, the cross, and weakness as power.

For Western Christian missions, grappling with economic power at the theological level will mean subjecting all personal, family, ecclesiastical, and strategic plans, policies, practices, and considerations to these three questions: (1) Does it reflect the incarnation, or is it essentially self-serving? (2) Is the cross both the message and the method, or is self-preservation the bottom line? (3) Are people more impressed by its stability and strength or by its weakness? The answers to these questions will provide some intimation of the future of Western missions as a vitally Christian spiritual force.

Contextualization from a
World Perspective

Robert J. Schreiter

The text of this article was an address to the 1992 Association
of Theological Schools' biennial meeting. In the first part of his
address (not included here) Schreiter is clear in identifying his
views as coming out of a Roman Catholic theological perspective. His insights, however, have much wider application.
Schreiter is professor of doctrinal theology at Catholic Theological Union, Chicago, Illinois. Source: *Theological Education*
1993 Supplement 1 (autumn 1993): 63-85.

As North American theological educators struggle to clarify their understanding of contextualization and its correlative form, globalization, the
perspective of the wider world, particularly the world outside the North
Atlantic region, can be of great use here. . . .

Globalization is inevitable;
hence contextualization becomes essential.

The United States (and to a lesser degree, Canada) is just beginning to
realize what other parts of the world have known for quite some time:
globalization is here and is a presence that cannot be escaped. Because of
its economic power, the United States has often been the agent of globali-

315

zation without having to feel its effects. Especially since the end of the Second World War, the United States has asserted its presence around the world. Other countries have had to come to terms with that, whether they wanted to or not. The U.S.'s neighbor to the North, Canada, is itself a rich and powerful nation, but was perceiving what globalization was about before the United States. The United States did not really come to understand the implications of globalization until it began to become "globalized" by other countries, notably those of the oil rich Middle East, Western Europe, and Eastern Asia. Most effectively, perhaps, globalization began for the United States in 1973, when the OPEC cartel began to impose prices on the worldwide market that the U.S. could not control. "Globalization" becomes a full reality when we realize that we are inevitably part of a worldwide flow of information, technology, capital, and goods — a flow over which no single nation has effective control any more.

This leads to a second reflection. The globalization that is now the subject of our discussion is but the latest round of globalization on our planet. As I will argue in the third section of this presentation, we are experiencing what may be the transition from the second to the third round of globalization to take place in the past five hundred years. . . .

Much of the reflection in this section has been devoted to the correlate of contextualization — globalization. But what of contextualization? In view of this perspective, for most of the world contextualization is a matter of finding one's voice and protecting oneself from the onslaughts of globalization. Both of these efforts are going on at the same time in many parts of the world. The ravages of colonialism and the disappointments of the independence movements following colonialism have continued to stifle the development of the authentic voices of many of the cultures of the world. Local cultures are considered inferior and backward to the shining world that the global media present. Women must not only struggle with the bonds of patriarchy present nearly everywhere, but must do so under the restraints of cultures that long told them they were not worthy vessels of "civilization." All of this happens at a time when markets are flooded with cola, denim jeans, and gym shoes, as well as music and entertainment, especially from the United States. The sight of children and adults wearing T-shirts with English sayings emblazoned upon them — sometimes fractured in grammar and not infrequently obscene in innuendo — bespeaks the invasion of cultures. This is especially the case when the glittering goods portrayed on television, or in the wealthy sections of a large city, or in tourist districts are goods far beyond the reach of the majority. The gap

316

between the two worlds reinforces the message of the inferiority of the local culture.

Contextualization becomes, therefore, a means to help hold up what is noble and immensely human and humane in a local culture against the onslaughts of forces — both historical and contemporary — that seek to undermine the dignity of the local culture. . . .

> *Contextualization is coming about slowly — more*
> *slowly than its correlate, globalization.*

Contextualization is coming far more slowly than had first been hoped. So what has gone wrong? Four things seem to play a major role. First of all, overcoming uniformities in previous practice, and the depredations of colonialism are taking far longer than any had realized. That is because these were not simply absences of local culture; they represented a local theology in themselves, a local theology of considerable cohesion and power. We know the pain of being robbed of one's culture, but we still do not understand the reach and the impact of that pain sufficiently clearly. Moreover, many suffered in throwing over local custom and culture to become Christian. Now they are being asked to take back what they had distanced themselves from at great pain.

Secondly, contextualization must contend with the overwhelming power of what is called global culture. This global culture is not "culture" in the same sense as local culture, but is so analogously. It carries many of the trappings of culture, but does not of itself create a culture in which one can live completely. However, it often embodies the aspirations of a local culture, and can seduce local cultures in trying to achieve the goods of this global culture and to neglect the development of the local culture. The power of globalization is so overwhelming as a technological, economic, and political force that it can make contextualization seem a weak agenda best relegated to the private sphere of a hobby, of tending one's garden. (It might be noted that a too-strong globalization would account for a too-weak contextualization, if the proposed hypothesis is correct.)

Third, the North seems to resist too much emphasis on building a more contextually sensitive world. Sometimes this emphasis is read by the North as a rejection of its values in favor of local ones (as indeed sometimes it is!). Other times there are fears that contextualization makes those interested in pursuing local values seem less flexible about moving around to service the new economic configurations. If people get too attached to one place, they may not be willing to pick up and follow where they are needed in the economy. But perhaps most of all, contextualization may mean simply doing things differently. And the inertia that greets the challenges of innovation (especially in an aging society) may be the greatest obstacle to contextualization.

Fourth and finally, there are ambivalences in the South. I have already mentioned the ambivalences those Christians face who are asked now to embrace what they once were asked to reject and so courageously did so. Another set of ambivalences arises out of a suspicion that the sudden Northern interest in contextualization after so many years of rejecting it is but another ploy to cut the South out of the future. "Are we yet again not good enough to be part of the new global culture?" they query. Moreover, the resources are often no longer there in the South to create the kind of context desired. Languages have been forgotten, customs destroyed, stories suppressed. And sometimes the sheer struggle for survival makes these kinds of questions utterly moot.

Viewed, then, from another angle, the quest for contextualization reveals itself as considerably more complex. It is, at this time in human history, linked closely to the forces of globalization. To fail to see this is to try to create *tableaux vivants* or cultural reservations rather than a truly contextual response to the gospel.

Three Concrete Issues Facing Contextualization

Among the many issues facing effective contextualization in the many cultural contexts around the world, I would like to focus upon three major ones that impinge upon cultural settings over and over today. These are by no means the only major ones. They do, however, represent issues at the crucial juncture between contextualization and globalization.

Deracination: The Uprooting of Peoples

Perhaps more than ever before, we have experienced in this century an uprooting of peoples. We have before us countless examples and cautionary tales of what happens when a people is wrenched out of its culture. Cultures are more than social relationships even as they include them; they involve language, familiar places, shared memories, food, a cycle of the year and a place to remember the dead. The three forms of uprooting that I wish to focus upon here as complicating contextualization are: colonialism, refugees, and urbanization.

There have already been several opportunities in this presentation to refer to the effects of colonialism on culture. While decrying the effects of colonialism, the gospel mandate to share the Good News with all people seems inevitably to create a colonizing opportunity, if not the colonial fact. Moreover, the gospel message is about transformation, about *metanoia,* hence change is about to happen. Some changes are definitely for the better. Gambian-born theologian Lamin Sanneh has assiduously pursued this side of the equation. The negative side has also been more than amply documented. Only recently have scholars tried to explore the nexus of ambiguity in wanting both to honor the dignity of a culture and to engage in changing it at the same time; such an example would be that of Australian-born anthropologist Kenelm Burridge. . . .

The second kind of uprooting is that of refugees. The United Nations High Commission on Refugees recently estimated that there are now more than twenty-one million political refugees forced out of their homelands into foreign exile. They are a presence here in the United States and Canada. And they are worldwide. If one adds to these the economic refugees, that is, those forced to leave their homes in order to support their families, the numbers would be even greater.

A third uprootedness is the urbanization of so much of the world. In Nicaragua, for example, a third of the entire population now lives (or better, struggles to survive) in Managua. This is a story repeated over and over again across the cities of Africa, Asia, and Latin America. Even as the cities become huge unsustainable and unsustaining megacities (Mexico City is now the largest, with a population of nearly twenty-four million people), people continue to flock to them, mainly because the situation in the countryside is even worse for them. Nineteenth century models of industrial economies simply do not fit. One finds most of the people surviving in the so-called "informal economies" and through what others have referred to as the "rurification of the cities." What does "context" mean in these settings where, if people find work, they must walk for miles each day from their location on the urban periphery in order to reach the place of employment? Are our models of "Christian community" not often models more suited to rural and village life than to the dislocation of the *favelas* and *pueblos jovenes* ringing these cities? The small ecclesial community movement and the planting of small Pentecostal churches have been the most effective responses, it seems, to create the new "contexts." Here there is still much to learn.

Reception: How the Gospel Message Is Received

Reception has to do with how the Gospel message is received in a culture, as opposed to how it is sent. Much literature about contextualization has focused upon the sending process, to assure that the evangelist or contextualizer is presenting an orthodox account of the biblical witness. But it is becoming increasingly apparent that the reception of that message needs more attention than we have given it in the past. The assumption has largely been that, if the message is clearly presented, it will be clearly perceived. What such an approach does not account for is the cultural universe in which the message is lodged: its semantic location (how it relates to other meanings in the culture) may be significantly different from where it was located in the universe of the sender. . . .

A noted Bible translator told of his experience of presenting a fresh translation of the Psalms and the New Testament to a Thai university student. The student was not a Christian, and the intent of the gift was to see if the translation was intelligible to a non-Christian, not just syntactically (at the level of the correct grammatical usage), but also semantically. A few weeks later the translator encountered the student again and asked what he thought. The student admitted to having read the four Gospels, and was at that point reading the Acts of the Apostles. "What a wonderful person, your Jesus!" the student exclaimed. The translator, clearly excited by the response (for he is also a devout evangelical Christian and saw a potential convert here), asked the student to elaborate. "What a marvelous story," he continued, "of how your Jesus was born, lived, died . . . was reborn, lived, died . . . was reborn, lived, died . . . was reborn lived, and then — in the Acts of the Apostles — ascends into Nirvana! Just four incarnations to reach Buddhahood, and it took our Gautama a thousand lives to achieve that!" No doubt the more exalted language of the Gospel of John contributed to this reading of the spiritual maturation of Jesus. . . .

Another way of misunderstanding how the reception process expresses itself is by labeling it in an uncritical way as "syncretism." We have often made distinctions between syncretism as a social process (which has to do with the shaping of religious identity), and syncretism as a theological judgment (which is understood as a distortion of the theological tradition).

320

But more and more, this distinction can be shown to be really unhelpful. It does not tell us why particular configurations of belief emerge and, more importantly, why they perdure. . . .

A way of opening up the syncretism question within contextualization is to ask: *whose* syncretism? The evergreen trees that bedeck our sanctuaries at Christmas time come from pre-Christian Germanic and Slavic religion. An interesting and somewhat embarrassing case arose some thirty years ago when the new Roman Catholic cathedral was built in Kyoto. One of the stained glass windows had a portrait of St. George slaying the dragon. This image of St. George goes back to an amalgam of pre-Christian, Eastern Mediterranean lore. The problem in its context in Kyoto was that the dragon is not a symbol of Satan or of evil. Throughout East Asia, the dragon is a symbol of royalty and of heaven! Needless to say, the window was removed.

Much still needs to be done here, not only to see how peoples are shaping the irreligious identities, but also to critique the syncretisms that have accrued within Western Christian beliefs. The Reformation was one attempt to do that, but that was an intracultural critique. We now have the resources in the Southern Hemisphere churches to have an intercultural critique of both Catholic and Reformation forms of Western European Christianity.

Ways of Belonging

In the shaping of identity, multicultural theorist James A. Banks suggests that belonging was one of three most defining characters of communities (the other two being the sources of moral authority for the community and the frameworks for explaining events for the community). Christians often cite believing as the criterion for authentic Christianity and can have a tendency to underestimate the role of ways of belonging.

A clearer emphasis on belonging is needed because people find themselves in multiple worlds of reference: they define themselves by a variety of communities to which they belong. These can include the communities of immediate and extended family, work, leisure activities, charitable activities, education, and so on. Belonging is rarely as simple as having one point of location.

In matters of contextualization, we see people struggling with multiple belonging in the irreligious worlds of reference. This phenomenon is sometimes referred to as "double belonging," since it often involves relating to two worlds. Three worlds are not uncommon in Southeast Asia, where one has local traditions, Confucian traditions, and Christianity. In many parts of the world multiple belonging does not pose a cognitive or emotional obstacle; Japan is the clearest example of that, where there are almost twice as many religious adherents as there are people in the population! But for Christians this has long posed a vexing and difficult problem.

Sometimes it is a matter of competing worlds (that is the world-view of many Western Christians). For many people in these situations, however, it may be a matter of complementary worlds or even objective, noncommunicating worlds — what cultural psychologist Richard Shweder has called "multiple objective worlds." An example might help here.

Some years ago, a Roman Catholic missionary pastor was visiting the villages in Northern Ontario. He paid a pastoral call on a native woman on the first anniversary of the death of one of her two sons; he had been killed in an oil-rig accident. He accompanied her and her surviving son to the cemetery outside the village to pray at the gravesite. As they were coming out of the cemetery, a buck walked slowly out of the woods and stopped, facing them only a few yards away. Both the woman and her son dropped to their knees and began to pray in their native tongue — she, wailing; he, muttering softly. The buck did not move, but continued to stare at them intently. After a few minutes, the prayers ceased and the buck turned around, walking slowly back into the forest.

When they all returned to the house, the mystified priest asked the young man what had happened. He explained patiently, "That buck was the guardian spirit of my deceased brother. He came to thank us for remembering my brother on the anniversary of his death. You see, my brother communed closely with his guardian spirit. In fact, the spirit came to warn my brother on his last visit home that he would not return alive. My brother confided that to me before he left for the last time."

Multiple worlds? False worlds? Obviously the mother and son saw no incompatibility in praying traditional Christian prayers for their dead son and brother one moment, and in addressing a guardian spirit immediately thereafter. Do these worlds relate, or are they separate dimensions of time and reality that break into each other's realms? Enlightenment North Atlantic types find difficulty making room for this kind of thing, but peoples elsewhere do it routinely. Yet we find parallel beliefs in the New Testament in Paul and the Letter to the Hebrews. There, too, is the belief that Christ has overcome the Powers and Principalities, but Paul and Hebrews do not deny their existence.

322

Not much research has been done to date on multiple belonging, but a few things are beginning. How to classify the varieties of such belonging has still not been resolved satisfactorily. I would suggest that there are at least three types that recur: (1) Multiple belonging out of protest — such would be the case of people forcibly Christianized who maintain their local ways as an act against the oppressor. These are found frequently among the native peoples of the Americas. (2) Multiple belonging out of the inadequacy of Christianity to deal with local spirits and immediate, quotidian issues such as healing. This is common in Africa. (3) Multiple belonging out of inevitability, where the religious culture is so strong that one cannot be a member of the culture without participating in some fashion in another world. This is the case throughout much of Eastern and Southern Asia. . . .

Globalization: The Long View

Along with our understanding of contextualization, we need a fuller understanding of globalization. I wish to sketch out a proposal here of how we might understand globalization from a perspective useful for theological education and ministry. . . .

To aid us in this, I want to make a rough adaptation of Immanuel Wallerstein's world-system theory as a basis for understanding globalization. I am proposing that globalization (as seen from the point of view of theological education) has gone through three stages. . . .

First Phase: 1492-1945 — Expansion and the Building of Empires

The first phase has its period of dominance from the European voyages of exploration down to the conclusion of the Second World War. It is a time of European expansion and the creation of new European territorial space on the other continents of the world. The *carrier* of this phase of globalization is an image of expansion and establishment of political power over wide areas of the world — empire. The mode of *universality* giving justification or credence to this expansion is the concept of civilization that is invoked. In the early stage, the peoples encountered are seen as either animal or demonic; in the later stage, as not fully evolved.

323

On the religious side, we see a concomitant development, reflecting the envelope of the carrier in which it acts, and the universality in which it works out its own understanding of globalization. Images of expansion of the church, of a *plantatio ecclesiae* come to the fore. There is a sudden interest in worldwide evangelization (first among Roman Catholics in Spain and Portugal; later among churches of the Reformation as England and the Netherlands become worldwide powers). The *theological mode* responding to this is *world mission,* understood as saving souls and extending the church. The *results,* by the height of European empire building in the nineteenth century, is a worldwide missionary movement. Globalization, at this point, means extending the message of Christ and His church through the whole world.

Second Phase: 1945-1989 — Accompaniment, Dialogue, Solidarity

The Second World War finished what the First World War began: the dissolution of the overseas empires of Europe. From the late 1940s into the 1960s, region after region was given independence (at least "flag" independence) and it looked as though the shackles of colonialism would be cast off. There was an optimism about a new world at that time, fueled by economic expansion in the North and a discourse of "development" of the newly formed nations. All of this presaged a new kind of world. The *carriers* of this second phase were *decolonialization, independence,* and *economic optimism.* The mode of universality was optimism about overcoming the evils of the past.

On the religious side, Reformation churches found themselves overcoming their old antagonisms (partially as a result of the student missionary movement and the experience of the Resistance in Europe during the Second World War), and they started coming together. The Roman Catholic Church abandoned at the official level its fortress mentality against the modern world and embraced that same modernity in the Second Vatican Council. Both of these Western embodiments of Christianity found themselves welcoming a new partnership with the churches of the South. The shift into the new phase called into question the dominant universalities of the previous phase. What "mission" meant came under close scrutiny. . . . The response toward ecumenism, the ambivalence toward mission, and a new attention to the churches of the South was developed in the carrier envelope of decolonization, independence, and optimism. The *theological modes* that emerged were those of solidarity, dialogue, and accompaniment. Solidarity bespoke the new partnership that led to a sense of mutuality and commitment to the churches on the churches' own terms; it gave birth to liberation theologies. Dialogue was a reaction to the evangelizing mode of the first phase, and emphasized respect for the other and left the possibility of conversion deliberately vague. Accompaniment was meant to overcome the hegemonic patterns of leadership from the colonial period, and replace them with greater mutuality. The *results* were a new definition of globalization as ecumenical cooperation, interreligious dialogue, and the struggle for justice.

Third Phase: 1989 — Between the Global and the Local

Paul Tillich and others said that the twentieth century began in August 1914 with the outbreak of the Great War. It could equally be said that it ended in 1989 with the fall of the Berlin Wall. But the conditions leading up to that political event were also shaping a larger understanding of what is sometimes called the postmodern world. The date of the OPEC oil embargo, 1973, is often given as the date when economic power and the concomitant modes of production began to shift. New technologies, especially in communications, marked a move away from largely industrial economies to economies involved more in the flow of information, technologies, goods, and services. Just when the South was struggling to attain nation-states, these states were becoming more and more superfluous as information and capital drew their own map of the world — one beyond the eighteenth century ideal of the nation-state.

The *carrier* of this new postmodern reality is a new *global capitalism*. As was noted earlier, the defeat of socialism left no alternative. But the liberal capitalism that had been seen as the implacable foe of Marxist socialism has largely disappeared now into a new form of capitalism that emphasizes the mobility of capital, information, and resources rather than building of large industrial bases. . . .

What becomes the theological *mode* of the third phase of globalization? Discussions of the meaning of mission continue. Worries about the stagnation of ecumenism, the possibility of genuine dialogue with the religiously other and a theology of religions, and speculation about the future of liberation theology in a no-alternative world bespeak the fact that even as we have moved into a new phase, the previously dominant modes continue with us. After all, most Christians still feel the need to spread the gospel, overcome the scandalous divisions in the body of Christ, understand other religious traditions better, and struggle for justice. But the optimism that marked those earlier discussions has been replaced by a sobered realism (the attitude of the postmodern phase). Can a new mode be identified?

I would suggest that the new *mode* will involve bridge building, finding symbols of hope, and seeking paths of reconciliation. In other words, the barriers in the third phase are not between empire and colony, or between older and younger church, but rather are barriers that run helter-skelter through our communities, created by attempts to hold the global and the local in critical correlation. Even to phrase it as between North and South is too simple, since the South lives in the North and the North in the South. We need to find the cracks yawning in our midst where the global and the local fail to connect. We need too to seek symbols of hope in a world that seems less and less able to hold out opportunities for another vision. Our hope is not the optimistic hope of the 1960s; it is a tempered, more sobered hope, but a hope nonetheless. Likewise, in the tensions and conflicts that emerge, we need to seek paths of reconciliation less an ecologically threatened earth fracture altogether. There are many false paths of reconciliation, to be sure. But in an ever violent world where the majority suffer, reconciliation — the discovery of the gift of true humanity — is something we cannot disdain to seek.

Globalization in this third phase, then, becomes a quest for the bridges between the global and the local. The global has changed; its economic face appears to be even less benign than in the recent past. This has prompted new expressions of the local — the eruptions in Central Asia and in Eastern Europe, the resurgence of native pride in the Americas, but also the rootlessness of much of affluent North America and Western Europe. How shall the global and the local be configured to one another, within communities and across continents? How shall prophetic challenge be maintained? If the hypothesis about the yoking together of the global and the local suggested above is correct, this could well be the shape that globalization will take in the ensuing period, even as we struggle to integrate the understandings of the first and second phase.

Implications for Theological Education

Let me conclude with just a couple of suggestions about what all of this means for theological education today. I make the suggestions in three points and a concluding remark about vision.

If the next phase of globalization finds us between the global and the local, we need to prepare ourselves and our students to:

1. *Understand the contextual.* Especially for uprooted peoples, for those who receive in a different way from how it is given, and who seek ways (and it is often plural) to belong. The world has shifted such that we can no longer presume (or perhaps should even presume) an Archimedean point.

2. *Build strong local communities.* Only communities confident of themselves and imbued with the gospel will resist the temptation to become enclaves or fortresses rather than the communities Christ intends.

3. *Interpret the global,* both in its hegemonies — how it destroys human life — and in its gifts of decentralization, democratization, and local empowerment.

To carry these out in the concrete may require some axial changes. The sin-and-forgiveness model that has dominated Western Christianity for so many centuries may need to give way to others. One being suggested from the South is a death-and-life model, since that hues closer to the day-to-day experiences of the poor of the world.

Certain biblical images have often undergirded, at least implicitly, our understandings of globalization. In the first phase, it was undoubtedly the Great Commission of Matthew 28:19-20. In the second phase, Luke may have provided the key: Luke 4:16-20 in the call to solidarity and justice; Luke 24:13-15 in the call to accompaniment.

The Scripture for this third phase may well be Ephesians 2:12-14: "Remember you were at that time without Christ, being aliens from the commonwealth of Israel, and strangers to the covenants of promise, having no hope and without God in the world. But now in Christ Jesus you who once were far off have been brought near by the blood of Christ. For he is our peace; in his flesh he has made both groups into one and has broken down the dividing wall, that is, the hostility between us."

Fundamentalisms Observed

Martin E. Marty and R. Scott Appleby

Martin E. Marty and R. Scott Appleby direct the Fundamentalism Project. Marty, the Fairfax M. Cone Distinguished Service Professor of the History of Modern Christianity at the University of Chicago, is an editor of *The Christian Century* and the author of numerous books, including the multivolume *Modern American Religion,* published by the University of Chicago Press. Appleby, a research associate at the University of Chicago, is the author of *"Church and Age Unite!" The Modernist Impulse in American Catholicism.* Source: *Fundamentalisms Observed,* ed. Martin E. Marty and R. Scott Appleby (Chicago: University of Chicago Press, 1991), vii-x.

Modern Religious Fundamentalism Defined

Modern, like the other two words, resists easy definition. It would not be possible to pursue the project if the scores of scholars involved with it had to agree on its meanings and usages. Yet consistently in these pages "modern" is a code word for the set of forces which fundamentalists perceive as the threat which inspires their reaction. Modern cultures include at least three dimensions uncongenial to fundamentalists: a preference for secular rationality; the adoption of religious tolerance with accompanying tendencies toward relativism; and individualism. From this perspective fundamentalisms are recently developed forms of traditionalisms, forms which agents of liberal cultures had not expected to see rise or flourish. They appeared at first to be residues, vestiges, or throwbacks, not active elements in an emerging and unsettling set of global changes. In these pages, however, it will become apparent at once that fundamentalists do not reject all features of the ways called modern. Rather they exist in a type of symbiotic relationship with the modern, finding, for example, technology, mass media of communications, and other instruments of modernity congenial to their purposes.

Religious, like the noun *religion,* equally eludes precise definition, but readers will see that the scholars tend to include in their use, among others, at least these elements: religion has to do with what concerns people ultimately, and provides them with personal and social identity. Religion leads adherents to prefer myth and symbol along with rite and ceremony, over other forms of expression. And religion tends to imply some sort of cosmic or metaphysical backdrop and to stipulate certain behavioral correlates.

The present point in adducing the term is to suggest that while there may be such a thing as a "fundamentalist mentality" which finds its expression in various ideological or scientific forms, here the prime interest has to do with fundamentalisms in which the religious dimension is foremost. In cases where it is epiphenomenal — the author of an essay on Japan, for instance, sees religion associated with political fundamentalism — the association must be very close and vivid.

Fundamentalism is at least as controversial an issue for definers as are the other two terms, which are less central to the present project, so it demands more attention.

Let it be said at the outset that the directors of the project have assured all authors herein that in this introduction and in all that follows, they will make it emphatically clear that "fundamentalism" is not always the first choice or even a congenial choice at all for some of the movements here discussed. Most of the essayists take some pains to say why they are uneasy with the term, and they say so often, with evident awareness that some of their colleagues who specialize in the same topics will criticize their assent to use the term. We have asked them to keep their apologias brief, since we would elaborate here.

Among the reasons for insistence on a single term are these:

First, "fundamentalism" is here to stay, since it serves to create a distinction over against cognate but not fully appropriate words such as "traditionalism," "conservatism," or "orthodoxy" and "orthopraxis." If the term were to be rejected, the public would have to find some other word if it is to make sense of a set of global phenomena which urgently bid to be understood. However diverse the expressions are, they present themselves as movements which demand comparison even as they deserve fair separate treatment so that their special integrities will appear in bold relief.

Second, when they must communicate across cultures, journalists, public officials, scholars, and publics in the parts of the world where these books have their first audience have settled on this term. Rather than seek an idiosyncratic and finally precious alternative, it seemed better for the team of scholars to try to inform inquiry with the word that is here to stay and to correct misuses.

With those two reasons goes a third: all words have to come from somewhere and will be more appropriate in some contexts than in others. Words which have appeared in these paragraphs — "modern," "religious," "liberal," and "secular" — are examples. It is urgent in all cases that these terms be used in such ways that they do justice to the particularities of separate realities, something which we are confident readers will find the present authors responsibly undertaking to do.

Fourth, having spent two of the five years set aside for research and study comparing "fundamentalism" to alternatives, we have come to two conclusions. No other coordinating term was found to be as intelligible or serviceable. And attempts of particular essayists to provide distinctive but in the end confusing accurate alternatives led to the conclusion that they were describing something similar to what are here called fundamentalisms. The prefix "ultra-" or the word "extremist" did not connote enough. When scholars made suggestions for replacements such as "revolutionary neotraditionalist Islamic (or Jewish, or Christian, or whatever) radicalism" and were then asked to define these alternatives, they came to describe pretty much what the other authors were calling "fundamentalism."

We early came to an agreement, then, that the authors could take some pains to mention any uneasinesses they had with the term, with the assurance that we editors would ask readers constantly to think of what we here call "fundamentalisms" as being equal to "fundamentalist-like" movements. It will be appropriate in virtually every case to picture individual quotation marks surrounding the term and then proceed with the inquiry and the reading.

If people cannot agree on cross-cultural terms like the chosen one, "fundamentalism," they are also not likely to agree on all features of its definition. Readers of these essays will find, however, that the authors have certain elements of definition in mind, without which they would not know what to seek. Someone proposed Ludwig Wittgenstein's concept of "family resemblances," and it seems appropriate.

To anticipate a key feature separating "fundamentalism" from, say, "traditionalism" or "conservatism," we take an observation from one essay in this book. The coauthors say that the members of the movement they observe "no longer perceive themselves as reeling under the corrosive effects of secular life. On the contrary, they perceive themselves as fighting back, and doing so rather successfully."

Fighting back. It is no insult to fundamentalisms to see them as militant, whether in the use of words and ideas or ballots or, in extreme cases, bullets. Fundamentalists see themselves as militants. This means that the first word to employ in respect to them is that they are reactive (though not always reactionary). These essays make clear a feature which in our inquiries to date have struck us with surprising force and have appeared with astonishing frequency: fundamentalists begin as traditionalists who perceive some challenge or threat to their core identity, both social and personal. They are not frivolous, nor do they deal with peripheral assaults. If they lose on the central issues, they believe they lose everything. They react, they fight back with great innovative power.

Next, they *fight for.* It will become clear that what they fight for begins with a worldview they have inherited or adopted and which they constantly reinforce. If there are assaults on the most intimate zones such as the family, they will respond with counteraction in support of such an institution. Along with this go certain understandings of gender, sex roles, the nurturing and educating of children, and the like. They will fight for their conceptions of what ought to go on in matters of life and health, in the world of the clinic and the laboratory. While some fundamentalists may be passive for a time, just wanting to be left alone, when the threat grows sufficiently intense, they will fight for a changed civil polity. If nothing else works, as a last resort they may fight for territory, or the integrity of their social group, by using the instruments of war.

Fundamentalists *fight with* a particularly chosen repository of resources which one might think of as weapons. The movements got their name from the choice: they reached back to real or presumed pasts, to actual or imagined ideal original conditions and concepts, and selected what they regarded as fundamental. The verb includes a clue: fundamentalists are selective. They may well consider that they are adopting the whole of the pure past, but their energies go into employing those features which will best reinforce their identity, keep their movement together, build

331

defenses around its boundaries, and keep others at some distance. These chosen practical or doctrinal fundamentals, to use terms which appear in these essays, often turn into icons, fetishes, or totems in the rituals of those who employ them.

Fundamentalists also *fight against* others. Those may be generalized or specific enemies, but in all cases, whether they come from without or within the group, they are the agents of assault on all that is held dear. The outsider may be the infidel, the agent of antithetical sacred powers, the modernizer; but he or she may also be the friendly messenger who seeks compromise, middle ground, or a civil "agreement to disagree." The insider as threat is likely to be someone who would be moderate, would negotiate with modernity, would adapt the movement. Many of the fundamentalists here described spend more energy focusing on the moderate or the apostate than on the polar opposites of their movement.

Fundamentalists also *fight under* God — in the case of theistic religions — or under the signs of some transcendent reference in the minority of instances, such as Buddhism and Confucianism. Particularly potent are those fundamentalisms whose participants are convinced that they are called to carry out God's or Allah's purposes against challengers. . . .

THE MISSION FIELDS

The Enduring Validity of Cross-Cultural Mission

Lesslie Newbigin

Newbigin, a former missionary to India and professor at Selley Oaks College in England, has been active in World Council of Churches affairs for many years. In this article he attempts to make the case that the proper response to pluralism is not relativism but restatement of the gospel in culturally sensitive ways. Thus, cross-cultural mission is difficult but still essential. Source: *International Bulletin of Missionary Research*, April 1988, 50-53.

Whatever may or may not have been the sins of our missionary predecessors (and of course it is much more relaxing to repent of one's parent's sins than of one's own), the commission to disciple all the nations stands at the center of the church's mandate, and a church that forgets this, or marginalizes it, forfeits the right to the titles "catholic" and "apostolic." If there was a danger of arrogance in the call for the evangelization of the world in that generation, there is a greater danger of timidity and compromise when we lower our sights and allow the gospel to be domesticated within our culture, and the churches to become merely the domestic chaplains to the nation. I am not impressed by those who thank God that we are not like the missionaries of the nineteenth century — which the beloved Yale historical Kenneth Scott Latourette called "the Great Century" — the century that made it possible for us to talk today of the world church. Of course it is true that there were elements of arrogance in the missionaries of that century, but that was just because in the preceding centuries Christianity had become so domesticated within Western culture that when we carried the gospel overseas it sometimes looked like part of our colonial baggage.

The truth is that the gospel escapes domestication, retains its proper strangeness, its power to question us, only when we are faithful to its universal, supranational, supracultural nature — faithful not just in words but in action, not just in theological statement but in missionary practice in taking the gospel across the cultural frontiers. . . .

The contemporary embarrassment about the missionary movement of the previous century is not, as we like to think, evidence that we have become more humble. It is, I fear, much more clearly evidence of a shift in belief. It is evidence that we are less ready to affirm the uniqueness, the centrality, the decisiveness of Jesus Christ as universal Lord and Savior, the Way by following whom the world is to find its true goal, the Truth by which every other claim to truth is to be tested, the Life in whom alone life in its fullness is to be found. . . .

Western culture was once a coherent whole with the Christian vision at its center. It has disintegrated. If we seek now, as we must, a coherent vision for the human race as a whole, it cannot be on the basis of a tired relativism that gives up the struggle for truth. Nor can it be by pretending that the scientific half of our Western culture can provide coherence for the life of the world. We are at present busy exporting our science and technology to every corner of the world in the name of "development" and "modernization." But we also know that if all the six billion of the world's people succeeded in achieving the kind of "development" we have achieved, the planet would become uninhabitable. There is an absurd irony in the fact that we are busy exporting our scientific culture to every corner of the world without any compunction about arrogance, but we think that humility requires us to refrain from offering to the rest of the world the vision of its true goal, which is given in the gospel of Jesus Christ. Relativism in the sphere of religion — the belief that religious experience is a matter in which objective truth is not involved but one in which (in contrast to the world of science) "everyone should have a faith of one's own" — is not a recipe for human unity but exactly the opposite. To be human is to be a part of a story, and to be fully human as God intends is to be part of the true story and to understand its beginning and its ending. The true story is one of which the central clues are given in the Bible, and the hinge of the story on which all its meaning turns is the incarnation, death, and resurrection of Jesus Christ. That is the message with which we are entrusted, and we owe it to all people to share it. If this is denied, if it is said that every people must have its own story, then human unity is an illusion and we can forget it.

I do not believe it is an illusion. I believe the word of Jesus when he said that being lifted up on the cross he would draw all people to himself. I believe it because the cross is the place where the sin that divides us from one another is dealt with and put away. But I believe that the truth is credible only when the witness born to it is marked not by the peculiarities of one culture, but by the rich variety of all human cultures. We learn to understand what it means to say that Jesus is the King and Head of the whole human race only as we learn to hear that confession from the many races that make up the human family. In the end we shall know who Jesus is as he really is, when every tongue shall confess him in all the accents of human culture.

We have already, in the ecumenical fellowship of churches, a first foretaste of that many tongued witness. We owe the existence of this worldwide family to the missionary faithfulness of our forebears. Today and henceforth all missionary witness must be, and must be seen to be, part of the witness of this worldwide, many cultured fellowship. Every culturally conditioned expression of the Christian witness must be under the critique of this ecumenical witness. The one Christ is known as he is confessed in many cultures. But we must reject the relativism that is sometimes wrongly called "the larger ecumenism." I am not referring to the fact, for which I thank God, that we are now much more open to people of other faiths, willing to learn from them, to share with them, to learn to live together in our one planet. I am referring to the fact that it is sometimes suggested that as the churches have come together to form one fellowship across their doctrinal differences, so — by a natural extension — the great world religions must move toward a fellowship of world faiths and that this latter movement would be a natural extension of the former.

In fact, such a move would not be an enlargement but a reversal of the ecumenical movement. That movement was not born out of a lazy relativism. It was born through the missionary experience of the nineteenth century, when Christians, divided by centuries of European history, found themselves a tiny minority in the midst of the great ancient religious systems of Asia. In this new situation perspectives changed. The issue "Christ or no-Christ" loomed so large that the issues dividing Christians from one another seemed small. They did not disappear. The long theological wrestlings of Faith and Order are witness to the seriousness with which they were treated. But — real though they were — they were relativized by a new realization of the absolute supremacy of Jesus Christ. The separated Christian confessions would never have accepted membership in the World Council of Churches without its firm Christological basis — Jesus Christ, God and Savior — a phrase later put into its proper trinitarian and biblical frame. It was only because the absoluteness of Jesus' Lordship was acknowledged that the confessional positions could be relativized.

What is proposed in the so-called larger ecumenism is the reversal of this. It is a proposal to relativize the name of Jesus in favor of some other absolute. We have to ask: What is that absolute in relation to which the name of Jesus is relativized? Is it "religion in general?" Then where — in the medley of beliefs and practices that flourish under the name of religion — is the criterion of truth? Let it be brought out for scrutiny. Or is it, perhaps, "human unity?" But if so, unity on whose terms? Andre Dumas has correctly pointed out that all proposals for human unity that do not explicitly state the center around which unity is conceived happen to have as their hidden center the interests of the proposer. We have a familiar word for this. "Imperialism" is the word we normally use to designate programs for human unity originated by others than ourselves. The center that God has provided for the unity of the human race is the place where all human imperialisms are humbled, where God is made nothing in order that we might be made one. It is an illusion to suppose that we can find something more absolute than what God has done in Jesus Christ. It is an illusion to suppose that we can find something larger, greater, more inclusive than Jesus Christ. It is a disastrous error to set universalism against the concrete particularity of what God has done for the whole creation in Jesus Christ. It is only through the specificity of a particular historic revelation that we can be bound together in common history, for particularity is the stuff of history, and we shall not find meaning for our life by trying to escape from history.

Christian Mission in the Pluralist Milieu: The African Experience

Lamin Sanneh

Sanneh, an African born in Gambia who teaches missions at Yale University, argues for the need for "reciprocal missions" in Africa today. Source: *Missiology: An International Review,* October 1984, 421-33.

One of the most extraordinary frontiers in cross-cultural encounter was that opened by missions in Africa in the nineteenth century. The ground was laid in the eighteenth century, but it was only in the nineteenth that a significant expansion took place, bringing mission to the very heart of Africa's pluralist heritage. The early decades of the twentieth century built on this momentum, with the difference that indigenous Christian movements and the churches they founded arrived on the scene with explosive force, the delayed consequence of the vernacular achievement of missions.

The view I am propounding of Christian missions as instruments of religious and cultural pluralism is admittedly unconventional. In the first place it disconnects the subject from what has until now been considered as the ideological motive force of mission, namely, Western political and cultural dominance. In the second place, it implies a radical shift from the attitude of statistical superiority that had allegedly characterized missionary endeavor. Nevertheless, such an overhaul as I am urging seems necessary in order to take adequate account of the real — not imaginary

— worth of mission. In the past, mission has been squeezed between the falling thrust of imperial subjugation and the rising force of Western cultural alienation, with missionary educational institutions supplying the social ranks necessary for cutting through local resistance. Thus a conspiratorial shadow came to rest on Christianity. The alternative view I am proposing departs from this in an abrupt way, perhaps too abrupt not to require further clarification.

Two types of evidence have been called upon to support the view of mission as imperialist conspiracy and as religious arrogance. One type is the material that documents individual missionaries and mission agencies as sharing a declared interest in the aims of colonialism. Some of the primary evidence on this point is beyond dispute, although, as we shall see presently, it is by no means entirely consistent. The other type of materials comprises some of the established classics in the field, works such as the multi-volume studies of Adolf von Harnack, Kenneth S. Latourette and C. P. Groves. In their distinguished ranks we also find some contemporary authorities whose membership in, for example, the American Society of Missiology, lends an august dignity to that body.

Together these two types of sources have dominated the field almost completely, with the result that Christianity is confirmed as a Western political ploy, and evidence of it elsewhere in the world is seized on as proof of Western reactionary collusion. Even contemporary nationalism has succeeded in exploiting this characterization of Christianity, and exacted a heavy price of Western guilt for the tenacity of the religion. I yield to none in my admiration for the pioneers of missionary scholarship for the one part, and, for the other, I would be the last to deny the justice of the case against Western exploitation. But, as this paper will attempt to demonstrate, those are separate issues, whatever their relevance to the course of Christian mission. With due respect to the past pioneers, we have, because of the thoroughness of their triumph, inherited a dubious intellectual foundation for assessing the significance of mission, with the effect that much current scholarly output is seriously out of step with the central categories of missionary endeavor.

When Christian mission arrived in Africa it stood on the frontier of a pluralist world, and the issue of the vernacular translation of the scriptures could not be avoided or postponed. It was engagement with that fact that secured for Christianity cultural pluralism as an inseparable component. Consequently, missionaries, often with inadequate preparation, were plunged into the deep end of such cross-cultural currents. Never in the

340

previous history of the religion had it come upon such a complex linguistic and cultural frontier. In west Africa this was particularly sharpened by what linguists have come to term as the "fragmentation belt" of a welter of seemingly unrelated language families, the most complex anywhere in the world. For example, Nigeria alone has over 380 languages.

Far from destroying indigenous cultures, mission infused a spirit of stimulus and conservation with its linguistic investigations and its adoption of local religious vocabulary to express Christian teaching. It is undeniable, of course, that missionary endeavors in this field were not completely bereft of self-serving motives, or that the spirit of triumphalist rivalry was entirely missing. But no one can deny the irrepressible repercussions in the wider culture of missionary action. A more adequate way to define this is to view mission with the pluralist milieu of local cultures. Christian mission would consequently cease to be seen as an arm of imperial combat or as an extension of Western cultural alienation. Instead mission would become a principle for indigenous reconstruction and an integral part of Africa's pluralist heritage.

Colonial Policy and Mission

Let me digress for a moment and suggest that a corresponding topological analysis of Western imperialism would produce a diametrically opposed picture. Colonial protagonists rated indigenous cultures extremely low on the Darwinian evolutionary scale, and a functional formula of usefulness to the progress of the imperial time-machine was foisted on them. At its most enlightened, colonial policy gave weight to indigenous institutions only as factors of stability which would be disproportionately expensive to try to replace with imported arrangements. In themselves these institutions were insufficient to invalidate the justice of the imperial cause. Lord Lugard, for example, the architect of Britain's imperial designs in Africa, was hard put to find any reason for admitting equality with Africans. Traditional African rulers he respected more as useful surrogates than as symbols of indigenous values. Only in the rarest of cases was knowledge of local languages made a condition of service at the top. In northern Nigeria, which Lugard took for the British in 1902, the inherent conflict between the Olympian logic of imperialism and the vernacular dynamic of mission came to the surface when Dr. William Miller, the Church Missionary Society pioneer and an uncompromising Puritan evangelical, urged the creation of a political association, the Northern People's Congress, to press African claims against imperial obduracy, thus reversing his own earlier robust championing of the colonial cause. This is the inconsistency I alluded to. Dr. Miller epitomized the contradictory relationship between mission and imperialism. The two forces, faced with the same phenomenon of how to manage an African populace, proceeded from different assumptions. The comparative study of mission as "imperialism at prayer" should be drastically revised to indicate the ultimate divergence in presuppositions and thus help shed light on the problematic relationship between civilization and Christianity as popularized by the exploits of Dr. David Livingstone. The historical confidence in their combination is not any longer justified, if it ever was, not at least in the high-minded terms of the original proponents. So much for the digression.

Missionaries as Indigenous Agents

We must at this stage shift our interest from the ideological assumptions of mission and their perpetuation in the great historical studies of our own day and earlier to a different set of assumptions that try to relate missionary action and local context in a more consistent and logical fashion. This requires us to see missionaries rather as indigenous agents than as historical transmitters. Another way of putting it is to say that the missionary became a figure of cross-cultural significance rather than one of determined foreign domination. At this point we must disregard for the most part the evidence gathered from missionary testimonies, for such self-interpretation can easily disguise a bearer of ideological assumptions with scant regard to the situation on the ground. Missionaries were themselves often mistaken about the significance of what they did, or thought they were doing. But, even more seriously, they might believe that it was their role to do battle against the unintended consequences of their actions, resorting to a highly refined theoretical reconstruction of their situation as pious substitute for the living context. Often such reformist zeal is inspired by a subtle form of self-justification when their foreign credentials have failed to matter for the task at hand. We must not allow missionaries to incriminate themselves because what is at stake is the legitimacy of mission as such, not the occasional lapses from it.

It is simpler to begin with the contemporary situation and see how nearly two hundred years of practice and reflection have changed little in our understanding. One present-day American missionary admitted that before he set out for Africa he had a pretty neat and settled idea of what Christianity was and what his role was going to be in introducing it. Summoned by the wraith of the much mythologized Dr. David Livingstone, he said he would represent civilization in Africa. That is what I have called the "hardware" view of mission, a complete package put together without reference to the different presuppositions of another culture. This missionary soon discovered, however, the limitations of his pre-packaged religion once he arrived in Africa. His exposure to the field resulted in shattering all illusions, and missionary "software" in the form of human agents began responding to the different acoustic space of cross-cultural encounter.

Why, we might ask, had this major reversal come about? This is a large question, but the fundamental answer lies with the vernacular character of Christianity, and the corresponding vernacular role missionaries must fill in spite of the heavy hardware baggage they might carry. This forces some sharp questions about the legitimacy of insisting on the specific Western cultural scaffolding as the accompanying support for the religion. Whether they perceived as clearly as they performed, missionaries in fact bore the brunt of this sharp disjunction. The words of our American missionary testify to this fact. He admitted, he said,

> that I was a response to Dr. Livingstone's call to come to Africa to help free and civilize and Christianize the Africans. . . . I didn't know any other civilization except the Western civilization, so that is the civilization I was talking about when I first went to Africa. If you stopped me on the street and asked me what I was going to impart to them, I would have told you, "Four years of theology and about six years of further study." That's what the gospel was, I thought. But now I know it's not that. . . . It's much simpler than that — yet much deeper than that. . . . I thought that maybe what the [people] were rejecting was not Christianity but our version of it. And then we began that . . . process of trying to peel away from everything that we learned in the seminaries, from everything that was Western and white and European and American, and we started to search for what we called the "naked gospel." That was the final and fundamental substance of the Christian message. I don't think we really discovered it but we are searching for it. The reason I say I don't think we discovered it is because I think we won't really discover it until we present it to every culture in the world and then have those cultures play it back to us. Then I think we'll know the gospel.

The missionary in question has mapped out the logical terrain of Christianity on cross-cultural frontiers. The act of historical transmission is really a secondary factor in the unveiling of the gospel, and the more critical stage is the vernacular embodiment of the message and the consequent "feedback." The image of mission in this view is radically recast from its status as impervious hardware to its responsiveness to local conditions. Yet even this realization appears to have failed to relieve the missionary of a statistical view of Christianity. The burden to present the message "to every culture in the world" remains a pre-condition of successful mission. The truth of the matter is that every cultural embodiment of Christianity is an authentic representation of God's historic mission in the world, partial only insofar as it falls woefully short of the Lord's utter brokenness, and not because it fails to complete the earthly jigsaw of cultural homogeneity. . . .

The Principle of Reciprocity

Genuine pluralism assumes the mutual benefit to be derived from shared responsibility. It does not demand superficial compatibility or a staged confrontation. The peaceful exposure of different cultures to each other and the deep history of human solidarity in fellowship and service across cultures are fruits of a matured sense of pluralism. Christian mission was God's instrument in raising the frontiers of the new humanity of the age. Many contemporary witnesses of this quiet, unpretentious revolution are even more handicapped than either the unsuspecting consumers of dung or the jet-setting correspondent with fluid pen.

This brings me to reciprocity as a factor of pluralism, which I should like to develop on the basis of what has been said thus far. But first, to recapitulate, I opened with Christian missions as instruments of pluralism, and suggested the unconventionality of that view. I said it gave us the ability to separate mission from imperialism and from a triumphalist enumeration of gains. I said that the impact of the vernacular Bible produced a cross-cultural milieu and the field setting of mission. The argument then moved forward to contrast the different assumptions of mission and imperialism, with one founded on the revival of the vernacular, and the other centered on the civilizing mandate as the grounds for conquest. I urged the importance of due caution toward missionary self-interpretation in order to better distinguish between living reality and constructed theory. Next I considered the contemporary situation, showing what residues have been deposited by generations of ideological accumulation. I drew attention to some of the strong signals that are still being relayed in the feedback of local participation. I presented the story of one contemporary missionary to illustrate the point.

I stressed the importance of field experience for missionary effectiveness. I said that field experience exposed the missionaries to the "naked gospel" *in situ*, employing the tanning metaphor to express the hidden dimensions of the experience.

I suggested, however, that individual missionary resistance may still occur, and considered the example of one Mennonite missionary who found himself caught between the demands of local expectation and the standards of his theological education. The price he paid was to forfeit local credibility and thus restrict his value for the vernacularization process which continued apace. I then took up the theme of the response of the institutional hardware. The controversy over Archbishop Milingo represented in part the unyielding force of the vernacular before a determination to impose supervised conformity. In that case, too, the local context is the principle of assimilation. Finally, I argued that pluralism thrives by the vernacular route and is the direct, even if unintended, result of the linguistic and cultural explorations of missionaries.

I am now in a position to move to the concluding stages of the discussion. Christian missions pioneered communities of pluralism by the attention they devoted to indigenous languages, working by the principle that whatever the social status of these languages, they represented the best and the most suitable form by which contact with God was possible. By implication, the mother tongue speakers themselves became the indispensable partners of the historical transplanting of Christianity, and, at a deeper level, the unrecognized pacesetters for the enterprise of mission. The term I should like to employ to represent all this is reciprocity. It was implied in another term, "feedback," and is certainly included in the concept of pluralism. It thus helps to summarize the limitations of the ideological hardware and to save the "software" of missionary personnel from the harsh mechanistic fate we noted earlier. What is even more significant is that it relates us at once to the central categories of missionary endeavor, describing both the *modus operandi* and the specific indigenous response.

Reciprocity has thus both a wide and deep resonance, and we can, for example, see its implications for a purely imperialist notion of mission. Yet its theological implications are even more radical. The missionary who testified that he did not really know the gospel until he saw it embodied in the indigenous idiom and played back to him was treading in the burning bush of reciprocity. Unspared from death to the acquired sensibilities of his hardware formation, he would rise eventually in the resurrection experience of another culture. That can be extended to describe the entire history of the church down the ages: the experience of stripping and baring is in inverse ratio to the reward and renewal assured in turn. At that point reciprocity makes our loss God's greater gain, which includes us. The words of the Catholic missionary in Africa demonstrate the familiar but still inexplicable truth of the supreme risk of putting faith in a living God whose presence by the sign of the cross in other cultures can arouse us in the deepest recesses of duty and obligation. The missionary testifies as

> With great reverence to the Masai culture, we went back to the naked gospel, as close as we could get to it, and presented it to them as honestly as we could. We let them play it back to us — that was the system, to let them play it back. As it was played back, we began to see different lights on the very message we were trying to bring them. . . . That would startle me. There was this constant playing it back and forth, until something emerged that I thought they or we never heard before. At the end, we began to see that what was emerging was the God of the gospel — one that we did not recognize before. . . . The God who finally comes to us at the heart of the naked gospel is the God who loves evil people. That's incredible. This is God who not only loves evil people, but loves me when I'm evil. A God who loves me no matter how good I am, no matter how evil I am. That's not the God of religion. That's the beginning and it's very, very difficult. It's not the God we normally worship — church officials and authorities can do nothing with a God like this.
>
> This shattered me as much as them. . . . I used to have the Sermon on the Mount memorized in their language because I went through it so many times. I would never interpret it. In our culture we say, "When someone strikes you on your cheek, you turn the other. That doesn't mean you can't defend yourself. That doesn't mean you can't take it to court." We water it down and the whole punch is gone.
>
> But the Masai were a conquering people; they defeated everyone they ever met. And I just gave them the Sermon on the Mount. "If someone hits you, turn the other cheek. If he takes your outer cloak, give him your inner cloak." They were silent.

A major shift in self-understanding followed this. The Christian creed, stiffened with Greek philosophical premises and encrusted with Western psychological assumptions about the *self* and individual autonomy, was reconstituted in the solvent of the field setting. When the missionary prepared to baptize a selection of individuals from among those in the catechumenate, he was resisted. The people insisted that everyone in the group should be baptized, for faith was a communal affair. The more advanced ones would help the others, and then all would help make the pilgrimage together. The missionary quickly understood the basis of this appeal and responded accordingly. It permanently modified his own understanding.

> I know now [he said] that if you asked me to describe belief, if I really wanted to be accurate, I could say that the faith I have depends on so many people whose faces I can see, whose names I know. It is a communal belief. I don't know how [he queried] we ever came to say about our faith, "*I* believe." It is really true that *we* believe.

At that point reciprocity merges into reconciliation, and the contiguous frontier of redemptive love looms up.

Christian Mission and the Peoples of Asia

D. Preman Niles

In order for missions to work in Asia, Niles argues, we must
avoid dichotomizing missions and theology (with theology always being done in the West) and realize that we must first do
theology in the Asian context, and then work out the missions
implications from that. Niles serves as professor of Old Testament at the Trinity Seminary in Singapore. Source: *Missiology:
An International Review,* July 1982, 279-99.

In Asian theology the term "people" would seem to have both ecumenical
appeal and significance. This explains why this term is beginning to figure
prominently in Asian theological thinking, and thus the subject "Theology
of People" was assigned to me.

Encounters with theologians and missiologists from outside Asia in
ecumenical arenas of debate have made me wonder about the wisdom of
approaching the subject of a theology of "people" without first discussing
the journey, "how did we get here," rather than deal purely with a theology
of people. Such a sketch would also explain the Asian context, helping us
understand what Asian theologians are saying.

Traditionally, Asia has been the object of mission while Asian churches
and Christians have been considered their products, and thus not the
subjects of mission or an integral part of church history (T. V. Philip).
Traditional missiological thinking had to do with mission fields out there
(in Asia, Africa, etc.). Usually, one would work out the missiological impli-

cations (out there) of a theology that had to do with the faith as it is lived in the church (in here). In Asia theology and mission have become almost coterminous. The world is at our doorstep. Hence it is difficult to think of our faith and its practice apart from mission. Whenever we have tried to practice faith apart from mission, we have borrowed our theology from the West and retreated into a ghetto — being content to fish souls from time to time, souls from a non-Christian world, putting them into a ghetto church.

A significant stream of Asian theological thinking has been a protest against this dichotomy of theology and mission and the traditional understandings of theology and mission. Thus these new theological positions and voices which began at the periphery kept asserting that the periphery is the center. . . .

Creation Rather than Redemption as a Basis for Doing Theology in Asia

In *Christian Mission Reconstruction — An Asian Attempt* (1975), C.-S. Song proposes creation rather than redemption or salvation history as a proper framework for doing theology in Asia, arguing that during the period of the exile, Israel saw itself as a part of the nations and that its history with Yahweh was part of a much larger history. It was during this time that Israel came to a more mature understanding of the theme of creation as the backdrop against which several histories of redemption, including the history of Israel, could be understood. Song perceives a similarity between the context of Israel in the midst of the nations during the exile and that of Asian churches in the midst of communities of other faiths. He therefore feels that creation rather than redemption history narrowly interpreted in terms of the ideology of Christendom would provide the tools to break away from a mission-compound Christianity.

It must be noted that the argument is not that we have creation rather than redemption as a theological center or a primary concept for theology in Asia, but rather that creation, not redemption history narrowly understood in terms of the ideology of Christendom, should prove the basic framework and emphases for doing theology in Asia. This is not a new proposal but the clarification of a basic Asian theological stance which undergirds missiological perceptions and theological constructions in Asia.

349

Towards a Deeper Understanding of Christian Mission in the Context of Other Faiths

This recognition of creation as a framework for theology and mission poses the problem of the relationship between the Christian faith and other faiths in a new way. There are three identifiable approaches to the issues of other faiths in post-Christendom thinking which I delineate as follows:

1) To set out a theological or philosophical basis for relating the Christian faith to other faiths which overcomes the traditional denigration of other faiths. "A theology or philosophy of pluralism" may aptly summarize this approach (cf. Hick 1973; Ariarajah 1976:88-97; Wickremasinghe 1978).

2) To delineate the methodology of dialogue and analyze the dynamic of dialogue as a style of living and discourse, which helps to clear past misunderstandings, creates new and deeper understandings of each others' faith positions, and works towards the building of community (Samartha 1981; de Silva 1977:3-8).

3) To discover the significance of other faiths for a deeper understanding of the Christian faith and its mission; this approach is becoming a primary concern of Asian Christians and theologians. . . .

Where in this scheme do Asian Christians belong? This is not an academic question but an existential problem, having to do with our identity as individuals who confess Jesus Christ as our Lord and Savior and as communities witnessing to the Lordship of Jesus Christ. This is more than a problem of identity in a particular context, it is a matter of confessing and witnessing, a missiological problem.

In Aloysius Pieris's article "Towards an Asian Theology of Liberation" (1980:21-42), he shows how the meta-cosmic or soteriological religions of Asia have fused with cosmic (wrongly termed "animistic") faiths, which are concerned with the world affairs of economics, politics and societal arrangements, to form the great Asian religions as we know them. While meta-cosmic religions have been immensely successful in absorbing cosmic religions to form new religious amalgams, they have hardly succeeded against each other. There have usually been only small movements from one to another. This explains why Christianity, a latecomer into the religious scene in Asia, had immense success in the Philippines and among various tribal religions in Asia, all of which were cosmic religions as yet uninfluenced by other meta-cosmic religions, but it had few gains elsewhere in Asia. Viewing this situation as a problem for mission in the present, one realizes that since Asia has already been missionized by the various meta-cosmic religions, there seems to be little room left for Christian missionizing or for producing a specifically identifiable Christian culture — a Christian meta-cosmic plus cosmic fusion to produce an Asian Christian civilization. There is therefore the need to work out a Christian approach to other faiths in the post-missionizing period.

Although in origin Christianity was an Asian religion, it came to Asia as a missionizing religion largely after it was culturally shaped in the West. Consequently in those cases where it fused with cosmic religions it maintained its heavy Western cultural identity, partly because this was the form in which it came, and partly because it came as the religion of the colonizing forces and was concerned to obliterate or suppress native religious sentiments and aspirations which could be inimical to Western Christianity. Then where Christianity won converts from other major faiths, there was the need to maintain a cultural separation (a phenomenon we call mission-compound Christianity) lest there be a reabsorption into the religious culture from which the converts came. Taking these two trends together, Christianity in Asia by and large has a Western cultural identity with some Asian.

Basically it was this problem of mission with its dual components — the need for a Christ-centered relationship with other faiths and the need for an Asian Christian cultural identity. . . . As Asian Christians we inherit two "stories" — one is that of the Bible which comes to us through the church and more specifically the Western missionary enterprise, the other is that of our own people and culture from which we have often been alienated. The theological/missiological task we face in Asia today is to discover ways of relating these two stories. . . .

By and large, the main cluster of symbols and themes which have emerged has to do with the motif of liberation from various forms of oppression. In this search there is the attempt to cut back behind the various institutionalized forms of religion to the liberational thrust of the life and teaching of the founder of a particular religious tradition, and to reappropriate this stance in the present. Also there are attempts to rediscover the moments in the history of the people where the symbols and motifs arising from the life and teaching of a religious founder have played a key role. Another important component in this search is the investigation of popular faiths and art forms of "people" as expressions both of their suffering and aspirations. This search is a response to the problems of massive poverty and oppression in Asia to which multireligious groups, sharing a common ideological commitment or stance, are responding.

351

The second cluster gradually beginning to reemerge in a Christ-centered approach to other faiths coheres in what we may call the mystic experience of the cosmic Christ. This is probably one of the earliest responses to the reality of other faiths particularly in Christian ashrams. But the monastic locus of this search seems to have been the reason for its being gradually left aside. A stance that was essentially apart from the world and seemingly "otherworldly" could find no real place in a milieu created by forms of historical thinking brought about by the impact of secular ideologies. . . .

This Christ-centered approach of Asian thinkers to other faiths was not simply to work out a theological or philosophical basis for understanding the place of other faiths in the divine economy, but rather the concern was deeply missiological, to discern and to respond to the presence and activity of Christ in other faiths. While such a search and response would take place in terms of a dialogical engagement within a particular religio-cultural tradition to which a particular Christian community belonged, the validity of such an engagement lay in the fact that it was taking place in the context of the presence and activity of the cosmic Christ. . . .

The Korean Example

In describing or sketching the emergence of a theological/missiological stance in Asia, we have concentrated on representative thinkers in the Indian subcontinent. This is not to deny the richness of other Asian theological developments or their relevance for understanding this emerging theological/missiological stance, but because at least at the beginning the challenge of other faiths was felt and responded to here more sharply than elsewhere. Also we find here the problems colonialism raised for Christian mission when both went hand in hand. . . .

As in the other colonial situation, a wrestling with the colonial and post-colonial contexts in Korea prompted a new understanding of mission. However, the colonial context here was different from that of Asian countries under Western colonial domination, for the colonial power was Japan which permitted foreign mission boards to work in Korea; its other colonies provided the mission boards and its missionaries remained apolitical.

To a great extent, the missionaries maintained this stance even under great provocation partly because their concern was to save souls that were being damned in the wretched conditions of sinful living and partly because their concern was to provide the necessary medical and educational services through which evangelization could take place. An apolitical stance was also needed to negotiate with the colonial government when there were instances of political harassment of local churches.

However, often factors militated against the strict separation of faith and politics advocated by the missionaries. As a foreign religion without the backing of a dominating power, Christianity won few converts from the upper echelon of society. With its promise of salvation and the offer of a new hope in Jesus Christ, it appealed more to the lower classes of society, the *minung* Christians, . . . [producing] two significant results:

1) Although the Christians separated themselves from the rest of the Korean population in living a socially pure life, the experience of colonial oppression affected them just as much as it did others, thereby creating a national consciousness in which there was a fusion of the hope of personal salvation with the hope for national liberation.

2) Since the target of evangelism was perforce the common people, the language used was not the Chinese script through which philosophical and theological concepts could be expressed more easily, but *hangul,* the script used by the common people. While it was difficult to express metaphysical ideas through it, its earthly character dealing with everyday affairs and its richness of metaphoric and poetic expressions made it an ideal vehicle for communicating the stories and parables of the Bible. In fact, the biblical narratives were so readily taken into Korea that without apparent contradiction Korean Christians viewed Korea as Israel and Japan as Egypt.

In brief, there was a considerable gulf between the theological concepts and dogmas the missionaries taught and through which they attempted to control Christian behavior and thinking, and the faith and thinking of Korean Christians. There was also a considerable gulf between the two in Christian identity. Consequently, the Korean appropriation of the gospel was much faster and the biblical language began to function more readily in the political thinking and aspirations of the Christian *minung*. This explains, for instance, the flowing together of the Donghak Messianic Movement and the Christian Messianic Movement to struggle against Japanese imperialism.

Apparently, the spiritual and theological strength of a church seems to depend on its political vulnerability. In such a situation, the church identifies itself more readily with the sufferings and aspirations of the people to which it belongs.

Such an identification produces an important shift in perspective. The culture and history to which the church or the Christian koinonia belongs is understood from the viewpoint of the "peoples" — those who share in a culture of oppression. . . .

This shift in perspective not only influences the way we reappropriate the Asian culture and history to which we belong, but also the way we understand the biblical story. The same affirmation goes on to state,

> Jesus lived with people *(ochlos)* and ministered to them. It was in living with people that Jesus understood the shape and the purpose of his own ministry. He put the outcasts, dispossessed and victimized at the very center of his teaching and proclamation of the Kingdom of God. It is from this perspective that we must view the deep aspirations of the people to be the subjects of their own history.

In brief, we are called to discern the presence and activity of the cosmic Christ as the Christ of the people in the sufferings and aspirations of the people themselves.

Thus in summary we can say that because of people's sense of belonging to a particular culture and history, the relevance of the gospel is seen in terms of and in reference to this totality. So one does not start with the gospel and attempt to work out its relevance for a situation, but rather the context itself is the starting point from which the relevance of the gospel is perceived and appropriated. To be sure, such a way of doing theology produces theologies. . . . This stance also permits "the riches of the cosmic Christ" to flow in from other faiths and historical traditions for a larger experience and understanding of the One we worship and serve.

Also there is a similar shift in missiological thinking. In its most radical form, we could say that the imperatives for mission are emerging not from within the church in terms of its inherited dogmas and doctrines, but from the world of our people in whose midst Christ is at work. . . . Only in this way can the church of the Christian koinonia as the bearer of the promise of the Messianic Kingdom and as witness to the presence and the activity of the cosmic Christ carry out its mission.

354

Contextual Evangelization in Latin America: Between Accommodation and Confrontation

Mortimer Arias

Mortimer Arias, a Uruguayan by birth, served as bishop of the Evangelia Methodist Church in Bolivia. This article is adapted from his 1977 George A. Miller Lecture at Scarritt College for Christian Workers, Nashville, Tennessee. Source: *Occasional Bulletin of Missionary Research*, January 1978, 19-28.

D. T. Niles once said the Gospel . . . is like a seed, and you have to sow it. When you sow the seed in Palestine, a plant that can be called Palestinian Christianity grows. When you sow it in Rome, a plant of Roman Christianity grows. You sow the Gospel in Great Britain and you get British Christianity. The seed of the Gospel is later brought to America, and a plant grows of American Christianity. . . . When the missionaries came to our lands they brought not only the seed of the Gospel, but their own plant of Christianity, flowerpot included. [Niles] concluded that what we have to do is to break the flowerpot, take out the seed of the Gospel, sow it in our own cultural soil, and let our own version of Christianity grow.

This has been called indigenization in missionary theory, and it is what contextualization is all about. . . . The Gospel doesn't come in a vacuum. Already in the New Testament what we have is not a pre-Gospel but a contextualized Gospel, Jewish or Hellenistic, and distinguishable versions from Peter, Paul, or John. . . . Some Latin American theologians are saying today that what we have in the New Testament is a "first reading of the Gospel," and we have to do our own reading from our own context. Rafael Avila, a Catholic lay theologian from Colombia, has put it this way: "We have to look at Latin America with the eyes of the Bible and the Bible with the eyes of Latin America." . . .

This contextualization may become mere accommodation, acculturation, domestication, or absorption of the Gospel as in syncretism or culture religion. The relationship between the Gospel and culture has to be dynamic and dialectic. . . . The Gospel, Jesus says, is also like leaven in the dough, like salt in the earth, like new wine. There is an explosive, renewing, subversive, revolutionary power in it. This is why true contextualization also implies confrontation. . . .

To use Shoki Coe's words, we want to ask if Latin American contextualization of the Gospel has been "prophetic contextualization," "a genuine encounter between God's world and his Latin American world . . . challenging and changing the situation through the rootedness in and commitment to a given historical moment." . . . [So] we shall look at our subject from an historical perspective.

1. The Catholic Conquest: Civilizing Evangelization

The first evangelistic penetration of Latin America came with the Spanish conquest in the sixteenth century. . . . The missionaries — priests and friars of the Franciscan and Dominican orders — came on the wave of the explorers, conquistadores, and colonizers. Evangelization was the spiritual side of the conquest.

This conquering evangelization pretended to transplant the Spanish version of Christianity, the flowerpot included. The flowerpot involved not only Catholic dogmas, liturgy, and ethics, but also the Spanish hierarchy, the foreign priesthood, and even the Inquisition. The cultural genocide, however, would never be completely accomplished. The old Indian cultures — some of them widely developed — would prove to be resilient, and the old religion survived under the mantle of Christianity and with Christian names, such as the worship of the Mother Earth or the fertility deity in the imported worship of the Virgin Mary. This fact of cultural resistance and survival added to mass conversions and baptisms without Christian instruction, plus the shortage of clergy and the great distances to be traveled, would issue in a syncretistic type of Christianity, the worst kind of accommodation. In this way, we can say that conquering evangelization became conquered evangelization and another instance of the historical fact of the "conquered conquerors." . . .

2. The Protestant Transplant: Missionary Evangelization

The second evangelistic penetration in Latin America came in the wave of Protestant missionaries from the Anglo-Saxon countries in the second half of the nineteenth century, particularly Methodist, Baptist, and Presbyterian missionaries from the United States.

The *seed* of the Gospel in its Protestant version was strongly biblical, Christocentric, ethical, and individualistic. This would become the novelty and the fertilizing value of Protestant missions, in contrast to traditional Roman Catholicism which was biblically illiterate, centered on Mary and the saints, liturgical and superstitious, and strongly authoritarian.

But the *soil* would prove to be resistant. The Roman Catholic hierarchy would fight by all means and on any ground this "intromission of Protestantism in what was considered Roman Catholic territory." . . .

The first method used by Protestants to sow the seed of the Gospel was the distribution of the Bible. The pioneers in this apparently stony field were colporteurs of the British and Foreign Bible Society, and later on agents of the American Bible Society. . . . The second method was preaching — first by missionaries, and soon by national and lay preachers, who put the fluency and beauty of the Spanish language and the fervor of their personal conversion to Christ at the service of communicating the good news. . . . A third approach to evangelization was through educational institutions, used to educate the Protestant children in freedom, to reach the elite of the country and to motivate and train prospective Christian workers. Distribution of tracts and circulation of Christian literature was also a favorite instrument of evangelization until the coming of the radio which became the principle medium of verbal proclamation for the Protestant groups.

Of course the Protestant seed came with its flowerpot — denominational doctrines and church structures, liturgy and hymnology, ethics and style of life, architecture, and even clerical composition. But there were also cultural components of the flowerpot — the worldview, the ethos and ideology of the prospering and expanding capitalistic Anglo-Saxon countries. And it was this flowerpot, and not the seed itself, that the liberal politicians, the members of the Masonic Lodges, and the young Latin American elite were looking at. In the nineteenth century, the old Spanish colonialism was being replaced by the commercial and diplomatic neocolonialism of Great Britain, and later on of the United States of America. . . .

3. The Pentecostal Sprout: Indigenous Evangelization

The Pentecostal movement in Latin America was one of the "multiple centers of the worldwide explosion of Pentecostalism" at the turn of the century, but it has become "the only authentic South American form of Protestantism," according to the French sociologist Christian Lalive d'Epinay. There are some Pentecostal missions (Assemblies of God, and others) from the United States and Sweden, but the bulk of the movement belongs to those indigenous forms of Pentecostalism having no connection with or dependence on outside churches or missions boards. . . .

This fantastic growth and the particularities of the movement have intrigued sociologists, missiologists, church executives, and experts from Catholic, Protestant, and secular circles. How is this phenomenon to be explained? Some give a spiritual reason: the free action of the Holy Spirit. Some find anthropological roots: people's hunger for God. Others offer a sociological explanation: the Pentecostal movement, in replacing the "hacienda" social pattern, responds to the need for belonging, support, and authority for those coming from the rural areas to the insecurity and anonymity of the big cities. Others find the answer in an appropriate pastoral methodology: lay participation, common people communicating the Good News to common people in their own situation and on their own terms; the practical training and selection of pastors through a long on-the-job process; and sound principles of self-support, self-government, and self-propagation. There are also psychological explanations: the freedom of expression in worship and the charismatic type of authority of leaders and pastors. Finally, the cultural dimension: the use of popular music and instruments, the indigenization of worship. Probably each one of these explanations has relevance, but one thing is clear: here we have an evangelistic movement thoroughly contextualized.

4. The Seasonal Vintage of Revival: Professional Evangelization

Latin America has proved to be a fertile or at least open field for parachurch groups from the United States such as the Billy Graham organization to experiment with interdenominational evangelistic campaigns. Crusades have been held by Billy Graham himself in Buenos Aires and São Paulo. . . . Professional evangelization of this type stirs the congregations a bit, produces a brief public impact, and probably attracts a few people from the margins of the church. But as Professor Rudolf Obermuller has said, the task is not "revival," because "revival" presupposes a certain knowledge of the Church and the Bible, and this is precisely what the masses do not have in Latin America.

What can we say of professional evangelization in terms of our inquiry? Is it prophetic contextualization? Hardly. In spite of all the modernization, in terms of the media, the theology is as old-fashioned as it can be — almost a carbon copy of the mini-theology developed in the American revivals 150 years ago, docetic, individualistic, otherworldly, emotional, socially conservative, politically blind, escapist. To be prophetic you have to take the whole biblical message seriously. That means taking seriously the context and people in their context. Revivalistic preaching is the same everywhere — in New York or Nairobi, in Rio de Janeiro or Singapore — it is disincarnated, timeless, ahistorical. . . .

5. Prophetic Contextualization

I want to conclude with a brief note on a new phenomenon in Latin American Christianity: the emergence of what could be called prophetic contextualization. As has been said, "The future Church historians will be puzzled in studying this period of the Church in Latin America, because, suddenly, Christians began to act out of character." For centuries the church has been the supporter of the status quo. But when Nelson Rockefeller visited Latin America and made his report to President Nixon, he pointed to the Church as one of the main forces for change in the continent. Strange as it may sound, the title of a recent release from the Latin American Press is quite true to the facts: "Right-wing dictators fear Christianity more than Marxism." These Christians are not using the *Communist Manifesto*. They are using their Bible, and releasing its liberating message. Not all Christians, but a growing and decisive minority, including laywomen and laymen, young people, pastors, priests, friars, nuns, and quite a few bishops are trying to respond prophetically to "the cry of my people" as Yahweh asked Moses to respond.

In one sense we are seeing the greening of the Church in Latin America. Springtime has come and a revitalizing breeze is blowing. The Roman Catholic Church has jumped over four centuries assuming finally the Reformation of the sixteenth century and embracing the impetus of the revolution of the twentieth century. Protestants are finally overcoming their reductionistic individualism and spiritualism, and they are gradually liberating themselves from their inherited cultural hang-ups. Pentecostalists are experimenting with a growing awareness of human needs and affirming the one Gospel, including the material and the spiritual. There is a converging thrust to recover the whole Gospel, for the whole person, and for the whole of Latin American society. The Bible is being read anew in thousands of small grass-roots *(comunidades de base)* in the Roman Catholic Church. The common people are commenting upon it from their own situation, and letting it speak to that situation, after generations for whom it was a sealed book. Christ is being met again — as he wants to be met and served — in the neighbor, in the man on the road. Christians are discovering the neighbor — individually and socially — and they are discovering that the Good News is really "good news to the poor" in our context. And from this discovery a new style of life, a new theology, and a new evangelization are emerging. . . .

A Great New Fact of Our Day: America as Mission Field

Craig Van Gelder

Van Gelder, who serves as professor of domestic missiology at Calvin Theological Seminary, identifies the shifts that have taken place within America both in the broader culture and in the churches working in that context. The result of these shifts is that America must now be seen as a mission field. Source: *Missiology: An International Review,* October 1991, 409-17.

We now find ourselves in a new landscape. The dominant culture, influenced for decades by both the rationalistic strains of the Enlightenment and the moral influences of Christianity, has now become globalized and pluralized. Many denominational churches, dependent for many decades on the symbiotic relationship between church and culture, have become marginalized and fragmented. In this context, the new landscape is often referred to as both postmodern and post-Christian. It is critical to understand something about how we arrived at this point and what influences are presently working to shape this new reality, if we hope to be responsive in ministry in the 1990s and beyond. This article will attempt to provide a historical and cultural context for understanding this new reality Christians face today.

The Development of the Modern Project
and Its Subsequent Demise

A cursory reading of history indicates that the modern societies which grew out of the Medieval world experienced a transformation to a fundamentally different worldview. This transition gave birth to the "modern project," that effort to construct a rational social order which was capable of human improvement and social program. Today we are becoming aware of yet another shift in worldview, to a postmodern reality, as we observe the uncentering of this modern project. Some differences between these three worldviews are illustrated in Table 1.

Both the Renaissance and Protestant Reformation played major roles in helping what became modern Western nation-states emerge from the Medieval period into the modern world. But the most formative influence came during that period from 1700 to 1850 which is known as the Enlightenment or Age of Reason. The critical contribution of this era was the fundamental shift away from the concept of truth coming to persons/society from the outside, to truth which could be discovered within the social order through reason and science. In this context, the role of God was dethroned as a valid claim to authority. This role was replaced by an emphasis on objective facts. The driving force behind the movement was the scientific method which studied the relationships between cause and effect. . . .

For many decades the modern project gave evidence that this system of thinking and organization was working. The quality of life improved for large segments of the population in Western countries. People began to live longer, travel faster, communicate more easily, work more productively, and enjoy more leisure time. But there was always a darker side to the modern project, which began to make itself felt by the mid-1880s. The breakdown of traditional social patterns, the loss of one's sense of community-based identity, the negative effects of industrial hardships and pollution, the devastation of modern warfare, and a consumer-based economy which required an endless supply of resources, all gave evidence that modernity came with a price tag.

Table 1 The Differences in Worldviews from Medieval to Modern to Postmodern

Medieval (pre-science)	Modern (Newtonian)	Postmodern (20th Century)
1. Fixed order	Change as rearrangement	Evolutionary emergent
2. Teleological	Deterministic	Law and chance
3. Substantive	Atomistic	Interdependent
4. Hierarchical	Reductionistic	Organic system
5. Dualistic (spirit/matter)	Dualistic (mind/body)	Multi-faceted
6. Kingdom	Machine	Community

The Collapse of the Modern Project — a Postmodern World

In the physical sciences, the development of quantum physics, the clarification of the theory of relativity by Einstein, and the discovery by Heisenberg of the "principle of uncertainty" challenged many of the core assumptions of the Newtonian worldview which undergirded the modern project. The world came to be understood as operating with both law and chance, both order and chaos. The social sciences went through similar effects of becoming relativized with the new disciples of Freudian psychology, Weberian sociology, and Boasian anthropology. With the emergence in the 1960s of the framework of general systems theory and the interdependency of all of life, all hope of preserving a rational, predictable social order rooted in the assumptions of logical positivism was dead. . . .

In the broader culture, the shift to a relativistic worldview has begun to be felt by the masses, especially since the threshold of social change which occurred in the 1960s. A variety of movements introduced elements of this change. The civil rights movement challenged the society to be consistent in balancing equality with freedom. The counter-culture dethroned the "shoulds" and "oughts" of Christian culture as the basis of guiding social behavior. The Vietnam War and anti-war movement reshaped our notions of the reliability of technology to render final solutions to social and moral complexities. And Watergate worked to demythologize the intrinsic authority of institutions over our lives. Changes such as these in the broader culture led irreversibly toward fragmentation and relativism. We see this trend expressed even within missiology with the current plethora of writing on religious pluralism (Hillman 1989, Knitter 1985, Kreiger 1991, Swidler 1987) and the heated debate over the centrality of Christ and Christology in Christian mission (D'Costa 1990, Hick 1974, Hick and Knitter 1987, Samartha 1991).

The assumptions of the Enlightenment-based modern project of rational order, historical progress, and the management of human life have all been found to be insufficient to provide meaning and direction for modern life. These assumptions have now been exposed as both inadequate and faulty. With this awareness the recognition has come that we are now living in a postmodern world. We have lost the grand narrative, the story line which gave direction and meaning to our lives as a society. We have begun to experience the implications of a pluralistic society where multiple perspectives now offer us conflicting truth claims, all of which are viewed as relative in value.

The shape of this emerging postmodern worldview is characterized by a collapse of the importance of history, with attention being given to an endless succession of "nows." There is a focus on surfaces and images, rather than depth and substance. The endless expansion and multiplication of choices now challenge our capacity to process information and make decisions. Patterns of relationships continue to expand around rootless associations, rather than around context and place. Change and flux are seen as normative and endless. And there is a recognition that all meaning systems are, in the end, only social constructions that have been shown to be inadequate for establishing the possibility of a grand narrative. The overarching story line has been lost and cannot be re-invented (Anderson 1990).

The implications of this shift can be visualized quite simply by contrasting the worldviews of the various generations of present day adults. The differences between generations and the core values which shape their identity are quite significant. People may still speak some of the same words, but they no longer share the same meanings. We are in a fundamentally different landscape, both within the secular culture and within the church, as illustrated in Table 2.

These worldviews stand in distinct contrast with one another. The traditional generation is looking for stability and rational order in a world which no longer offers such a viewpoint. The early boomers, oriented toward trying to change the social order, now find their social ideologies

Table 2   Multiple Worldviews of Contemporary Generations

Area	Traditional	Early boomers	Late boomers	Emerging
Born	Pre-1945	1945-55	1956-65	1966-75
Age today	46-older	36-45	26-35	16-25
Worldview	Progress	Competing	Fragmentation	Pluralism
View of church	Preserve heritage	Instrument for change	Pragmatic meets needs	Place for acceptance
Key values	Tradition Family Community Stability	Relationships Relevance Equality Justice	Me Now How Wow	Relational Compassion Accepting Entitled

somewhat sidelined and out of touch compared to the more conservative and materialistic late boomers. These late boomers turned inward toward their own pragmatic welfare in the midst of the fragmentation of world-views in the 1970s. And the emerging generation, also known as vidiots, is giving evidence of being the first generation raised with a pluralistic world-view, tending to be nonjudgmental toward ideological differences in the midst of their own personal search for relational acceptance.

Changes and Challenges for the Church in Keeping Pace with Change

Local churches have always tended to reflect the particular context and time period in which they were begun. In this regard, the development of local churches in the story of American Christianity can be understood as having passed through a number of phases. A typology of these changes is displayed in Table 3.

The geographic practice of local church life, where there was a natural fit between the church and its community, lasted through the period of time when the suburban neighborhoods expanded our cities after World War II. By the 1960s, this type of church was becoming increasingly obsolete as a viable approach to reaching and serving people. Both the mobility offered by modern forms of transportation and the shift to people grouping

Table 3 Typology of Local Churches in the Development of American Church Life

Type of Church	Model	Shaping Influence
Geographic churches	Village church (1800s)	Family networks
	Old first (1890ff.)	Institutionalism
	City neighborhood (1900ff.)	Urbanization
	Family Suburban (1940ff.)	Suburbanization
Life-style churches	Alternative (1960s/70s)	Changing society
	Ministry centers (1970s/80s)	Meeting needs
	Seeker centers (1980s/90s)	Reaching the lost

by affinities rather than geography shifted the patterns of local church life to a new model of life-style churches.

These life-style churches tend to follow the pattern noted earlier regarding the differences between generations. The early boomers were the ones who started the alternative churches in seeking to deal with racial reconciliation and community development. The later boomers were attracted to the ministry centers of the 1970s and 1980s to have their needs met. And it is the secularized version of the late boomers which the seeker centers are attempting to reach in the 1980s and 1990s. What will be interesting to watch is the style of church which will develop in the 1990s and following, to serve the emerging generation which is looking for relational acceptance.

A Church Seeking to Reposition with a Search for New Rules

In light of the shifts which have taken place in the broader culture and the specific patterns of change within churches, it is becoming evident that many local churches are struggling to reposition themselves within their contexts. This repositioning is somewhat complicated at the present time by two different strains at work in the church. On the one hand, many churches are aggressively trying to become needs-oriented, market-driven, and user-friendly by relying on all of the latest technologies and methods available to reach their target populations. The question this raises is whether these churches have themselves become a reflection of a set of postmodern processes. On the other hand, some churches are having to examine seriously the core relationship between gospel and culture, and are working to disengage from the dominant culture. The question this raises is whether these churches will be able to reposition adequately without retreating from an effective engagement of the broader culture(s).

While churches are in the process of either trying to adapt to the new context or reposition themselves within it, many pastors are having to focus on retooling in order to stay relevant in ministry. There are a series of new rules which are emerging within this retooling process.

Rule 1: From "denominational loyalty" to "shared vision": The primary glue which used to bond a local church together in the form of institutional, denominational loyalty has shifted and is being replaced by a commitment to a shared vision. This vision concept is at the core today of almost all new church development starts, as well as the majority of renewal efforts.

Rule 2: From "professional minister" to "missionary pastor": There has been a clear shift from the days of a churches culture when the world was seeking out the church to the reality today that the church must seek out the world (cf. Callahan 1990). This has significant implications for the role of the minister. It is no longer adequate for the minister to function primarily within the professional role of being the preacher, administrator, and counselor. Pastors must now lead local churches in significant ministry to engage the world and seek out the unchurched.

Rule 3: From "administrative decision making" to "participation planning": In light of the decline of institutional loyalty and the continued fragmentation in worldviews and social meanings, local churches are finding that they are having to shift their patterns in making decisions. It is no longer possible for a church council or board to make decisions, announce them, and expect compliance. Members today must be involved in helping to shape the strategic decisions which influence the direction of the church, if they are to have a sense of ownership in its ministry.

Rule 4: From "single cell" to "multi-form" congregations: The local church which seeks to serve its members and reach the unchurched today has to develop a multi-form program model to accomplish this. The practice of offering the same program on the same schedule to all the members worked well within a churched culture. Today, people expect and need choices if they are to become involved in the life of the local church.

Rule 5: From "cultural uniformity" to "unified diversity": It is clear that both the broader culture and the local churches are becoming increasingly diverse. Different people hold multiple viewpoints, many of which are not easily wrapped within one expression of faith. One major challenge facing many local churches in the postmodern world is that of trying to find an adequate basis for creating a unified diversity without having to insist upon uniformity.

Summary

We are living in a new day in America. The shifts in the cultural context have presented a new challenge for the churches to address America as a mission field. The awareness of this is rapidly growing within many denominations that are now attempting to retool in order to respond to this shift. This awareness is also growing among many who are seeking to start new forms of the church outside of the historic denominations with community-based models. It is not yet clear what will happen to the churches involved in these two trends, but it is clear that Christianity as we have known it in America is undergoing a systemic shift.

THE MISSION CHALLENGE

Vision for Mission

David J. Bosch

Bosch argues that we are in the process of developing a new paradigm for Christian world mission. He states in succinct form five key elements he believes must be part of the new paradigm. Bosch is also author of a significant new book on missions, *Transforming Mission: Paradigm Shifts in Theology of Mission* (Orbis Books, 1991), which expands on the themes of this article. Source: *International Review of Mission,* January 1987, 8-15.

The philosopher of science, Thomas S. Kuhn, has put forward the theory that science only progresses when one theoretical structure is replaced by another. This he calls a "paradigm change," a paradigm being made up of the general theoretical assumptions and laws and techniques for the application that the members of a particular scientific community adopt. Paradigms, however, become obsolete; once a paradigm has been weakened and undermined to such an extent that its proponents lose their confidence in it, the time is ripe for a scientific revolution that gives birth to a new paradigm.

Hans Küng has applied Kuhn's theory to the history of the Christian church and of theology. During the past twenty centuries, he contends, we have had five successive paradigms, namely the early Christian apocalyptic, the Hellenistic Byzantine, the medieval Roman Catholic, the Protestant Reformation and the modern Enlightenment paradigms. With the advent of dialectic and existential theology (Barth, Bultmann, Tillich) this last paradigm was fundamentally challenged; a new paradigm was beginning to emerge, the contours of which are only now beginning to become clear. This new paradigm Küng and others provisionally call — for lack of a better word — the "contemporary" or "postmodern" paradigm.

I believe that Küng's (and Kuhn's) suggestions can be applied not only to theology in general but also to mission and missionary thinking. Since the first issue of the *International Review of Mission* was published in January 1912, in the wake of Edinburgh 1910, a fundamental "paradigm shift" has taken place in mission and missionary thinking. Then Europe and North America were the solid beacons of orientation, the models for the "non-Christian" world still to be brought into the orbit of Christianity; today we are involved (at least theoretically!) in "mission in six continents." Then the Christian missionary movement was molded by the West's religious and cultural self-consciousness; today mission is faced with a world in which the West's prestige counts for little. Then the missionary was a giver and an initiator, in a position of power (also "secular" power) in a world of fixed and evident values; today the missionary is regarded as a throwback to a bygone era and the message he or she has to offer is, at best, having to compete on equal terms with every other message.

Many have tried and some are still trying simply to revive the traditional (read: "modern Enlightenment" in the Küngian sense) paradigm of mission. After all, clinging to yesterday's images provides solace. It provides little else, however, for artificial respiration will in this case yield little more than the semblance of returning life. What is called for, rather, is recognition that a new paradigm is needed, a new vision to break out of the present stalemates toward a different kind of missionary involvement. The bravest among missionary thinkers have already for some time begun to sense that a new paradigm was emerging. To mention only one example: In 1959 Hendrik Kraemer said that we had to recognize a crisis in mission, even an "impasse." Yet he continued: "we do not stand at the end of mission"; rather, "we stand at the definite end of a specific period or era of mission, and the clearer we see this and accept this with all our heart, the better." We are, in fact, called to a new "pioneer task which will be more demanding and less romantic than the heroic deeds of the past missionary era."

Since these words were uttered twenty-eight years ago, the contours of the new missionary paradigm Kraemer had vaguely alluded to have gradually become more distinct. Even so, what mission should be during the coming decades is far from being a foregone conclusion. We can, at best, sketch only very tentatively some of its characteristics. To this I now turn — even if with a great degree of hesitation. What follows is, in a sense, nothing but a series of "I believe" statements, put forward for others, to be considered, challenged — and perhaps rejected.

1. We have to find a new way of developing what has traditionally been referred to as "the biblical foundations for mission." We can no longer appeal to specific biblical statements for a one-to-one legitimation of our missionary involvement. This approach has become impossible for two reasons. First, the contemporary missionary enterprise in all its ramifications and with all its paraphernalia is so vastly different from what the New Testament calls "mission" (under different names) that it is plainly dishonest to appeal directly to the latter as justification for what we do today. Second, the contemporary debate on hermeneutics has taught us that, in our efforts to understand a text, much more is involved than just what the text "originally meant"; the application ("Anwendung") of a text is integral to the whole experience of understanding it.

Without developing this any further let me just say that the permanent validity of the Christian mission should not be traced back to authoritative biblical commissions but rather to the recognition of the fact that the Christian church is missionary by its very nature (to use the formulation of *Ad Gentes*). What we therefore have to demonstrate, to the church and to the world, is that the Christian faith is a missionary faith or it is no faith at all. One irrefutable conclusion to be made from the New Testament documents — particularly the pauline corpus — is that it is intrinsic to the Christian faith to cross frontiers, to concern itself with those outside, to reach out in compassion to those who are lost or marginalized. Of course, in certain periods of its history the church, or segments of it, lost this essential missionary dimension. Where this happened, however, it was no longer truly and fully the church but, at best, only an approximation of what it was intended to be.

Today we know — or ought to know — that we can never give up the inherent missionary nature of the church. Moreover, it is with this understanding that we approach the historical documents of the church, including the oldest document, the Bible, in an attempt to better appreciate the nature of the church. It is when we study the Bible from within a missionary context that we discover the biblical validity of mission. The Bible then opens our horizons and unlocks "envisioning possibilities" to us.

2. If it is true that the church is "by its very nature missionary," it is

equally true that the church is one. It was no coincidence that, when the church began to rediscover its missionary nature, it also rediscovered its essential oneness. There is a creative and dynamic relationship between mission and unity; indeed, "it is impossible to choose in favor of either mission or unity. The only possible choice for the Church, or any part of the Church, is *for or against both*."

It could be argued that the peculiar phenomenon of denomination-alism, particularly in North America, is, in fact, an institutionalized mani-festation of a missionless Christianity and theology. In the words of H. R. Niebuhr: ". . . that peculiar institution, the American denomination, may be described as a missionary order which has turned to the defensive and lost its consciousness of the invisible catholic church." Denominationalism led, in its early stages, to pointless rivalries and subsequently to "churches" turned inward, where the pastor's only responsibility was to look after the faithful while the faithful sat back to be looked after.

The denominational principle, strangely enough, manifests itself in two very different ways.

(a) The denomination becomes a voluntary association of the like-minded individuals who do not claim any ultimacy for their point of view. The denomination to which a group of people belong offers just one of several options of belief and ethos; their having chosen a particular denom-ination does not suggest that other denominations are wrong or inadequate. They have joined their group for "practical" reasons. They were looking for a place in which to feel at home religiously and culturally. Their denomi-nation provides a shelter for all who have made the same choice. And the validity of other denominations is magnanimously conceded.

Needless to say, such a denomination has no missionary vision; it is fully content with other people believing what they choose to believe.

(b) The opposite manifestation of the denominational principle is for a group to identify its understanding of the truth with the truth. This was, *inter alia,* the official Roman Catholic position from the Council of Trent to Vatican II. In October 1962, however, Pope John XXIII broke with the Tridentine frame of mind when he stated: "Truth is greater than any of our formulations." Many Roman Catholics and many Protestant groups, for all practical purposes, however, still adhere to the Tridentine position. These groups are, moreover, ever eager to foist their views on what the truth is on others. It is seriously to be questioned, however, whether this activity can be termed "mission" or "evangelism"; it may, in effect, be neither but rather be a manifestation of proselytism, through which a religious group sets out to transform other people into carbon copies of themselves.

Both manifestations of the denominational principle, in fact, militate against the idea of being *one* as well as *missionary*. Missionary ecumenicity, on the other hand, means meeting as equal partners in order to challenge, correct, enrich, inspire and support each other. It means that we cannot live without one another precisely because of our missionary calling, that the problems and joys of one of us are the problems and joys of all of us. It also means that we cannot evangelize the world if we Christians are at loggerheads with one another. The church is both one *and* apostolic. In the years to come the essential and reciprocal relationship between unity and mission will have to receive serious attention. I agree with Willem Saayman: "a firm theological integration of thinking on the unity of the Church and its mission . . . has yet to take place."

3. If the spirit of ecumenism is basic to our understanding of mission, it is also basic to the way we view other religions and their adherents. No longer can we state categorically — as we used to do — that there is light only in the church and darkness outside. No longer dare we say that God is at work only in the church. We have to recognize light and God's presence also in other faiths. This recognition undoubtedly calls for a thorough overhaul of the traditional understanding of mission and of its methods.

I do not believe, however, that this implies the demise of mission and evangelism. I subscribe to the view expressed in the report of Section III of the Nairobi Assembly of the WCC: "While we do seek wider community with people of other faiths, cultures and ideologies, we do not think that there will ever be a time in history when the tension will be resolved between belief in Christ and unbelief." There are still millions of people who have not yet heard the message of liberation and salvation in Christ. The church cannot acquiesce in this. Conversion to Christ remains an essential focus and aim of mission. It is not enough to say that the "central purpose of mission is being realized as long as, through mutual witnessing, all are converted to a deeper grasp and following of God's truth" and that the goal of missionary work is achieved when the Christian is made a better Christian and the Buddhist a better Buddhist.

Christians must indeed show a profound respect for other faiths (and this has often been glaringly absent in the past; sometimes we have proclaimed other religions' "falsehoods" rather than Christ), but such respect in no way militates against witnessing to Christ with a view to winning others to faith in him. Respect is, in fact, a presupposition for authentic evangelistic witness. If I take Christ seriously I'll also take the beliefs of others seriously.

As I see it, the relationship between the Christian faith and other faiths and the legitimacy of Christian evangelism will be among the major issues facing us in the next decades. The Christian faith will have to compete in the marketplace of religions as never before. And it will have to do this in total humility, at the same time repenting of the arrogance and intolerance that characterized much of its evangelism in the past. But it would turn against itself, its origin, nature and history, if it ceases to challenge people of all persuasions to put their trust in Christ and join a community of his disciples. To state this is not to suggest — as has often happened in the past — that baptism is a magical rite conferring grace, nor that the church is the ark of redemption. It is simply saying that the church is a sign of salvation, a sign, moreover, that shall be spoken against, like its Lord, a sign that some may discover but that others may not.

4. We have moved from an exclusively confessional and denominational to an ecumenical era, from a Europe-centered to a humankind-centered epoch. We no longer talk about the "Christian world" vis-à-vis the "non-Christian world"; we talk about "mission in six continents." No longer can we export a ready-made and definitive version of the faith from the West and "implant" it among third world peoples. In the West and in the East, in first, second and third worlds the church is struggling equally hard to indigenize and contextualize the gospel. For it was an illusion ever to have believed that the gospel had been fully indigenized in the West. It had not. And in fact it never will; indigenization (by whatever name we wish to call it) is always unfinished, a process, an ideal to strive towards.

The discovery of this had precipitated a new self-understanding among Christians, both in the West and in the East. The Roman Catholic Church has abolished the *ius commissionis*: missionary orders may no longer dictate the pattern of evangelism in the third world. The one-time missionary who "brought" the "gospel" has been substituted for the brother or sister who together with us all struggle to discover the relevance of the gospel. The rugged heroes of the faith of an earlier era have been exchanged for partners who hope to have their own faith strengthened and who are prepared to share their doubts with others. This implies, *inter alia,* that the missionary is not central to the life and future of the younger churches. As a matter of fact, in country after country, and particularly in China, it has been demonstrated that the missionary is not only not central but that he or she is not even essential. The future of the world church neither lies with nor depends on missionaries from the West. People the world over are challenged to be "missionaries to themselves." But — and this is important — it is precisely as they become missionaries to themselves that they may also be missionaries to others and go to the ends of the earth in humble boldness.

5. I have to go one step further; the time has come for mission "in reverse," from the third world to the first. In the year 1900 — according to David Barrett's calculations — one half of the world's Christians lived in Europe and only two percent in Africa. In 1980 Europe had about one quarter of the world's Christians, and Africa fifteen percent. By the end of this century Europe and Africa will each have about twenty percent of the world's Christian population. In Europe and North America, an average of 53,000 people leave the Christian church from one Sunday to the next. In Africa the net increase of Christians is about 115,000 per week.

In view of such statistics, which is the mission field? Africa or Europe? Lesslie Newbigin rightly asks: "Can the West be Converted?" In fact, his latest book is nothing but a sustained investigation of this question and a reflection on his conviction "that there is no higher priority for the research work of missiologists than to ask the question of what would be involved in a genuinely missionary encounter between the gospel and . . . modern Western culture." In the decades to come the church in the West and in the third world will be increasingly called upon to respond to this challenge.

6. I am concluding with what I believe to be a sixth priority for the church-in-mission in the coming decades: In a world in which poverty, oppression, exploitation and discrimination are endemic diseases like never before in the history of humankind, the church-in-mission is called upon to give witness to peace, justice, healing, reconciliation and love. Evangelism means calling people to Christ and to a commitment to a vision of a society radically different from what we see around us. To make disciples means to call people to be signs and agents of God's love and just in all human affairs: signs of love *and* justice, for justice without love can be demonic. The church is the sphere of those who confess Christ as head of both the church and the cosmos, as the epistles to the Ephesians and the Colossians and also the writings of the early Greek fathers teach us. In the church's mission Christ lays claim to all the world.

I am writing these lines from the South African context of late 1986. In this country, ravaged by the apartheid ideology and currently going through the convulsions of violence and counter-violence, of repression and resistance, of thousands detained without trial and many others in hiding, of brutal force and desperate protest, the yearning after peace and justice and reconciliation is a silent sigh in the hearts of millions.

What will mission mean in South Africa, in Lebanon, in Northern Ireland in 1987 and subsequent years? What will it mean to the millions languishing in the famine-stricken Sahel? What will it mean to the many more millions of refugees from a score of third world countries? What will it mean to the destitute in the *favelas* of Latin America?

Mission is the church's participation in the work of the Spirit to renew the face of the earth. It also means confronting the state with the claims of Christ's kingdom, calling upon it to be human, to treat all its citizens equally or, rather, to be biased towards the less privileged.

The church is called to exercise this ministry with total commitment. About this there can be no doubt. And yet, we have to sound a note of warning here. The virus of megalomania can easily infect the church. It then believes that, through its own efforts and involvement, it has the means of creating a new political order. But this would simply be the latest version of the heresy of millenarianism, of wishing to replace the existing political, economic and social order by some sort of theocracy. This heresy is both theologically unsound and practically misleading. The church will not inaugurate the kingdom of God on earth; neither is it called to do that. Its calling is a different one: holding up before all people the vision of the kingdom, challenging them to strain their eyes as they focus on the vision and take resolute steps in beginning to realize it.

The church, however, will not achieve more than that. Indeed, it should not, for the simple reason that it has never been given the tools to coerce people. The church cannot rule, it can only appeal. The rulers of this world lord it over their subjects; the church, however, has no subjects and exercises no authority. Like the one it follows it has come into the world as the servant of all.

On the evening of 16 June 1976, the day policemen began to shoot at demonstrating but unarmed school children in Soweto, the members of the executive committee of the South African Council of Churches were summoned to an emergency meeting. Speaker after speaker denounced the government and called upon the church to show its muscle, to do this and that and the other thing so as to immediately change the deplorable situation in South Africa. After a while Desmond Tutu spoke. He said: "We have been so inveigled with the success ethic that we have forgotten that, in a very real sense, the church is a failing community." This is what Fr. Sebastian Rodrigues in Shusaku Endo's disturbing novel *Silence* had also discovered.

So as to stop the torture of Japanese Christians, he was asked to apostatize: he had to trample on the *fumie,* the image of Christ laid before him. For many months he refused to do so and fervently prayed to Christ to speak to him and tell him what to do. There was no answer to his prayer, however, only silence. Still, in the end the silence was broken. Christ spoke. Not, however, the beautiful and serene Christ of his devotions, but the Christ of the *fumie,* the trampled, suffering Christ, who said to him: "Trample, trample! It is to be trampled on by men that I was born into this world. It was to share men's pain that I carried my cross."

The church is the community of those who follow the one who was nailed to a rugged cross on a barren hill. In this world it is and remains a *paroikia,* a people with an emergency resident permit only, a pilgrim community. It does not change and save the world; still, it is a sign and sacrament of salvation to the world. It is the community of the Epiphany, nothing more (and nothing less!), which in its mission holds up Christ for the entire world to see.

As I see it, the hardest lesson the church-in-mission will have to learn in the coming years is how to become again what it originally was and was always supposed to be; the church without privileges, the church of the catacombs rather than of the halls of fame and power and wealth. In country after country in the second and third worlds the church is, in fact, already learning this lesson. And the church of the first world? Since Constantine's victory over Maxentius at the Milvian Bridge on 28 October, AD 312, the church in the West has always been compromised to power and privilege in one form or another. To this day it has not yet been liberated from the guilt of privilege. It would, of course, be masochism for the church in the West to pray to be persecuted, but it would be faithfulness to the gospel to pray for it to take on — also in its mission — the form of a servant and become truly solidary with its suffering and persecuted sisters and brothers elsewhere.

Justice, Peace and the Integrity of Creation

World Council of Churches

The Seoul Convocation (March 5-12, 1990) was an important milestone in the conciliar process of committing WCC member churches to a mutual covenant for "Justice, Peace and the Integrity of Creation" (JPIC). . . . . Cited here are the ten affirmations on justice, peace, and the integrity of creation, and four "concretizations" of the act of covenanting among the churches. They express a concrete program of action which parallels the spiritual vision of the kingdom as the goal of God's mission. Source: *New Directions in Mission and Evangelization 1: Basic Statements 1974-1991*, ed. James Scherer and Stephan Bevans (Maryknoll: Orbis Books, 1992), 82-83.

Ten Affirmations on Justice, Peace and the Integrity of Creation

1. We affirm that all exercise of power is accountable to God.
2. We affirm God's option for the poor.
3. We affirm the equal value of all races and peoples.
4. We affirm that male and female are created in the image of God.
5. We affirm that truth is at the foundation of a community of free people.
6. We affirm the peace of Jesus Christ.
7. We affirm the creation as beloved of God.

8. We affirm that the earth is the Lord's.
9. We affirm the dignity and commitment of the younger generation.
10. We affirm that human rights are given by God.

Four Commitments from the Act of Covenant

1. For a just economic order on local, national, regional and international levels for all people; for liberation from the foreign debt bondage that affects the lives of hundreds of millions of people. We commit ourselves to work and to engage our churches to work. . . .

2. For the true security of all nations and peoples; for the demilitarization of international relations; against militarism and national security doctrines and systems; for a culture of nonviolence as a force for change and liberation. We commit ourselves to work and to engage our churches to work. . . .

3. For building a culture that can live in harmony with creation's integrity; for preserving the gift of the earth's atmosphere to nurture and sustain the world's life; for combating the causes of destructive changes to the atmosphere which threaten to disrupt the earth's climate and create widespread suffering. We commit ourselves to work and to engage our churches to work. . . .

4. For the eradication of racism and discrimination on national and international levels for all people; for the breaking down of walls which divide people because of their ethnic origin; for the dismantling of the economic, political and social patterns of behaviour that perpetuate and allow individuals to consciously and unconsciously perpetuate the sin of racism. We commit ourselves to work and to engage our churches to work. . . .

SECTION III

DIALOGUE AND MINISTRY

Interreligious Dialogue as a Christian Task

In a thoughtful and provocative book entitled *Remembering Esperanza: A Cultural-Political Theology for North American Praxis*, Mark Kline Taylor describes what he calls a "postmodern trilemma" that confronts humankind at the present juncture of our history. That is, our contemporary situation presents a three-pronged tension, three demands to which we are called to respond simultaneously: "to acknowledge some sense of tradition, to celebrate plurality, and to resist domination."[1] Taylor writes primarily with North American theologians in mind, but his problematic goes beyond geographical boundaries.

As individuals and communities living in various cultural-political contexts in different parts of the world, we in the church now find ourselves confronted with this shared trilemmic challenge. In an increasingly complex world beset by serious problems that impinge on the very survival of our planetary community, therefore, we first need to get in touch more deeply with the roots of our spiritual heritage, with our tradition that goes back to the apostolic community that received and bore witness to the good news in the person and message of Jesus Christ. Moreover, we must continue to ask what this Good News means for us and demands of us in this day and age. At the same time, we need to acknowledge that we coexist with many other religious communities which have their own claims to ultimate truths that often appear to be radically different from our own. Yet the mere recognition of "coexistence" no longer suffices; increasingly, we find it necessary in our

1. Mark Kline Taylor, *Remembering Esperanza: A Cultural-Political Theology for North American Praxis* (Maryknoll: Orbis Books, 1990), 23.

interdependent world to communicate with, cooperate with, and relate to one another across our differing belief-systems. We recognize that all of us remain, on many different levels, under the influence of structures of domination that tend to our dehumanization. Such a situation calls for courageous acts of resistance, for sincere commitments to seek paths of liberation for ourselves and for our fellow beings. Our own Christian resistance to domination is grounded in our ministries of reconciliation in the world, our covenant responsibilities as bearers of God's Good News.

This trilemmic tension summarizes the contextual issues which the readings collected in this book seek to address. The introduction to the book has offered us a summary of the contemporary global situation and the numerous eco-justice challenges that the Christian community faces in living out its mission. It has described how mass poverty and injustice, structural and physical violence, and ecological deterioration on an ever wider scale pose challenges of vital concern for the church and for the entire global community. These represent concrete manifestations of the "structures of domination" that all humans are called to resist.

As Christians, we have a particular vocation that does not permit us to ignore these problems, although Christian responses to our trilemma understandably take many forms. In view of the inaugural sermon of Jesus as he began his public ministry, all of us are called to consider in what ways, in the paradigmatic footsteps of our master, we too might bring good news to the poor, proclaim release to the captives, announce recovery of sight to the blind and freedom for the oppressed (Luke 4:18-19).

Unfortunately, religion has often been more a part of the problem than of the solution. Leaders within all of the world's religions, including Christianity, have recognized this more clearly in recent decades and have encouraged believers to enter into new measures of reflection and critical self-examination. Religious persons within many communities have been challenged to seek the spiritual resources for responding to the global crises of our wounded world.

The coexistence of multiple religious traditions in the world, of course, has always presented a practical theological issue for the church; the renewed vitality of other religious communities in our time and the minority status of Christians has encouraged a renewed questioning of our global mission in light of "the Great Commission" (Matt. 28:19-20). The first and second sections of this textbook have presented a variety of perspectives on understanding and recovering our tradition in the context of the cultural and religious diversity of the global community.

This third section, through its collection of readings, presents interpretations of interreligious dialogue as a vital and constitutive dimension of Christian mission and ministry in the world. The first set of five readings presents arguments on why and how such dialogical endeavors are important. The next set of five offers views on the fruits of dialogue, such as a renewed commitment to and deeper understanding of one's own religious tradition, as well as a greater openness to and appreciation of other traditions, leading participants toward a transformation of consciousness and what Ewert Cousins calls a *global spirituality.* The last set of essays outlines some of the concrete tasks of interreligious dialogue and cooperation as understood by Jewish, Muslim, Hindu, Buddhist, Native American, and Christian authors. A brief look at the essays in this section may help to highlight their contribution to our Christian quest for forms of faithful discipleship.

Why Dialogue?

In the first article of the section, David Lochhead outlines attitudes Christians have taken vis-à-vis people of other faiths. He further notes how these various attitudes have been expressed in different types of relationships and have been related to different theologies of mission. That is, different attitudes regarding the "other" and various ways of interaction have contributed to different theological interpretations or images of the mission of the church vis-à-vis the world. According to Lochhead, for example, a theology of *isolation* is related to an attitude that considers the rest of the world to be a realm of darkness and the church to be the sole bearer of the Light of Truth to the world still lost in ignorance. A theology of *hostility* judges the world to be a realm fundamentally inimical to God, destined to perdition; the task of Christians, therefore, is to rescue people from a sinful world into the church, wherein only can be found the salvific work of God's grace. A theology of *competition* recognizes elements of truth and goodness in the world, but emphasizes that these are inadequate for ultimate salvation. The church is thereby entrusted with the task of bringing the fullness of Truth and Goodness, which can be found only in God's revelation in Jesus Christ. A theology of *partnership*, in contrast to the above three modes of relationship, sees the world in a positive way as the field of God's activity, wherein the Christian community is called to exercise its unique and proper role, together with many other religious communities, all of whom maintain their own claims to legitimacy as ways to ultimate healing or salvation.

Lochhead notes that these four theologies — which are at the same time attitudes and modes of relationship — can each find biblical support, as the New Testament itself presents ambivalent attitudes toward "the world." Yet he argues that they are inadequate insofar as they share one thing in common: an understanding of the church's role as a "monological activity" vis-à-vis the world. In other words, the four theologies of mission described above in terms of isolation, hostility, competition, and partnership fail in not being able to take fully into account the dialogical nature of God's way of relating to the world, upon which the church's mission is to be modeled. Thus, he describes what he calls the "dialogical imperative" as central to Christian mission.

Dialogue in this context does not simply mean "amiable discussion" or a kind of noncommitted conversation, as is often misunderstood or caricatured in some circles, but a fundamental acceptance of a mode of relationship wherein one embraces the world. "It is precisely as Christians have embraced the world, in openness and concern, that the Christian critique of the world's structures has developed," observes Lochhead. A dialogical relationship with the world, and consequentially, with other religious traditions, does not, therefore, preclude a stance of critique or confrontation.

This is also the thesis of John R. Stott, who invites those who identify with the evangelical Christian tradition to consider dialogue as something in which they can engage in a way that is fully consistent with the belief in the finality of Jesus Christ. Stott asserts that true dialogue is a mark of authenticity, humility, integrity, and sensitivity on the part of the Christian. He urges evangelicals to seek a genuine encounter, and even confrontation, with members of other faith traditions in relation to their commitment to the truth revealed in Jesus Christ.

Following Stott's essay, included is a short account of an actual conversation between an Orthodox Jewish scholar, Pinchas Lapide, and a prominent Roman Catholic theologian, Karl Rahner, who provide us with a moving example of how disagreements on the level of the intellect can be pursued and maintained, while remaining in a spirit of mutual respect, trust, and love.

David Tracy reinforces the point that at this stage of world history "dialogue among the religions is no longer a luxury but a theological necessity." Outlining the reasons why, he also describes the possible significance of such an engagement in dialogue with other religious traditions for the Christian community. It can lead, he claims, not only to the retrieval of the great mystical traditions of Christianity itself, but also to the enhancement of the prophetic dimension of the Christian mission in the world.

David Hesselgrave's article enumerates the kinds of dialogue in which Christians are called to engage, and especially addresses evangelical Christians who express concerns and hesitations about dialogue. In fact, he describes five kinds of dialogue in which evangelicals need not hesitate to participate: (a) dialogue on the nature of interreligious dialogue; (b) interreligious dialogue that promotes freedom of worship and witness; (c) interreligious dialogue concerned with meeting human need; (d) interreligious dialogue designed to break down barriers of distrust and hatred in the religious world; and (e) interreligious dialogue that has as its objective the mutual comprehension of competing truth claims. He emphasizes that "if the Christian message is to be understood it must be framed with reference to the context of competing world views and faiths."

This last type of dialogue defined by Hesselgrave is one that demands considerable time and effort. A special kind of commitment is required to engage another religious tradition in order to comprehend more adequately its truth claims. The truth claims of any given religious community are not to be taken in isolation, and can only be adequately understood in the light of the whole framework within which the given tradition presents and comprehends itself. To engage another tradition in dialogue in an adequate way thus would require effort toward an understanding of the historical backgrounds in which it arose and the development of its central doctrinal formulations. It would demand, too, an endeavor to understand the ethical and ritual practices of the communities of its adherents as the tradition moved across cultures and historical periods, as well as an appreciation of the different expressions by its adherents about their own mission in the world. Such forms of engagement undertaken by Christians can lead not only to more nuanced levels of mutual understanding and appreciation, but to what John Cobb Jr. has called a "mutual transformation."[2] The next set of essays give us some glimpses of what this might mean.

Toward Inner Transformation

Minoru Kasai's essay is an intimate account of the author's own encounter with the reality of God in Christ, in and through his personal encounters and spiritual communion with persons of the Hindu tradition. Although

---

2. John B. Cobb, Jr., *Beyond Dialogue: Toward a Mutual Transformation of Christianity and Buddhism* (Philadelphia: Fortress Press, 1982).

not spelled out in detail in this cryptic essay, originally presented to a Zen-Christian colloquium in Japan, he is suggesting a way toward addressing the basic problem of the rootlessness and hopelessness of a world intoxicated with itself. That way lies precisely in the refreshing experience of returning to the source of what is authentically human — a source that cuts across religious boundaries. For Kasai, as a Christian, it is no other than the encounter with the reality of Christ, present and manifest in the living spirituality of persons of other religious traditions.

Bettina Bäumer, also a committed Christian who has had close contact with Hindu spirituality over a long period of time, writes of the pitfalls and perils of "adopting practices from other faiths" in an arbitrary or utilitarian kind of way. She stresses the importance of taking seriously and respecting the integrity of the traditions involved. In doing so, the question inevitably arises: can one receive nourishment from two (or more) spiritual traditions in a way that does not compromise the essential aspects of either? Her essay offers suggestive hints in considering such a question, noting that "one of the results of an interreligious experience is that the 'names and forms' lose their importance and one necessarily becomes more attentive to the reality indicated by them." Bäumer's essay resonates in part with that of David Tracy in pointing out that interreligious encounter may provide a basis for the recovery of the mystical tradition within Christianity.

Yamada Koun Roshi, a Zen master who had many Christian disciples, writes from his Buddhist perspective about the key elements involved in the practice of Zen. He encourages those engaged in this practice to deepen their own Satori-awakening or Zen enlightenment and to embody and actualize this enlightenment in their daily lives. He specifically invites Christians to continue to explore and expound the meaning of such an enlightenment experience and its actualization in daily life from their own Christian perspectives. This invitation from a Buddhist Zen Master is, in fact, being taken up by an increasing number of committed Christians toward the enrichment of their own spirituality in the context of an encounter of traditions.[3] This kind of encounter Raimundo Panikkar has called "intra-religious dialogue," to distinguish it from "inter-religious dialogue" as that is ordinarily understood.[4] Intra-religious dialogue involves the meeting of

---

3. See Ruben L. F. Habito, "No Longer Buddhist or Christian: A Tribute to Yamada Koun Roshi," *Buddhist-Christian Studies* 10 (1990): 231-37.

4. See Raimundo Panikkar, *The Intrareligious Dialogue* (New York: Paulist Press, 1978).

traditions within one and the same person's inner life in a way that enables a mutual challenge and mutual fertilization to take place, while respecting the integrity of the traditions involved. Such are encounters that are now forging the frontiers of self-understanding among members of the different religious traditions, and spurring not only spiritual enrichment but also theological creativity among Christians as well as those of other traditions.[5]

Joanna Macy's essay includes a concrete set of prescriptions and meditative exercises that can be taken up by the reader irrespective of religious affiliation. This is included to provide examples of particular religious practices coming from another tradition (in this case, Buddhist) which may be taken up by Christians in a way that not only does not compromise their own faith commitment, but more positively, enhances their own commitment to and living of the gospel in a wounded world such as ours.

Ewert Cousins' essay maps out the implications, highlights the significance, and lays out the challenges of interreligious and intrareligious encounters for our world as we enter the twenty-first century (i.e., according to a Western calendar). Noting how we have entered a new mode of awareness ever since astronauts who were sent out into space were able to catch a glimpse of Earth as a unified and interconnected whole, Cousins takes the astronaut's vantage point as foundational for what he calls a new global consciousness emerging in humanity. This global consciousness will have a horizontal dimension: new horizons opened in the meeting of religions and cultures coexisting on the surface of the globe as these engage one another in creative encounters. It will also have a vertical dimension: a deepened sense of interconnectedness with all beings that emerges as members of the various traditions "plunge their roots deep into the earth and far into the universe" and live in a way that is ecologically sound and is grounded upon principles of justice and peace. A spirituality nurtured by this global consciousness, with its twofold (horizontal and vertical) thrust, Cousins suggests, "is not only a creative possibility to enhance the 21st century; it is an absolute necessity if we are to survive."

Yet the question remains for Christians and others: will such a "global spirituality" be an outcome of the melding of elements of different religions in a way that would diminish, compromise, or even do away with a com-

---

5. Consult, for example, John P. Keenan, *The Meaning of Christ: A Mahayana Theology* (Maryknoll: Orbis Books, 1989) and Francis Clooney, *Theology After Vedanta: An Experiment in Comparative Theology* (Albany: State University of New York Press, 1993).

mitment to and appreciation of one's own tradition, or will it perhaps lead to a blotting out of the boundaries and distinct differences between the traditions? The last set of selected essays indicates that it need not necessarily be either.

Tasks for Interreligious Cooperation

The final set of essays are written by committed adherents of their respective traditions — Jewish, Muslim, Hindu, Buddhist, Native American, and Christian — who seek to address concrete tasks which we all face in our troubled global community. The authors write from their own religious standpoints, while acknowledging that their views are not the only ones within their communities. They each try to delineate basic issues that need to be addressed by members of their particular spiritual communities. However, in so doing, they also address the wider human family, and especially members of other religious traditions, inviting all of us toward greater participation in shared goals and tasks as an interconnected Earth community, nourished, enlightened, and empowered by our own respective traditions.

Jacob Neusner, for example, considers the key notion of *shalom* in the Jewish tradition, which means peace "in the sense not merely of the absence of war, but the presence of a whole and complete state of complementarity." If genuine *shalom* is to be realized in this world of conflicting truth claims and clashing interests, he suggests, it is imperative for all of us, especially adherents of the different religious traditions, to include the "other" within our religious framework. Much of the distrust and violence of human history, he charges, may be traced to attitudes that have excluded the "other" from our horizons. In this context, therefore, mere "tolerance" — which he defines as "a theory of the other that concedes the outsider is right for the other but not for me" — is totally inadequate because it invokes a "meretricious relativism" which is not compatible with genuine religious commitment. The task of developing a "theory of the other" within the framework of one's own religious commitment is a task that falls especially upon the intellectuals of all spiritual traditions and is one that presents itself with urgency in the light of our current situation.

Chandra Muzaffar begins his essay with a consideration of a number of specific issues that present challenges to the peace and well-being of the human community. Among these, he says, are (a) imperialism, understood as "the control of the destinies of other human beings and other societies";

(b) the overbearing power of the modern state, understood as the one institution that has control over our very identity; (c) the denial of basic rights to many people in many societies all over the world; (d) the exploitation of multitudes of human beings, whereby they are deprived of their basic human needs; (e) discrimination of women; and (f) the threat to the environment. Confronted with these realities and aware of their interdependence, he asserts, adherents of the different religions of the world are especially challenged to consider them from the perspective of their own spiritual traditions. As a Muslim and a social activist, Muzaffar suggests ways in which members of his own religious community can harness the spiritual wealth of Islam, looking to the Qur'an and to Islamic tradition for resources for empowerment in addressing the urgent issues of our contemporary world. Yet Muzaffar's challenge to his own religious community is also heard clearly across traditions as he asks provocatively: how can Islam contribute to a universal spirituality, to "a universal spiritual vision of human dignity and social justice" that can become the basis of a new global civilization?

G. Shanta looks at her Hindu tradition for resources in her own struggle for women's rights in the larger context of her participation in the protest against oppressive structures throughout the world. What she offers is a re-reading of texts of the Upanishads, the Bhagavad Gita, and the epic Ramayana, all formative influences in her own culture, which would bring to fresh relief the liberative dimension of the message of these sacred texts. The re-readings that she attempts puts in question those institutionally sanctioned readings that tend on religious grounds to rationalize, legitimize, and reinforce oppressive socio-political and economic structures, such as those that discriminate against women in her society. Her own endeavor can be seen as a parallel to the attempts at re-reading religious texts in order to uncover their liberative dimension currently being undertaken by those within other religious traditions, including Christians who re-read the biblical message in order to address contemporary situations of oppression. This is an area where persons from different traditions can learn from and mutually enlighten one another on various levels, including basic methodological as well as concrete practical issues, in their endeavors to re-read their own religious texts and redirect their own religious communities.

Sulak Sivaraksa takes a look at the basic tenets of Buddhism beginning with the Four Noble Truths, and interprets them in the light of the liberative tasks confronting his fellow Buddhists in contemporary society. He calls upon members of other religious traditions to overcome tendencies to take their religions in a tribal way, and instead to look at their own religious heritages with a renewed vision and a renewed commitment. He calls for parallel quests for the original vision of the liberative message within one's own religious tradition in order to foster engagement in tasks of liberation from all kinds of unjust and oppressive structures in the world today. It is in the fostering and nurturing of such a renewed vision and commitment that members of different religious traditions can mutually support and inspire one another.

Audrey Shenandoah, a clan mother of the Onondaga nation, speaks from a Native American experience of living in close harmony with the natural world, in constant awe at its wonders, in a spirit of thanksgiving for its gifts. The basic attitude and way of life underlying her vision as presented in this selection can be a source of inspiration and learning for all of us as we confront and struggle with the devastating effects of our technological civilization that has lost this sense of awe and gratitude regarding the world of nature. In the next to the last excerpt included in our collection, Jocele Meyer lays out ten global issues specifically for Christian reflection, issues that cannot be ignored or taken lightly by Christians who seek to live in a way that is faithful to the gospel message of Jesus Christ. To live as a Christian is to follow Jesus, and to follow Jesus, she argues, is to live as Jesus lived, totally open to one's neighbor. The issues she names are those which concern our "neighbor" from a global perspective. The practical question, then, is how concern with these large global issues translates into concrete action in each local situation as Christians seek to follow Jesus. This is where Meyer's invitation to "Christian reflection" needs to be followed up.

The tasks outlined by our authors affect each of us; they should be of great concern to all of us. As we meet sincerely committed persons of other traditions from near or far who are likewise concerned and engaged in similar tasks, we may frequently experience a moving sense of affinity that cuts across our religious differences. This does not mean that our religious differences are of no importance. However, such encounters do offer us glimpses of new possibilities for relating to one another in non-divisive ways in which our differences, rather than increasing alienation, will serve as continual challenges for us to deepen our roots in our own tradition while broadening our vision by including "others," true "others" who nevertheless are embraced as our own.

Perhaps this is the abiding paradoxical question of our time: how to embrace the other *as* other, and yet no longer as "mere" other. For many

Christians this will involve, in part, finding innovative ways to move beyond the stereotypes of exclusivism, inclusivism, and pluralism. For all, surely, it will require forging new living relationships that offer viable answers to our "postmodern trilemma" by creatively recovering our traditions, meaningfully celebrating our unity in the midst of our diversity, and resolutely resisting forms of oppression that diminish our humanity and impoverish our future. Upon the possibility of responding to this trilemma through grace hinges our very survival as Earth community.

Questions for Discussion

1. In what way does the triple need (a) to recover tradition, (b) to celebrate plurality, and (c) to resist domination constitute a "trilemma" for our postmodern age?

2. What does Lochhead mean by "the dialogical imperative"?

3. In what way can dialogue also include confrontation?

4. What are some types of dialogue that evangelicals are especially challenged to consider?

5. How are the prophetic and the mystical dimensions of Christianity brought to greater relief in dialogue with other religious traditions? Give examples.

6. How can Christian spirituality be deepened and enhanced in interreligious dialogue? Give examples.

7. Describe some of the tasks of dialogue from the perspectives of other religious traditions as presented in the essays in part 3 of this section.

8. What are some of the tasks of dialogue as you perceive it in the context of your local congregation?

For Further Reading

Arai, Tosh, and Wesley Ariarajah. *Spirituality in Interfaith Encounters.* Geneva: World Council of Churches, 1988.

Berthrong, John. *Interfaith Dialogue: An Annotated Bibliography.* Wofford Heights, Calif.: Multifaith Resources, 1993. (Includes nearly two hundred titles on interfaith dialogue, with short descriptions of their contents. For copies, write c/o Multifaith Resources, P.O. Box 128, Wofford Heights, CA 93285-0128).

Clooney, Francis. *Theology After Vedanta: An Experiment in Comparative Theology.* Albany: State University of New York Press, 1993.

Cobb, John B. Jr. *Beyond Dialogue: Toward A Mutual Transformation of Christianity and Buddhism.* Philadelphia: Fortress Press, 1982.

Habito, Ruben. *Total Liberation: Zen Spirituality and the Social Dimension.* Maryknoll: Orbis Books, 1989.

————. *Healing Breath: Zen Spirituality for a Wounded Earth.* Maryknoll: Orbis Books, 1993.

Keenan, John. *The Meaning of Christ: A Mahayana Theology.* Maryknoll: Orbis Books, 1989.

Küng, Hans. *Theology for the Third Millennium: An Ecumenical View.* New York: Doubleday, 1988.

Lochhead, David. *The Dialogical Imperative: A Christian Reflection on Interfaith Encounter.* Maryknoll: Orbis Books, 1988.

Mollenkott, Virginia Ramsey. *Women of Faith in Dialogue.* New York: Crossroad, 1990.

Muck, Terry C. *Those Other Religions in Your Neighborhood.* Grand Rapids: Zondervan, 1992.

Panikkar, Raimundo. *The Intrareligious Dialogue.* New York: Paulist Press, 1978.

Taylor, Mark Kline. *Remembering Esperanza: A Cultural-Political Theology for North American Praxis.* Maryknoll: Orbis Books, 1990.

Walker, Susan, ed. *Speaking of Silence: Christians and Buddhists on the Contemplative Way.* Mahwah, N.J.: Paulist Press, 1987.

Wells, Harry, comp. *Resources for Buddhist-Christian Encounter: An Annotated Bibliography.* Wofford Heights, Calif.: Multifaith Resources, 1993. (Includes listings of books, articles, directories, as well as audiovisual and other educational material usable for local church congregations).

World Council of Churches. *Guidelines on Dialogue with People of Living Faiths and Ideologies,* rev. ed. Geneva: WCC Publications, 1990.

THE WHY AND HOW OF DIALOGUE

Cosmic Dialogue

David Lochhead

In his book *The Dialogical Imperative,* David Lochhead argues that a stance open to dialogue is the only one that can be deemed true to the Christian gospel imperative to love our neighbor. The following excerpt is from a chapter of this book, describing dialogue first and foremost as "a fundamental relationship into which we are called with our neighbor." Source: *The Dialogical Imperative: A Christian Reflection on Interfaith Encounter* (Maryknoll: Orbis Books, 1988).

To consider dialogue as a categorical imperative, as a relationship that is its own purpose, is to ascribe something of an unconditional character to it. One of the implications of this is that there is no situation in which dialogue is not an appropriate relationship. There may indeed be situations in which dialogue is so undercut by our own resistance to dialogue that the relationship is never established. However, there is no situation in which we escape from the dialogical imperative. If we are not in dialogue, we ought to be.

That conclusion calls into question many of the traditional attitudes about mission. Mission, as I use the term here, refers to the calling of the Church by God into the world. The question of mission is the question of the nature of that call. When God calls the Church into the world, what does God intend the Church do there? How does God intend the Church to relate to the world?

Types of relationship that we can describe as isolation, hostility, competition, and partnership have all been expressed, at one time or another, as a theology of mission. In a theology of isolation, for example, the world is seen as a realm of darkness. The mission of the Church is to take light into darkness, knowledge to the ignorant. This view has been prominently represented in the literature of the missionary movement of the last few centuries.

A theology of hostility is expressed in the missiology of many sectarian movements. The world is the enemy of God. It is itself not capable of redemption but is doomed to ultimate destruction in the final victory of God. God, through the work of people of genuine faith, calls people out of the world. The mission of the Church, therefore, is a rescue mission. The community goes into the world in order to pull people out of it.

A theology of competition stresses that Christians have to live "in" the world, but that they ought not to be "of" the world. This is a theology of the "church" type rather than the "sect" type of religious community. If people have to live in the world, they nevertheless have to be wooed away from the temptations of "worldliness." The Church is thus called into competition with the world, the stakes being the ultimate loyalty of individual souls.

A theology of partnership represents the world positively. As the creation of God, the world is good. The goodness of the world and the call of the Church are synonymous. Consequently, the world can be allowed — indeed *ought* to be allowed to set the agenda for the mission of the Church. The mission of the Church is to name and to support the signs of God's activity in the world.

Each of these theologies of mission can appeal to the Bible for support. The fact is that the Bible, particularly the New Testament, uses the term "world" ambivalently. On the one hand, the world is God's creation and the object of God's love. On the other hand, the world is evil, the organized body of human and spiritual rebellion against God. An adequate biblical doctrine of the world would have to deal carefully with the tension that is inherent in this ambivalence. If one wants to pick and choose, however, it is not difficult to find biblical support for quite different theologies of mission. One can color the world white or black as one chooses. One can appeal to the Bible for confirmation of one's choice.

Most theologies of mission have tended to treat mission as a monological activity. The Church, it is argued, is called to preach, to teach, to heal, and to baptize. These are primarily activities in which the Church does something to and for the world. The Church gives, the world receives. The Church speaks, the world listens.

In all of that, there may be a reciprocal listening of the Church to the world. But the listening is justified primarily because it helps the Church to speak better. The Church listens in order that it might understand better what the world hears when the Church speaks. When the Church proclaims the Gospel, it wants the world to get the message right. If the world understands the wrong thing when the Church says "God," the Church needs to know about it. By listening to the world, the Church improves the way that it tells the world what the world needs to hear.

This approach to mission assumes, in one way or another, that the Church knows about the world prior to the Church's engagement with the world. The Church may not know the details. Therefore, the Church has to listen. The decisive things, however — what the world needs, and the answers to the needs of the world — the Church knows a priori. In missions, the Church has the diagnosis and the prescription for the world's ills all ready to administer. The diagnosis is ignorance and the answer is revelation. The diagnosis is sin and the answer is redemption in Christ. The diagnosis is oppression and the answer is liberation.

With this view of the mission of the Church, dialogue can be no more than one aspect, among others, of the things that are done by the Church in mission. Dialogue has to fit in with other priorities. Whatever priority dialogue is given at some point or other, we must go beyond dialogue and engage in activities that are usually described by the words "witness" or "proclamation." Dialogue is granted a certain value but, it is argued, the Church fulfills its mission only as it is faithful to its mandate to witness and proclaim.

The problem with this approach is not with its insistence that the Church has a mandate to witness and proclaim. One could deny this only at the price of a radical falsification of the biblical record. The problem lies with the assumption that insofar as one witnesses and proclaims one must step out of the dialogical relationship. The problem is that the view ends in an exaltation of monologue.

Consider this statement from the Lausanne Occasional papers, which represent a conservative evangelical perspective on mission:

> The use of dialogue in reaching people has to be carefully considered. This method paves the way for a sharing of experiences, and provides an opportunity for frank interchange in conversation. It provides an atmosphere in which both parties can understand each other, and creates a mutual bond of friendship and appreciation. However, it must not end there. It must lead to proclaiming Christ as Lord.

In spite of the limited appreciation of dialogue expressed in this statement, mission is assumed to be ultimately and primarily monological. Dialogue is seen as a means, not of meeting people but of "reaching" people. The point of reaching people, of course, is expressed in the last sentence. At some point in the relationship, dialogue must be superseded by "proclamation." The representatives of other religious communities must be told that Christ is Lord.

Against the representation of dialogue as a means to evangelization, we can only reiterate that a conversation in which one of the parties has an ulterior motive cannot be genuinely dialogical at all. This kind of conversation may prove to be very effective in preparing the ground for evangelization. But it is not genuine dialogue.

The Lausanne papers reflect what is best described as a moderate conservative evangelical point of view. However, the assumption that witness and proclamation are "beyond dialogue" is represented by the World Council of Churches as well. The World Council is concerned to make witness as dialogical as possible. In the final analysis, however, witness and dialogue are distinct activities:

> Witness may be described as those acts and words by which a Christian or community gives testimony to Christ and invites others to make their response to him. In witness we expect to share the good news of Jesus and be challenged in relation to our understanding of, and our obedience to that good news.
>
> Dialogue may be described as that encounter where people holding different claims about ultimate reality can meet and explore those claims in a context of mutual respect. From dialogue we expect to discern more about how God is active in our world, and to appreciate for their own sake the insights and experiences people of other faiths have of ultimate reality.

The Vancouver Assembly of the World Council of Churches attempted to resist any position that would make witness and dialogue into antithetical activities. The report repeatedly refers to mutual witness and to the hearing by Christians of the witness of those of other traditions. Nevertheless, the monological assumptions of this definition of witness cannot be hidden. Dialogue consists of mutual exploration of visions of ultimate reality. In witness, by contrast, we "speak" and then we listen to the feedback that pertains to what *we* have said. In the World Council report, witness and dialogue are interrelated. But at some point, the Church in mission must go beyond dialogue and engage in a different activity called "witness."

The problem stems in part because witness and dialogue are conceived as "activities" or "events." As an activity alongside other activities, dialogue is relative and must take its place as one priority among many. So long as we tie the words "dialogue" and "witness" to specific types of "happenings," then the problem of finding a place for both activities will persist.

When we speak in terms of the dialogical imperative, however, we are talking of attitude and relationship rather than activity. What is universally binding is not a life of going from one "dialogue" to the next "dialogue" but entering into relationships marked by openness, honesty, and the search for understanding.

Dialogue is not just an activity among other activities. It is, first and foremost, a fundamental relationship into which we are called with our neighbor. Unless dialogue is selective — that is, unless we are called into dialogical relationships with some people but not with others (which could only be the case if dialogue were not universally binding) — we must say further that dialogue is a fundamental relationship with the world to which we are called.

If this is the case, we ought not ask how we balance dialogue and witness as activities that are sometimes complementary, but often in competition among the priorities of the Christian community. The question ought rather to be what "witness" and "proclamation" mean within a dialogical mode of being and within a dialogical relationship with the cosmos. We have allowed "witness" and "proclamation" to be defined from the perspective of ideologies that exalt monologue. The difficulty may not be with the mission to which the Church is called by Jesus Christ, but with ideologies that have limited our vision of what witness and proclamation can be.

The question that is raised by these ideologies is whether proclamation and witness are antithetical to dialogue. The question is serious because, as we have admitted, proclamation and witness are clearly activities that are constitutive of the mission of the Church. If the Church's mission is what is mandated in scripture, and it is difficult to see how it could be other than what is mandated in scripture, then an adequate missiology has to make sense of witness and proclamation as central to the calling of the Church in the world.

Whether we are conservative evangelicals or liberal universalists or something in between, we tend to have a stereotype of witness and proclamation as a kind of arrogant dogmatic pronouncement. We imagine these activities as a kind of announcement of a truth that no amount of listening to others could ever touch. The person who hears our witness or proclamation has the option of accepting what we pronounce or of remaining in his or her ignorance and error.

Having named that stereotype, let us set it aside to focus on the way that the concepts of witness and proclamation meant in the apostolic and postapostolic Church. What we find there is an understanding of mission — of witness and proclamation — that is not as clearly opposed to dialogue as our modern stereotype would suggest.

Both witness and proclamation in the New Testament are forms of storytelling. The witness reminds us of a witness in a court of law. The witness is a person who tells a story that, when supported by other witnesses, creates a presumption of the credibility of the story. Similarly, proclamation is the telling of the kerygma. The kerygma has the form of a story. It tells of God's activity in the history of Israel and in the person and work of Jesus Christ.

Witness and proclamation are very closely related activities. If they are to be distinguished at all, both are still fundamentally the telling of the Christian story.

Why, we need to ask, does it seem that witness and proclamation are antithetical to dialogue? As a genre, story is not at all monological. Story is an invitation to the listener to participate actively. Story both engages the imagination of the listener and leaves the listener free. It is difficult to imagine a dialogue that does not include the sharing of stories.

The tension that we perceive between witness and dialogue is closely related to the fact that we tend not to associate witness and proclamation with storytelling. Rather, the words connote to us images of the lawgiver, the moralizer, the dogmatist. In our operative images of witness and proclamation, the hearer is not left free. A story does not attempt to prescribe the response of the hearer, even though it does invite response. Legalism, moralism, or dogmatism tends to narrow acceptable responses to "yea" or "nay," "obey" or "disobey," "accept" or "reject."

The story is told of a Zen Master who, on hearing a passage from the Sermon on the Mount, remarked that "Whoever said that is not far from Buddhahood." It is important to see in that remark a positive response to the proclamation of the Gospel. It is not the response that the Christian community would sometimes like to prescribe for its proclamation. Nevertheless, it is a positive and genuine response to the very question that Christians have generally identified as central to the proclamation: "Who do you say that I am?"

The necessity for proclamation to invite response does not exclude proclamation or witness from dialogue. In dialogue, we always respond to each other's stories. In genuine dialogue, this response is reciprocal. If the Zen Master is able to respond to Jesus, so Christians, hearing the Buddhist story, also respond to the Buddha. Furthermore, our response to the Buddha is not without its impact on the way that we tell the Christian story. Our telling of our stories in witness and proclamation is never as mono-logical as we often make it appear.

In Christian tradition the witness, the proclamation, is the telling of a shared story. The way that the story is told is not fixed or eternal. It has been told differently as the secular and historical context has changed. The story has always been told in dialogue with the world. Despite some ap-pearances, the storytelling of the Christian community has not and cannot be abstracted from the continuing dialogue of the community with its worldly context.

The proclamation of the Christian community developed a relatively fixed form quite early in the history of the tradition. This form is probably best summarized in the Apostles' Creed. The story tells of God's creation of the world, of God's dealings with Israel, of the ministry, death, and resurrection of Jesus, and of the culmination of history at the end of time. This relatively fixed form of the story obscures the fact that the telling of the story has differed markedly at different times and in different places. Some elements of the story are glossed over. Other elements are given special emphasis. The concrete form that the story takes in any telling of it reflects the ongoing dialogue in which the storyteller is engaged with his or her world. That the kerygma assumed a Hellenistic dress in the early Church is not so much a compromise of its Hebrew roots (as is often intimated). The Hellenistic form that the telling of the story took in the early Church is the result of the necessary dialogue of the early Christian community with its own time and place.

The dialogue with other religious communities is only a special case of the dialogue with the cosmos into which the Church is called. This point cuts two ways. First, it implies that the Christian community, like other religious communities, cannot see its mission as primarily confined to the sphere of "religion" (whatever that might mean). Secondly, it implies that

405

our relationship with other religious communities is not qualitatively different from our relations with the various secular communities whom we encounter in the world we live in. Let us look at each of these points in a bit more detail.

First, then, the Christian community (like other religious communities) cannot construe its mission as narrowly "religious." In the present historical context, the suggestion that religious communities should "stick to" religion is expressed in the light of religious communities' involvement in important political and economic issues. The view proposed suggests that as governments are in the political sphere and corporations are in the economic sphere, so religious communities are in the religious sphere. Consequently, this view suggests, religious communities should not become involved in questions of justice, peace, and human rights.

This view is generally rejected by religious communities. The issue, for the religious communities, is not ideology but "faithfulness." This is true whether the religious community be represented by the World Council of Churches, the Moral Majority, or the Shi'ite Muslim community in Iran. Faithfulness, for religious people, typically involves an ongoing concern for and dialogue with the wider community of the world.

The sense of religious communities as having a secular mission implies that the question of dialogue with other religious communities does not hinge on the fact that the various religions are in "the same business." The case for dialogue with other religious communities is *not* based on the assumption that all religious communities have something in common, namely, religion. Religious communities don't simply engage in dialogue with each other. The call to dialogue is a call to dialogue with the whole world.

The second point, that the relation between religious communities is not qualitatively different from the relation between a religious community and its secular neighbors, provides the corollary to the first point. In many situations, there is an attempt to do just that — to prescribe one type of relation between "church" and "world" and another type of relation between "church" and "church." In many churches, for example, the relation between church and world (i.e., the secular community) is viewed as fundamentally dialogical. In the World Council of Churches, and in many of its member denominations, it is a fundamental dialogical stance in relation to the world that underlies its political critique of peace and justice issues.

The dialogical openness to the secular community that is characteristic of the World Council of Churches is not necessarily applied to the relation of the churches to non-Christian religious communities. While dialogue with secular communities may be affirmed, other religious communities may be viewed as competitors. The dialogical relationship affirmed as appropriate in the secular realm is suddenly reversed when we enter the realm of religion.

The view that religious communities have a special interest in dialogue with each other and the view that religious communities exist in essential competition with each other are both rooted in the same assumption. Both views assume that religious communities have "something in common" with each other that they do not share with nonreligious communities. Both views assume that religious communities are "in the same business" and that, consequently, either "partnership" or "competition" are the appropriate relationships between them.

Against that view, we have here been proposing the view that mission is fundamentally dialogue with the world. This view is proposed as an interpretation of Christian mission without, thereby, precluding the possibility that it might also be true of other religious communities.

To describe mission as cosmic dialogue does not rob mission of its critical element. If we take the secular dialogues of the churches as an example, we can understand this point clearly. In the sphere of human rights, of justice and of peace, the churches have time and time again been drawn into critiques of racism, of classism, of sexism, of militarism. The point to be understood is that these critiques do not issue from an arm's-length relationship with the world. On the contrary. It is precisely as Christians have embraced the world, in openness and concern, that the Christian critique of the injustice of the world's structures has developed.

A dialogical relationship with the world does not entail the suspension of judgment. Neither does it preclude anger. Dialogue places judgment and anger in a new context. Dialogue may require that we search for a new style of expressing ourselves on those occasions when we may need to speak a negative word. What we need to insist is that prophetic criticism ought not to be a pretext for avoiding the dialogical imperative.

Dialogue, Encounter, Even Confrontation

John R. Stott

ANGLICAN

Evangelical Protestants have had sharp, negative reactions against some expositions of dialogue with people of other faiths. An acknowledged evangelical leader, one of the framers of the 1974 Lausanne Covenant, presents here a biblical basis for "true dialogue," as well as the historical background for the "conservative Christian's argument against dialogue" which considers it as "bordering on treason against Jesus Christ." John R. Stott, a minister in the Church of England, argues that "true dialogue" is a mark of Christian authenticity, humility, integrity, and sensitivity. However, there is need also for encounter, even confrontation (what he calls "elenctics"), "in which we seek both to disclose the inadequacies and falsities of non-Christian religion and to demonstrate the adequacy and truth, absoluteness and finality of the Lord Jesus Christ." Source: *Christian Mission in the Modern World* (Downers Grove: InterVarsity Press, 1975).

"Mission" denotes the self-giving service which God sends his people into the world to render, and includes both evangelism and socio-political action. Within this broadly conceived mission a certain urgency attaches to evangelism, and priority must be given to it; "evangelism" means announcing or proclaiming the good news of Jesus. . . . Is there any room for "dialogue" in the proclamation of the good news? It is well known that during the past decade or two the concept of "dialogue with people of other

408

faiths" has become the ecumenical fashion, and that evangelicals have tended to react rather sharply against it. Is our negative reaction justified? And what are the issues anyway?

Extreme Views

Extreme positions have been taken on both sides of this debate. Evangelical Christians have always — and in my judgment rightly — emphasized the indispensable necessity of preaching the gospel, for God has appointed his church to be the herald of the good news. An eloquent summons to proclamation has been issued by Dr. Martyn Lloyd-Jones in his book, *Preaching and Preachers* (Hodder and Stoughton, 1971). His first chapter is entitled "The Primacy of Preaching," and on its first page he writes: "to me the work of preaching is the highest and the greatest and the most glorious calling to which anyone could ever be called. If you want something in addition to that I would say without any hesitation that the most urgent need in the Christian Church today is true preaching, as it is the greatest and most urgent need also" (p. 9). Indeed, because man's essential trouble is his rebellion against God and his need of salvation, therefore "preaching is the primary task of the Church" (p. 25). To his passionate advocacy of preaching Dr. Lloyd-Jones has sometimes added his distaste for the concept of dialogue: "God is not to be discussed or debated. . . . Believing what we do about God, we cannot in any circumstances allow Him to become a subject for discussion or debate or investigation . . . as if He were but a philosophical proposition" (pp. 46, 47).

And the same goes for the gospel: the gospel is suitable for proclamation, not for amiable discussion. Now if by "discussion" we have in mind the work of clever diplomats at the conference table, whose objective is to satisfy (even appease) everybody, and whose method is to reach consensus by compromise, I find myself in whole-hearted agreement with Dr. Lloyd-Jones. The gospel is a non-negotiable revelation from God. We may certainly discuss its meaning and its interpretation, so long as our purpose is to grasp it more firmly ourselves and commend it more acceptably to others. But we have no liberty to sit in judgment on it, or to tamper with its substance. For it is God's gospel not ours, and its truth is to be received not criticized, declared not discussed. Having said this, however, it is necessary to add that, properly understood, "dialogue" and "discussion" are two different things.

At the other extreme there is a growing dislike for preaching, or at least for preaching of an authoritative or dogmatic kind. Proclamation is said to be arrogant; the humble way of communication is the way of dialogue. It would be difficult to find a more articulate exponent of this view than Professor J. G. Davies of Birmingham. In his small book *Dialogue with the World* (SCM, 1967) he writes: "Monologue is entirely lacking in humility; it assumes that we know all and that we merely have to declare it, to pass it on to the ignorant, whereas we need to seek the truth together, that our truth may be corrected and deepened as it encounters the truths of those with whom we are in dialogue" (p. 31). Further, "monologue . . . is deficient in openness" (p. 31), whereas "dialogue involves complete openness" (p. 55). Professor Davies goes on:

> To enter into dialogue in this way is not only difficult, it is dangerous. Complete openness means that every time we enter into dialogue our faith is at stake. If I engage in dialogue with a Buddhist and do so with openness I must recognize that the outcome cannot be predetermined either for him or for me. The Buddhist may come to accept Jesus as Lord, but I may come to accept the authority of the Buddha, or even both of us may end up as agnostics. Unless these are *real* possibilities, neither of us is being fully open to the other. . . . To live dialogically is to live dangerously. (p. 55)

For myself I regard this as an intemperate overstatement. It is true that good Christian preaching is always dialogical, in the sense that it engages the mind of the listeners and speaks to them with relevance. But it is not true to say that all monologue is proud. The evangelist who proclaims the gospel is not claiming to "know all," but only to have been put in trust with the gospel. We should also, as I believe and shall soon argue, be willing to enter into dialogue. In doing so we shall learn from the other person both about his beliefs and also (by listening to his critical reaction to Christianity) about certain aspects of our own. But we should not cultivate a total "openness" in which we suspend even our convictions concerning the truth of the gospel and our personal commitment to Jesus Christ. To attempt to do this would be to destroy our own integrity as Christians. . . .

The Place of Elenctics

We do not deny that there are elements of truth in non-Christian systems, vestiges of the general revelation of God in nature. What we do vehemently deny is that these are sufficient for salvation and (more vehemently still) that Christian faith and non-Christian faiths are alternative and equally valid roads to God. Although there is an important place for "dialogue" with people of other faiths (as I shall shortly argue), there is also a need for "encounter" with them, and even for "confrontation," in which we seek both to disclose the inadequacies and falsities of non-Christian religion and to demonstrate the adequacy and truth, absoluteness and finality of the Lord Jesus Christ.

This work is technically called "elenctics," from the Greek verb *elengchein*, to "convince," "convict," or "rebuke," and so call to repentance. J. H. Bavinck devotes the whole of part 2 of his book *An Introduction to the Science of Missions* (Hodder and Stoughton, 1954) to this subject, and describes the nature, place, task, and main lines of elenctics. . . .

First, the purpose of elenctics is not to "show the absurdity of heathendom," still less to ridicule other religions or their adherents. It refers chiefly "to the conviction and unmasking of sin, and to the call to responsibility." "In all elenctics the concern is always with the all-important question: 'What have you done with God?'"

Second, the justification for this task is the Bible itself, for "the Bible from the first page to the last is a tremendous plea against the heathenism, against the paganizing tendencies in Israel itself, in short, against the corruption of religion." The Bible also teaches us "concerning the human heart and its sly attempts to seek God and at the same time to escape him."

Third, elenctics is not the harsh or negative activity it may sound. It "can actually be exercised only in living contact with the adherents of other religions." . . . Further, this contact must be a loving contact. . . .

A fourth and final point is that ultimately elenctics is the work of the Holy Spirit. It is he who "convicts" of sin, righteousness and judgement (John 16:8-10). "He alone can call to repentance and we are only means in his hand."

The very concept of "elenctics" is out of accord with the diffident, tolerant mood of today. But no Christian who accepts the biblical view of the evil of idolatry on the one hand, and of the finality of Jesus Christ on the other can escape it. Further, only those who see the need for elenctics can also see the need for dialogue and can understand its proper place.

411

Only when we are assured that a true Christian dialogue with a non-Christian is not a sign of syncretism but is fully consistent with our belief in the finality of Jesus Christ, are we ready to consider the arguments by which it may commended. They are four.

The Argument for Dialogue

First, true dialogue is a mark of *authenticity*. Let me quote the Uppsala statement:

> A Christian's dialogue with another implies neither a denial of the uniqueness of Christ, nor any loss of his own commitment to Christ, but rather that a genuinely Christian approach to others must be human, personal, relevant and humble. In dialogue we share our common humanity, its dignity and fallenness, and express our common concern for that humanity. (Report II, par. 6)

If we do nothing but proclaim the gospel to people from a distance, our personal authenticity is bound to be suspect. Who are we? Those listening to us do not know. For we are playing a role (that of the preacher) and for all they know may be wearing a mask. Besides, we are so far away from them, they cannot even see us properly. But when we sit down alongside them like Philip in the Ethiopian's chariot, or encounter them face to face, a personal relationship is established. Our defenses come down. We begin to be seen and known for what we are. It is recognized that we too are human beings, equally sinful, equally needy, equally dependent on the grace of which we speak. And as the conversation develops, not only do we become known by the other, but we come to know him. He is a human being too, with sins and pains and frustrations and convictions. We come to respect his convictions, to feel with him in his pain. We still want to share the good news with him, for we care about it deeply, but we also care now about him with whom we want to share it. As the Mexico report put it, "true dialogue with a man of another faith, requires a concern both for the Gospel and for the other man. Without the first, dialogue becomes a pleasant conversation. Without the second, it becomes irrelevant, unconvincing or arrogant" (*Witness in Six Continents*, 1964, p. 146). Dialogue puts evangelism into an authentically human context.

Secondly, true dialogue is a mark of *humility*. I do not mean by this

412

that proclamation is always arrogant, for true proclamation is a setting forth of Jesus Christ as Savior and Lord, and not in any sense or degree a parading of ourselves. What I mean rather is that as we listen to another person, our respect for him as a human being made in God's image grows. The distance between us diminishes as we recall that if he is fallen and sinful, so are we. Further, we realize that we cannot sweep away all his cherished convictions with a brash, unfeeling dismissal. We have to recognize humbly that some of his misconceptions may be our fault, or at least that his continuing rejection of Christ may be in reality a rejection of the caricature of Christ which he has seen in us or in our fellow Christians. As we listen to him, we may have many such uncomfortable lessons to learn. Our attitude to him changes. There may after all have been some lingering sense of superiority of which we were previously unconscious. But now no longer have we any desire to score points or win a victory. We love him too much to boost our ego at his expense. Humility in evangelism is a beautiful grace.

Thirdly, true dialogue is a mark of *integrity*. For in the conversation we listen to our friend's real beliefs and problems and divest our minds of the false images we may have harboured. And we are determined also ourselves to be real. Bishop Stephen Neill distinguishes between dialogue and an "amiable discussion." In an article about Bangkok published in *The Churchman* in December 1973 he wrote:

> Anyone brought up in the Platonic tradition of dialogue knows well the intense seriousness involved; Socrates and his interlocutors are concerned about one thing only — that the truth should emerge. This is the concern of the Christian partner in dialogue. If Christ is the Truth, then the only thing that matters is that Christ should emerge, but Christ as the Truth makes categorical demands on the individual for total, unconditional and exclusive commitment to himself. It may well be that I may discover in dialogue how inadequate my own self-commitment is; but, out of respect for the freedom and dignity of the partner, I may not hope and ask for him anything less than I ask and hope for myself. As experience shows, it is extremely difficult to find in any of the non-Christian religions and anti-religions a partner who is prepared to engage in dialogue on this level of seriousness.

Yet such integrity is essential to true dialogue.

Fourthly, true dialogue is a mark of *sensitivity*. Christian evangelism falls into disrepute when it degenerates into stereotypes. It is impossible to evangelize by fixed formulae. To force a conversation along predetermined lines in order to reach a predetermined destination is to show oneself grievously lacking in sensitivity both to the actual needs of our friend and to the guidance of the Holy Spirit. Such insensitivity is therefore a failure in both faith and love. Dialogue, however, to quote from Max Warren, "is in its very essence an attempt at mutual 'listening,' listening in order to understand. Understanding is its reward" (from an unpublished paper entitled *Presence and Proclamation,* read at a European Consultation on Mission Studies in April 1968). It is this point which was picked up in the Lausanne Covenant, which contains two references to dialogue. On the one hand it says firmly that we "reject as derogatory to Christ and the gospel every kind of syncretism and dialogue which implies that Christ speaks equally through all religions and ideologies" (par. 3). But on the other it says with equal firmness that "that kind of dialogue whose purpose is to listen sensitively in order to understand" is actually "indispensable to evangelism" (par. 4). The principle was stated centuries ago in the book of Proverbs: "If one gives answer before he hears, it is his folly and shame" (Prov. 18:13).

Speaking the Truth in Love

Pinchas Lapide and Karl Rahner

Pinchas Lapide, an Orthodox Jewish scholar, and Karl Rahner, a Roman Catholic theologian, sat down and discussed various issues involved in Jewish-Christian relations. This section is excerpted from that illuminating discussion. Source: *Encountering Jesus — Encountering Judaism: A Dialogue* (New York: Crossroad, 1987).

Lapide: When I sit with you like this, I am overcome for a moment by the feeling of the all-encompassing fellowship of God. The centuries of alienation dissolve, and two sons of one father sit across from one another — two sons who have seriously argued and drifted apart, but who finally come to the insight that the fatherly benefaction envelops them both. Gradually it dawns upon them that this contending among themselves may admittedly have thousands of humanly valid reasons, but nevertheless does not accord with the redemptive intentions of their common creator. Such an overview can scarcely harm our dialogue.

Rahner: Naturally I am basically in agreement with the description you have given of our mutual relationship. But that still doesn't change the fact that presumably there are fundamental religious and ideological differences between us that we cannot simply pass over. Whether a deeper unity lies hidden behind these religious differences (which must be taken seriously) — and how one interprets it — is still another question. In any case, we are simply not yet united in what we will probably say to one another. We can therefore only postulate in hope that behind that in which we are not united there is nevertheless a fundamental unity. But despite the hope at this level, about which we can speak with one another with human words, we must take the religious differences seriously.

Lapide: So seriously that none of us should renounce one iota of his religious position. The dialogue frequently doesn't concern the faith itself, but the angle of vision, the way of seeing, and the manner of articulation. In all these modalities the motto of Pope John XXIII hovers before me: *veritas in caritate.* We owe each other the truth — but in love.

Rahner: After all, "speak the truth in love" is already found in Paul.

Lapide: In accepting the Reuchlin Prize of the City of Pforzheim in 1965, you said: "A Christian will conduct the dialogue earnestly in the knowledge of the danger that within himself the sin of pride, of stubbornness, of false self-security, of brutality poisons the dialogue and causes social lies. . . . The Christian knows . . . that one must be able to say of his dialogue what the apostle said of love: In true dialogue one is patient, kind, not jealous, one does not boast, one is not arrogant, one does not insist upon one's own way, one does not play the hypocrite, one does not become resentful, one does not resent the evil suffered, one hopes all things, one endures all things, for one knows — even in the conviction of one's own truth — that one still sees as in a mirror dimly and in part." I could wish for no better guiding word for a Christian-Jewish religious dialogue.

Rahner: I hope that in the present dialogue between us this description of a true dialogue is not denied. One never knows for sure reflexively whether this description is being lived up to or not. For on the one hand, one must represent a definite, clear conviction in the face of one's dialogue partner who is of another conviction. And on the other hand, one should do so precisely in the manner just described. To unite both, though, is difficult, and whether one actually brings it off always remains unclear.

Lapide: When I endeavor to survey the entire terrain of the Christian-Jewish discussion *sub specie aeternitatis* — all two millennia of divergence — it appears to me that from an initial brotherly argument developed a still fruitful rivalry ("a struggle over heaven") that all too quickly dissolved into opposition and finally degenerated into hostility. In Buber's German one could say: from *Be-gegnung* (encounter) came *Ent-gegnung* (objection), then *Ver-gegnung* (reprisal) and finally destructive *Zer-gegnung* (antagonism). Is it not time for us to ask ourselves the basic question: Where is HE, our Father in heaven, who separates and divides us? What has alienated Jews and Christians for such a long time? And where are we, with our

416

handiwork and our human faculties, erecting the walls that put barriers in the way and prevent an actual coming together?

Rahner. I believe one must make a distinction between two questions: On the level of what can be expressed, can one come to an agreement through the dialogue described above? And what do I accept as already given in the dialogue partner, then and there, when this desired agreement is not yet given on the level of what can be expressed?

Dialogue and the
Prophetic-Mystical Option

David Tracy
Roman Catholic

Encounters between different religious traditions have led participants of these encounters to focus on the mystical dimension
of the traditions as an area of mutual resonance. David Tracy
looks at the prophetic element of religion as a dimension thrown
light upon in interreligious encounters. Source: *Dialogue with
the Other* (Grand Rapids: Eerdmans, 1990).

Christian Theology and Dialogue

Dialogue among the religions is no longer a luxury but a theological necessity. The praxis of dialogue demands primacy before any rush to
theoretical revisions within theology. To be sure, true theory is also
grounded in praxis — the praxis of critical reflection. Still the move to any
serious theological revision open to the demands of religious pluralism
suggests a need to be wary of theoretical reflection not grounded in both
the demanding praxis of the kind of critical reflection proper to all theory
and the transformative praxis of interreligious dialogue where the "other"
becomes not a projected but a genuine other.

Theoretical reflection on dialogue itself, moreover, suggests that only
where the subject-matter and not the subject's consciousness is allowed to
take over does true dialogue happen. Every subject inevitably enters that

unnerving place, the dialogue, with certain expectations on what the relevant questions are and who the other may be. It cannot be overemphasized that, if genuine dialogue is to occur, we must be willing to put everything at risk. Otherwise, we do not allow attention to the logic of questioning elicited by this particular subject matter (however different or other — even, at times, terrifyingly other, as Levinas correctly insists). For my part I cannot but enter an interreligious dialogue as other than a Christian. Even my willingness to enter is, for me, a result of a two-fold commitment: a faith commitment to love of God and neighbor — the heart of Christianity in that command and empowerment of the God decisively manifested in Jesus Christ; and an ethical commitment to these honorable (Western) meanings of what genuine dialogue is (from Plato to Gadamer).

A Western ethical commitment to what reason-as-dialogue and my Christian commitment to the ethical-religious praxis of interreligious dialogue as one of the "works-of-love" may unite to impel one to enter that *fascinans et tremendum* place, the pluralistic and ambiguous dialogue among the religions in our day. For many of us, our prior theological self-understanding as modern Christians had already occasioned an abandonment of any purely "exclusivist" understanding of the revelation of Jesus Christ. For some (myself included) one or another liberal version of Christian "inclusivism" and "finality" once seemed adequate to the pluralistic situation as well as appropriate to a revised understanding of the tradition. Liberal inclusivism seemed adequate insofar as it provided one honest Christian way to affirm other revelations and ways of salvation as real ways. Theological inclusivism seemed appropriately Christian by providing a theological account of how these other ways could be included, in principle, either as constituted by or normatively judged by the Christian belief in general revelation and the universal salvific will of the God disclosed with finality in Jesus Christ.

But the liberal inclusivist ways, too, I now realize, must also be put at risk in the new interreligious dialogues. The new question is to find a way to formulate a Christian theological question on religious pluralism in such manner that a genuinely new answer may be forthcoming without abandoning Christian identity. The "answer" is unlikely to be, as some suggest, by shifting from a "christocentric" to a "theocentric" position. This Christian response seems more a postponement of the issue rather than an adequate response to it. For insofar as Christians know the God (as pure, unbounded Love) that all Christian models of theocentrism demand, they know *that* God in and through the decisive revelation of God in Jesus Christ.

Correlatively, insofar as Christians are willing to enter dialogue they are thus willing either because of their prior ethical commitment to reason-as-dialogical or, more likely, their Christian understanding of *Christian* faith-working-through-love as now demanding interreligious dialogue (that new work of love).

Like many others I now find myself in the uncharted territory of the new interreligious dialogue aware that both our present situation demands that entry and, as suggested above, so does Christian faith. Is it possible to have an adequate theological response to the full implications of inter-religious dialogue for Christian theological self-understanding yet?

For some, the answer is yes. For myself, I have no such confidence at present. That we should examine critically all prior Christian theological answers in the light of the interreligious dialogue I do not doubt. That we should risk articulating new Christian theological answers (like the move past "christo-centrism" to "theocentrism") I also do not doubt. Yet if we have good reason to think that "theocentrism" simply recalls the issue of "christocentrism" by another name, then we may need to ask more questions in actual dialogues with others and ourselves before announcing a new christology or a new theocentrism. It is, in fact, more exact to speak of two crucial and related dialogues: first, the interreligious dialogue which provides the principal new religious praxis which is transforming all of us and which gives rise to new theological thoughts and theories; and second, the inner-Christian dialogue, where Christian theologians attempt to report to others what possibilities they now foresee.

My own attempts at the first form of interreligious dialogue have been serious but modest: with Jews; with Buddhists; with the archaic or primal religions through the work of Mircea Eliade and other colleagues, especially in history of religions; and, in a strange way unnecessary to spell out here, with new work in ancient Greek religion — and not only ancient Greek philosophy. I hope that each of those dialogues as well as other needed dialogues will increase over the years. The praxis of interreligious dialogue itself, I believe, does not merely bear a "religious dimension." It *is* a religious experience; hence, the "mutational person" demands of Raimondo Pan-nikar and other Christians makes far more sense to me now than ever before.

Each dialogue is likely to make it possible to revise aspects of the tradition which need revision and to discover other forgotten, indeed often repressed, aspects of the great tradition. Some examples: the post-Holocaust Jewish-Christian dialogue has provoked, for me, a greater realization not only of the irretrievably Judaic (and especially prophetic-eschatological) character of Christianity. That crucial dialogue has also made me more aware of needed revisions in christology (as in the language I now employ of the always-already, not yet Christ), while also making me aware of the revolting underside of christology in the history of Christian anti-Semitism. The work of Jewish theologians has also occasioned a needed Christian theological reappropriation of the other *tremendum* aspects of the covenantal God. Indeed, many Christian formulations of God as love begin to seem, at best, unfinished — as *Lamentations* and much of the Wisdom literature suggests, as Luther's *deus nudus* insisted, as Barth's attempted recovery of the "wrath of God" suggests, and as post-Holocaust Jewish theology suggests with even greater force.

Moreover, the primal religions (too often ignored in theological interreligious dialogue) occasion further reflection on the primal (or manifestory) character of both Christianity and Judaism. Minimally, primal manifestation should be the necessary dialectical counterpart to the more familiar prophetic and proclamation trajectories — as the prophetically oriented Latin American liberation theologians who are presently rethinking "popular religion" see. A rethinking of the ancient Greek religions (including pre-classical goddess religions) have occasioned, for me, new reflections on the diversity of resources in the Greek side of our heritage. That diversity historically has been often violently suppressed by the early Christian theological decision to follow Plato (rather than, say, Sappho or Hesiod or Herodotus or Aeschylus) in the reading of classical Greek and pre-classical (e.g., goddess) religion. Finally, the Buddhist-Christian dialogue can occasion, it is true, a new appreciation (as in John Cobb's work) of the possibilities of "mutual transformation" in dialogue with traditions like Amida Buddhism and the Boddhisattva traditions. It can also occasion the discovery of aspects of the Christian tradition like the radically apophatic traditions as well as thoughts on the fuller implications of a "kenotic christology."

Yet that same Buddhist-Christian dialogue, especially when it turns to Zen Buddhism, seems to call all sanguine language of commonality and complementarity into very serious question. I am not aware of *any* strand of Christianity, however forgotten or repressed, that answers the profoundly religious question of transience as the Buddhist does. Is the Buddhist simply wrong? Or is the Buddhist way a disclosure of another "way" (for the Christian, therefore, some revelation and salvation) not previously glimpsed in the Christian way — but open to, challenging to, transformative of our way? How, if at all, we might be able to include so different an other as the Buddhist only further dialogical praxis will be able one day to suggest. Then and only then will we begin to know how such Buddhist praxis may relate to Christian soteriology and thereby to any christological claim. It is true that Buddhist notions of Ultimate Reality as emptiness do help to break any dualism in Christian notions of God and creation. Yet, for the Christian and Jew, some duality (not dualism) between Creator and creation will always be affirmed. Buddhists can also force Christian theologians to realize that theism can be a subtle way to "cling" and not let go to God. As suggested earlier, Buddhists can occasion for Christians a rediscovery of the insights of Eckhart. Yet, however radical Eckhart's language of the Godhead-beyond-God for Christian self-understanding is, even that is not Nagarjuna's view of either language or Ultimate Reality. They are and remain radically different.

It is true, as John Hick argues, that all great traditions seem to occasion a radical turn from self-centeredness to Reality-centeredness. Yet the differences at every step in these different turns — of the understandings of self, salvation-enlightenment, and Ultimate Reality — seem so striking, so different and other, that all I really know is that I do not know (and that with a relatively *indocta ignorantia*). With such differences as these how can a plausible generalization — on either commonality or complementarity or dialectical relationships or sheer difference — be made? The future may tell, but the present, as far as I can see, provides many hints and guesses but no adequate Christian theological answer. Perhaps another generation or two of thinkers who take the interreligious dialogue for granted as a necessary religious and intellectual praxis for all serious religious thinkers in our day is needed before any adequate response is possible. In the meantime, we should all try to articulate some tentative suggestions for change. . . .

. . . I remain convinced that one signal opportunity for Christian theology as a result of serious religious dialogue is the retrieval of the great Christian mystical traditions: the image tradition of Gregory of Nyssa and Origen and their development of a cosmic Christianity; the Trinitarian mysticism of the Cappadocians and Augustine and, above all, Ruysbroeck; and the great love mysticism tradition of the classic Cistercians and Bernard of Clairvaux to the great Spanish Carmelites, Teresa of Ávila and John of the Cross.

But it is also clearly time to try to restore the balance from an almost exclusive emphasis on retrieving the mystical traditions, to recover the central prophetic core of Christianity in the context of the interreligious dialogue. Here the need is for any prophetic tradition (even one rethought as prophetic-mystical) to establish, beyond the "no-self" of Buddhism and the "death of the subject" of postmodern thought alike, a Christian agent with enough freedom to allow for a commitment to the prophetic struggle for justice. The Christian agent, as we shall see, is also the prophetic agent of the Bible. . . .

. . . It is the singular achievement of the liberation and political theologians that their prophetic, indeed prophetic-mystical, theological return into real history — more exactly into the history of those whom official historical accounts, including Christian theological accounts, have too often disowned as non-persons, non-groups, non-history: the oppressed, the marginalized, the suffering — now empower new prophetic-mystical theologies. That strategy has allowed the liberation, political and feminist theologians to retrieve in and through their very suspicions of earlier modern theological interpretations of scripture the repressed moments of the New Testament: the profound negations in the genre of apocalyptic — so embarrassing to the liberals, so unnecessary to neo-orthodox eschatologies; the dangerous memory of Jesus as eschatological prophet — dangerous, above all, for those who claim his memory as their own.

Here a new hermeneutics of mystical retrieval through prophetic suspicion is clear: the retrieval of the sense of history as rupture, break, discontinuity in apocalyptic; the retrieval of the social systemic expressions of sin over individual sins; the retrieval of the concrete praxis of discipleship in and for the oppressed.

With the prophets, Christians must ask how is it possible to say we have really entered history — that muddle, that ambiguity, even, at times, with Joyce, that nightmare from which we are attempting to awaken — and not have a prophetic-mystical theology? The alternative is not the theological silence of some mystics on concrete history. This much, however, does seem clear on the contemporary Christian theological horizon: the interreligious conversation will only become fully serious when the historical events of our century are taken with full theological seriousness. Christian theology will not be the same when that finally occurs. Christian theology in dialogue at last with Jewish thought will then begin to learn the lessons of Jewish thought through the centuries — the lessons of the need for radically new interpretations after radically new interruptive events — the destruction of the Second Temple, the expulsion of Spanish Jewry, and eclipsing them all with its *tremendum* horror and its radically revisionary demands, the Holocaust.

Despite the important revisionary mystico-political work by many Christian theologians in our historical situation, I do not believe that any of us can even guess at the moment where the new Christian theological hermeneutics of both retrieval and suspicion empowered by a new religious mystico-prophetic *via negativa* on both history and nature will eventually lead. Yet this much does seem sure. Those differences will render pale the kind of shifts we are already familiar with. They will prove more radical for Protestant theology than the radical shift that once occurred when the generation of Barth, Tillich, and Bultmann returned from those trenches of World War I where earlier liberal illusions had collapsed. . . .

. . . Every Christian theological hermeneutic today — no matter how powerful and believable its retrievals of its authoritative passion narratives, no matter how fierce and unrelenting its suspicions of the history of the effects of its own readings of those narratives — must now endure as not merely unfinished but as broken. Yet theology is broken only in order to allow for some new beginning of a retrieval of hope. The new theological beginning must this time be in real concrete history, because it has been chastened by the theological seriousness of the actual history we have witnessed.

The great artists of the Flemish Catholic tradition help see our need for both the mystical and the prophetic with singular clarity. As postmodern Christian thought recovers a new and healing sense of transience after its welcome dialogues with Buddhists, the unexampled genius at transience of Watteau may render that reality for postmodern Christian eyes. The classical mystical resonances in the great Flemish traditions of art and thought may help us all to retrieve anew our own half-forgotten archaic heritage, our own Christian archetypes, and our own need to recover both Eckhart and Ruysbroeck. Like our Flemish forebears, we postmoderns also sense that any serious retrieval of the classic mystical readings of our prophetic texts must not retreat from history and the sense of personal and communal responsibility for the struggle for justice. Any responsible theology today must be what classic Flemish thought, art and spirituality once exemplified: mystical and prophetic; aesthetic and ethical-political; contemplative and committed to action.

Evangelicals and Interreligious Dialogue

David J. Hesselgrave

The author points out that there are different levels of dialogue in which Christian evangelicals are invited to participate, precisely in following their task of witnessing to the gospel of Jesus Christ. Source: *Faith Meets Faith,* ed. G. H. Anderson and T. F. Stransky (New York: Paulist Press, 1981).

Evangelicals are being challenged to demonstrate a new kind of bravery today. If the Christian messenger is to be taken seriously, he or she must demonstrate an interest in those great human concerns which are the topics of contemporary discussion. If the Christian messenger is to be heard, he or she must not be too timid to enter the forums of world opinion. If the Christian message is to be understood it must be framed with reference to the context of competing worldviews and faiths in which it is to be preached. If the Christian mission is to progress, its advocates must be prepared to advance in a new world of resurgent non-Christian religions.

Unless as evangelicals we are willing to risk locking ourselves up in a closet of monologue where we speak primarily to one another, the question for us is not, "Shall we engage in dialogue?" but, "In what kinds of dialogue shall we engage?" *Scriptural precedent clearly enjoins — and the Christian mission entails — interreligious dialogue that answers the questions and objections of unbelievers, proclaims the good news of Jesus Christ, and beseeches men to repent and believe.* Scriptural principle clearly precludes — and the Christian conscience condemns — any dialogue that compromises the gospel or countermands the great commission. Within these boundaries there are various types of dialogue which merit consideration by evangelicals.

Type 1: Dialogue on the nature of interreligious dialogue. It is to be deplored that the evangelical point of view has not been adequately represented in dialogues on dialogue. That lack of participation is due to several factors. First, for reasons of conscience evangelicals do not often hold membership in communions and organizations sponsoring such dialogues. Second, ecumenists are often predisposed not to include evangelicals in such dialogues lest predetermined purposes be jeopardized. Third, evangelicals are suspicious that little or no good can come from their participation. Fourth, because of lack of exposure to this kind of forum, evangelicals sometimes feel ill-prepared to engage in it. One could wish, therefore, that ecumenists would exhibit the same irenic spirit toward evangelicals that they do toward non-Christians. But one could also wish that, when the conditions are right, evangelicals thought it as important to faithfully expound their understanding of biblical teachings within the forums of Christendom as to faithfully proclaim those teachings in the contexts of heathendom.

Type 2: Interreligious dialogue that promotes freedom of worship and witness. There can be no question but that religious freedom is being challenged in one way or another among vast populations of people today. To accede quietly to totalitarian repression of religious faith, or to claim freedoms and privileges for one's own faith that are refused to others — such approaches are tacit denials of the most basic of men's inalienable rights. By what means will we implore the world's rulers and remind ourselves to respect those rights? The pursuit of that question may well merit interreligious conversation and even action.

Type 3: Interreligious dialogue concerned with meeting human need. This is similar to Eric Sharpe's "secular dialogue," but it is not necessarily the same. In the first place, "secular dialogue" may not be the best nomenclature. Though definition of the term resolves some problems, it raises others. In the second place, from a Christian point of view it may be necessary that this dialogue stop short of complete cooperative action because it is incumbent upon the Christian that all he does in word and deed be done in the name of his Lord Christ (Col. 3:16). Nevertheless, discussion of ways and means may be invaluable in view of overwhelming and increasing human need.

Type 4: Interreligious dialogue designed to break down barriers of distrust and hatred in the religious world. If hatred is enjoined by any religion at all, it is certainly not enjoined by Christianity. Christians are admonished to love not only one another but all men. Canon Max Warren seems to imply that interreligious dialogue is basically of this type (or of Type 5, below). It will be apparent that I have some difficulty with this understanding, but my disagreement is not with the idea that this kind of dialogue indeed can be profitable in breaking down barriers. There are excellent examples — too few, to be sure — that dialogue of this type can be used to dissolve distrust and break up log jams that have deterred the conversion of large groups of non-Christians.

Type 5: Interreligious dialogue that has as its objective the mutual comprehension of conflicting truth claims. This is close to Sharpe's "discursive dialogue" (especially as he has elaborated in one context), but in contrast to discursive dialogue it is not committed to dialectic and the proposition that reason alone is a sufficient guide to truth. Its objective is to arrive at a common meaning, not necessarily a common faith. Evangelicals should give serious consideration to proposing and participating in this kind of dialogue because apart from it (in *some* form — so why not face-to-face?) real communication of the Christian faith becomes exceedingly difficult. It is apparent that our Lord and Paul understood the religious systems of their respondents and adapted to them. For altogether too long evangelical missionary communication has been monological because of a lack of this understanding.

Conclusion

The Christian mission in the closing decades of the twentieth century challenges both the ecumenist and the evangelical to make a reappraisal of their attitudes toward, and participation in, interreligious dialogue.

Now is the time for ecumenists to review the direction that dialogue has taken and subject it to the standards of the revealed will of God in the Scriptures. Any form of dialogue that compromises the uniqueness of the Christian gospel and the necessity that the adherents of other faiths repent and believe it should be rejected and supplanted by forms of dialogue that enjoin conversion to Christ.

Now is the time for evangelicals to review their attitude of disinterest and nonparticipation in dialogue. To insist upon the uniqueness of the Christian gospel and the need of all people for salvation in Christ is not tantamount to engaging in biblical dialogue. Something new is needed.

While it may be in the interest of the Christian mission to participate in those types of dialogue that have positive benefits and do not require abandonment or obfuscation of the Christian message, it definitely would be in the interest of the Christian mission to participate in those types of dialogue that enable evangelicals to enter the forums of the world with the understanding, commitment, and courage that characterized the apostolic era.

In a world of religious pluralism evangelical witness, preaching, and teaching would become increasingly dialogical — answering those questions and objections raised by non-Christian respondents rather than simply answering questions of the evangelical's own devising. In the words of my colleague and friend, Carl F. H. Henry, "The only adequate alternative to dialogue that deletes the evangelical view is dialogue that expounds it. The late twentieth century is no time to shirk that dialogue."

FRUITS OF DIALOGUE: TOWARD INNER TRANSFORMATION

Meeting Other Religious Traditions and Rethinking My Own

Minoru Kasai

Kasai, a Japanese history professor, recounts the transformation in his own consciousness and the deepening of his own Christian faith occasioned by the encounter with members of other religious traditions during a trip to India. Source: *A Zen Christian Pilgrimage* (Tokyo: Zen Christian Colloquium, 1981).

The encounter with another religious tradition is in itself a religious experience; it is to return to the root of one's own religion. This religious encounter is like a seal which makes its indelible mark upon my soul and is confirmed as I go through life. This is for me the most fundamental truth. The conclusive moment and the mainspring for this seal to make its mark is the time of encounter and communion with those who live in other religious traditions.

In 1976, I had the opportunity of a month's travel in India. The most joyful part of that journey was my reunion with old friends, one of whom was Professor A. K. Saran, head of the Department of Sociology at Jodhpur University in Rajashtan. Professor Saran invited me to stay in his home for six days and he welcomed me as a member of his family. I observed that Professor Saran's daily life reflected the depth of the Hindu tradition. His way of life was a symbol pointing to the transcendental reality of the Upanishad and the presence of Christ in the Bible. Professor

Saran's central concern is the destiny of human beings. This word "destiny" which he would mention from time to time, is a word which cannot easily be translated into Japanese. He seems to use the word in the context of what Isak Dinesen meant by it. If it is translated, it will be "Who am I?" instead of "What is the human?" He identifies this with A. K. Coomaraswamy's "autological question." Professor Saran distinguishes this from the self-centered "autotelic question," typically modern humanity's concern. In the reality of this destiny, God's grace is all. The endurance of suffering as a way of life holds immense significance in this context. When a human being living in this mystery says, "I am your friend," it is real and logically consistent, there is not the slightest hint of ambiguity. According to Professor Saran, the "autological question" is the core of theoretical frame of reference of self-understanding in the Hindu tradition. Without this question, the Hindu religion is dead as it is. Professor Saran is severely critical of modern civilization which denies transcendental reality and accepts sociology, anthropology and religion based on science and its certification.

Professor Saran's journey of life has called me to return to the source of life, and surprisingly enough, with this Indian sociologist and follower of the Hindu tradition I received a bond of deep communion. Although geographically we are now far apart, he is continuously here with me. Moreover this communion was neither planned nor manipulated, but it was given to me as a blessing in spite of my unworthiness. The reality of this friendship is for me the reality of Christ. I cannot but affirm that this friendship has the power to break down all barriers.

This Indian friend cites Mahatma Gandhi as the most typical example of a contemporary Indian who has lived faithfully according to the Indian religious tradition. On the same journey I was able to satisfy a long-standing wish to visit two of Gandhi's ashrams, and I was astounded at the down to earth, dynamic, transcendental way in which Gandhi lived. Just to mention the form of housing, as an example, I traveled from Sabarmati Ashram to Sevagram Ashram and noticed the housing conditions became more and more primitive. An ordinary person, particularly a city-dweller, would not be able to endure life under such conditions. During the rainy season the dampness would be harmful to one's health, and the intense summer heat at the Sevagram Ashram would be unendurable.

Chimanlal, who accompanied Gandhi since 1916, in spite of his age and poor health is still in charge of the Sevagram Ashram today. According to this person, Gandhi became more and more down to earth as the years

432

went by. In order to keep up with Gandhi's way of living, it was necessary to constantly negate and conquer oneself. However, at Sabarmati Ashram Gandhi was like a father, and at Sevagram Ashram he acted as a mother.

Kosambi, a famous Buddhist scholar and follower of Gandhi, chose the Sevagram Ashram as a place to die. One Hindu member of the Ashram looked after him till the very end. Kosambi could foretell the actual time of his death, and he made this known beforehand to the Hindu, who saw to it that Kosambi would pass away peacefully. This is an example of the dynamic destiny and this has been an unforgettable event for this Ashram.

A leader of Gandhi's village movement, and one who had Gandhi's full trust, was J. C. Kumarappa, a devoted Tamil Christian. He gave up an affluent business life in Bombay to dedicate his life to Gandhi's movement. Kumarappa's home was just as simple as Gandhi's Sevagram Ashram. These two people had a deep spiritual bond.

For me, of decisive importance was the genuineness of this kind of friendship which not only called me to reflect on the root, but to come to grips with basic truth.

I know a person who has lived this reality. Swami Abhishiktananda was French by birth and left for India at the age of 38. He died three years ago without ever returning to his homeland for thirty-one years. He was an ardent lover of India, and became an Indian citizen. As a sannyasi searching for the roots of India's religions' traditions, he built himself a shelter beside the Ganges at Gyansu in the Himalayas and spent his time in meditation for a certain period of a year. He was a faithful Christian and lived accordingly. His manuscripts are being published posthumously by his dedicated friends, and I think these writings will throw light on my groping in the dark. I was fortunate enough to make a pilgrimage together with this Swami in 1971 from Varanasi, through Lucknow, Delhi and Harudawar to Rishkeshi. When we finally parted at Dehra Dun station, he took my hands in both of his, and looked into my eyes affectionately and intensively. That scene has been vividly impressed in my mind. Swami Abhishiktananda has shown me the reality of communion in Christ. This Swami belonged to the Roman Catholic Church, but to those Indians who desired to become Christians, he would point out that they were not to become superficial church members, but rather encouraged them to work outside the church and become true Christians in the Indian world. He was painfully conscious of the church being blind to the reality of Christ.

With this background, I am now quietly recalling my conversation with the late Zen Master Zenkei Shibayama during the Zen-Christian Colloquium, and his words, "See the cosmic light which fills the universe, listen to the voice that fills the universe." I remember how this distinguished Roshi listened from beginning to end, while I, a young man of no importance, recounted my experience in India. I feel that the encounters I had at the colloquium are budding within me, their roots are limitlessly deep and in some way are joined to that experience I had at the Manikarnika Ghat in Varanasi along the Ganges, when I saw the light of death burning in the still darkness.

By lending one's ear to the existence of this root, the encounter with humans, nature, and all existence leads to the reality of God. This to me is more fundamental than the air I breathe. Just as one does not think nor conceptualize the air one breathes, so God's reality is a fundamental truth. Paul's words "For in him we live, and move, and have our being" (Acts 17:28), are indubitable.

The genuine realization of God's presence, omnipresence and perpetuity, even if it should occur just for one moment, leaves an indelible mark upon one's soul. Encounter is seeing God in the encounter itself, in the voice of nature, and in fellow beings. When one thinks of the root of a small plant, one is seized in the mystery of God's existence. This truth is firmly wedged in my life and my emotions can do nothing about it. However, because of my illusions, my ignorance and egoism, I reject this, and therefore at such times God's revelation becomes "Jesus on the cross" or "Jesus waiting for Veronica." Suffering and love are expressions of the mystery of God's existence.

At this point I cannot refrain from saying that the mystery of God's existence is Love. This word "Love" has become idolized, and has lost its symbolical nature of pointing out God's reality, so that one wishes to do away with that word. However, it is clear that as a result, another idol will come into being. What I wish to convey through the word "Love" is that my Indian friends are continuously here with me. At times they speak to me, and at other times they are in silence with me. Love is expressing this reality of prayer.

Looking at the world from this standpoint, it is obvious that the world has chosen a path of rootlessness, and seems to be intoxicated by its fruits. Moreover, because the intoxication has exceeded its limits, the possibility of a reawakening seems beyond hope and self-ruin seems to be our destiny.

The question before us then, is this: How will religious encounter, which for me has revealed the root of religious traditions, deal with this hopelessness?

A Journey with the Unknown

Bettina Bäumer

The problem with "adopting" practices from other religions'
traditions, says Bettina Bäumer, is that it presupposes that these
practices can be isolated; spiritual life in her view is a "totality."
"If one allows it to unfold with all its implications," she says,
"one may be surprised at the transformation taking place."
Source: *Spirituality in Interfaith Dialogue*, ed. Tosh Arai and
Wesley Ariarajah (Geneva: WCC Publications, 1989).

Dialogue at the spiritual level is certainly not sufficient if spirituality is only talked about. But the moment one gets involved in living spirituality in the meeting with another religious tradition, one discovers that spiritualities are not closed vessels. They may be different ways of letting the Spirit take possession of one's life, but we cannot talk of the Spirit in the plural. If spiritualities, of whatever denomination, are authentic, they cannot but be living means of communication since what they communicate in is the Spirit.

This, however, does not imply a chaotic confusion of ways and traditions, for it is valid only at the deepest level. As a stone thrown into still water creates circular waves on the surface, any deep spiritual experience has its repercussions increasingly at the external levels of religion. Even within one tradition, for instance the Christian one, a stone thrown into the depth can create an explosion on the surface, as is evident from the lives of most mystics and saints, much more so when this happens in and through contact with another faith. Swami Abhishiktananda, who had lived such an experience in two traditions with the utmost sincerity and depth, spoke about such "explosions" towards the end of his life. Maybe the outer rings of the waves created by his experience are yet to appear and become effective in the church. It is much more comfortable for any institution, the churches not excluded, to look at such an experience from a safe distance and go on with business as usual, than to take it seriously and accept the consequences.

If I am to say something about my own experience, after living in close contact with Indian — mainly Hindu — spirituality for twenty-four years, I only want to stress a few points which seem important to me.

My attitude at the beginning, and the attitude of my teachers and predecessors on this path, i.e., Christians wanting to incorporate some of the spiritual values of Hinduism or Buddhism in their own way, was certainly one of openness, wanting to learn and being ready to receive inspiration from Indian spirituality for my own inner life as a Christian. But I was not conscious of the full implications of entering into another spiritual world. I felt fairly firm in my Christian faith and wanted to deepen and enrich my spiritual life in India (by "India" I do not mean the geographical reality, but a living spiritual tradition, predominantly "Hindu"). I can still feel this attitude in many of my good Christian friends. We could compare it to somebody wanting to bathe in a river without getting wet!

First of all the questions may be asked, why was I attracted towards Hindu spirituality to such an extent that I wanted to immerse myself in this spiritual dialogue? One may find many reasons — psychological, sociological, theological — but the main reason seems to me that I was not satisfied with the way Christian spirituality is lived today. I had discovered the mystical dimension of Christianity, but I could not help feeling that this dimension was suffocated by and suppressed under heavy institutional (legal) and theological (mental) structures. In Hindu spirituality I found that breath of freedom which is so necessary for the full inner growth of the spirit.

What I came to realize was that "adopting practices from other faiths" was not completely honest towards "other faiths" — as if one had the right to extract certain beautiful experiences, practices or teachings from another tradition in order merely to incorporate them in one's own. No wonder that this attitude of "appropriation" or "utilization" practiced by Christians has now led to the suspicion on the part of Hindus and Buddhists that this is a kind of spiritual theft. After all, Christians would also feel apprehensive

436

if some Hindus started celebrating the mass without understanding the totality of meaning of which the mass is a part. If we take another tradition seriously, we must also accept its premises — in the case of the Hindu tradition one such premise is what is called *guruparampara,* the living transmission from master to disciple which alone bestows the *adhikara,* the right to do certain spiritual practices, as well as the power and promise that they will be fruitful.

Another reason why the "adoption of practices from other faiths" is not satisfactory is that it seems to presuppose that these practices can be isolated, whereas spiritual life is a totality. I could have easily said that what I learnt from Hinduism was a way of meditation — but in fact this meditation leads to a transformation of life itself, of one's experience of oneself, of others, of nature, of God. Meditation is not a particular yoga technique, or a Zen way of "sitting," taken out of their context. If one allows it to unfold with all its implications, one may be surprised at the transformation that is taking place.

Once I accept all the implications, the next question will be justified: how can one belong to two spiritual traditions at the same time? Does it not lead to either schizophrenia or dishonesty? It is precisely here where I am completely naked and exposed and depend on nothing but divine grace. There is no *a priori* scheme which I can fit into. Swami Abhishiktananda underwent this excruciating and blissful experience, remaining faithful to both traditions, and he found his freedom by transcending both. But I have to tread the way myself in all sincerity, in spite of the tremendous encouragement received from him and others. My conviction is that only such an experience can really build bridges between the old and still persisting misunderstandings among the diverse spiritual traditions.

What happens when one has jumped into that melting-pot? On the one hand, my Christian faith is reduced to its essentials. After all, the fear of losing one's faith means that it has not reached the level of reality, that there is still something to be lost. It is like climbing a high mountain along a narrow path: you cannot take much baggage. First you may think that all this baggage is necessary, but higher up you realize that it is only a burden, and the lighter you walk, the easier you will reach the peak. First of all, renunciation applies not only to worldly but also to religious possessions. Secondly, in real renunciation one does not give up any real value, one only pierces to the core and so one does not feel the need for the externals any longer. In a sense I do not feel that I have lost anything, though it may appear so. On the contrary, the deep Christian archetypes reappear often

437

in a different and unexpected context. I could cite examples from the realms of religious expression, ritual, etc., in the relation between guru and disciple, in spiritual experience or insights. For example, several times I had the experience of communion in the full sense in a Hindu context, where the participants never had any direct contact with Christ. There was no need to use the name, the spiritual reality was there. Christian churches are not yet ready for an intercommunion among themselves — but to my mind, intercommunion should go far beyond the narrow boundaries of Christianity, a real sharing of religious values in theory and practice. In fact, one of the results of an interreligious experience is that the "names and forms" lose their importance and one necessarily becomes more attentive to the reality indicated by them. This is an exercise in sensitive awareness. This deep attentiveness leads sooner or later to a complete transcending of the names and forms, and a piercing through to what lies behind them. Is not this transcendence the very purpose of any religious expression or doctrine?

If somebody asks (or I ask myself): how can you believe in Christ and Shiva at the same time? my answer will be a further question: who is Christ? who is Shiva? and, who am I? Shiva is not a name or any mythological personality, he is the "gracious one," the great Lord *(Parameshvara)*, the ultimate Reality *(anuttara)*, the most intimate I-consciousness of every conscious being. Christ is not merely the historical personality, otherwise I would not have cared to follow him. He is "the Way, the Life and the Truth" — but not in an exclusive sense; on the contrary. Even beyond that he is essentially the "I am": "Then you will know that 'I am.' " How can one limit the "I am" to only one person? Here I learn from Kashmir Shaivism or Ramana Maharshi that the ultimate "I" of every conscious being is the divine "I." The ultimate realization is not of some "objective" truth: "This is He," but the personal discovery: "I am He." In this way every spiritual practice in the interreligious context leads to a kind of purification from mere conceptions.

The theological implications of such an experience, which is certainly not without suffering and conflict, will have to be worked out. Though such a double experience cannot be imitated or generalized, it is also far from being individualistic. Any authentic inner experience is lived in solidarity — with the church, with humanity or whatever one may call it. If it is not somehow universal or all-embracing, it cannot be called an authentic spiritual experience. Are we Christians not too much concerned with labels instead of contents? A spiritual dialogue should precisely go beyond labels — only to discover that perhaps the unknown pilgrim on the dusty and hot Indian road in whose presence we feel "our hearts burning," is in reality He, the Risen One.

In the present spiritual situation, East and West, I could perhaps define my situation by describing possible and actual positive and negative attitudes. The present meeting of spiritualities can be the greatest source of enlightenment as well as the most dangerous source of confusion and distortion. Starting with the negative:

1. I do not feel comfortable with most of the imitations of Eastern religious practices in the West. They lack the background on which those practices make sense and when superimposed on a Western psyche they can create the greatest confusion. I am not only referring to the neo-Hindu "sects" and guru-cults, but even to the grafting of such authentic traditions as Tibetan Buddhism for example on Western soil. What is required here is: (a) knowledge of the background, and (b) a kind of integration with the Western and Christian tradition. The churches are doing very little to help people in understanding and integrating such experiences.

2. I am ill at ease with fundamentalist Christians who are scared of any kind of contamination. They are not only living in an ivory tower, but are also creating a terribly distorted image of Christ and Christianity which makes a spiritual dialogue with other faiths difficult if not impossible.

3. I am also not at ease with the so-called "inculturation" of the church in India (I cannot speak about other countries), because most of the time it is only a superficial adaptation of elements of Indian traditions, just to show that "we are also Indian." No real spiritual transformation accompanies the external adaptations. Hindus are probably right in their criticism that this kind of "adaptation" is only another manifestation of the same old missionary mentality.

"Inculturation" is only authentic if it springs from a real inner need and if it is accompanied by a sincere spiritual dialogue within and without. No Hindu or Buddhist will object to an authentic spirituality, but they are very sensitive to imitations and make-believe.

4. What I find equally unsatisfactory is a syncretism which is practiced mostly in Western countries where people jump from yoga to shamanism, from the Jesus prayer to Hare Krishna, from Tantric practices to Zen Buddhism, etc. It has become a kind of spiritual supermarket where one can pick and choose (and pay for it, too!), but nothing goes really deep or is carried forward in all seriousness.

Examples of possible positive attitudes are:

1. One may be a practicing Christian and receive inspiration in all

openness from other spiritual traditions, through books, meetings, exposure, etc.

2. One may sincerely and fully accept another spiritual tradition, without giving up one's own roots. This vocation may be rare, and it is not easy, but it can be pioneering also for others.

3. A Christian may reach a point in his or her experience where the externals of religion are transcended, and thus touch also upon the experience of other traditions. This has been called "transcending religions" in a mystical experience, where the labels do not matter any longer.

These three positive attitudes are in reality not so clearly distinguishable, because one may lead to another, yet I consider them as authentic ways of relating to other spiritualities.

Christians and the Practice of Zen

Yamada Koun Roshi

An address delivered to a group of Christians at San-un Zendo, Kamakura, Japan, on May 9, 1975, by an authentic Zen Master who has led many Christians in Zen practice. Source: *Dialogue*, September-December 1976.

I am often asked by Christians whether they can practice Zazen, and still preserve the beliefs of Christianity. To that question I usually answer that Zen is not a religion, in the same sense that Christianity is a religion. Therefore, there is no reason why Christianity and Zazen cannot coexist.

Almost all Buddhist sects can be called religions. Zazen however, is quite different in this respect. Quite simply, it is the *core* of all Buddhist sects. As you know, there are many sects in Buddhism, but the core or essence of them all is the experience called Satori or Self-Realization. The theories and philosophies of all the sects are but the clothing covering the core. These outer wrappings are of various shapes and colors, but what is inside remains the same. And the core, this experience, is not adorned with any thought or philosophy. It tastes the same to Buddhists as it does to Christians. There is no difference at all.

You may ask what makes this experience happen. Well, quite simply, it is when certain conditions are present to the consciousness of a human being, and a reaction of this experience is always the same, regardless of the beliefs we may hold, or the color of our skin. It could be compared to playing billiards. When we hit the balls with the same amount of power,

441

and in the same direction, all the balls roll along the same course and at the same angles, regardless of their color.

Now you may ask, what are the conditions that bring our consciousness to the experience. It is to concentrate with our mind in one-pointedness, and to forget ourselves in it. The one-pointedness is achieved sometimes in breath-counting, sometimes in what we call "following the breath," sometimes just sitting, and sometimes working on so-called koans. You will notice that all these ways point inwardly. It is a very interesting fact, but when we concentrate on an object outside ourselves, for example as in archery where we aim at a target, no matter how strong the concentration may be, we cannot attain the Zen experience. So, in Zen practice, when we want to attain Satori, we have to be absorbed inwardly.

Here you must remember that the experience attained by Zazen practice is not a thought or a philosophy or a religion, but merely a fact, a happening. And strange as it may seem, the experience of that fact has the power to free us from the agonies of the pains of the world. It emancipates us from the anxiety of all worldly sufferings. No one knows why that experience has such wonderful power, but it does. This is the most important point, and it's the most difficult to try to explain.

In the Zen experience, a certain unity happens, subject and object become one, and we come to realize our own Self-Nature. This Self-Nature cannot be seen, it cannot be touched, it cannot be heard. Because of these characteristics, we refer to it as "empty" (in Japanese *ku*), but its activities are infinite. So, we say the Zen experience is the realization of the Empty-Infinite of our Self-Nature or our Essential Nature, as it is often called.

When this happens, the fact is accompanied by a great peace of mind. At that moment, we feel as though the heavy burdens we have been carrying in our head or on our shoulders, indeed all over our body and soul, suddenly disappear as if thrown away. The joy and happiness at that time is beyond all words. And there are no philosophies or theologies attached to it.

Should such a fact be called a religion? I don't think so. It is called Satori, or Self-Realization, or Enlightenment. Catholics are attaining the Satori experience here in this Zendo. I feel that in the future they should do research into the meaning or the origin of the fact of Satori from the Christian's point of view. This should be the work of Catholics and not mine.

Having discovered this new world, the Zen student must learn that it is essentially one with the phenomenal world we all know so well. In my

442

teaching I often use a fraction as an illustration to show that all things have two aspects, but are essentially one. In the fraction, the numerator is anything in the phenomenal world, a dog or cat, a finger or a flower, or Mary or Jiro, etc. The denominator is the world of the Empty-Infinite which we call the Essential World. Since the horizontal 8 expresses infinity in mathematics, I use it encircled by a zero as the denominator. The fraction is a way of expressing two aspects as one.

Regarding the relation between Christianity and Zen, I think it can be thought of as two highways, going in separate paths, but crossing at an interchange. The two roads may seem quite apart, but where they cross is common ground. Now, if we take Zen as a religion, Christianity and Zen do seem to be quite different. But their teachings have as their interchange, a common area which belongs to both. That is the area of religious experience. I'm sure that a lot of words and phrases in the Bible can never be uttered outside a true religious experience. That, it seems to me, is not irrelevant to the Satori experience in Zen.

Now it is of utmost importance for beginners in Zen to comprehend its aims clearly. What are we going to attain by doing Zazen? There are three categories: (1) Developing concentration of the mind; (2) Satori-awakening, Enlightenment; and (3) Personalization of Satori.

The first, to develop concentration, is of utmost importance in establishing and maintaining a successful life in this world. The ability to concentrate calms the surface of our consciousness. This is most necessary in making correct decisions, and for receiving external impressions and information the right way. Also, when the mind is deeply absorbed, it does not easily yield to the influences of external circumstances. And moreover, when we want to actualize ideas which arise in our heart, or when we want to accomplish some work or business, a strong concentration of mind is indispensable.

The second, Satori, is the most important to a Mahayana Zen Buddhist. Dogen Zenji, the great Zen Master who brought Soto Zen to Japan, has clearly stated that without enlightenment there is not Zen. This Satori does not happen necessarily by mere concentration. This is especially true if the mind is brought to one-pointedness in the objective world. And even if this is achieved inwardly, our life problem, the problem of life-and-death, cannot be solved fundamentally by concentration. It can only be resolved by enlightenment and the personalization of that experience. So, if we want to free ourselves from the anxiety of the sufferings of life through Zazen, the Satori experience should be our main purpose for practicing Zazen.

Dogen Zenji has told us that we should pray for the help of Buddhas and Patriarchs. This resembles Christianity's prayers of intercession.

The third aim of Zazen, the personalization or embodiment of Satori, comes as a matter of course, only after having attained Satori. To attain this experience of Enlightenment is not very difficult. For some people, only one session is necessary. But to accomplish our ultimate personality is very difficult indeed, and requires an extremely long period of time. The experience itself is only the entrance. The completion is to personalize what we came to realize in the experience. After washing away all the ecstasy and glitter in the experience the truly great Zen person is not distinguishable in outward appearance. This is one who has experienced deep enlightenment and consequently extinguished all illusions, but is still not different externally from an ordinary human being. Through Satori and Zazen, you should not become a strange person, not an eccentric or an esoteric person. You should become a normal person, a real person, and as far as it is possible, a perfect human being. I think the truly great Christian is not much different.

Taking Heart: Spiritual Exercises for Social Activists

Joanna Macy

A Buddhist active in socio-ecological concerns, Macy presents the elements of a spirituality of contemplation in actions that Christians can resonate with and from which they can learn. Source: *Fellowship*, July/August 1982.

To heal our society, our psyches must heal as well. The military, social, and environmental dangers that threaten us do not come from sources outside the human heart; they are reflections of it, mirroring the fears, greeds, and hostilities that separate us from ourselves and each other. For our sanity and our survival, therefore, it appears necessary to engage in spiritual as well as social change, to merge the inner with the outer paths. But how, in practical terms, do we go about this?

Haunted by the desperate needs of our time and beset, as many of us are, by more commitments than we can easily carry, we can wonder where to find the time and energy for spiritual disciplines. Few of us feel free to take to the cloister or the zafu to seek personal transformation.

Fortunately, we do not need to withdraw from the world, or spend long hours in solitary prayer or meditation, to begin to wake up to the spiritual power within us. The activities and encounters of our daily lives can serve as the occasion for that kind of discovery. I would like to share some simple exercises that can permit that to happen.

I often share these mental practices in the course of my workshops. Participants who have found them healing, energizing, and easy to use in their daily activities have urged me to make them more widely available. I have been reluctant to put them in writing; they are best shared orally, in personal interaction. This is especially true of these forms of what I call "social mysticism," where the actual physical presence of fellow human beings is used to help us break through to deeper levels of spiritual awareness.

The four exercises offered here — on death, compassion, mutual power, and mutual recognition — happen to be adapted from the Buddhist tradition. As part of our planetary heritage, they belong to us all. No belief system is necessary, only a readiness to attend to the immediacy of one's own experiencing. They will be most useful if read slowly with a quiet mind (a few deep breaths help), and if put directly into practice in the presence of others.

Meditation on Death

Most spiritual paths begin with the recognition of the transiency of human life. Medieval Christians honored this in the mystery play of *Everyman*. Don Juan, the yaqui sorcerer, taught that the enlightened warrior walks with death at his shoulder. To confront and accept the inevitability of our dying releases us from attachments and frees us to live boldly — alert and appreciative.

An initial meditation on the Buddhist path involves reflection on the two-fold fact that "death is certain" and "the time of death, uncertain." In our world today, the thermonuclear bomb, serving in a sense as a spiritual teacher, does that meditation for us, for we all know now that we can die together at any moment, without warning. When we deliberately let the reality of that possibility surface in our consciousness, it can be painful, of course, but it also helps us rediscover some fundamental truths about life. It jolts us awake to life's vividness, its miraculous quality as something given unearned, heightening our awareness of its beauty and the uniqueness of each object, each being.

> As an occasional practice in daily life: Look at the person you en-counter (stranger or friend). Let the realization arise in you that this person may die in a nuclear war. Keep breathing. Observe that face, unique, vulnerable . . . those eyes still can see; they are not empty sockets

. . . the skin is still intact. . . . Become aware of your desire, as it arises, that this person be spared such suffering and horror, feel the strength of that desire . . . keep breathing. . . . Let the possibility arise in your consciousness that this may be the person you happen to be with when you die . . . that face the last you see . . . that hand the last you touch . . . it might reach out to help you then, to comfort, to give water. Open to the feelings for this person that surface in you with the awareness of this possibility. Open to the levels of caring and connection it reveals in you.

Breathing Through

Our time assails us with painful information about threats to our future and the present suffering of our fellow beings. We hear and read of famine, torture, poisonous waters, the arms race, animals and plants dying off. Out of self-protection, we all put up some degree of resistance to this information; there is fear that it might overwhelm us if we let it in, that we might shatter under its impact or be mired in despair. Many of us block our awareness of the pain of our world because our culture has conditioned us to expect instant solutions: "I don't think about nuclear war (or acid rain) because there is nothing I can do about it." With the value our society places on optimism, our contemplations of such fearful problems can cause us to feel isolated, and even a bit crazy. So we tend to close them out — and thereby go numb.

Clearly, the distressing data must be dealt with if we are to respond and survive. But how can we do this without falling apart? In my own struggle with despair, it seemed at first that I had to either block out the terrible information or be shattered by it. I wondered if there wasn't a third alternative to going numb or going crazy. The practice of "breathing through" helped me find it.

Basic to most spiritual traditions, as well as to the systems view of the world, is the recognition that we are not separate, isolated entities, but integral and organic parts of the vast web of life. As such, we are like neurons in a neural net, through which flow currents of awareness of what is happening to us, as a species and as a planet. In that context, the pain we feel for our world is a living testimony to our interconnectedness with it. If we deny this pain, we become like blocked and atrophied neurons, deprived of life's flow and weakening the larger body in which we take being. But if we let it move through us, we affirm our belonging; our collective awareness increases. We can open to the pain of the world in confidence that it can neither shatter nor isolate us, for we are not objects that can break. We are resilient patterns within a vaster web of knowing.

Because we have been conditioned to view ourselves as separate, competitive, and therefore fragile entities, it takes practice to relearn this kind of resilience. A good way to begin is by practicing simple openness, as in the exercise of "breathing through," adapted from an ancient Buddhist meditation for the development of compassion.

> Relax. Center on your breathing . . . visualize your breath as a stream flowing up through your nose, down through windpipe, lungs. Take it down through your lungs and, picturing a hole in the bottom of your heart, visualize the breath-stream passing through your heart and out through that hole to reconnect with the larger web of life around you. Let the breath-stream, as it passes through you, appear as one loop within that vast web, connecting you with it . . . keep breathing. . . .
>
> Now open your awareness to the suffering that is present in the world. Drop for now all defenses and open to your knowledge of that suffering. Let it come as concretely as you can . . . concrete images of your fellow beings in pain and need, in fear and isolation, in prisons, hospitals, tenements, hunger camps . . . no need to strain for these images, they are present to you by virtue of our interexistence. Relax and just let them surface, breathe them in . . . the vast and countless hardships of our fellow humans, and of our animal brothers and sisters as well, as they swim the seas and fly the air of this ailing planet. Breathe in that pain like a dark stream, up through your nose, down through your trachea, lungs and heart, and out again into the world net . . . you are asked to do nothing for now, but let it pass through your heart . . . keep breathing . . . be sure that stream flows through and out again; don't hang on to the pain . . . surrender it for now to the healing resources of life's vast web. . . .
>
> With Shantideva, the Buddhist saint, we can say, "Let all sorrows ripen in me." We help them ripen by passing them through our hearts . . . making good, rich compost out of all that grief . . . so we can learn from it, enhancing our larger, collective knowing. . . .
>
> If you experience an ache in the chest, a pressure within the rib cage, that is all right. The heart that breaks open can contain the whole universe. Your heart is that large. Trust it. Keep breathing.

This guided meditation serves to introduce the process of breathing through, which, once experienced, becomes useful in daily life in the many situations that confront us with painful information. By breathing through the bad news, rather than bracing ourselves against it, we can let it strengthen our sense of belonging in the larger web of being. It helps us remain alert and open, whether reading the newspaper, receiving criticism, or simply being present for a person who is suffering.

For activists working for peace and justice, and those dealing most directly with the griefs of our time, the practice helps prevent burnout. Reminding us of the collective nature of both our problems and our power, it offers a healing measure of humility. It can also save us from self-righteousness. For when we can take in our world's pain, accepting it as the price of our caring, we can let it inform our acts without needing to inflict it as a punishment on others who are, at the moment, less involved.

The Great Ball of Merit

Compassion, which is grief in the grief of others, is but one side of the coin. The other side is joy in the joy of others — which in Buddhism is called *muditha*. To the extent that we allow ourselves to identify with the sufferings of other beings, we can identify with their strengths as well. This is very important for our own sense of adequacy and resilience, because we face a time of great challenge that demands of us more commitment, endurance and courage than we can ever dredge up out of our individual supply. We can learn to draw on the other neurons in the net, and to view them, in a grateful and celebrative fashion, as so much "money in the bank."

The concept here resembles the Christian notion of grace. Recognizing our own limitations, we cease to rely solely on individual strength and open up to the power that is beyond us and can flow through us. The Buddhist "Ball of Merit" is useful in helping us see that this power or grace is not dependent upon belief in God, but operates as well through our fellow beings. In so doing, it lets us connect with each other more fully and appreciatively than we usually do. It is most helpful to those of us who have been socialized in a competitive society, based on a win-lose notion of power. "The more you have, the less I have." Conditioned by that patriarchal paradigm of power, we can fall prey to the stupidity of viewing the strengths or good fortune of others as a sign of our own inadequacy or deprivation. The Great Ball of Merit is a healthy corrective to envy. It brings us home, with a vast sense of ease, to our capacity for mutual enjoyment.

449

The practice takes two forms. The one closer to the ancient Buddhist meditation is this:

> Relax and close your eyes, relax into your breathing. Open your awareness to the fellow beings who share with you this planet-time . . . in this room . . . this neighborhood . . . this town . . . open to all those in this country . . . and in other lands . . . let your awareness encompass all beings living now in your world. Opening now to all time as well, let your awareness encompass all beings who ever lived . . . of all races and creeds and walks of life, rich, poor, kings and beggars, saints and sinners . . . like successive mountain ranges, the vast vistas of these fellow beings present themselves to your mind's eye. . . . Now open yourself to the knowledge that in each of these innumerable lives some act of merit was performed. No matter how stunted or deprived the life, there was a gesture of generosity, a gift of love, an act of valor or self-sacrifice . . . on the battlefield or workplace, hospital or home . . . from each of these beings in their endless multitudes arose actions of courage, kindness, of teaching and healing. Let yourself see these manifold and immeasurable acts of merit . . . as they arise in the vistas of your inner eye, sweep them together . . . sweep them into a pile in front of you . . . use your hands . . . pile them into a heap . . . pat them into a ball. It is the Great Ball of Merit . . . hold it and weigh it in your hands . . . rejoice in it, knowing that no act of goodness is ever lost. It remains ever and always a present resource . . . a resource for the transformation of life . . . and now, with jubilation and gratitude, you turn that great ball . . . turn it over . . . over . . . into the healing of our world.

As we can learn from modern science and picture in the holographic model of reality, our lives interpenetrate. In the fluid tapestry of space-time, there is at root no distinction between self and other. The acts and intentions of others are like seeds that can germinate and bear fruit through our own lives, as we take them into awareness and dedicate, or "turn over," that awareness to our empowerment. Thoreau, Gandhi, Martin Luther King, Dorothy Day, and the nameless heroes and heroines of our own day, all can be part of our Ball of Merit, on which we can draw for inspiration and endurance. Other traditions feature notions similar to this, such as the "cloud of witnesses" of which St. Paul spoke, or the Treasury of Merit in the Catholic Church.

The second, more workaday, version of the Ball of Merit meditation helps us open to the powers of others. It is in direct contrast to the commonly accepted, patriarchal notion of power as something personally owned and exerted over others. The exercise prepares us to bring expectant attentions to our encounters with other beings, to view them with fresh openness and curiosity as to how they can enhance our Ball of Merit. We can play this inner game with someone opposite us on the bus or across the bargaining table. It is especially useful when dealing with a person with whom we may be in conflict.

> What does this person add to my Great Ball of Merit? What gifts of intellect can enrich our common store? What reserves of stubborn endurance can she or he offer? What flights of fancy or powers of love lurk behind those eyes? What kindness or courage hides in those lips, what healing in those hands?
>
> Then, as with the breathing-through exercise, we open ourselves to the presence of these strengths, inhaling our awareness of them. As our awareness grows, we experience our gratitude for them and our capacity to enhance and partake. . . .

Often we let our perceptions of the powers of others make us feel inadequate. Alongside an eloquent colleague, we can feel inarticulate; in the presence of an athlete we can feel weak and clumsy. In the process, we can come to resent both ourselves and the other person. In the light of the Great Ball of Merit, however, the gifts and good fortunes of others appear not as judgments, put-downs or competing challenges, but as resources we can honor and take pleasure in. We can learn to play detective, spying out treasures for the enhancement of life from even the unlikeliest material. Like air and sun and water, they form part of our common good.

In addition to releasing us from the mental cramp of envy, this spiritual practice — or game — offers two other rewards. One is pleasure in our own acuity, as our merit-detecting ability improves. The second is the response of others, who — while totally ignorant of the game we are playing — sense something in our manner that invites them to move more openly into the person they can be.

Learning to See Each Other

This exercise is derived from the Buddhist practice of the *Brahmaviharas;* it is known as the Four Abodes of the Buddha, which are lovingkindness, compassion, joy in the joy of others, and equanimity. Adapted for use in a social context, it helps us to see each other more truly and experience the depths of our interconnections.

In workshops, I offer this as a guided meditation, with participants sitting in pairs, facing each other. At its close, I encourage them to proceed to use it, or any portion they like, as they go about the business of their daily lives. It is an excellent antidote to boredom, when our eye falls on another person, say on the subway. It charges that idle movement with beauty and discovery. It also is useful when dealing with people whom we are tempted to dislike or disregard; it breaks open our accustomed ways of viewing them. When used like this, as a meditation-in-action, one does not, of course, gaze long and deeply into the other's eyes, as in the guided exercise. A seemingly casual glance is enough. The guided, group form goes like this:

> Sit in pairs. Face each other. Stay silent. Take a couple of deep breaths, centering yourself and exhaling tension. Look into each other's eyes. If you feel discomfort or an urge to laugh or look away, just note that embarrassment with patience and gentleness toward yourself and come back, when you can, to your partner's eyes. You may never see this person again: the opportunity to behold the uniqueness of this particular human being is given to you now.
>
> As you look into this being's eyes, let yourself become aware of the powers that are there . . . open yourself to awareness of the gifts and strengths and the potentialities in this being. . . . Behind those eyes are unmeasured reserves of ingenuity and endurance, wit and wisdom. There are gifts there, of which this person her/himself is unaware. Consider what these untapped powers can do for the healing of our planet and the relishing of our common life. . . . As you consider that, let yourself become aware of your desire that this person be free from fear. Let yourself experience how much you want this being to be free from anger . . . and free from greed . . . and free from sorrow . . . and the causes of suffering. Know that what you are now experiencing is the great loving-kindness. It is good for building a world.
>
> Now, as you look into those eyes, let yourself become aware of the pain that is there. There are sorrows accumulated in that life's journey. . . . There are failures and losses, griefs and disappointments beyond the telling. Let yourself open to them, open to that pain . . . to hurts that this person may never have shared with another being. What you are now experiencing is the great compassion. It is good for the healing of our world.

As you look into those eyes, open to the thought of how good it would be to make common cause . . . consider how ready you might be to work together . . . to take risks in a joint venture . . . imagine the zest of that, the excitement and laughter of engaging together on a common project . . . acting boldly and trusting each other. As you open to that possibility, what you open to is the great wealth: the pleasure in each other's powers, the joy in each other's joy.

Lastly, let your awareness drop deep, deep within you like a stone, sinking below the level of what words or acts can express . . . breathe deeply and quietly . . . open your consciousness to the deep web of relationship that underlies and interweaves all experience, all knowing. It is the web of life in which you have taken being and in which you are supported. Out of that vast web you cannot fall . . . no stupidity or failure, no personal inadequacy, can ever sever you from that living web. For that is what you are . . . and what has brought you into being . . . feel the assurance of that knowledge. Feel the great peace . . . rest in it. Out of that great peace, we can venture everything. We can trust. We can act.

In doing this exercise we realize that we do not have to be particularly noble or saintlike in order to wake up to the power of our oneness with other beings. In our time, that simple awakening is the gift the Bomb holds for us.

For all its horror and stupidity, the Bomb is also the manifestation of an awesome spiritual truth — the truth about the hell we create for ourselves when we cease to learn how to love. Saints, mystics, and prophets throughout the ages saw that law; now all can see it and none can escape its consequences. So we are caught now in a narrow place where we realize that Moses, Lao-Tzu, the Buddha, Jesus, and our own inner hearts were right all along; and we are as scared and frantic as cornered rats, and as dangerous. But the Bomb, if we let it, can turn that narrow *cul-de-sac* into a birth canal, pressing and pushing us through the dark pain of it, until we are delivered into . . . what? Love seems too weak a word. It is, as St. Paul said, "the glory that shall be revealed in us." It stirs in us now.

For us to regard the Bomb (or the dying seas, the poisoned air) as a monstrous injustice to us would suggest that we never took seriously the injunction to love. Perhaps we thought all along that Gautama and Jesus were kidding, or their teachings meant only for saints. But now we see, as an awful revelation, that we are all called to be saints — not good, necessarily, or pious or devout — but saints in the sense of just loving each other. One wonders what terrors this knowledge must hold that we fight it so, and flee from it in such pain. Can it be that the Bomb, by which we can extinguish all life, can tell us this? Can force us to face the terrors of love? Can be the occasion for our births?

It is in that possibility that we can take heart. Even in confusion and fear, with all our fatigues and petty faults, we can let that awareness work in and through our lives. Such simple exercises as those offered here can help us do that, and to begin to see ourselves and each other with fresh eyes.

Let me close with the same suggestion that closes our workshops. It is a practice that is corollary to the earlier death meditation, where we recognize that the person we meet may die in a nuclear war. Look at the next person you see. It may be a lover, child, co-worker, postman, or your own face in the mirror. Regard him or her with the recognition that:

> This person before me may be instrumental in saving us from nuclear war. In this person are gifts for the healing of our planet. In him/her are powers that can resound to the joy of all beings.

Toward the Meeting of Mystical Paths

Ewert Cousins

Ewert Cousins is editor of a twenty-four volume series entitled *World Spirituality: An Encyclopaedic History of the Religious Quest*. This article outlines a vision of the fruits of the encounter between the religious traditions in our age and the tasks they must undertake toward what can be called a global consciousness for a transformed humanity. Source: *Global Spirituality: Toward the Meeting of Mystical Paths* (Madras: Radhakrishnan Institute for Advanced Study in Philosophy, 1985).

... Situating ourselves within the Western calendar, we can ask the question: What is the religious phenomenon on the eve of the twenty-first century? To answer this question, we must extend our view not only of time but also of space. On the eve of the twenty-first century, the religious phenomenon can no longer be viewed within one religious tradition, within one geographical region, even within one continent, or one hemisphere. It must be viewed globally, for the religious phenomenon of our time is a global phenomenon. The religions of the world can no longer live in isolation, nor can they rightly live in tension or hostility. The organic interaction of the human race is becoming so extensive that the religions of the world must seek new ways of mutual understanding and interrelation.

An Astronaut's Perspective

To observe the religious phenomenon, then, on the eve of the twenty-first century, we need a new perspective — one which would not have been necessary or even possible on the eve of the twentieth century or of any previous centuries in human history. We need a perspective analogous to that of the astronauts who traveled into outer space and looked back upon the earth. From outer space they could see the earth as whole. It is true that they observed the earth's clouds, oceans, and continents, but these appeared not as separate units, as would be the case if viewed within limited horizons on the earth's surface. Rather they were part of an interrelated whole. To the astronauts the earth appeared as a single unit of remarkable beauty — a blue and white globe, shining against the black background of the universe. For the first time in history, human beings had a sense impression of the earth as a whole. For centuries scientists had known the spherical shape of the earth and its place in the universe through mathematical speculation, but no one had actually seen the earth as a single unit. Now through the photos taken from outer space, all the people of the world can share this sense impression. I would like to propose that this new sense image of the earth as a whole can become the concrete symbol for the entire human race of the global consciousness that is emerging on the eve of the twenty-first century.

From our astronaut's position, what do we observe? As we look at the earth as a whole, we can perceive two phenomena that are deeply affecting religions on the eve of the twenty-first century: the meeting of world religions and the secularization of culture. As a result of the industrial revolution, the development of technology and travel, a communication network has encircled the earth. The religions of the world can no longer remain in isolation. Inevitably they are meeting each other through contact of individual followers, through the spread of books and academic studies, through interreligious conferences, and through official dialogue of the leaders of various traditions. Fortunately this meeting is occurring in an atmosphere of mutual respect and understanding. Although religions are still embroiled in political conflict — for example, in the Middle East, in Northern Ireland, and in Iran — there is emerging an ecumenical atmosphere for the peaceful encounter of the world's religions. In this atmosphere, the old attitudes of isolation, hostility, domination, and colonialism are breaking down and being replaced by respect and spiritual sharing. In fact, there is reason to claim that the meeting of spiritual paths is itself becoming a spiritual journey for the human race, in which the encounter of spiritual paths is the catalyst that will transform religious consciousness to become truly global. . . .

. . . But another facet of our situation calls our attention: the thrust of human civilization, through industrialization and technology, has threatened the survival not only of the religions but of the human race itself. In its negative form, it has led to the pollution of the environment, the exhaustion of natural resources, and ultimately to the threat of nuclear holocaust. All of these problems have become global problems, threatening the human race as a whole. What should be the response of the religions to these problems? In cultivating the spiritual, the religions have been accused of neglecting the material dimension of life. Can the religions remain silent on these issues now? Can they make a creative contribution to the solution of these problems from their spiritual resources? It may well be that this last question is the ultimate challenge to religions on the eve of the twenty-first century.

From our astronaut's perspective, we can penetrate more deeply into these phenomena, perceiving them as dimensions of a larger transformation of consciousness that is taking place in this present period of history. I will examine these phenomena and the underlying transformation of consciousness, from the standpoint of Karl Jaspers' theory of the Axial Period, and then I will explore their implications for religions and philosophy, specifically for the cross-cultural, interreligious study of mysticism. . . .

The Axial Period

. . . Some thirty years ago in his book, *The Origin and Goal of History,* Karl Jaspers gathered together a number of facts into a comprehensive theory of the transformation of consciousness in the first millennium B.C. He pointed out that in three geographical areas a remarkable alteration in consciousness occurred which produced the form of consciousness that has dominated in the world to the present. Jaspers discovered an axis at the "point in history which gave birth to everything which, since then, man has been able to be." He observes that "this axis of history is to be found in the period around 500 B.C., in the spiritual process that occurred between 800 and 200 B.C. It is there that we meet with the most deepcut dividing line in history. Man, as we know him today, came into being. For short we may style this the 'Axial Period.'"

During this period spiritual teachers emerged heralding this transformation of consciousness. This occurred in three separated geographical regions without indiscernible influence of one on the other: in China, in central Asia, and in the eastern Mediterranean. In China Lao-Tze and Confucius appeared, from whose teaching emerged the schools of Chinese philosophy. In India the Upanishads were transforming the ancient cosmic, ritualistic Hinduism of the Vedas, while the Buddha and Mahavira inaugurated two new spiritual traditions. In the same geographical area, Zoroaster taught in Iran, describing the struggle between good and evil. In the eastern Mediterranean the Jewish prophets — Elijah, Isaiah, and Jeremiah — were effecting a transformation of Judaism from an emphasis on ritual observance to individual moral consciousness. In Greece, Socrates effected a similar awakening of individual moral consciousness. Here the birth of moral awareness was part of the dawn of Western philosophy, in which the pre-Socratic cosmologists searched for a rational explanation of the universe, and Plato and Aristotle produced metaphysical systems.

In this Axial period were shaped the great religions of the world, as they have perdured to this day. Jaspers observes: "In this age were born the fundamental categories within which we still think today, and the beginnings of the world religions, by which human beings still live, were created." . . .

. . . At the root of Axial consciousness is an awareness of an individual self, which is the center of moral consciousness and is capable of an individual spiritual journey. In Greece, seekers of wisdom drew their motto from the inscription over the temple of Delphi: Know thyself. The Jewish prophets preached to the people that it was not animal sacrifice that pleased God, but a pure heart. In India the Upanishads testified to the *atman*, the deeper transcendent self. Even the reaction of the Buddha against the doctrine of the self was not a return to archaic consciousness. If we study . . . the major religions, we will see that their spirituality is based on this notion of the self. The self can come to a critical realization that its consciousness is distorted: that it is chained in a cave, that it is deceived by the illusions of the phenomenal world. It can seek liberation from the cosmic process of birth and death; it can purify itself from its entrapment in matter, embarking on an individual spiritual journey that ultimately leads to union or identification with the divine.

If we look at the spirituality of pre-Axial peoples, we will find a different form of consciousness. The archaic peoples do not have a sharply defined notion of the individual self. Rather their consciousness is embedded in the cosmos and the cycles of nature. It is closely tied to the inorganic world and the animal kingdom. Out of this harmony with nature flows a rich mythic lore and tribal rituals which situate archaic peoples in the universe and nourish their spirit. Their consciousness is also fused with the tribe so that they cannot take radical stance against the group, nor can they easily survive psychologically, or even physically, when separated from their people. Archaic consciousness is capable of a rich spirituality, but it is different from that of Axial consciousness. In fact, the archaic spirituality survives in varying degrees as a substratum of Axial consciousness. . . .

. . . Although Axial consciousness brought many blessings, it created problems as well. By heightening self-awareness, it severed the connection with nature, alienating the human person from the cosmos and the community. The exercise of his analytic and critical powers turned his attention away from the wisdom available through the mythic imagination and the practice of ritual. The Axial transformation of consciousness, it is true, released enormous spiritual energy, opening a spiritual journey into the depths of the self and up the ladder of the hierarchical universe to the transcendent. It made possible direct union or identification with the divine, making available a whole range of mystical experiences, forms of meditation and contemplation, and spiritual disciplines. But this release of spiritual energy tended to draw the Axial person into the spiritual realm and away from the earth, from the life cycles, and the harmony with nature which formed the essence of archaic spirituality. As a result Axial humans lost the spirituality inherent in the earth itself. Although the extent of this split varies significantly within the traditions, the spirituality of the Axial Period tends to otherworldliness in a movement away from the earth and into heaven.

The Second Axial Period

Let us return now to our astronaut's position in outer space, and look at the earth on the eve of the twenty-first century. From this vantage point I believe that we can discern a transformation of consciousness as significant and far-reaching as that of the Axial Period. In view of this, we can call the eve of the twenty-first century the Second Axial Period. Unlike the transformation of the First Axial Period, this is a transition from individual to global consciousness. . . .

. . . The world religions are the product of the First Axial Period and the forces of divergence. Although in the first millennium B.C. there was a common transformation of consciousness, it occurred in diverse geographical regions within already differentiated cultures. In each case the religion was shaped by this differentiation in its origin and developed along differentiated lines. This produced a remarkable richness of spiritual wisdom, of spiritual energies, and of religious cultural forms to express, preserve, and transmit this heritage. Now that the forces of divergence have shifted to convergence, the religions must meet each other in center to center unions, discovering what is most authentic in each other, releasing creative energy toward a more complexified form of religious consciousness.

Such a creative encounter has been called by Raimundo Panikkar the "dialogic dialogue" to distinguish it from the dialectic dialogue in which one tries to refute the claims of the other. This dialogic dialogue has three phases: One, the partners meet each other in an atmosphere of mutual understanding, ready to alter misconceptions about each other and eager to appreciate the values of the other. Two, the partners are mutually enriched, by passing over into the consciousness of the other so that each can experience the other's value from within the other's perspective. This can be enormously enriching, for often one discovers in another tradition values which are submerged or only inchoate in his own. It is important at this point to respect the autonomy of the other tradition: in Teilhard de Chardin's terms, to achieve union in which differences are valued as a basis of creativity. Three, if such a creative union is achieved, then the religions will have moved into the complexified form of consciousness that will be characteristic of the twenty-first century. This will be a complexified global consciousness, not a mere universal, undifferentiated, abstract consciousness. It will be global through the global convergence of cultures and religions and complexified by the dynamics of dialogic dialogue.

This global consciousness, complexified through the meeting of cultures and religions, is only one characteristic of the Second Axial Period. The consciousness of this period is global in another sense: namely, in rediscovering its roots in the earth. At the very moment when the various cultures and religions are meeting each other and creating a new global community, our life on the planet is being threatened. The very tools which we have used to bring about this convergence — industrialization and technology — are undercutting the biological support system that sustains life on our planet. The future of consciousness, of even life on the earth, is shrouded in a cloud of uncertainty by the pollution of our environment, the depletion of natural resources, the unjust distribution of wealth, the stockpiling of nuclear weapons. Unless the human community reverses these destructive forces, we may not see the twenty-first century. The human race as a whole — all the diverse cultures and the religions — must face these problems squarely. In this Second Axial Period we must rediscover the dimensions of consciousness of the pre-Axial Period. As we saw, this consciousness was collective and cosmic, rooted in the earth and the life cycles. We must rapidly appropriate that form of consciousness or perish from the earth. However, I am not suggesting a romantic attempt to live in the past, rather that the evolution of consciousness proceeds by way of recapitulation. Having developed self-reflective analytic critical consciousness in the First Axial Period, we must now, while retaining these values, reappropriate and integrate into that consciousness the collective and cosmic dimensions of the pre-Axial consciousness. We must recapture the unity of tribal consciousness by seeing humanity as a single tribe. And we must see this single tribe related organically to the whole cosmos. This means that the consciousness of the twenty-first century will be global from two perspectives: (1) from a horizontal perspective, cultures and religions are meeting each other on the surface of the globe, entering into creative encounters that will produce a complexified collective consciousness; (2) from a vertical perspective, they must plunge their roots deep into the earth and far into the universe in order to provide a stable and secure base for future development. This new global consciousness must be organically ecological, supported by structures that will insure justice and peace. In the Second Axial Period this twofold global consciousness is not only a creative possibility to enhance the twenty-first century; it is an absolute necessity if we are to survive.

Task of Religion

What does this mean for religions on the eve of the twenty-first century? It means that they have a double task: to enter creatively into the dialogue of religions and to channel their energies into solving the common human problems that threaten our future on the earth. It means that they must strip away negative and limiting attitudes towards other religions. They must avoid both a narrow fundamentalism and a blind universalism. They must be true to their spiritual heritage, for this is the source of their power and their gift to the world. They must make every effort to ground them-

461

selves in their own traditions and at the same time to open themselves to other traditions. In concert with the other religions they should commit themselves to creating the new complexified global consciousness we have been exploring.

But to meet, even creatively, on the spiritual level is not enough. They must channel their spiritual resources toward the solution of global problems. For the most part, this calls for a transformation of the religions. Having been formed in the First Axial Period, the religions bear the mark of Axial consciousness: in its turning toward the spiritual ascent away from the material. The religions must rediscover the material dimensions of existence and their spiritual significance. In this they can learn from the secular: that justice and peace are human values that must be cherished and pragmatically cultivated. But they must not adopt an exclusively secular attitude, for their unique contribution is to tap their reservoirs of spiritual energy and channel this into developing secular enterprises that are genuinely human. . . .

. . . In this Second Axial Period on the eve of the twenty-first century, is there a special task for the academic community? What can that community contribute through its study of religion and philosophy? The process of the transformation of conscious-ness of the Second Axial Period involves three stages: (1) the retrieval of tradition; (2) dialogue with other traditions in the light of this retrieval; (3) the transformation of this shared wisdom for resolving human problems in a global context. The academic community can indeed contribute in a significant way to each of these phases in exercising its functions centered on critical reflection.

TASKS FOR INTERRELIGIOUS COOPERATION

Shalom: Complementarity

Jacob Neusner

Jacob Neusner, a widely known scholar in Judaic Studies, writes of an urgent task facing religions today: to go beyond mere tolerance toward understanding of the outsider from within one's own religious framework, in a way that would enable members of the different religious traditions to relate with one another and cooperate with one another in the common tasks or peace-building. Source: *Jews and Christians: The Myth of a Common Tradition* (Philadelphia: Trinity Press International, 1991).

The conception of "shalom," as we all know, involves peace in the sense not merely of the absence of war, but the presence of a whole and complete state of complementarity. Peace is peace when both parties affirm peace, meaning, when each party affirms the other.... Peace is possible only when a whole and complementary understanding among different religions is attained. There can be no peace, nor even a truce, so long as one side within the framework of its religious convictions can make no sense of the other side within the framework of its religious convictions....

... At this very moment we confront an example of the future task of all religious intellectuals, which is to try to think through a religious theory of the other, a theory framed by each religion within its own terms but suitable for guiding the insider on how to think about the outsider. The single most important problem facing religion for the next hundred years, as for the last, is that single intellectual challenge: how to think through difference, how to account within one's own faith and framework for the outsider, indeed, for many outsiders. True, people think that the most important problem confronting religion is secularity or falling away; but it is clear from all studies, religious affiliation remains constant. Not only so, but when we look at the evidence of our own eyes, we find the vital signs of religion attested in the headlines every day: Christian civil war in Ireland, monotheist civil war in the Middle East, the breakup of the Soviet Empire by reason of religious conflict — these attest to the power of religion. They also remind us of its pathos, which is the incapacity of religions to form for themselves a useful theory of the other. That, not secularization, defines the critical task facing religions: their excess of success in persuading the believers so that believers not only love one another, they hate everybody else.

The commonplace theory of religious systems concerning the other or the outsider finds ample illustration here. What do you do with the outsider? Find the other crazy (as we did Ayatollah Khomeini and Jim Jones of Jonestown), or declare the other the work of the devil (as the Ayatollah did with us), or consign the other subject to such metaphors as unclean, impure, dangerous, to be exterminated, as the Germans — Christians, ex-Christians alike — did with the Jews. . . . It is incomprehension of the other, the inability to explain the other to oneself in one's own terms, that transforms religion from a force for peace and reconciliation into a cause of war and intolerance.

Tolerance does not suffice. A theory of the other that concedes the outsider is right for the other but not for me invokes a meretricious relativism that religious believers cannot really mean. Religions will have to learn how to think about the other, not merely to tolerate the other as an unavoidable inconvenience or an evil that cannot be eliminated. For reasons I shall explain, they face the task of thinking, within their own theological structure of the other outside of it. And that is something no religion has ever accomplished up to this time.

Religions have spent their best intellectual energies in thinking about themselves, not about the outsider. Why should this be so? The reason is that religions form accounts of a social world, the one formed by the pious; they set forth a worldview, define a way of life that realizes that worldview, and identify the social entity that constitutes the world explained by the worldview and embodied in the way of life: world without end. The this-worldly power of religion derives from its capacity to hold people together

466

and make them see themselves not as a given but a gift: special, distinctive, chosen, saved — whatever. But the very remarkable capacity of religions to define all that is important about a person, a family, a group also incapacitates religions in a world in which difference must be accommodated. For in explaining the social world within, religions also build walls against the social world without, and in consequence religions impose upon the other, the outsider, a definition and a standing that scarcely serve the social order and the public interest.

For theories of "the other" that afford at best toleration, at worst humiliation and subordination, may have served in an age of an ordered society, but they do not fit a time in which social change forms the sole constant. It is one thing to design a hierarchical society defined by religion when one religion is on top, all others subordinated, as was the case in the Islamic nation(s) from the seventh century and as was the case in Christian Europe until the rise of the nation-state. A hierarchy based upon religion — with Islam at the apex, and with Christianity and Judaism tolerated, but on the whole well-treated minorities — served so long as all parties accepted their place. So, too, Christian European society before the Reformation had its dual theory of religious difference within the social order: the Christian state headed by the pope, Christ's deputy; and the monarch, the secular Christian counterpart. In such an order, Judaism found its place as testimony, Islam was kept at bay across the Pyrenees or Mediterranean and then forced back in the Near East itself, and paganism was eliminated. But with the shaking of the foundations in the Reformation, for instance, the social order trembled. Christianity in the West became two, then many, and the hierarchical structure tottered. Then what of the other? Jews were driven to the East, to the more tolerant pioneering territories of Poland, Lithuania, White Russia, the Ukraine; Islam would then be ignored; and Christians would spend centuries killing other Christians. Some theory of the other! Some theory of the social order!

The solution of the seventeenth century was simple: the head of state defines the governing church. That served where it served. The solution of the eighteenth century was still more simple: tolerate everything, because all religions are equally ridiculous. But no religion accepted either theory of religious difference, and it was with no theory of the other that the West in the nineteenth and twentieth centuries entered its great ages of consolidation and expansion and fruition, then dissolution and civil strife. The civil war of Western then world civilization proved no age for thinking about the social order, and the pressing problem of religious accommodation of religious difference hardly gained attention. The reason is that from 1914 to nearly the present day, it was by no means clear that humanity would survive the civil war fought at such cost and for so long. With a million killed in one battle in 1915, with twenty million Soviet citizens killed in World War II after a prior ten million Soviet citizens were killed by their own government in the decade preceding the war, with six million Jews murdered in factories built to manufacture death — with humanity at war with itself, religions could hardly be expected to reconsider long-neglected and scarcely urgent questions.

Yet it is obvious that religious theories of religious difference — theories formed within the framework of a religious worldview, way of life, and social entity — about those beyond that framework, do impose upon us an urgent task now. Part of the reason is the simple fact that we have survived the twentieth century.

That adventitious fact by itself would hardly precipitate deep thought within religion on the requirements of the social order: how to get along with the outsider. But a more important fact does. It is that the two hundred year campaign against religion on the part of forces of secularization has simply failed. Faith in god, worship of God, life with God — these testimonies to the vitality of religions are measurable: people go to church or synagogue, they observe this rite and that requirement, they make their pilgrimages, and by these quite objective measures of the fact of human action the vast majority of most of the nations of the world is made up of religion believers of one kind or another. All claims that secularization is the established and one-way process and the demise of religion forms the wave of the future have defied the facts of religion power and (alas) worldly glory. Not only is religion strong in its own realm, religious affiliations and commitments define loyalties and concerns in the larger social world of politics and culture. Anyone who doubts it had better to explain without religion the intense opposition to abortion manifested by from one-third to nearly one-half (depending on the framing of the issue) of the voting population of this country — like it or not. In the formation of social groups, for instance, religion remains a critical indicator as to where we live, how we choose our friends, whom we marry.

That brings us back to the century rushing toward us, an age of parlous peace, a time in which, for the first time in human history, we have the opportunity of a period of sustained peace — but only if. . . . We can have peace on earth only if we find sources of good will for one another, for in the end, moved by hatred, we may well bring down upon ourselves the roof of the temple that is over us all. Hatred of the other, after all, forms a powerful motive to disregard love of self, and anyone who doubts that fact had better reconsider the history of Germany from July 1944 through May 1945. At that time, when everyone knew the German cause was finished, hatred of the other sufficed to sustain a suicidal war that ended with the absolute ruin of all Germany; more people died in the last nine months of World War II than in the first five years. All that kept Germany going on the path to its own complete destruction was hatred: drag them all down with us. So much for the power of hatred. There is good reason to tremble when we consider how hatred, brewed within religious theories of the other as the devil, for example, leads nations to act contrary to all rational interest. . . .

So there really is a considerable and urgent task before religions today, the task of addressing a question long thought settled by the various religious systems that now flourish. It is the question of the other. And the question is to be framed in terms that only religions can confront, that is, the *theological* theory of the other. The theological question of the other has been framed in these terms: how, as a believing person, can I make sense of the outsider with not mere tolerance of difference but esteem for a faith not my own?

To expand the question, How can I form a theory of the other in such a way that within my own belief I can respect the other and accord to the outsider legitimacy within the structure of my own faith?

I say very simply that no Western religious tradition has ever answered those questions. None has tried. The hierarchical theory of religions has served, by which Islam at the apex made room for Christianity and Judaism and eliminated everything else; or Christianity at the apex (always in theory, sometimes in practice) found a cave, a cleft in the rock, for Judaism, kept Islam out of sight, and eliminated everything else. Judaism for its part expressed its hierarchical counterpart by assigning to undifferentiated humanity (Islam and Christianity never singled out for special handling) a set of requirements for a minimal definition of a humane and just social order, with holy Israel, God's first love, responsible for everything else. Of you God wants civility; of us, holiness — a hierarchy with one peak and a vast flat plain, no mountain of ascent in between.

When we take note of how religions in the past and present have thought about the other, we may perceive the full weight of the task that is now incumbent upon us. Looking backward, all our models tell us what not to do, but we have scarcely a single model to emulate. A Christian theology of the other in terms of the other for faithful Christians; a Judaic theology of the other in terms of the other for believing Jews — these have no precedent in either Christian or Judaic theology. That effort at treating as legitimate and authentic a religion other than our own and treating religious people different from ourselves as worthy of respect because of their religion, we have never seen on this earth before, though in the past quarter century the beginnings of the work have been attempted — so far as I know solely by Roman Catholic and mainstream Protestant theologians.

I assign to the future the task of thinking about a religious theory of the other, because I can find in the past no suitable examples of how that thought might unfold or what rules of intellect may govern. In the case of Judaism, for example, Judaism thought about Christianity when, in the fourth century, it was forced to do so. In the case of one Christianity, the British one, Christianity thought about Buddhism when, in the nineteenth century, it found it required a theory to make sense of chaotic facts. In both cases, we see religions thinking about the other solely in terms of themselves.

The case of Judaism tells us when and why a religion must frame a theory of the other. It is when political change of a fundamental character transfigures the social world that a religious system addresses, thus imposing an urgent question that must be addressed. In the case of Judaism that change, at once political and religious, came about when in the fourth century Christianity became the religion of the Roman Empire. At that moment, the new faith, long ignored as a petty inconvenience at best, required attention, and more to the point, the fundamental allegations of the new faith, all of them challenges to Judaism, demanded response. Christians had long told Israel that Jesus is Christ, that the Messiah has come, and that there is no further salvation awaiting Israel; that Christians were now bearers of the promises of the Old Testament, and in them, the Israelite prophets' predictions were realized; that Christians were now Israel and Israel was now finished. The political change in government made it necessary for the people of Israel, particularly in the Land of Israel ("Palestine"), to respond to Christianity as in the prior three centuries they had not had to.

What they did by way of response was not to form a theory of Christianity within the framework of Judaism, but to reform their theory of Judaism — of who is Israel and what is its relationship, through the Torah, with God. To that theory, Christendom was simply beside the point. Within that theory — that religious system defining the holy way of life,

470

worldview, and social entity that was Israel — Christianity did not find any explanation at all. Nor has it ever since. But at least, for a brief moment, Judaism thought about Christianity. Forced by political change, that stunning shift in the political circumstance of a religion affected that religion's thought about, among other enduring questions, the outsider, the other, the brother, and the enemy. And as a matter of fact, in thinking about the other, that same religion reconsidered the enduring and long-settled issues concerning itself as well. The fact that thinking about the other means we have also to rethink the truth about ourselves explains, I think, why we are so reluctant to do so. . . .

. . . Ours is an intellectual task, for if we cannot in a rational and rigorous way think religiously about the other, then the good works of politics and the ordering of society will not be done. And the dimensions of our task are formidable. For we have seen what does not serve. Tolerance works only in a climate of indifference; when you care, so it seems, you also hate. Toleration works where law prevails, but the limits of the law are set by sovereign power, and the range of difference on the other side of the border stretches to the last horizon. So are we able in wit and imagination, mind and intellect, to form a theory of the other coherent with the entire structure of the world that our religious worldview, way of life, account of the "us" that is the social entity, comprise? The issue of coherence is critical, and that matter of cogency with the whole religious system explains why at stake are theological propositions. Tolerance is a mere social necessity, but we all recognize, simply not a theological virtue. Anyone who doubts should recall the ridicule that met the position, "It does not matter what you believe, as long as you're a good person," not to mention, "It does not matter what you believe, as long as you believe something."

Beyond tolerance and before theology — that is where we now stand. The history of religion is teaching us about the failures of the past, so closing off paths that lead nowhere. Can religious systems make sense of what lies beyond the system? In my judgment the answer must be affirmative, because the question comes with urgency. . . .

. . . This, then, is a time for intellectuals to do their work courageously. The events at Oswiecim have turned a chronic into an acute problem, and it will be a *Qiddush Hasham* — an act, like the act of martyrdom, that is a sanctification of the name of God — on the part of religious intellectuals, both Judaic and Christian ones, to meet that challenge as an urgent example of an enduring religious dilemma: making sense of the other in the intellectual tools provided by one's own religion and its theology.

Social Activism and Spiritual Alternatives — An Islamic Perspective

Chandra Muzaffar

A Muslim intellectual and social critic from Malaysia, Muzaffar looks at his own religious tradition and finds resources for engaging in tasks of social transformation. Source: *Liberation, Religion and Culture: Asian-Pacific Perspectives* (Bangkok: ACFOD Booklet, 1989).

In this paper I want to analyze how one could apply values and principles from spiritual traditions to the challenges and the sort of issues which social activists are confronted with, and have to come to terms with, from time to time. I will provide examples of how these values and principles can be applied from an Islamic perspective, but I will also make a number of references to other spiritual traditions with which I have some familiarity.

Let me begin by taking some of the broad issues as far as the contemporary situation is concerned and see how these broad challenges can be approached from a spiritual perspective. First, the question of imperialism which is undoubtedly one of the major challenges of our times. It has been a challenge which has confronted a huge segment of humanity for a very good part of this century in one form or another.

Imperialism

If imperialism is, in essence, the control of the destinies of other human beings and of other societies, then we can argue that there is a clear response from the spiritual traditions. The very fact that almost all the Semitic traditions (Judaism, Christianity and Islam) have taken clear-cut stances against slavery can be used as a basis to argue that there is no acceptance of imperialism because the essence of slavery is control and dominance. If slavery was wrong, it was not because slavery per se was a widespread practice in all these societies. But what made slavery abhorrent, what made is so obnoxious, was because it allowed total dominance and control of another human being. And in early Islam, freeing slaves was regarded as one of the most noble acts. The Prophet Muhammad set the example. It is a practice which is sanctioned in the Qur'an itself. Many slaves joined the Islamic struggle in the early years. They viewed Islam as a liberator. But institutional slavery was not abolished, just as none of the Semitic traditions abolished slavery as such. The attitude towards slavery, however, was a very clear manifestation of how the great spiritual traditions felt about control and dominance of someone else or some other group. I would therefore argue — as it has been argued by Muslims like Hassan Hanafi, the Egyptian philosopher — that the liberation of slaves is perhaps one of the proofs that we have of the attitude of Islam towards imperialism, why it regards imperialism as wrong. Human beings in the ultimate analysis must have control over their own destinies, over their own lives: they must never be left to the mercy of other people. And in the Islamic tradition, it is supported by a number of other injunctions. For instance, there is a very clear verse in the Qur'an that says that in the affairs that concern a human being or his group, he must have control. He must be consulted in the affairs which concern him. His own position is important. It is this consultation, this participation, which determines his dignity. It is also laid out in the Qur'an that without participation and consultation, his destiny as a human being is affected.

The State

A second example (which is again very relevant to our times) is the power of the state. We are confronted with this reality all the time, not least social activists. People in political parties are also confronted with this reality.

This is a reality that faces every individual living in our time and age, even if some of us are not conscious of this and are not able to articulate this in a certain way. But the power of the modern state has no parallel in human history. The modern state demands total loyalty. The modern state sees itself as the only source of a person's destiny. The modern state determines our identity. What we are is determined by the state. The state gives us an identity card. The state says that you are a national of a particular place. And the state tells you what your culture should be. The state tells you, for instance, whether you can move from one place to another or not. The state determines almost everything. Your rights and obligations are determined, your responsibilities to your fellow human beings are determined, by the state. The state sometimes even says what sort of food you can eat! The state is all pervasive. It is powerful. It is the source of loyalty. It is that one institution which has control over your very identity. This is the power of the modern state. Not many of us realize what this reality of the modern state really means to us — the tremendous influence, the impact of the modern state. This is true of not just the non-communist states in the Asia-Pacific region. This reality of the state, which affects the psyche of every individual, confronts every one of us. It is a reality that is sometimes even harder in the case of the communist states of the Third World and the Second World.

Is there a spiritual response to this reality, the reality of the state? If religion cannot respond to this reality of the state then it will not be able to meet any of the other contemporary challenges. I would argue that religion can respond to the question of the overwhelming power of the modern state. And religions' response is in some ways very ancient, and yet it is perennial, it is eternal. The argument from a religion perspective would be that there is a loyalty that transcends the loyalty to the state. There is a loyalty that is much more important than the loyalty to the modern state. And this is the loyalty to God. It transcends loyalty to the state and is so strong that every other loyalty should be weighed and considered against this loyalty to God, whether it is loyalty to the state or loyalty to one's cultural community, or loyalty to one's religious group or loyalty to the family or loyalty to a friend. Loyalty to almost everything else has to be weighed and considered against this very important loyalty to God which transcends everything else. The concept of God itself may be expressed in different ways. We need not have a common notion of what God means — some may see it as the Ultimate Reality, some may see it as the Divine Presence, some may see God in some other way. But that loyalty transcends loyalty to the state. And that, I think, is a very important factor. . . .

Political Rights

A third point that I want to make is this. If we look at some of the realities that we are confronted with in this day and age, in many societies, very basic rights are denied to people. This is a reality all over the Third World, in the Second World and even in the First World.

Here again, one would begin to wonder whether religion has got a response, whether our spiritual traditions are able to respond to this challenge. And I would argue that there is a response. From the Islamic perspective, for instance, there are very clear enunciations in the Qur'an on the right of free speech, on the right of assembly and association. The right of free speech is contained in one of its most famous Suras: Sura Al-i-Imran line 104 which advises humankind to "have amongst you a group that would enjoy what is right and forbid what is wrong." That is a clear call to the exercise of freedom of expression. You must exercise this freedom on behalf of justice, on behalf of what is right — you must speak out. And that particular verse also asks you to associate, to form an association. It asks you to struggle against injustice.

There is a famous hadis (saying of the Prophet Muhammad) that says that the greatest Jihad (meaning to struggle against oneself) is expressing a word of justice before an unjust ruler. That is the greatest Jihad! A great person's commitment to a struggle is manifested in this. In another hadis it is noted "If you see an injustice, try to change it with your hands (which means through action). And if you fail to do that then at least condemn it in your heart." This is the Islamic attitude toward injustice. The importance attached to speaking out, to standing up for justice, is crystal clear. And yet if you look at the great paradox that we are confronted with, there is hardly a single nation anywhere in the Muslim world where Muslims and others can speak the truth without suffering the consequences. Not a single country where you can speak the truth! This is a measure of the tremendous gap that exists between ideal and reality everywhere in the Muslim world. And this is true of many other societies as well. . . .

Basic Needs

Now let me move from these examples which are all political in a sense to some of the economic examples from Islam and other traditions. In many of our societies there is tremendous exploitation of the ordinary human being: of the poor, the oppressed, the helpless and hopeless. What is the spiritual response to this?

Again, using the tradition that I am familiar with (though I am sure that these things can be applied to other traditions, too), you will realize that in Islam, there is a very clear view that the basic needs of every human being must be provided for. That is a priority. The Qur'an itself states that the basic needs of food, shelter, clothing, education and health must be made available to every human being. There is also the concept of Zakat in Islam. The Zakat is sometimes misinterpreted as the poor tax, but it is more than that. It is the surplus after you have satisfied your basic needs which goes into the common pool which would be used by the community as a whole. It becomes the wealth of the entire community. That is what the Zakat is supposed to be.

If you look at the way it was used in the early period of Islam, it was for the good of the community as a whole. Ordinary human beings were entitled to the wealth of the community. Leaders could not use the wealth as they liked. They had to account for it. There is a very well-known episode in Islam where the Caliph Omar Ibn Khattab wanted to use a little bit of olive oil that was kept in the Baitul Mal (public treasury). Omar was ill as a result of starvation. This was because there was a famine in his empire at that time and a lot of people were suffering, and he had taken a vow that he would be the last person to eat because he was the Caliph. It was only after every other person had been looked after and their needs had been looked after that he would eat. Consequently, he fell very ill and he needed this olive oil to cure his illness. He went up to the congregation and asked their permission to use that olive oil so that he could cure himself of his illness.

Now this was the notion of how the wealth of the people should be used, how leaders should account to the people, how the people should have priority over their leaders. There is also a very well-known story about the first Caliph of Islam, immediately after the Prophet Muhammad's time. He was a very rich man. He was a merchant who had given up a lot of his wealth to serve the cause of Islam in that period. When he died, it is said that he had only one dirham — the Arabian money at that time — left because he had given up everything for the cause of justice. Now if you look at the contemporary situation of modern politicians in the Muslim world, when they begin their political careers they have only a dirham, but when they end their political careers they have millions and millions of dirhams. It is just the opposite now. The way things have changed. Even "interest" (or usury) which Islam bans is again related to justice because the argument is that one should not be allowed to make money in an idle manner, that wealth must circulate and be reproductive. In the Qur'an, in Sura al-Hashr, line 7, it is said "Don't allow wealth to circulate only among the rich." In other words, wealth must circulate within the larger community. These are some of the values and principles that show that we should never ever allow wealth to be monopolized by a small elite. . . .

Women

Let us look at yet another question that we are confronted with, the question of women and sexual discrimination. Here again, one of the great myths is that in Islamic thought women are looked down upon, that women are inferior. And yet, if you look at the Qur'anic spirit, this is not true at all. The Qur'an recognizes very clearly that in all their social and spiritual obligations there is no distinction between male and female. In all those verses concerned with the sexes the Qur'an says it over and over again that there is no distinction between male and female, men and women. Whether it is in the performance of rituals or in their social obligations there is no distinction at all. There is only one line in the Qur'an that does say men are — depending on how you translate it — either "greater than" or "more important than" or "superior to" women. But it clarifies why this is so: men are supposed to look after women in their material needs. Great Muslim thinkers have argued that if women play an equal role in the provision of material needs, if women are also bread-winners and bring in income, then that distinction has no relevance anymore. One of the greatest contemporary Muslim thinkers, Fazlur Rahman, has argued that there is no sexual discrimination at all in the Qur'an. The greater importance of men alluded to just now, according to Fazlur Rahman, is linked to economic function and nothing else. Once economic roles change, it would be wrong to accord economic superiority to the male. In like fashion, people who say that only men can hold positions of importance and women cannot become leaders are distorting the truth. Nowhere in the Qur'an is it said that women cannot become leaders or hold public office. And yet these prejudiced ideas about women have developed in Islam as in all other religions. . . .

Environment

Let me give a final example of an area of importance to social activists, the question of environment. How do we approach this question?

In Islam, environmental degradation is condemned. You cannot destroy the environment because you are part of it, you are part of the whole cosmos, the total unity. That unity is not confined to human beings or to the relationship between the sexes alone, it also includes nature. It includes, in fact, not just this universe but other universes too. Even in the Sura "Fatihah," that particular verse which is regarded as the mother of the Qur'an, it is made very clear that God is the Lord of the universes. Modern astronomy is also of the view that there is not just this Universe but many other universes. The Qur'an also recognizes that there are living creatures in other planets. We must respect all living creatures and nature. For, the human being, nature and the Universe are one. This is the concept of Tauhid in Islam. Everything is part of an integrated Whole. No part of it should be destroyed. One of the first instructions that Muhammad gave after he returned to Mecca was to ask the people not to cut down even a single tree. You can compare that with Buddhism where there is a clear-cut concept of harmony with the environment. It has its roots in the relationship between Gautama Buddha and the Bodhi tree under whose shade he received enlightenment. You will find it in other traditions, too. In Christianity — contrary to what modern writers have said — harmony with nature is very crucial. The best example of this would be Saint Francis of Assisi, the man who talked to birds and other animals. If you look at many of his writings, the way he eulogized nature reveals a profound respect for all creation. In Taoism this tradition was so powerful at one time that the construction of every city had to emphasize the beauty of nature. Buildings, architecture took second place while the beauty of nature had priority.

Own Womb

I have tried to show that Islam, like the other spiritual traditions, has its own character, its own autonomy. Ideas on social change must emerge from its own womb. By ideas here we mean the basic philosophical ideas, what constitutes the fundamental framework of a particular spiritual tradition. . . .

. . . But the point must also be made that once you have established that framework, and your framework is authentic, coming out of your own womb, your own history and your own background, then the next thing to do is to absorb all that is good and worthwhile from outside that framework. It is like building a house. Once you have got the foundation and have put up the pillars, there is nothing wrong in getting designs, ideas, on how to do your bedroom, sitting room or living room from other traditions. Let's absorb from the great traditions of our times. From the Left, the good ideas from socialism; they will certainly enrich this framework of ours. Even in the market economies, there are certain ideas that we can absorb. Because it would be very naive of us to believe that the market economies could exist for so long merely by exploiting the labor of the weak. There are also other reasons. You must be able to develop an intelligent critique of capitalism, which exposes its weaknesses while acknowledging its strengths.

Once the basic framework, the foundation is clear, once selective absorption from other sources is taking place, we should be able to develop a spiritual perspective on human dignity and social justice which would be relevant to all of us, whatever our particular religious affiliation. I see this as a challenge facing Muslims and Islam at this juncture in history: how to develop from the essence of Islam a universal spirituality as the basis of a global civilization. Indeed, this is a task facing all the other religions experiencing a resurgence at this point in time, it is only Catholicism which seems to be responding to this challenge of developing a universal spirituality. But even then, it is also caught up in certain theological and structural problems.

A universal spirituality, a universal spiritual vision of human dignity and social justice — this is the challenge facing us social activists. As our present materialistic civilization with all its artificial glitter and glory comes to an end, humankind awaits the birth of a new spiritual dawn which will mark the triumph of human compassion and social justice in God's universe.

Hinduism and Social Action from Women's Perspective

G. Shanta

G. Shanta is a Hindu woman from Bali (Indonesia) who has founded an ashram in her own country and is leading and encouraging others toward a way of life in community and in harmony with nature. She is also active in women's issues, and in this article looks at her own religious tradition as a resource for feminist perspectives. Source: *Liberation, Religion and Culture: Asian-Pacific Perspectives* (Bangkok: ACFOD Booklet, 1989).

Reviewing Women's Status in Hinduism

Hinduism has an elaborate heritage of many sects, subsects and various philosophies as it ran through different historic phases. Scriptures like the Veda, Upanishads and Bhagavad Gita can be referred to. We cannot forget the role of the great epics like Mahabharata and Ramayana which people quote frequently in their day-to-day life.

Hindu tradition is broad based with regard to women's position. The place of the creator is also addressed as "she." We have seen women goddesses in Hindu tradition who have partaken in overthrowing the oppressors. Moreover, in Hinduism women are not primarily looked at in limited areas like marriage and the home alone. The tenth mandala of the

Rig-Veda holds "woman is the highest power of the world." Brihadaranyaka Upanishad tells about Gargi, the woman seer, who led the intellectual debate and inquiry with Yajnavalkya.

Woman-Man Concept

The recognition that women and men are inseparable parts of the creation is one of the great hopes of the Indian feminist movement.

Upanishads

Prasna Upanishad says "Prajapati created a pair of matter and energy, so that the two together would between them produce a multiple of creatures." "Prajapati" here refers to the cosmic principle of intelligence or cosmic consciousness. Matter and energy symbolize man and woman.

This is further enforced by the Shiva-Sakti concept of the Vedanta: "Shiva is the flawless reality in which cosmic conscious energy exists in a state of quiescence." Devi Bhagavata (XI-12-21) glorified sakti as "the supreme being who is the inexhaustible reservoir of energies." Because all the gross and subtle elements and the whole world composed of them are being constantly created by Sakti and being shown to Shiva. In all living objects and phenomena, Sakti alone is manifested and is the only reality enveloping the whole world. Without Sakti, Shiva is not important and unproductive of anything (Bharatiya Sanskrati IV, 90).

In fact, Shiva and Sakti are not two separate principles, but two aspects of one and the same, "like the moon in the moonlight and the moonlight in the moon." (Chandra-chandrikayoriva) Shiva-Sakti dance, the energy dance and cosmic dance or dance of creation and destruction, is an interesting feature of this unitary principle.

Vedic Thought

In Vedic thought, "Purusha" and "Prakriti" — the "male" and the "female" — are two opposite principles accounting for the manifestation of the material universe. Though apparently opposites, they are not antagonistic but complementary to each other. They are almost identical with the prin-

481

ciple of Shiva-Sakti except for the significant fact that the Shiva-Sakti principle is active more in the nature of interaction between consciousness and energy. The principle of purusha-prakriti is active more in the nature of interrelationship through mutual attraction of these two "opposites," thereby actualizing the process of manifestation of all material phenomena. "Animated by Prakriti, I project again and again in this world of multitude of beings" declares Purusha himself (Bhagavad Gita, 8).

The universe is evolved through the interaction of Purusha and Prakriti. Hence, there was no sex discrimination of man as superior and woman as inferior. . . .

Protest Against Oppressive Structures

Upanishads

There are two types of knowledge to be acquired by human beings — one pertaining to the material world and the other to the transcendental which leads to imperishable reality.

In the scriptural story of Ganesha running a race with his brother Shanmukha, both are to go round the earth three times and return to their parents, Shiva and Parvati, waiting for the winner. As the story goes Shanmukha flies fast in space on his peacock's back while Ganesha only circumambulates three times around his parents and won the prize. In this story Shanmukha symbolizes one who traveled on the relative plane while Ganesha moves in the space-time continuum of the Shiva-Sakti principle of matter and energy. This story symbolizes the made race of mechanized development or material development, in other words consumeristic culture.

This story further illustrates the triumph of the Absolute over the materialistic culture. This would indicate man's present capitalistic worldview and man's selfish and indiscriminate desire for quick material prosperity which forgets the wholistic-human development. So feminism should not aim at a reform movement only for economic equality or equality for women alone but should look critically at all forms of oppression which are hurdles for a complete true humanity. . . .

Bhagavad Gita

. . . In the Gita, Arjuna asked why God did not keep everyone equal — why the few are powerful and wealthy while others are not. Krishna gives an excellent example: in winter people light a fire and sit around. Only people who are closer to the fire get the warmth. It is not the fire which is biased. The fire and warmth are common to all. A few people keep it for themselves and alienate others. Likewise God's creation of nature and wealth are common to everyone. People are responsible for the unequal distribution of wealth. God did not discriminate as between man or woman, poor or rich, low or high from birth, more educated and less educated and so on.

Krishna Lila (play and dance of Krishna with shepherd women) symbolizes the simplicity of spirituality. It further implies God taking the side of the poor and being in close touch with the oppressed. Here again they are women. He played with women. But women are depicted as temptresses and are condemned as seducers standing in the path of enlightenment. Spirituality is not meant only for the intellectuals. God is easily accessible to anyone who is just and compassionate. Hindu tradition holds the view that service to humanity is the perfect way of attaining enlightenment — the liberation of the soul. Human beings can attain Moksha or liberation by doing rightful actions. This is the message of the Gita (2,12).

Ramayana

The epic Ramayana and the symbol of Sita is a great controversial debate among contemporary reformers. While Gandhi used the symbol of Sita for women's awakening, others like to discard it as it is an oppressive symbol of unquestioned obedience and subservience. To Gandhi, the symbol of Sita is an embodiment of personal courage and a sense of suffering. Let us look at the original text of Ramayana written by Valmiki and see how the interpreters acted as they wish to. To enslaved Sita Hanuman says: "after your separation Rama does not eat meat, does not drink wine and lives in your memory eating only ordinary food."

The later interpreters could not imagine how Rama, the incarnation of God, can eat meat and drink toxic drinks. Hence, they interpreted "meat" as mango pulp and "wine" as honey. The original text depicted Rama only as a man with all human follies. In the same story after Rama's victory over Ravana, Sita is released. Rama asked Sita to go through the raging fire to prove her chastity during her enslavement at Ravana's palaces. Hearing this Sita gets angry, as any normal individual would. The dramatic scene was:

> "Sita is coming out of Ravana's palace. She looked at Rama with love and passion because of long separation."

To her Rama says:

> "I won the enemy. I have taken vengeance. I did everything a man would do as an answer for an insult he bore. These deeds are not for your sake (to release you) but to safeguard my image from getting defamation. Now you can go wherever you want, Janaka's daughter! Turn your mind to Lakshman, Bharath, Sukriva or Vibeshman. You will live with any one of them as you please."

Further he asks her to go through the fire. Sita gets angry and utters:

> "How can you use these words, wise man! It is like a bloody stupid talking to his wife."

Yes, Sita, the obedient Indian woman, calls Rama "stupid" in the midst of a big crowd where well-known people are assembled!

It looks as if Sita is not scolding him but that Valmiki, the epic writer of Ramayana, is scolding Rama for his shameful behavior. It is not only a blow to Rama alone but to all male chauvinists all over the world. But in the later version of Kambaramayana (one of five Tamil classics) in the same context Sita spoke like this: "My life, my penance and my femininity and my past married life with you were all meaningless and madness as I did not understand you before." Here, she did not scold Rama with words as Sita did in Valmiki's Ramayana. By that time temples had come and they had started worshipping Rama as God's incarnation. So Kamban could not use more strong words to abuse Rama directly.

The above are all elements of protest in the Indian tradition. We must look into these liberative elements in Hinduism as a basis for feminism in this tradition.

Buddhism and Social Values

Sulak Sivaraksa

A well-known Thai Buddhist intellectual and writer, Sulak
Sivaraksa founded the International Network of Engaged Buddhists in the late 1980s. For over three decades he has been a
leading figure and social critic in his own country, and is also
internationally known for his efforts in human rights, justice,
peace, and ecology, promoting interreligious cooperation in
these areas. Source: *Liberation, Religion and Culture: Asian-
Pacific Perspectives* (Bangkok: ACFOD Booklet, 1989).

. . . The first of the Four Noble Truths of Buddhism is suffering. In our
context any religion which does not deal with suffering is not worthy. It is
just an escape from suffering.

To know how to confront suffering is not enough. You must know
the cause of suffering: that is the second truth. Once you know the cause
of suffering then the third is the cessation of suffering, getting rid of
suffering. And finally the fourth truth is really the whole fabric of Buddhism
known as the noble Eight-Fold Path; in fact it is the way to get rid of
suffering. This is, of course, not exclusively Buddhist; anybody can use it.
It is common to many traditions; Buddhism does not have copyright on
it. To get rid of suffering is what "liberation" means. The word "moksha"
— again a Hindu and Buddhist word — means "liberation." To be liberated
means "nirvana" (or "nibanna") — the stage of cessation of suffering.

Hence liberation is the key word in Buddhism. If we do not lead our lives towards liberation it is not worth being a Buddhist.

Anybody can be a Buddhist in this sense, because — unlike in other religions — you do not have to declare that you will join Buddhism; you do not have any special rights or privileges if you actually join. If you want to join it is O.K., if you do not want to join it is also O.K. This is the strength and weakness of Buddhism, perhaps because there is not dogma in Buddhism. You are not required to believe in anything; you are told to challenge every teaching, even if it is the teaching of the Buddha — the word of Buddha, any sacred scripture — unless that teaching helps you to realize the truth, leads you to liberation and shows you the way to do it. That means that to be liberated, you must be able to get rid of the three root causes of suffering.

That is, first of all, greed and lust which go together. Then hatred, which tends to link with power, evil and all kinds of affinities. These two are very important, but the worst one is delusion or ignorance. Many people think they are clever, but in Buddhism, unless you understand the reality of things you are ignorant or deluded. You are deluded because you have egocentricity or selfishness. Selflessness, and how to overcome selfishness, is the key to Buddhism.

In order to get liberated from suffering, that is to overcome selfishness, every human being should first of all know who he himself or she herself is. We tend to feel that we are somebody permanent or great. In Buddhism that is delusion. If we get up in the morning aiming at changing the world and do all kinds of things we often get back into anger, greed and delusion. That is why if you want to practice Buddhism first of all every person has to find out who he or she is. That is why meditation is important. Reflect five or ten minutes how to restructure your mind from a selfish being to a selfless being. That is not easy but it is essential.

That is the first step if you want to be a seriously practicing Buddhist. It is related to the second step. If you restructure yourself to be less selfish you relate to others. The less you exploit yourself the less you exploit others. Exploitation always begins with exploiting oneself. Those of us who smoke very heavily realize how they exploit themselves and others. Maybe sometimes we think we have to do it because we are nervous. How you exploit yourself and how you exploit others always go side by side. Thus personal development and social development must be side by side. You cannot play one against the other. The understanding that Buddhism is only to calm ourselves is wrong. The more calm you are the more society remains unjust and selfish. You should be calm in order to be mindful and to tackle injustices in society more meaningfully. So in this way personal liberation and social liberation must go side by side. We have three steps: first mindfulness, which is known as "samadhi."

Samadhi is reflection for constructive self-criticism. The second is "sila," that is the precept of how to deal with society and not to exploit others and oneself. You can do that properly only when you have wisdom "panna" or "prajna." All this is relative unless you see the truth, unless you get rid of selfishness. Then all these relative values "sila," "samadhi," "panna" become absolute values. That is where mundane and the supra-mundane come together.

When you are no longer selfish then you can really be liberated. But on the way towards that state you can also be on the way of liberation. We respect others more. For instance in the Tibetan tradition to meditate is meditation on your enemy. Your enemy is the best friend you have. I find that very difficult because I have so many enemies. Without them you are without challenges. You feel sometimes they say many bad things about you — sometimes true, sometimes false. However you have to attempt some change trying not to hate the enemy, so that the enemy can become your friend. But unless you have wisdom you do not know how to change the structures. To kill the enemy is not a help. You have to kill hatred and the system which creates hatred and exploitation. That is the essence of the liberative element in Buddhism as I see it.

The man Gautama became Buddha because he had liberated himself and he wanted to liberate society. When he became liberated he became the Buddha, the Enlightened and Awakened One. He discovered the "dhamma," the truth. He and the truth became one — the "Buddha-Dhamma." You may identify "dhamma" not as a person but as a universal law which is justice and truth. If we understand and walk along the Buddha-Dhamma we walk along the path of liberation.

But you cannot do that alone, and therefore the Sangha was founded. The Sangha is the ideal Buddhist society, founded, first of all, among those who had become enlightened and liberated. It was also founded to help people who wanted to be liberated and to join the Sangha. And eventually the Sangha became divided into four categories: one is the monks, a very bad translation of "bhikkhu"; the second one is the "bhikkhuni," for whom I do not want to use the word "nun" as unfortunately this word has become regarded as lower. Male and female monks are equal. The laymen and laywomen make up the third and fourth categories and are all equal too.

To be liberated means not to exploit anything at all. You have to become a Bhikkhu or Bhikkhuni in order not to exploit at all. But in our daily lives unfortunately we have to exploit, we have to kill animals for our living. We do not kill directly, we kill indirectly. Even those who became vegetarians kill vegetation, which also has life. So the vegetarians are not generally better beings than non-vegetarians. Of course it is good to be a vegetarian; it is good not to smoke; but it does not mean that one is better. I remember that Alan Watts, an Anglican priest who became a Zen master in California, once said that the reason he became a vegetarian was that cows cry louder than cabbages. You see, if you go to the extreme not to exploit you might end up like those religious teachers during the time of Buddha who only ate fruit that had fallen from the tree because to pluck was also violent. . . .

To summarize the first part of my argument: in Buddhism you must walk individually towards liberation but cannot do so unless society is peaceful and righteous. Buddhism works best in small communities. In Siam you can see many temples where monks live. Although the monks also compromise, they are still an example for us; they eat less, they possess fewer things than us, they lead a celibate life and spend their time meditating on the truth. Of course, they also work on indigenous medicine, they teach and so on; the stress is always on the individual in community, with a harmonious natural surrounding.

Regarding the state: the Buddha said the state or the king is like a snake: keep them at arm's length but you cannot get away from them; do not kill them as that would be violent. Handle the state as you handle the snake: be kind and cautious. If you want to deal with the snake, go behind it, not in front of it.

Regarding trade: a rich man can also be liberated, but as in Christianity it is more difficult for a rich man. That is why a monk does not own anything: he can be liberated easier. But if you are rich it depends on how you acquire your wealth. If you acquire it righteously you might achieve liberation, but if you do not do so you will not achieve it. If you spend your wealth selfishly that is also wrong. You must spend it generously. The richer you are the more you can be generous. And generosity in Buddhism means first of all to be generous with your property. But that is only one and not even the major aspect of it. Generosity means to be generous with your time and with your mind which you should share with others. That is much more important. Similarly charity in Buddhism is "dana" which means giving away but not only wealth. You give away selfishness while the most meaningful gift to others is giving the truth for liberation. . . .

We must also note that there are quite a number of negative elements in this country (Siam) making use of Buddhism. Buddhism has become part and parcel of the state, dominated by the military; Buddhism has become part and parcel of capitalism. Even the temples have become rich for the first time in history; they now get quite a good amount of money with which they build more big temples which, however, do not really help the people.

Though there are elements in our Buddhist society which militate against liberation, there are nevertheless also elements of liberational attitudes. The most important one started in 1932 by Buddhadasa Bhikkhu, which translates as "servant of the Buddha." He pointed to what went wrong with Buddhism. Regarding society, Buddhadasa said that one has to deal with the state but also remain critical of it. In his book *Dhammic Socialism* he said that all socialist societies are wrong because they have state capitalism instead. Dhammic socialism means that each community should be more socially oriented, should be self-contained, and should be more decentralized; it is very similar to Gandhi's village republic. But you must have mindfulness, not competition, but collaboration.

In 1960, the Venerable Prayudh, a young monk from Suphanburi province, communicated the essential teachings of the Buddha with a social dimension. He and Buddhadasa Bhikkhu have a tremendous appeal with the young people. People are now coming back to Buddhism in a big way. Up to now they saw Buddhism as something related to state ceremonies, as something dead or conformist, but now they realize that Buddhism is beyond the state. In his book *Looking to America to Solve Thailand's Problems* he said that we follow the Americans far too much, and they interfere far too often. Yet also in America there is a movement to change people's lifestyles. When we look at the West we usually look at the materialistic aspects only but never look at the liberative elements. But more importantly, he said, we should look into our own culture. Our Buddhist culture has enough liberative elements to free ourselves from mental colonialism. . . .

There is also a lay person, Ms. Chatsumarn Kabilsingh, who emphasizes that we must revive the order of female monks. They existed for 800 years but then disappeared. Her commitment to revive the female order helps a good deal. Now the poorest of the poor join the monkhood as they cannot even afford to go to school. But by putting on a yellow robe people respect you culturally and you can have education. And if you are clever you can move from your village to the town, from the town to Bangkok. The community supports you while the state does not. They even send you to be educated in India. Now if we can revive the female monkhood I am pretty sure a lot of prostitution will go down. They sell their bodies because they have nothing else. Now luckily the first Thai woman ordination has taken place, fortunately or unfortunately in Los Angeles. You have to do that there because the hierarchy here is still very conservative. Perhaps they also feel threatened. In a way it is good that it started in Los Angeles because in this country they blindly admire the West. If we start female ordination in the West and then come home with it, it will be accepted much easier.

The most important things, however, are the up-country monks. They have now realized that in the name of progress and development the state told us to believe that economic development was good. Those monks have realized that this is all a lie. They realized that their lives have become much worse: the environment is spoilt, the animals have gone, there are more roads and dams and more electricity. Yet only the rich reap the benefit. To counter the wrong trends of development, these monks who are working with the people bring Buddhism back to life for the masses. Meditation has become collective meditation, meditation with social analysis. They want self-reliance, not growing for sale, and they revive their old traditions. Instead of going after tractors, they work together with buffaloes. What we need now in this country is to link all these liberative elements together, those up-country monks of whom we have more than twenty now. Seri Phongphit, a Catholic friend, has written a book on them (Religion in a Changing Society: Buddhism, Reform and the Role of Monks in Community Development in Thailand).

Secondly there is the urban problem: how Buddhism can be meaningful in the urban setting. In Bangkok Buddhism has become very ceremonial. How can we help in the urban area? Twenty percent of Bangkok is now slums. We have a monk now working in the slums, but moreover we have to have some analysis to understand society. So while we are firm using the Buddhist way, we need to understand how exploitation in our society works. We have to link all this together into a movement. That is why we have to learn from other ideologies. We must learn from other traditions because nowadays Buddhism alone is not sufficient. We have to learn from the Muslims, the Hindus and the Christians. In this country we luckily do not have many antipathies against the Christians. We are working together. Of course the conservative Christians and the conservative Buddhists do not like that. On the one hand they join together to support the status quo, on the other hand they are afraid to lose their own followers. But we who live and work on the liberative elements have to work together to help liberate ourselves and our societies. . . .

... Consumerism is a disease against which we should build up our communities. In this, so far all religions have failed. We have not yet succeeded in building up a new culture. We talk so much about liberation but do not ask ourselves why in Latin America they have been successful. And I think they were successful because they offered a new culture. When a bishop gives up his palace that is something! It is easy to say "Get back to the roots!" unless you really change your lifestyle and mental attitude to be more simple. That is why Gandhi was successful. He changed his lifestyle. He changed his attitude and he was fairly radical. I think if we want liberation we have to be radical. But so far we have not been able to build up a new culture. The culture you see everywhere is a feudal culture. We claim to be progressive and very scientific but it is a feudal culture. Siam is the only Buddhist country which has not done away with the monarchy system. But if this system is going to remain it ought to be the Buddhist concept of monarchy, that is, elected by the people, serving the people, near to the people, with the people and in righteousness. Otherwise the people have the right to overthrow the monarchy. This is all in the Sutras. We need a new culture with spiritual dimension. I think this is where we are different from others when we talk about liberation, religion and culture. Otherwise philanthropic organizations, Marxists and socialists are much better than us in many respects but I think they lack that spiritual dimension. But I feel the need for this dimension is coming back. If the Green Party is to survive — and I hope they will survive — I think they will reach this spiritual level. The Christian Democrats have become reactionary. Or you have a Buddhist party as in Sri Lanka which is also nationalistic and lacks spiritual depth. We do not want religious political parties but a spiritual dimension in politics and society. Why should we not take from Mahayana and from Christianity?! In this area you cannot have only one religion anymore. At one time the missionaries told us that they have the only true religion. Now some Buddhists seem to have adopted this opinion. But we have to coexist together and we must learn from each other. But we can only learn from those who are on a similar wave-length struggling with the people to overcome the common problems. ...

... Each community — firm in its roots, related through a movement within and outside the community — should try to bring together Buddhists, Christians and Muslims, all those who work on liberation. It has to be done. At the same time we must develop some common culture of simplicity. Socialism in England failed because they could not produce a new social culture. They still used the feudal culture. Capitalism also uses feudal culture to oppress people. Unfortunately when socialists have no culture they become capitalists themselves. I see that in Australia very clearly: the Labor Party is in power on a capitalistic venture. And that is also why our commitment to religion fails. We think of our own religion too much in a tribal way. Buddhism with a capital "B" has become tribal: Sinhalese Buddhism against the Tamil. Unfortunately, Christianity has also been tribal with its notion of the selected people, the chosen people. They used to be the Jews but now the white men are the selected ones. For me that is a fallacy. Christianity appeals to me because of the aspect of universal love, and the image of Christ appeals to me because he sacrificed himself. In any religion we have universal love in order to overcome suffering, and thus we can be together.

A Tradition of Thanksgiving

Audrey Shenandoah

One of the principal Native American traditions is that of the Haudenosaunee or Iroquois Confederacy, which includes the Mohawk, Oneida, Onondaga, Cayuga, Seneca, and Tuscarora nations. Elder Audrey Shenandoah is a Clan Mother of the Onondaga nation and has devoted much of her life to preserving and sharing the sacred teachings that lie at the heart of traditional Iroquois culture. The Haudenosaunee believe that if society at large is to address the environmental crisis effectively, it must first undergo a spiritual transformation and embrace the spiritual principles and attitudes associated with these teachings.

The following comments were made after Elder Shenandoah offered a thanksgiving prayer naming and acknowledging the various elements of creation beginning with our mother, the Earth, and concluding with a thanksgiving address to the Creator. Source: *Spirit and Nature,* ed. Steven C. Rockefeller and John C. Elder (Boston: Beacon Press, 1992), 17-23.

This is the thanksgiving address that our people have every time we get together, no matter how many or how few. And at every ceremony this is done. It is done at the beginning, and it is done at the closing.

You notice the very first component of this address is people. So people must be very important in the eyes of our Creator, if we should first give thanksgiving to each other and for each other. But all of the elements within this cycle of creation work together harmoniously, in balance, and our place is to keep the balance, to use them right, to use them wisely, and to remember to give thanksgiving.

Many of the elements are now out of balance, and we have forgotten in many instances to give the proper thanksgiving. Water is life. Water is very important to all living things. Without clean water there will be no life. Money should not be asked for water, for it is a gift given freely from our Creator. Technology and industry I am sure could find the ways to purify the water that has been polluted and abused. Technology and industry I am sure could do much research and find out how to correct quite a bit of the imbalance that is happening in our world today.

We are responsible for seven generations in my tradition, seven generations into the future. Our leadership must not make decisions that are going to bring pain or harm or suffering seven generations in the future. As individuals, we have the same mandate. This is a cause for great concern among my people, for we live in a society that feels dominant over the rest of the elements of the creation. But we are not. All the rest of the cycle could continue, if we were to drop out. It would probably continue very well, and the earth could heal itself. Other creatures would continue in their work. But if any single one of the rest should drop out from the cycle, we would be crying, we would be suffering, and our children would be suffering.

It is one of the main thoughts within the Thanksgiving Prayer that there be much repetition. It is purposely repeated over and over again, that we must put our minds together, and that we must give a thanksgiving for all of life, for all that gives us sustenance here on this earth. So much repetition allows for one to absorb the thoughts and in that way they become a part of one's being.

There are many, many people on the earth today who are poor and hungry. There are also many, many stockpiles of material wealth, people in business only for making money and not caring about the harm that may come to the people, the consumers of their products. They do not care whether what they are selling is healthful or beneficial, or what it is going to be used for in the future.

This is one of the main components of our thanksgiving address, that we must give thanks, and remember that we are responsible for seven generations into the future. I think this is a thought well worth looking into by all of industry and technology. But I ask, and we ask, will they, are they capable of doing this? Are they capable or willing to use a Good Mind, humane thought, as they continue to be producers of goods?

494

We cannot wait for multinationals, we cannot wait for huge programs to do all of this. It is up to each and every individual, once you have heard the message. Then you have the responsibility to teach it. This is the philosophy of the tradition that I come from. That is why there is so much repetition, so that you cannot say I do not know that, I did not hear that.

In today's times, we have a very difficult situation. Many of our young people no longer speak and understand our native language. And so we have to do a very difficult task, like today, putting this message into a foreign language, the English language. Our own language is still connected to the land. But in the English language, you have to use a whole bunch of cold words to try to describe what in any native language, because it's a land language, can be said completely, rounded out and whole.

So we have a difficult time giving our young people this understanding, and at the same time trying to teach the language. Because like any other language, there is the language of the ceremony, and there is the everyday language that you use as you move about with your friends. And so we have this very, very difficult time, not only among my own people, who are the Haudenosaunee, but among our native brothers all over this Turtle Island.

And I think that indigenous peoples all over the world have this basic principle of a respect, a deep love for the land, a very real connection, a relationship to all of those elements that are mentioned in our thanksgiving. I believe somehow we have to try to reach the people in power, to try to get them to listen to the indigenous people, no matter where they are. We had a meeting with some very interesting spiritual people this August in my own territory. There were indigenous peoples from several parts of the world, and the message was always the same. We were not surprised, because we have met before with those from other native lands, people who still feel related to the land and the components of the cycle of life. The message is the same, that we should respect our Mother, the Earth, and all of the components of the cycle of creation and that we should not continue the abuse that has been going on for so many years. Much technology can be used in a good way, but it has to be thought over. It has to be looked at. Proper changes and alternatives need to be acted upon in order to ensure well-being and peace of mind for future generations. There is a spiritual foundation that all of us were born with. It is inherent to every kind of people, a spiritual connection to this earth, to this land. This word "culture" is very much overused, I say. It is our way of life, and it is our connection to all of the rest of creation. That is our way.

We dance, we sing, expressing thanksgiving, expressing good feelings, strong spirits. We are misunderstood by many, many people. We have been portrayed as people who worship the sun, who worship elements of the creation, and this is incorrect. We give thanks, we respect, and we acknowledge all the rest of the creation. And this is what our ceremonies are for. This is what our ceremonies are all about.

They take up a whole lot of our time. We just finished one ceremony that lasted six days. And we will have another coming up very soon. We have a thanksgiving celebration for everything in its season. We also have a thanksgiving celebration for what many people are afraid to think about and to approach, even though it is a very important part of our life. And that is what in English is called death. We have a celebration for a person passing from this world into the other. And it has equal stature in our minds to any of the other of our thanksgiving celebrations.

We do not shelter our little ones from that thing that is called death, and so feared by so many people. It is a part of our life; it is a part of our lives. And so our little children are not shocked and frightened and driven into all kinds of emotional disturbances when death comes close to them. And it is right in the speeches, it is right in the ceremony, that we should instruct our children from the time of reason in thanksgiving, respect, acknowledgment, and also in what is called passing from one world to the other. And so it is really a complete cycle, if we will take the time to look at it. This passing comes in its time. We do not have to know the time, but it comes in its time. Our prophecies tell us of a time when the principal ones of all these elements will face destruction.

As we flew over the mountains from New York to Vermont, it was pretty cloudy. But I watched — because I've never seen the Adirondacks and the maple forests from the air, coming in this direction. Our prophecies from a long, long time ago tell us that this Chief of the Woodlands, the Maple, will begin dying from the top. I think a lot of people have heard this, since it began happening.

We were also told a long, long time ago that things would happen to the animal life. This was before the invasion of the foreigners to this land, and while things were still what you call "a wilderness." In our world there is no such thing as a wilderness. It is only a free place. It was not feared, and there is no need to fear it now. People no longer know what is in that one-time free wilderness. So many things that we have to be on guard about.

So I ask that everyone here have this thanksgiving in our minds. Somehow we have to get the message, as I said before, to those who are in

496

command of the technology and the industry. We have to reach and soften their thinking if it is possible, letting as many people as we can know that we must make a turnabout now. *Dane'tho.*

Following Elder Shenandoah's talk, she responded to questions from the audience. Several of those questions and answers follow.

Q: Could you please say something about how children are given guidance in your culture so that they grow up with this love and reverence for life?

Shenandoah: Within our longhouses, and within our ceremonies, I know of only two ceremonies where children are not allowed. Our children are brought with their mothers when they are new babies to get their names, for one, and also to do our sacred feather dance for the first time. And so the children are brought from the time they are infants to the longhouse, by their mothers, or their grandmothers, or their aunts.

Many of the young parents do not know the language. So we have to spend time with these young parents, so that they can in turn instruct their children. I guess this makes our job three times harder.

We have an extended family within our longhouse tradition. We are not like the nuclear family — mother, father, children, perhaps grandparents. We still carry on the tradition of clanship. Clan families meet, and the traditions are passed on at these times. During some of our ceremonies, we have to meet at people's houses in clans before we go to the longhouse. This is another time that traditions are passed on.

Then there are the storytelling times. They are not held as often as they used to be when I was a little girl, but we still have them. Children learn by listening to the elders and to their teachers in school.

Q: Please tell us a little more about your people's vision of the other world, and perhaps the word for death.

Shenandoah: Our Creator is a loving creator. Our Creator is not one who is vengeful, or who is going to punish. We punish ourselves if we do not follow the instructions. We bring punishment upon ourselves here on this earth. Our ways teach us that we should try in this time on earth not to have any disharmony within our own space. Each person has his own space that he is responsible for. Your responsibility is to keep peace within that space around you, within your own space. You know this would do a great deal toward world peace today, if we all knew that, if we all practiced that.

When we pass from this earth, we pass into what is called the spirit world. And there, all of the ceremonies that we do at our longhouses are also done. We are told that the minute a person takes his last breath here on this earth, a singer there, whoever it is, beats down on the sacred turtle rattle, and the ceremony begins. So if you are faithful to ceremonies, if you are faithful to the teachings of our ways, these are the things that you will have around you in the spirit world, around you all the time. And whatever your way is here on this earth, that is the way that you will be there unless you find yourself and correct yourself. But only you can correct yourself.

Q: I have two questions. You mentioned the prophecy that the maples would begin dying from the top down. I wonder if the prophecy went further and spoke to a remedy for that situation? And second, I wondered if there was a word for religion in your language.

Shenandoah: There is a word for what they call Christianity. Otherwise, no. I guess because it is so much a part of the people to live this way that it was not considered a religion. It is just the way to live. And the maple tree. No, not a physical remedy. Except that we should do our ceremonies. We have a ceremony for healing, which we do. But at the very end of one of our teachings, it says it is up to the people how long this all will continue, how long this will be. How long we will have the maple is up to the people. How long we will have the strawberry is up to the people. How long we will have water to survive is up to the people. Every individual can make a difference!

Ten Global Issues for Christian Reflection

Jocele Meyer

Jocele Meyer writes as a Christian concerned with living the implications of her faith, which leads her to an engagement in the concerns of Earth community. She outlines these areas of concern that call for interreligious cooperation. Source: Art and J. Meyer, *Earthkeepers: Environmental Perspectives on Hunger, Poverty, and Injustice* (Scottdale, Penn.: Herald Press, 1991).

As our world of five billion people becomes increasingly interdependent, more global issues emerge that are complex and interrelated. Our perspective is that of Christians trained in science, who did international research in the areas of hunger, poverty, and injustice. We have identified ten key issues facing humankind as the twentieth century comes to a close.

We rank and briefly describe these situations, starting with ones that seem to have the most global significance:

1. Environmental degradation

We consider the insidious destruction of the natural systems that support all life on earth to be the number one global problem. Overpopulation in developing countries and overconsumption and waste of natural resources in industrialized countries is putting great stress on the earth's ecosystems

— land, air, and water. We have forgotten that the earth is the Lord's and our mandate is to maintain it for his glory. Who else on earth can manage the creation?

2. The worldwide arms race and the nuclear threat

In 1988 an estimated $1 trillion was spent on arms (an amount equal to a stack of $1,000 bills 67 miles high). This money is sorely needed for human development programs and to reverse environmental damage. The two superpowers spend over half the world's arms budget and are responsible for two-thirds of the arms exports to the Third World.

Some people might call the threat of nuclear annihilation the world's number one problem. That's understandable, but the nuclear problem is so apparent and so focused today that we believe it will be resolved. Degradation of the environment is so subtle that we believe it constitutes more danger than the nuclear threat. Of course, the arms buildup contributes to environmental destruction, too. War and military preparation for war are the world's worst destroyers of natural resources.

3. Blind adherence to political-economic systems that are incompatible with natural laws

Most present economic systems — capitalist, communist, or socialist — disregard fundamental laws of nature. They pay little attention to ecological principles, such as "everything is connected to everything else," "everything must go somewhere," "nature knows best," and "there is no such thing as a free lunch."

Because of this disregard, our societies are building up dangerous environmental debts. Present political-economic systems promote an untenable free-lunch mentality. When implemented, these systems exploit nature or people or both.

4. The hunger scandal

Estimates of the hungry in our world today range from 450 million to more than one billion persons. At the same time industrialized countries are awash in grain. The major problem is that industrialized countries produce food at a cost beyond what hungry people can afford to pay. There are many other issues related to hunger, including food and agriculture policy, poverty, loss of crop land, access to land, policies of multinationals, and export cropping.

5. Providing full and meaningful employment for all who are able to work

This must be done without further destruction to the natural resource base — an incredible challenge. The World Resources Institute describes this problem as its basic purpose: "How can we meet basic human needs and nurture economic growth without undermining the natural resources on which life, economic vitality, and international security depend?"

Other related issues include world trade structure and monetary systems, automation and jobs, and the military-industrial complex and jobs.

6. The rapidly increasing gap between the rich and the poor

The economic gulf between the haves and the have-nots, both among and within countries, is increasing. Access to improved communication through computers and other technology by the wealthy and powerful allows them to exert control over the poor. Failure to narrow this gap will result in further injustice to the poor.

7. Inappropriate food and agriculture policies worldwide

Industrial agriculture as practiced in the developed world and introduced into the Third World during the green revolution is not sustainable in the long term. It uses up limited supplies of fossil fuels, it degrades the soil, and it pollutes the environment. The extension of industrial agriculture by use of modern biotechnology and genetic engineering (a new green revolution?) will not solve the food problem in the long term. A food and agriculture policy is needed that promotes production within the constraints of nature's rules — a sustainable agriculture.

501

8. *The family-farm crisis*

In the U.S. this involves farm bankruptcy, concentration of farmland ownership, loss of farmland by African-Americans, and deterioration of rural communities. Worldwide, industrialization of agriculture and cash cropping for export forces peasant farmers off the land. This results in migration to Third World cities where these farmers are more economically and socially vulnerable.

9. *The human population explosion*

This is related to all the other issues. The expected doubling of the world's population in forty years will put increasing stress on political-economic systems worldwide. The earth cannot sustain the present rate of human population growth — or growth in consumption — indefinitely. Over-population, overconsumption, and poverty continue to be important issues in need of resolution as the twenty-first century approaches.

10. *The colonial legacy, multinational corporations, and Third World political leaders*

In Asia, Africa, and Latin America, European colonists have consolidated their earlier power by doing development via multinational corporations in conjunction with the new elite in those countries. More often than not, the elite are part of an oppressive military regime which controls the poor like the colonials used to.

Other issues that have global dimensions include human rights, racism, sexism, problems of the elderly and the disabled, the hazardous waste problem, abortion, health care of the poor, and criminal justice.

Earthkeepers' Response

Christians want to follow the example of Jesus — to help those who are in need. How do we best help the needy? By getting to know them first, of course, but also by knowing the reasons behind their need. As we understand how many issues are connected, we see more clearly how many of our decisions affect the poor who may be across town or across the seas.

Pastoral Recommendations on Dialogue: A Joint Statement by Protestant and Catholic Churches in Asia

The following is a joint statement on interfaith dialogue by representatives of the WCC-related Christian Conference of Asia (CCA) and the Federation of Asian Bishops' Conference (FABC). These representatives met July 5–10, 1987, in Singapore for a consultation on collaborating with people of other faiths in Asia. This was the first time that such a joint statement was made by Christian leaders in Asia, and their message applies in other parts of the world as well. Source: *Buddhist-Christian Studies* 10 (1990): 213-15.

The urgent need to seek new relationships with neighbors of other religious traditions brought together representatives of the member churches of the Christian Conference of Asia (CCA) and of the member conferences of the Federation of Asian Bishops' Conferences (FABC) to consider the theme "Living and Working Together with Sisters and Brothers of other Faiths in Asia." The first such CCA/FABC initiative, this gathering involved fifty-five participants from fourteen countries. All were conscious of the significance of this historic event, giving thanks to God for his gift in Jesus Christ who brought them together. Many insights emerged from our common deliberations. From them we highlight a few which we believe to be particularly significant for our churches.

1. Asia's dominant reality is, on the one hand, the massive presence of diverse religious traditions and ideologies, and, on the other, its widespread poverty and political oppression. Further, with the increasing politicalization of religions and the frequent clashes between religious communities, there is an increasing awareness that peace within and between nations is not possible without peace between religions. Conscious of their respective spiritual resources, people of all traditions share a responsibility to work for a new society (2 Cor. 5:17). In such a context, dialogue becomes an urgent priority for the churches.

2. Dialogue, then, is not primarily a matter of talking. It is, in the first instance, an attitude, an openness to the neighbor, a sharing of spiritual resources as people stand before the great crises of life and death, as they struggle for justice and human dignity, as they yearn for peace (John 14:27). In this, Christians have a contribution to make. In dialogue, Christians and their neighbors enter into a reciprocal relationship which becomes a process of mutual learning and growth.

3. We enter such relationships of dialogue on the basis of our faith in God through Jesus Christ, conscious that the Holy Spirit is guiding us toward an enrichment of human life and deeper appreciation of truth. This faith gives us our identity as Christians and empowers us to share with the neighbors our faith and vision, our words and silence.

4. As "mission," "evangelism" and "evangelization" have different nuances for Christians of different traditions, so too has the relation between dialogue and mission. However, we affirm that dialogue and mission have their own integrity and freedom. They are distinct but not unrelated. Dialogue is not a tool or instrument for mission and evangelization, but it does influence the way the church perceives and practices mission in a pluralistic world. Mission invites us to participate in God's continuing activity through the Spirit to mend a broken creation, to overcome the fragmentation of humanity and to heal the rift between nature, humanity, and God. God's recreating activity is prior to and more comprehensive than the church's mission, and it directs our attention beyond the church to the Kingdom.

5. Dialogue offers opportunities for Christian witness. Christians, while sharing insights from their faith, will be attentive to the insights of sisters and brothers of other religious traditions. Thus, the way is open for mutual criticism and mutual enrichment among all those who bring a religious perspective to the human quest. All life has a pilgrim character, and neighbors of other religious traditions are our fellow pilgrims on the

way. In humanity's shared pilgrimage, the church is called to be an effective sign and symbol of the Kingdom of God.

Dialogue is a lifestyle, which can be learned only by doing. At the same time interreligious dialogue has theological underpinnings. The following pastoral recommendations are made:

i. It is important that persons in leadership positions in the churches take the theological understanding of, and participation in, interreligious dialogue seriously.

ii. The theological basis of interreligious dialogue and courses on religions outside Christianity should be included and strengthened, in the curriculum of the seminaries and other houses of formation. Not only seminarians but bishops and clergy as well as lay people should at this point be given opportunities to update themselves.

iii. Christian institutions like schools and hospitals could become centers for interreligious dialogue, not for the sake of evangelism, but within an enlarged theological-religious framework. The public schools, too, in some areas, could become places where interreligious understanding may be furthered.

iv. A commission on interreligious relations could be established or activated at the local, regional, and national levels to work alongside other religious bodies so as to foster interreligious understanding and cooperation. Insofar as possible, these efforts should be carried out in an ecumenical spirit.

v. Christian groups (youth, women, and men) and their counterparts in other religions should be encouraged to visit one another, cooperate in community development, and participate in people's movements for human rights issues and promotion of justice and peace (dialogue of life).

vi. Interreligious gatherings for prayers and meditation on important national and international days, as well as occasions of religious festivals, should be encouraged.

vii. Guidelines for interreligious dialogue (such as those which have been prepared by CCA and FABC, and other national and international Christian bodies) should be widely distributed, studied and used, revised and adapted if necessary.

viii. Careful thought should be given by the proper religious authorities to the pastoral problems of mixed religious marriages and funeral services for a multireligious family.

ix. Attention should be given through the appropriate channels to the religious phenomena of fundamentalism and fanaticism.

x. The mass media should be used to promote interreligious understanding and harmony.

Acknowledgments

The editors and publisher gratefully acknowledge permission to include material from the following sources:

I. Toward a Christian Theology of Religions

Pre–Twentieth-Century Views

Saint Augustine, *The Fathers of the Church: Saint Augustine, Letters,* Volume II. Catholic University of America Press, 1953. Used by permission.
Nicholas of Cusa, *Nicholas of Cusa on Interreligious Harmony: Text, Concordance and Translation of "De Pace Fidei,"* ed. James E. Biechler and H. Lawrence Bond (Lewiston, N.Y.: Edwin Mellen Press, 1991). Used by permission.
Friedrich Schleiermacher, "The Conception of the Church: Propositions Borrowed from Ethics," from *The Christian Faith,* ed. H. R. Mackintosh and J. S. Stewart (Edinburgh: T&T Clark, 1928). Used by permission.

Contemporary Roman Catholic and Eastern Orthodox Views

Theological Investigations, vol. V: *Late Writings* by Karl Rahner. This translation © 1966 Darton, Longman & Todd, Ltd. Reprinted by permission of the Crossroad Publishing Company.

ACKNOWLEDGMENTS

Georges Khodr, *Living Faiths and the Ecumenical Movement,* ed. Stanley J.
Samartha (Geneva: World Council of Churches, 1971). Used by permission.

Raimundo Panikkar, *The Unknown Christ of Hinduism: Towards an Ecumenical Christophany,* revised and enlarged ed. (Maryknoll: Orbis
Books, 1981). Used by permission.

Hans Küng, "Towards an Ecumenical Theology of Religions: Some Theses
for Clarification," from *Christianity Among the World Religions,* ed.
Hans Küng and Jürgen Moltmann (Nijmegen, Holland: Stichting
Concilium; Edinburgh: T&T Clark Ltd., 1986).

The Myth of Christian Uniqueness: Toward a Pluralistic Theology of Religions,
edited by John Hick and Paul F. Knitter (Maryknoll: Orbis Books,
1987). Used by permission.

Gavin D'Costa, *Christian Uniqueness Reconsidered: The Myth of a Pluralistic
Theology of Religions* (Maryknoll: Orbis Books, 1990). Used by permission.

Contemporary Protestant Views

Ernst Troeltsch, *Christian Thought: Its History and Application,* ed. Baron
F. von Hügel. Used by permission of Hyperion Press, Inc.

Karl Barth, *Church Dogmatics,* vol. 1/2 (1932), trans. G. T. Thomson and
H. Knight (Edinburgh: T&T Clark, 1956). Used by permission.

Hendrik Kraemer, *Why Christianity of All Religions?* (Philadelphia: Westminster Press, 1962). Reprinted by permission of Westminster Press.

Paul Tillich, *Systematic Theology,* vol. 2 (Chicago: University of Chicago
Press, 1957). Used by permission.

Excerpt from *The Future of Religion,* edited by Jerald C. Brauer. Copyright
© 1966 by Hannah Tillich. Reprinted by permission of HarperCollins
Publishers, Inc.

Problems of Religious Pluralism by John Hick. Copyright © 1985. Reprinted
with permission of St. Martin's Press, Incorporated, and Macmillan
Press Ltd.

God Has Many Names by John Hick. Copyright © 1980, 1982 John Hick.
Used by permission of Westminster John Knox Press and Macmillan
Press Ltd.

Reprinted from *Beyond Dialogue* by John B. Cobb, Jr. Copyright © 1982
Fortress Press. Used by permission of Augsburg Fortress.

John B. Cobb, Jr., "Is Christianity a Religion?" in *What Is Religion? An Inquiry for Christian Theology*, edited by Mircea Eliade and David Tracy. Reprinted by permission of The Stichting Concilium.

Choan-Seng Song, *Tell Us Our Names: Story Theology from an Asian Perspective* (Maryknoll: Orbis Books, 1984). Used by permission.

The Myth of Christian Uniqueness: Toward a Pluralistic Theology of Religions, edited by John Hick and Paul F. Knitter (Maryknoll: Orbis Books, 1987). Used by permission.

Diana L. Eck, "The Religions and Tambaram: 1938 and 1988," *International Review of Mission* 78, no. 307 (July 1988). Used by permission.

James A. Borland, "A Theologian Looks at the Gospel and World Religions," *Journal of the Evangelical Theological Society* 33, no. 1 (March 1990). Used by permission. A subscription to this journal may be obtained by writing to 112 Russell Woods Drive, Lynchburg, VA 24502-3530.

Donald A. Pittman, "Testing a Two-Eyed Truth," *Encounter* 53, no. 4 (autumn 1992). Used by permission.

II. Mission and Ministry

Pope John Paul II, "Redemptoris Missio," taken from *New Directions in Mission and Evangelization: Basic Statements 1: 1974-1991*, edited by James Scherer and Stephan Bevans (Maryknoll: Orbis Books, 1992). Reprinted by permission of the Vatican.

Arthur F. Glasser and Donald A. McGavran, *Contemporary Theologies of Mission* (Grand Rapids: Baker Book House, 1983). Used by permission.

"Mission and Evangelism — An Ecumenical Affirmation," as approved by the Central Committee of the World Council of Churches, July 1982. © 1982 WCC Publications, World Council of Churches, Geneva, Switzerland. Used by permission.

L. Grant McClung, "Theology and Strategy of Pentecostal Missions," *International Bulletin of Missionary Research*, January 1988, pp. 2-6. Used by permission.

Swami Palimi, "Mission-Minded Hindus Going Global," reprinted from *Pulse* (8 February 1991), Box 794, Wheaton, IL 60189. Used by permission.

Frank Whaling, "A Comparative Religious Study of Missionary Transplantation in Buddhism, Christianity, and Islam," *International Review of Mission*, October 1981, pp. 314-33. Used by permission.

ACKNOWLEDGMENTS

Isma'il al-Faruqi, "On the Nature of Islamic Da'wah," *International Review of Mission,* October 1976, pp. 391-409. Used by permission.

Alexandre Ganoczy, "The Absolute Claim of Christianity: The Justification of Evangelization or an Obstacle to It?" from *Evangelization in the World Today,* edited by Norbert Greinacher and Alois Müller, Concilium Secretariat General, 1979. Used by permission.

Michael Amaladoss, "Dialogue and Mission: Conflict or Convergence?" *International Review of Mission,* July 1986, pp. 222-41. Used by permission.

James Engel, "We Are the World," *Christianity Today,* 24 September 1990, pp. 32-34. Used by permission.

Jonathan J. Bonk, "Mission and Mammon: Six Theses," *International Bulletin of Missionary Research,* October 1989, pp. 174-81. Used by permission.

Robert J. Schreiter, "Contextualization from a World Perspective," *Theological Education* 1993 Supplement 1 (autumn 1993), pp. 63-85. Used by permission.

Fundamentalisms Observed, edited by Martin E. Marty and R. Scott Appleby. Copyright © 1991 The University of Chicago Press. All rights reserved. Used by permission of The University of Chicago Press.

Lesslie Newbigin, "The Enduring Validity of Cross-Cultural Mission," *International Bulletin of Missionary Research,* April 1988, pp. 50-53. Used by permission.

Lamin Sanneh, "Christian Mission in the Pluralist Milieu: The African Experience," *Missiology,* October 1984, pp. 421-33. Used by permission.

D. Preman Niles, "Christian Mission and the Peoples of Asia," *Missiology,* July 1982, pp. 279-99. Used by permission.

Mortimer Arias, "Contextual Evangelization in Latin America: Between Accommodation and Confrontation," *Occasional Bulletin of Missionary Research,* January 1978, pp. 19-28. Used by permission.

Craig Van Gelder, "A Great New Fact of Our Day: America as Mission Field," *Missiology,* October 1991, pp. 409-17. Used by permission.

David J. Bosch, "Vision for Mission," *International Review of Mission,* January 1987, pp. 8-15. Used by permission.

"Justice, Peace and the Integrity of Creation," in *New Directions in Mission and Evangelization 1: Basic Statements 1974-1991,* ed. James Scherer and Stephan Bevans (Maryknoll: Orbis Books, 1992), pp. 82-83. Used by permission of the World Council of Churches, Geneva, Switzerland.

III. Dialogue and Ministry

David Lochhead, *The Dialogical Imperative: A Christian Reflection on Interfaith Encounter* (Maryknoll: Orbis Books, 1988). Used by permission.

Christian Mission in the Modern World by John R. W. Stott. © 1975 by John Stott. Used by permission of InterVarsity Press, P.O. Box 1400, Downers Grove, IL 60515. Used by permission.

Encountering Jesus — Encountering Judaism: A Dialogue by Karl Rahner and Pinchas Lapide, translated by Davis Perkins. Originally published under the title *Heil von den Juden? Ein Gespräch.* © 1983 by Matthias-Grünewald-Verlag, Mainz. English translation © 1987 by The Crossroad Publishing Company. Reprinted with permission of The Crossroad Publishing Company, New York.

Bettina Bäumer, *Spirituality in Interfaith Dialogue*, ed. Tosh Arai and Wesley Ariarajah (Geneva: WCC Publications, 1989). Used by permission.

Yamada Koun Roshi, "Christians and the Practice of Zen," *Dialogue*, September-December 1976. Used by permission.

Joanna Macy, "Taking Heart: Spiritual Exercises for Social Activists," *Fellowship*, July/August 1982. Used by permission.

Jacob Neusner, *Jews and Christians: The Myth of a Common Tradition* (Philadelphia: Trinity Press International, 1991). Used by permission.

Audrey Shenandoah, "A Tradition of Thanksgiving," from *Spirit and Nature* by Steven C. Rockefeller & John C. Elder, pp. 17-23. Copyright © 1992 by Steven C. Rockefeller and John C. Elder. Reprinted by permission of Beacon Press.

Reprinted by permission from *Earthkeepers: Environmental Perspectives on Hunger, Poverty, and Injustice* by Art and Jocele Meyer (Scottdale, Pa., 1991). All rights reserved.

"Pastoral Recommendations on Dialogue: A Joint Statement by Protestant and Catholic Churches in Asia," *Buddhist-Christian Studies* 10 (1990), pp. 213-215. Used by permission of the Federation of Asian Bishops' Conference.

Index of Subjects and Names

Abel, 206
Abhishiktananda, Swami, 9, 433, 436, 437
Abraham, 68, 75, 95, 96, 200
Activism, social, 472-84
Adam, 49, 75, 248
Ad Gentes, 373
Adhikara (Hinduism), 436
Aeschylus, 421
al-Faruqi, Isma'il, 229, 230, 232
Amaladoss, Michael, 224, 226
Ambrose, 47
American Bible Society, 357
American Society of Missiology, 340
Amida Buddhism, 421
Amitabha cult, 279
Amos, 160
Ananias, 69
Anderson, Norman, 205, 206
Anglicans, 276, 304
Anonymous Christians, 91-93, 108, 197, 303
Anselm, 198
An Shih-kao, 278, 281
Anuttarai (ultimate reality), 438
Apollinaris, 168
Apostles' Creed, 405
Appar (Hindu), 274
Aquinas. *See* Thomas Aquinas

Areopagus, 105, 243-45
Ariarajah, Wesley, 199
Arias, Mortimer, 225, 227
Aristotle, 128, 458
Arjuna (Hindu), 483
Ashram, 352, 432-33
Asoka (Indian emperor), 278
Assemblies of God, 269-70, 276, 358
Association of Theological Schools in the United States and Canada, 23
Atheism, 68, 107-8
Augustine of Hippo, 47-49, 114, 422
Authority of the Faith, The (Tambaram report), 191
Avila, Rafael, 356
Axial Period: First, 457-59, 462; Second, 459-62
Azarias, 69
Azusa Street Credential Committee, 267

Baby boomers, 304-8, 364-65
Banks, James A., 321
Baptists, 357. *See also* Southern Baptists
Barrett, David B., 377
Barth, Karl, 108, 110, 157, 192, 193, 372, 424
Bäumer, Bettina, 390
Baur, F. C., 167
Bavinck, J. H., 411

Berlin Wall, 325

Bernard of Clairvaux, 422

Bhagavad Gita, 25, 190, 393, 480, 482-83

Bhikkhu, Buddhadasa, 489

Bhikkhu (Buddhism), 487-88

Bhikkhuni (Buddhism), 487-88

Bible: authority of, 43, 248, 266; translation of, 340-41, 344, 345

Boddhisattva tradition, 421

Bodhi tree, 478

Boff, Leonardo, 119

Bonk, Jonathan, 9, 232

Bosch, David J., 18, 22, 48, 314

Brahma Kumari sect, 274

Brahmaviharas (Buddhism), 451

Brahmin, 96

British and Foreign Bible Society, 357

Brow, Robert, 205

Buber, M., 416

Buddha, 111, 112, 164, 174, 278, 405, 410, 453, 458, 478, 486, 487

Buddhism, 27-28, 39-40, 135, 164, 229, 232, 332, 375, 436, 441, 445-54, 470, 478; and Christianity, 174, 391, 421-22, 490; Four Abodes of, 451-52; missions of, 277-82; Tibetan, 439; values of, 280, 393-94, 485-92. See also Amida Buddhism; Four Noble Truths; Mahayana Buddhism; Pure Land Buddhism; Sangha; Zen Buddhism

Bultmann, Rudolf, 110, 372, 424

Burridge, Kenelm, 319

Cabasilas, Nicholas, 97

Caliph, 476

Calvin, John, 52

Celsus, 45

Chaitanya (Hindu), 274

Chao, T. C., 194

Chimanlal (Hindu), 432

Ching-ling (Chinese prince), 280, 282

Cho, Paul Yonggi, 267

Christian Conference of Asia, 503, 505

Christian Democrats, 491

Christianity: absolute claims of, 87-88, 107-11, 149-54, 183-85, 223-24, 291-96, 336, 338; comparison of, with other religions, 82-84, 133-40; development of, 94-99, 138-39, 335-36, 351; and dialogue with other faiths, 201, 250-51; missions of, to other faiths, 262-64, 350-52, 375-76; traditions of, 18-21, 134, 422-24; and views of other religions, 24-25, 42-43, 54-61, 87-93, 149-54, 175

Christianity and Buddhism, 174, 391, 421-22, 490

Christianity and Hinduism, 100-106, 128, 389-90, 431-40

Christianity and Islam, 49-50, 56, 284-87

Christianity and Judaism, 49, 172-74, 415-17, 420-21, 465-71

Christianity and World Religions: The Challenge of Pluralism (Anderson), 205, 206

Christianity and Zen Buddhism, 390, 404-5, 433-34, 441-44

Christian Message in a Non-Christian World, The (Kraemer), 191-93

Christian Messianic Movement (Korea), 353

Christocentrism, 118, 170-71, 237-39, 351-52, 419-20

Church, 216, 359-60, 365-68, 401; missionary attitude of, 148, 238-45, 375-76; and its place in the world, 95-99, 126, 268, 365-67, 401, 406; planting of, 226, 249-55, 268

Church Missionary Society, 42, 341

Church on the Way, 307

Clement of Alexandria, 45, 113

Cobb, John B., Jr., 10, 43, 54, 117, 389

Coe, Shoki, 356

Colonialism, 316-17, 319, 324, 340, 357-58, 502; and missions, 341, 352

Committee on Global Theological Education, 23

Communication, 244, 269, 275, 278, 281, 357; new technologies in, 260, 329

Communism, 251, 275. *See also* Marxism

Communist Manifesto, 359

Competition, theology of, 387-88, 399-400

Confucianism, 135, 279-82, 322, 332

Confucius, 51, 458

Conscientization, 6, 7

Consciousness: archaic, 458-59, 461; global, 317, 326, 391, 455-57, 459-62; moral, 458-59, 462

Constantine, 47, 221, 379

Constitution on the Church. See Lumen gentium

Consumerism, 309, 491

Contextualization, 34, 315-23, 355-56, 358-60, 376

Conversion, 225, 257

Coomaraswamy, A. K., 432

Cooperation, interreligious, 392-95, 456

Cornelius, 207

Cousins, Ewert, 387, 391

Cultures: local, 275, 317-20, 326, 356, 491-92; global, 317, 326

Cyprian, 46

Cyrenius, 68

Daly, Herman, 10

Damboriena, Prudencio, 266

David, 96

Davies, J. G., 410

Da'wah (Islam), 230, 283-87

Day, Dorothy, 450

D'Costa, Gavin, 118

Decentering, 7-15, 17

Declaration on the Relation of the Church to Non-Christian Religions. See *Nostra Aetate*

Decree on Ecumenism. See *Unitatis redintegratio*

d'Epinay, Christian Lalive, 358

Deracination, 318-20

Devi Bhagavata, 481

Dhamma (Buddhism), 487

Dhammic Socialism (Bhikkhu), 489

Dharma, 278, 279, 281

Dialogue, 100-101, 201-2, 325, 358, 415-17, 460; Buddhist-Christian, 421-22; Catholic view of, 245-46, 302-3; and conversion, 179-81; evangelicals and, 251-52, 388-89, 408-14, 425-28; and faith, 111-14, 198, 435-40; as an imperative, 399-407, 412-14, 504; Jewish-Christian, 420-21; and justice issues, 116-18, 126, 183, 185-87, 214; and mission, 173, 174, 297-303, 399, 401-5, 504; Muslim-Christian, 285; mutuality in, 21-22, 185, 190-91, 389; risks of, 172, 410, 419, 439; and truth testing, 210-16. *See also* Interreligious dialogue

Dialogue with the World (Davies), 410

Din al-fitrah (natural religion), 284, 285

Dinesen, Isak, 432

Document on Religious Freedom (Second Vatican Council), 298

Donatist controversy, 48

Donghak Messianic Movement (Korea), 353

Don Juan, 446

Dumas, Andre, 338

du Plessis, David J., 266

Eastern Orthodox, 23, 25

Eckhart, Meister, 422, 424

Eco-justice, 16-17, 22, 500-501

Ecumenism, 108-10, 256-64, 325, 337-38, 456

Edinburgh 1910, 372

Eight-Fold Path (Buddhism), 485

Einstein, Albert, 363

Elenctics, 411-12

Eliade, Mircea, 420

Elias, 69

Elijah, 458

Endo, Shusaku, 378

Engel, James, 226

Enlightenment, 50, 361, 362, 364, 371

Environmental issues, 12-14, 478, 494-95, 499-500

Epistle to the Hebrews, The (Saphir), 206

Ethnicity, 35-37, 163-64

European Consultation on Mission Studies, 414

Evangelicals, 23, 225; and dialogue, 251-52, 388-89, 408-14, 425-28; and missions, 247-53, 401-2, 408-14; and other religions, 204-5

Evangelism, 43, 56, 222-23, 244, 252-53, 256, 292-96, 376, 401-5, 408; types of, 357-59, 404

Eve, 248

Everyman (medieval play), 446

Exclusivism, 25, 54-57, 124, 129, 149-54, 181, 196, 202, 204-9, 395, 419

Extra ecclesiam nulla salus, 44, 108

Faith of Other Men (W. C. Smith), 205

Federation of Asian Bishops Conferences, 503, 505

Feminism, 182-88, 481, 482

Fetishism. *See* Idol worship

First World, 475. *See also* Second World; Third World

Florence, Council of (1442), 44, 46, 50, 108

Fo-tu-t'eng (Chinese Buddhist Missionary), 280, 281

Four Noble Truths (Buddhism), 393, 485

Francis of Assisi, 478

Freire, Paulo, 6

Fundamentalism, 328-32, 439, 505

Gadamer, H., 419

Gandhi, Mahatma, 275, 432, 450, 483, 489, 491

Ganesha (Hindu), 482

Ganoczy, Alexandre, 223, 224

Gargi (Hindu), 481

Gautama. *See* Buddha

Geertz, Clifford, 37

George, St., 321

Globalization, 8, 23-24, 219-21, 315-17, 323-27, 394, 499-502

Grace of God, 89-93, 143-47, 197-98, 201, 202

Graham, Billy, 359

Green movement, 275, 491

Gregorios, Paulos Mar, 223, 224

Gregory of Nyssa, 422

Groves, C. P., 340

Guruparampara (Hinduism), 436

Hanafi, Hassan, 473

Han Empire, 278-82

Hanuman (Hindu), 483

Hare Krishna, 274, 439

Harnack, Adolf von, 340

Haudenosaunee (Iroquois Confederacy), 493-98

Hayford, Jack, 267

Hegel, G. W. F., 53, 134, 159, 293, 294

Heisenberg, W. K., 363

Henry, Carl F. H., 428

Heraclitus, 45, 68

Hercules, 168

Heretics, 70-72

Hermeneutics, 115-16, 127, 281, 424

Herodotus, 421

Hesiod, 421

Hesselgrave, David, 389

Hick, John, 202, 422

Hinduism, 25-28, 111, 163-64, 189-91, 195, 229, 232, 282, 392-93, 458, 480-84, 490; and Christianity, 100-106, 128, 389-90, 431-40; missions of, 273-76. *See also* Bhagavad Gita; Ramayana; Rig-Veda; Upanishads; Vedas; Vedic tradition

Hindu View of Life, The (Radhakrishnan), 274

Hodges, Melvin L., 268

Hogg, A. G., 193-94

Holistic evangelism, 252-53

Holocaust, 420, 423

Hosea, 160

Hostility, theology of, 387-88, 399-400

Hua-hu theory (Taoist), 282

Hui-yüan (Buddhist missionary), 279

Ibn Khattab, Omar, 476

Idol worship, 83-84

Imperialism, 353, 392, 472-73

Incarnation, 167-69, 171, 195, 314

Inclusivism, 25, 54-59, 87-93, 108, 111, 123-29, 185, 197, 202, 213-15, 395, 419
Inculturation, 439
Indigenization, 34, 128-29, 279, 282, 355, 376
Indigenous Church, The (Hodges), 268
Indigenous Church and the Missionary, The (Hodges), 268
Individualism, 104, 136, 138-39, 200, 328, 359, 360
Inquisition, 356
"In Search of Justice" (Suchocki), 214
International Pentecostal Press Association, 269
International Review of Mission, 372
Interreligious dialogue, 20-21, 59-61, 170-74, 390-91, 418-23, 505; conditions of, 3, 116, 118-19, 179-80; tasks of, 27-29, 385, 387-91. *See also* Dialogue
Introduction to the Science of Missions, An (Bavinck), 411
Irenaeus, 45, 97
Isaiah, 458
Isasi-Diaz, Ada Maria, 5
ISKCON (International Society for Krishna Consciousness), 274
Islam, 19, 27-28, 57, 83-84, 116, 135, 189-92, 229-30, 232, 392-93, 467, 469, 472-79, 490-91; and Christianity, 49-50, 56, 284-87. *See also* Qur'an
Isolation, theology of, 387-88, 399-400

Jacob, 95
Jaspers, Karl, 457-58
Jeremiah, 458
Jesus Christ, finality of, 119-22, 388, 411, 419
Jesus — God and Man (Pannenberg), 167
Jews, 164, 238, 421-23, 466-70, 492. *See also* Judaism
Jihad (Islam), 475
John, 96, 126-28, 205, 208, 300, 356
John of the Cross, 422

John Paul II, 225, 237-46, 301
John the Baptist, 257
John XXIII, 374, 416
Jones, Jim, 466
Judaism, 19, 28, 44-49, 57, 83-84, 100, 125, 135, 160, 165, 388, 392, 458; and Christianity, 172-74, 415-17, 420-21, 465-71. *See also* Jews
Jupiter (god), 168
Justice, 8, 11, 120-21, 377, 380-81, 407, 475; and dialogue, 116-18, 126, 183, 185-87, 214; and missions, 225, 393
Justification. *See* Salvation
Justin Martyr, 45

Kabilsingh, Chatsumarn, 489
Kairoi, 158-59, 161
Kambara mayana (Tamil classic), 484
Kaniska (Kushan leader), 278
Kant, Immanuel, 50, 53, 159
Karma, 277, 279. *See also* Dharma
Kasai, Minoru, 389-90
Kennedy, John F., 306
Kerygma, 404, 405
Khomeini, Ayatollah, 466
"Kin-dom," 3-6, 8, 15-23
King, Martin Luther, 275, 450
Knitter, Paul, 36, 54, 61, 170, 171, 214
Ko-i (matching concepts), 279, 281-82
Kosambi (Buddhist scholar), 433
Koyama, Kosuke, 6, 16
Kraemer, Hendrik, 191-94, 202, 372
Krishna, 195, 483
Krishna Lila (Hindu dance), 483
Kristensen, Brede, 191
Kuhn, Thomas S., 371, 372
Kumarajiva (Buddhist translator), 280, 281
Kumarappa, J. C., 433
Küng, Hans, 47, 117, 184-86, 199, 214, 371-72
Kushan Empire, 278, 281
Kyoto school, 303

Lao-Tze, 458
Lao-Tzu, 453

Lapide, Pinchas, 388
Lateran Council, Fourth (1215), 108
Latourette, Kenneth Scott, 53, 335, 340
Lausanne Covenant, 262, 414
Lausanne Movement, 304
Lausanne Occasional Papers, 401, 402
Levinas, E., 419
Liberation theology, 7, 115-22, 182,
   185, 325, 421, 423
Livingstone, David, 342, 343
Lloyd-Jones, Martyn, 409
Lochhead, David, 387-88
Logos, 68, 106, 127, 165-69, 216, 300
*Looking to America to Solve Thailand's
   Problems* (Prayudh), 489
Lossky, Vladimir, 97
Lugard, Lord, 341
Lumen gentium, 57, 298
Luther, Martin, 52, 114

McClung, Grant, 225, 226
McCracken, Horace, 269
McGavran, Donald, 223, 225, 232, 269
Macy, Joanna, 391
Madras Christian College, 193
Mahabharata, 480
Maharshi, Ramana, 438
Mahavira (Buddhism), 458
Mahayana Buddhism, 174, 278, 281,
   443, 491
Mainstream, 23, 110, 470. *See also* Prot-
   estants
Maitreya (Buddhist cult), 280
Mammon, 309-14
Manikarnika Ghat, 434
Marxism, 251, 252, 325, 359, 491. *See
   also* Communism
Mary, 57, 238, 248, 356, 357
Masai, 346
Masonic Lodges, 358
Mass media, 244, 260, 329, 505
Matthew, 96, 260
Maxentius, 379
Meditation, 437, 486, 487, 490
Merton, Thomas, 116, 117
Meta-cosmic religions, 350-51

Methodists, 357
Meyer, Jocele, 394
Milingo, Archbishop, 345
Millenarianism, 378
Miller, Keith, 20
Miller, William, 341, 342
Milvian Bridge, 379
Misael, 69
Missionaries, 226-29, 267, 295-96, 306-
   7, 342-44; and Western values, 309-14
Mission compound, 349, 351
Missions, 26-27, 98-99, 178, 222-26,
   364, 372-79; and colonial policy, 340-
   44, 352; and dialogue, 173-74, 297-
   303, 399, 401-5, 504; mandate for,
   56, 209, 255-56, 335; moratorium
   on, 262; and other religions, 53, 92,
   138, 339-51, 353; to the poor, 231-
   32, 307, 310-11, 314, 377; theologies
   of, 349, 387-88, 399-400; to the West-
   ern world, 220-21, 229, 377
Mitchell, Robert Byrant, 226, 268
Moksha (Hinduism), 483, 485
Moral Majority, 406
Moses, 17, 73, 96, 111, 112, 299, 360,
   453
Moses, D. G., 189
Muditha (Buddhism), 449
Muhammad, 111-13, 135, 164, 475, 476
Muzaffar, Chandra, 392
*Mystical Theology of the Eastern Church,
   The* (Lossky), 97
Mysticism, 160, 422, 436, 446
Myth of Christian Uniqueness, The
   (Hick and Knitter), 214

Nagarjuna, 422
Narayaniyam (Hinduism), 190
National Conference of Catholic Bish-
   ops in the U.S.A., 225
Native Americans, 387, 392, 394, 493-98
Neill, Stephen, 413
Neo-Taoists, 279-82
New Age movement, 275
Newbigin, Lesslie, 18, 21, 190, 194, 224,
   230, 377

Nicholas of Cusa, 50, 292
Nichol, John Thomas, 269
Nicodemus, 260
Niebuhr, H. Richard, 15, 374
Niles, D. T., 355
Nirvana, 181, 278, 279, 320, 485-92
Nirvanasutra School, 280
Nishitani (Japanese philosopher), 303
Nixon, Richard, 359
Noah, 95
No Other Name (Knitter), 214
Northern People's Congress, 342
Nostra Aetate, 57

Obermuller, Rudolf, 359
Ogden, Schubert M., 33
On Being a Christian (Küng), 184, 199
Onondaga nation, 394
OPEC, 316, 325
Origen, 45, 95, 113, 422
Origin and Goal of History, The
    (Jaspers), 457
Orthopraxis, 101, 119-21, 329
Oswiecim (Poland), 471
Other, theory of the, 465-71
Oxtoby, Willard, 44

Palami, Swami, 229, 232
Panikkar, Raimundo, 117, 204, 390,
    420, 460
Panna (Buddhism), 487
Pannenberg, Wolfhart, 167-68
Parachurch groups, 359
Parameshvara (Hinduism), 438
Partnership, theology of, 387-88, 400
Parvati (Hindu), 482
Paul, 22, 44, 45, 105, 154, 160, 202, 205,
    206, 208, 243, 259, 300, 312, 322,
    356, 416, 427, 434, 450
Paul VI, 244
Pelagian debates, 48
Pentecostals, 225, 265-70, 319, 358, 360
Peter, 56, 205, 207, 238, 356
Philip, 206-7, 267, 412
Philip, T. V., 348
Phongphit, Seri, 490

Pieris, Aloysius, 350
Pius IX, 52
Plato, 69, 419, 421, 458
Platonism, 134
Pluralism, 182-88, 197, 202, 395; in
    Africa, 339-47; religious, 25, 36, 43,
    54, 59-61, 78-80, 162-67, 298-99,
    364, 418, 419; theology of, 123-24,
    129, 170-76, 344, 345, 350
Polytheism, 83-84
Pontius Pilate, 68
Population growth, 11-12, 502
Postmodern reality, 362-65, 372, 395,
    424
Poverty, 118, 252-53, 258, 260-61, 380,
    475-77, 500-504
Prajapati (Hinduism), 481
Prajna (Buddhism), 487
Prakriti (Hinduism), 481, 482
Prasna Upanishad, 481
Praxis, 6, 16, 117-22, 125, 418, 420
Prayudh, Venerable, 489
Preaching. *See* Proclamation
Preaching and Preachers (Lloyd-Jones),
    409
Presbyterians, 357
Presence and Proclamation (Warren),
    414
Prime Directive, 231
Proclamation, 401-5, 409-10, 413
Protestants, 25, 52-53, 113, 160, 165,
    358, 360, 374. *See also* Anglicans;
    Assemblies of God; Baptists;
    Ecumenism; Evangelicals; Main-
    stream; Methodists; Pentecostals;
    Presbyterians
Ptolemaic theory, 166
Pure Land Buddhism, 279, 282
Purusha (Hinduism), 481, 482

Qiddush Hasham, 471
Qur'an, 164, 190, 213, 283, 284, 285,
    393, 473, 475-77, 478

Radhakrishnan, S., 274
Radhasoami movement, 274

Rahman, Fazlur, 477
Rahner, Karl, 116, 197, 199, 202, 292, 293, 300, 303, 388
Rama (Hindu deity), 483-84
Ramanuja (Hindu teacher), 128
Ramayana, 393, 480, 483-84
Rationality in dialogue, 213-15
Ravana (Hindu), 484
Read, William R., 268
Reciprocity, principle of, 344-47
Redemptor Humanis (John Paul II), 171
Redemptoris Missio (John Paul II), 225-26
Reformation, 321, 324, 360, 362, 467
Relativism, 108, 111, 149-54, 175, 298, 336, 337; cultural, 227, 251, 328, 363-64; and dialogue, 183, 185, 211, 214; meretricious, 392, 466
Religion, 34-42, 329, 461-62, 468; absolute claims of, 135-37, 162-67; and politics, 456, 504; and truth, 35-38, 41, 109-11, 143-48. *See also* Religions
Religion in a Changing Society: Buddhism, Reform and the Role of Monks in Community Development in Thailand (Phongphit), 490
Religion of the Concrete Spirit, 160-61
Religions: history of, 39, 42, 157-61; theology of, 54, 115-22. *See also* Religion
Remembering Esperanza: A Cultural-Political Theology for North American Praxis (Taylor), 385
Renaissance, 362
Revelation, 142-44, 151-53, 156, 158, 178, 251, 411; in Christianity, 192, 194-95, 409, 419; and non-Christian religions, 191-93
Ricci, Matteo, 51
Rig-Veda, 105, 481
Rockefeller, Nelson, 359
Roman Catholic Church, 23, 25, 41, 57, 163, 240, 321, 433, 470, 479; as absolutist, 165, 324, 374; and dialogue with Jews, 172, 415-17; and dialogue with Protestants, 113; history of theology in, 47-52; and other religions, 245-46, 298-302; and view of missions, 226, 304, 356-60, 376. *See also* Florence, Council of; Inquisition; Lateran Council, Fourth; Trent, Council of; Vatican Council, Second
Roman Empire, 470
Roshi, Yamada Koun, 390
Ruether, Rosemary, 163
Ruysbroeck, Jan van, 422, 424

Saayman, William, 375
Sacraments, 49, 92, 103-4, 160
Sai Baba movement, 274
Salvation, 21, 25, 41, 55-58, 60, 102, 143, 155-56, 196-200, 202, 223; Augustine's view of, 47-49, 73-75; in Buddhism, 181; Catholic view of, 41, 44, 46-50, 238, 246, 298-99; in Christ, 204-9, 299-300, 375, 411, 421; in early church, 45-47; Enlightenment views of, 51-53; evangelical view of, 88-89, 165, 179, 248-49; history of, 156-58, 173; in Islam, 287; in non-Christian religions, 58, 90, 96, 102-5, 111, 193-94, 197, 302; Reformation views of, 52-53; as universal, 55, 108, 125, 165
Samadhi (Buddhism), 487
Sanatana Dharma (Hinduism), 163
San Chiao, 282
Sanctification, 143
Sangha (Buddhism), 277-79, 282, 487
Sankara (Hindu teacher), 101, 128
San-lun School, 280
Sanneh, Lamin, 227, 319
Sanskrit, 277
Saphir, A., 206
Sappho, 421
Saran, Professor, 431-32
Satori-awakening, 390, 441-44
Satyasiddha School, 280
Schleiermacher, Friedrich Daniel Ernst, 53
Second World, 474, 475. *See also* First World; Third World

Secularization, 456, 468
Self-Nature, 442. *See also* Zen Buddhism
Self-Realization. *See* Satori-awakening
Sermon on the Mount, 346, 404
Sexism, 183-84
Shaiva Siddhantin, 193
Shaivism, Kashmir, 438
Shalom, 392, 465-71
Shamanism, 439
Shankara, Adi, 274
Shanmukha (Hindu), 482
Shanta, G., 393
Shantideva (Buddhist saint), 448
Sharpe, Eric, 426, 427
Shenandoah, Audrey, 394
Shibayama, Zenkei, 433
Shi'ite Muslims, 406
Shiva (Hindu deity), 438, 482
Shiva Purana, 190
Shiva-Sakti concept, 481, 482
Shri Vaisnava, 193
Shweder, Richard, 322
Sila (Buddhism), 487
Silence (Endo), 378
Silk Route, 278, 281
Sin, 197-98, 252
Sita (as Hindu symbol), 483
Sita (Hindu), 483-84
Sivaraksa, Sulak, 393
Smith, Jonathan Z., 34, 37
Smith, Wilfred Cantwell, 25, 38-40,
    170, 193, 194, 204
Sobrino, Jon, 119
Socrates, 45, 68, 413, 458
Song, Choan-Seng, 21, 202, 349
Soteriocentrism, 116-21
Soto Zen, 443
South African Council of Churches, 378
Southern Baptist Foreign Mission
    Board, 307
Southern Baptists, 304, 307
Soviet empire, 466
Spanish Carmelites, 422
Spirituality, 435-40, 445, 479
Stackhouse, Max, 15, 24
Star Trek: The Next Generation, 231

Stott, John R., 388
Strauss, D. F., 167
Streng, Frederick, 35
Suchocki, Marjorie Hewitt, 214
Sullivan, Francis, 46, 49
Syncretism, 175, 320-21, 356-57, 414,
    439

Tantric practices, 439
Taoists, 278, 282
Task Force on Globalization, 23
Tauhid. See *Tawhid*
Tawhid (Islam), 286-87, 478
Taylor, Mark Kline, 27, 385
Teilhard de Chardin, 159, 460
Tell Us Our Names (Song), 202
Teresa of Ávila, 422
Tertullian, 45, 177
Thanksgiving, 394, 493-98
Theocentrism, 170-71, 239, 293, 419-20
Theologians in Transitions (Wall), 163
Theology: Asian, 348-54; and concept of
    evolution, 107-14, 134, 348-54, 418-
    24; Third World, 474-75, 500, 502. *See
    also* First World; Second World
Theology for the Third Millennium
    (Küng), 214
Thomas Aquinas, 47, 49-50, 114, 128
Thomas, Owen C., 54
Thoreau, H. D., 450
Thusing, Wilhelm, 292
Tillich, Paul, 110, 325, 372, 424
Tiruvacakam (Hinduism), 190
Tolle, Jim, 307
Torah, 470
"Toward a Philosophy of Religious Plu-
    ralism" (Hick), 171
Toward a World Theology (W. C.
    Smith), 194
"Towards an Asian Theology of Libera-
    tion" (Pieris), 350
Toynbee, A., 159
Tracy, David, 388, 390
Transcendental Meditation, 276
Trent, Council of (1545-63), 374
Trinity, 123-29, 164, 167, 171, 266

Troeltsch, Ernst, 53
Truth, 202-3, 210-16, 362, 374, 413; in religions, 135-36, 139, 150, 177-78, 180, 283, 291-94
Tutu, Desmond, 378

Unitatis redintegratio, 57
United Nations, 274; Fund for Population Activities, 12; High Commission on Refugees, 319
Universalism, 108, 157, 198, 230
Unknown Christ of Hinduism, The (Panikkar), 204
Upanishads, 190, 393, 431, 458, 480, 482
Urbanization, 319-20, 490

Vaishnavas, 195
Valmiki (Hindu author), 483, 484
Van Gelder, Craig, 231
Vatican Council, Second (1962-65), 57, 108, 241, 298-99, 324, 374
Vedas, 163-64, 458, 480
Vedic tradition, 213, 276
Verryn, Trevor, 313
Vietnam War, 306, 363
Visser 't Hooft, W. A., 199
Vivekananda, Swami, 276

Wagner, C. Peter, 269
Wall, James M., 163
Warren, Max, 42-43, 414, 427
Watergate, 363
Watts, Alan, 488
Wealth, 6, 8-11, 15, 488-89
Wei dynasty, 280
Whaling, Frank, 229, 232

What Is Religion? An Inquiry for Christian Theology (Knitter), 171
Wheaton College Graduate School, 305-6, 308
Witness in Six Continents, 412
Wittgenstein, Ludwig, 331
Women's issues, 267, 270, 393, 477, 480-84, 489-90
World Council of Churches, 20, 23, 108, 380-81, 406, 503-5; Central Committee, 254-64; Nairobi Assembly (1975), 375; Uppsala Assembly (1968), 412; Vancouver Assembly (1983), 402
World Resource Institute, 501
World War: First, 324-25, 424; Second, 316, 323-24, 365, 468
Wu (emperor of China), 280

Yajnavalkya (Hindu), 481
Yankelovich, Daniel, 305
Yoga, 274, 276, 437, 439
Youth With a Mission, 307

Zacchaeus, 260
Zakat (Islam), 476
Zazen. *See* Zen Buddhism
Zen Buddhism, 303, 421, 437, 439, 488; and Christianity, 390, 404-5, 433-34, 441-44. *See also* Buddhism
Zen enlightenment. *See* Satori-awakening
Zenji, Dogen, 443, 444
Zinzendorf, Nicholas von, 53
Zoroaster, 458
Zoroastrianism, 135
Zwingli, Ulrich, 52

Index of Scriptural References

OLD TESTAMENT

Genesis
15:6	206
49:10	104

Exodus 95

1 Samuel
4:21	10

Job
4:12	105

Psalms 320
27:1	22
85:7-13	254

Proverbs
18:13	414

Song of Songs
3:1-3	99

Isaiah 207
6	152
32:17-18	254
45:15	104
58:6-7	258

65:17-25	254

Jeremiah
49:7	105

Lamentations 421

Hosea
6:4-6	258

NEW TESTAMENT

Matthew
3:11	266
5:45	104
6:33	121, 225, 253
7:21	179
11:28	261
24	249
24:14	250
25:31-46	60
25:40	20
25:41	44
28:19	208
28:19-20	258, 327, 386

Mark 43
1:8	266

1:14	293
8:36	253
9:37	105
9:43-48	253
10:17-22	17
16:15-16	44, 208

Luke
2:14	104
3:16	266
4:16-20	327
4:18	293
8:1	293
10:25-37	4, 60
18:1	18
24:13-15	327
24:46-47	209
24:47	19
24:49	266

John 43, 167-68
1:33	266
3:15	207
3:18	208
4:14	207
4:38	105
5:40	207
6:29	207
6:35	207

6:40	207	17:23	104	**Ephesians**	377
6:47	207	17:28	434	1:10	105, 200, 238
6:53	207			2:12-14	327
7:38	208	**Romans**	45, 106	3:9-10	258
8:24	208	1–2	206	4:19	312
8:32	23	1:18-23	251	5:3-5	312
10:9	208	8:23	22	6:12	258
10:16	105	8:31	22		
11:25-26	208	10:9-13	208	**Philippians**	
13:16	260	10:14-15a	206	1:29	208
14:6	43, 205, 208,	10:17	206	2:5-7	6
	238, 245	10:20	104	3:4-9	154
14:27	504	11:28-29	60	3:7-8	312
15:26	266	11:33	22	3:8	313
16:8-9	208	15:21	104		
16:12-15	127			**Colossians**	71, 377
16:13	216	**1-2 Corinthians**	106	1:17	106
16:14-15	266			1:20	200
17:11	21	**1 Corinthians**		3:16	426
17:20-21	208	1:23	256		
18:36	239	3:11	205	**1 Timothy**	
20:21	259	7:30-31	313	2:4	19, 49, 58
20:31	208	11:26	259	2:5	205
		13:12	129	3:30	312
Acts	44, 320	15:22	97	6:5-11	312
1:8	20, 266	15:24-28	200	6:6-19	313
1:11	256	15:52	248		
2:17	97			**Hebrews**	75, 322
4:10, 12	238	**2 Corinthians**		1:1	105
4:12	44, 205	5	143	**James**	
8	267	5:14	122	1:22	20
8:5	206	5:17	256, 504		
8:12	206	5:19	19	**1 Peter**	
8:35	207	6:14-15	44	3:15	20
10:15	105	7:10	17		
10:22	207	8:9	256	**1 John**	
10:32	207	12:9-10	312	2:2	105
10:43b-44	207			5:11b-12	205
10:45	97	**Galatians**	106	5:12	208
11:13-14	207	1:6-9	206		
14:7	60	2:16	208	**Revelation**	
14:16	58	2:20	208	3:17-20	10
14:17	21	3:22	208	21:1-2	254
17:16-34	105	3:26	208	22:3	98
17:22-31	244